CONCEPTUALIZING IRANIAN ANTHROPOLOGY

CONCEPTUALIZING IRANIAN ANTHROPOLOGY
PAST AND PRESENT PERSPECTIVES

Edited by
Shahnaz R. Nadjmabadi

Berghahn Books
New York • Oxford

First published in 2009 by

Berghahn Books

www.berghahnbooks.com

Library of Congress Cataloging-in-Publication Data

Conceptualizing Iranian anthropology : past and present perspectives / edited by
Shahnaz R. Najdmabadi.
    p. cm.
  Includes bibliographical references and index.
  ISBN 978-1-84545-626-9 (hardback : alk. paper)
  1. Anthropology—Iran—History. 2. Anthropology—Iran—Philosophy.
3. Anthropology—Iran—Methodology. 4. Islam and culture—Iran. 5. Iran—
Social life and customs. I. Najdmabadi, Shahnaz R., 1947-
  GN17.3.I7C66 2009
  955—dc22

                                      2009025362

British Library Cataloguing in Publication Data

A catalogue record for this book is available from the British Library

Printed in the United States on acid-free paper.

ISBN: 978-1-84545-626-9 Hardback

❧ Contents

v

ॐ Tables

ᴥ Introduction

Shahnaz R. Nadjmabadi ᴥ

These days, when anthropological understanding is praised as 'a modern form of expert knowledge' (Restrepo and Escobar 2005), it is worth asking how far this assertion is valid at an international level and what the state of affairs is regarding the quality of this knowledge produced by the world's various national anthropological traditions. In their article entitled 'Other Anthropologies and Anthropologies Otherwise', Restrepo and Escobar argue that a discipline characterized by plurality and diversity requires thinking within multiple spaces and in a broader frame – that of a 'world anthropologies': 'rather than assuming that there is a privileged position from which a "real anthropology" (in the singular) can be produced and in relation to which all other anthropologies would define themselves, "world anthropologies" seeks to take seriously the multiple and contradictory historical, social, cultural and political locatedness of the different communities of anthropologists and their anthropologies' (Restrepo and Escobar 2005: 100).

A decade earlier others had asserted the need for a debate on the 'anthropology of anthropology' that would take into consideration other anthropologies, forms of knowledge, modalities of writing, political and intellectual practices (Kuper 1991; Patterson 2001; Lem and Leach 2002). Likewise, Scholte ([1969] 1974) had already stated in the 1960s that emancipatory anthropology starts by taking itself seriously as an anthropological object, recognizing that all anthropological traditions are culturally mediated and contextually situated. Today there are many anthropologists from indigenous communities that question anthropological knowledge about their society produced by non-indigenous scholars and who themselves have begun to produce anthropological knowledge about their own and other societies. Among the international anthropological community, however, there is limited awareness of the challenge and the emergence of other anthropologies and their impact on the reconsideration of anthropological discipline.

I have been inspired by these reflections and thoughts and possibly also affected by the fact that I started my anthropological research in Lorestan and Khorassan during the 1970s, when the discipline was thriving and a large number of Iranian and foreign anthropologists were enthusiastic about their ongoing projects. After the Revolution of 1979 all anthropological activities declined, and communication with other anthropologists became extremely difficult. There was a prevailing spirit of isolation and seclusion. Out of this situation I felt the urgent need to trace the history of anthropological research in Iran during the twenty years after the Revolution – a period of political turbulence and considerable social changes – to review and reconsider the process of devolution and the rather tangled history of the discipline's early development together with those who had played a formative role in the establishment of the discipline from its beginnings.

This common desire to reflect upon the emergence and history as well as the future development of a particular, in this case Iranian, anthropological tradition brought together fifteen scholars as part of a three-day symposium hosted by the Institute für Historische Ethnologie at Johann Wolfgang Goethe University, Frankfurt am Main, with the kind financial support of the Volkswagen Stiftung. All contributors to the symposium had started their anthropological field studies in Iran prior to the Revolution and had continued their research up to the present: the Western scholars Lois Beck (Washington University, St. Louis U.S.), Christian Bromberger (Institut d'Ethnologie Méditerranéenne Et Comparative, Aix-en Provence, France), Jean-Pierre Digard (CNRS Paris, France), Mary Elaine Hegland (Santa Clara University California, U.S.), Ulrich Marzolph (Akademie der Wissenschaften, Göttingen, Germany) and Richard Tapper (SOAS London, U.K), were joined by the leading Iranian anthropologists Sekander Amanolahi (Shiraz University), Ali Asghar Bulookbashi (The Centre for the Great Islamic Encyclopaedia, Tehran), Nasser Fakouhi (University of Tehran), Nematollah Fazeli (Allameh Tabatabai University, Tehran), Mohammad Mir-Shokraei (Cultural Heritage Institute, Tehran) and Soheila Shahshahani (Shahid Beheshti University, Tehran), all of whom played important parts in assuring the continuation of anthropological studies in Iran during the difficult postrevolutionary period. Finally, six more participants, now affiliated with Western institutions but of Iranian descent, also participated: Fariba Adelkhah (Centre d'Études et de Recherches Internationales, Paris), Shahram Khosravi (Centrum för forskning om internationell migration och etniska relationer, Stockholm University), Ziba Mir-Hosseini (Senior Research Associate at the Centre for Islamic and Middle Eastern Laws (CIMEL), SOAS, London) and Mohammad Shahbazi (Associate Professor of Public Health, JSU School of Public Health, Jackson, MS, U.S.).

For the first time since the Revolution of 1979, Western and Iranian anthropologists met to exchange their ideas and views about how anthropological knowledge in Iran is shaped, how it emerged and what are its salient features. The problems of, and obstacles to, anthropological research in Iran and their resolution on the personal or institutional level were considered, and new challenges to and tasks for anthropological research in Iran were identified. All participants contributed in one way or another to these questions; thus an image of the evolution of this discipline emerged that includes the personal touch and provides an account of individual experiences from the viewpoints of the speakers. Though some of the contributions overlap, especially concerning historical matters, I decided that the respective authors' concerns and arguments put them into different enough contexts to warrant the inclusion of duplication. It was of great importance to me to accept each contributor's position and not to attempt to derive from the complex discussions a coherent picture of *one* Iranian anthropological vision.

The present publication has two parallel aims: by tracing the development of anthropology in Iran through previous turns, making visible certain processes and practices of disciplinization, professionalization and institutionalization, I am trying to make a case for the pertinence of Iranian anthropological knowledge. Secondly, I would like to outline a framework that, going beyond a critique of past and current anthropological research, sets the direction for future collaborative research between anthropologists in Iran and their colleagues abroad. As emphasized a number of times in the contributions, it is only through international cooperation that Iranian anthropology will gain more academic and societal weight. The preconditions of such cooperation, however, should be subject to thorough reflection and ensure the equality of both partners. The present publication is meant as a first step towards this intended practical cooperation.

The volume comprises four parts. The first, 'From Folklore to Anthropology: The Passage', presents the historical and cultural setting and discusses the epistemological space established by literary and folklore studies long before anthropological research was undertaken by native and foreign anthropologists in Iran. Ali Bulookbashi, in his essay ' The Contribution of Foreign Anthropologists to Iranology', discusses the development of Iranian studies (Iranology) and how it was influenced by Western scholars, and also examines the conduct of ethnological and folkloric research in Iran. The first section of the chapter includes a short historical account of European travellers' reports on the sociocultural life of the Iranian people since the early seventeenth century and of the first anthropologists to carry out ethnographic fieldwork in Iranian societies. He then introduces the current research of foreign anthropologists who have focused their work on specific areas of Iranian culture. The final section sketches cooperative efforts between foreign and Iranian anthropologists carrying out field research in tribal, rural and urban societies before the Islamic Revolution. The concluding remarks are dedicated to the future development of anthropology, the impediments to its growth and the challenges it faces in achieving recognition of its status as an accredited scientific and academic discipline.

Ulrich Marzolph, who has extensive experience in research on Iranian folk narratives in both pre- and postrevolutionary Iran, provides in his chapter 'Storytelling as a Constituent of Popular Culture: Folk Narrative Research in Contemporary Iran' a short definition of folk narrative research, a discipline that in his understanding bridges the fields of folklore and anthropology. After sketching the discipline's historical development in Iran from the nineteenth century up to the present, he identifies the key issues in Iranian folk narrative research as follows: (1) the interaction between foreigners and locals; (2) research methods; (3) ethical problems. A fourth point, dealing with the problematics of folk narrative in Iran, is followed by a tentative assessment of current problems and their solutions. Marzolph sketches the discipline of folk narrative research as a highly active one and draws particular attention to the fact that folklore and folk narrative hold a strong potential for future research, whatever the conditions of both practising and studying folklore will develop to be.

Mary Elaine Hegland provides a detailed bibliographic overview of the anthropology of Iran via English-language publications. In her essay 'Iranian Anthropology – Crossing Boundaries: Influences of Modernization, Social Transformation and Globalization', she traces the history of anthropology in Iran by providing names, dates and project descriptions. She discusses more recent trends in the anthropology of Iran that tend to transgress existing scholarly fields to move into new types of research arenas, fieldwork sites, anthropological methods and ethnographic genres. Moreover, she discusses the career paths of scholars who were not able to return to Iran in the postrevolutionary period and also examines the research strategies of those who manage to continue their commitment to the study of anthropology of Iranian society and culture but face various challenges to conducting fieldwork. Finally, she offers an outlook onto the field's future prospects by summarizing the research of the new generation of anthropologists.

The second part of the volume, 'Voices From Within: Institutions and Professions', outlines the perspectives of anthropologists from within Iran, their academic and institutional practices (training, research, writing, publishing, etc.) and their critical perspectives on the shortcomings regarding the development of an assertive indigenous anthropology. Nematollah Fazeli examines the state of 'Anthropology in Postrevolutionary Iran'. The first part is devoted to an overview of the history of anthropology in the twentieth century prior to the Islamic Revolution, followed by an account of the state of the discipline at the beginning of the Revolution in the 1980s. The complex political forces and the sociopolitical changes in Iranian society, which set certain limits and constraints on the development of the discipline today, are sketched. It is against this background that Fazeli then examines the role of anthropology in the conflict between tradition and modernity and explains the political encounter of Islamism with secularism in terms of anthropology in contemporary Iran.

Nasser Fakouhi regards anthropology as an established and at the same time a new discipline in Iranian academia. In his chapter 'Making and Re-making an Academic Tradition: Towards an Indigenous Anthropology in Iran', he examines the relationship between anthropology, sociology, folk-lore studies and ethnic and regional studies, and discusses the extent to which anthropological research was marginalized with respect to sociology. The present situation of anthropology at Iranian universities is addressed through an assessment of faculty composition, their training and academic careers, the quality of the students, the focus of student research topics and the number and level of academic degrees awarded, and finally via an analysis of the material published in Iran as well as the literature available to scholars there more generally. The author stresses that there is both a potential and a crucial need to promote anthropological teaching and research in Iran. The conclusion presents proposals that would foster the development of an indigenous version of the discipline.

In her essay entitled 'Iranian Anthropologists Are Women', Soheila Shah-shahani emphasizes the gendered nature of the anthropological enterprise and underlines the role women have played in anthropological research and teaching. Focusing on issues in contemporary anthropology in Iran, she dis-cusses the political and cultural pressure on the discipline. Her perspective is broadened by comparing conditions in Iran with those in other Middle Eastern countries. For good academic and theoretical work to be possible, she argues, freedom of opportunity and non-interference in the conduct of research are indispensible.

The following part, 'Anthropological Practice: Constraints and Possi-bilities', addresses the wider context of anthropological research and prac-tices as experienced by both Iranian and foreign anthropologists, reflecting particularly on the possibilities and constraints under which anthropologi-cal research was undertaken in the past and continues to be conducted at the present time. Jean-Pierre Digard argues in 'Applied Anthropology in Iran?' that Western anthropologists working in Iran have had to cope with obligations vis-à-vis the government to make their expertise available to state authorities and to conduct research at its request. The role of anthropol-ogy in solving social problems and designing models for development is the main topic in this article. Although applied projects are welcomed in Iran and certainly not discouraged, the government questions the applicability of certain research results. To support his view the author gives several ex-amples of applied projects in Iran and concludes that the choice of whether to actually engage in applied anthropology always rests with the anthropolo-gist himself.

Mohammad Shahbazi refers to his anthropological fieldwork and health-related research conducted among the Qashqai tribes. In his chapter 'Past

Experiences and Future Perspectives of an Indigenous Anthropologist on Anthropological Work in Iran', he discusses the challenges he experienced in using ethnographic research methodologies and stresses issues facing the 'native anthropologists' and indigenous anthropology. He explains why he attaches such importance to the idea of an indigenous anthropology and concludes by offering several recommendations to create a more optimal environment for the future of anthropology and anthropological work in Iran.

In the chapter 'Anthropological Research in Iran', Lois Beck outlines a range of interlinking issues in past and current anthropological research in Iran and, based on her experiences as a cultural anthropologist in Iran and among Iranians living in other countries over a span of forty-four years, suggests improvements for the discipline to future researchers. She examines the purposes of anthropological research and writing, the applicability of Western theories and methods and the ethical issues involved in research and writing. She outlines comparative, problem-oriented, and local-level studies and urges writers to include discussions of the wider sociocultural context.

Ziba Mir-Hosseini, in her essay 'Being From There: Dilemmas of a "Native Anthropologist"', explores the ways in which the developments in anthropology and her own involvement in the politics of gender in Islam shaped her experience and the ethnographies (two of them documentary films) that she has produced since completing her doctoral thesis in 1980. She narrates the stories behind the production of her ethnographies, not because she considers her own trajectory particularly important or representative of Iranian anthropology, but because she thinks it highlights some of the issues central to the theme of anthropological perspectives on Iran. The central questions she addresses are: What kind of ethnography can she produce as a 'native feminist' anthropologist? What does it mean to be a 'native' ethnographer? In what ways, if any, do the fieldwork experiences and the ethnographic accounts of 'insider' and 'outsider' anthropologists differ?

Finally, the fourth part of the volume, 'Past and Present Perspectives: Challenging the Future', considers the discipline in its broader context by critically examining new fields of research such as problem-oriented projects, applied anthropology and anthropology and the media in the Iranian context, and by identifying strategies for future anthropological research. Christian Bromberger, in 'Usual Topics: Taboo Themes and New Objects in Iranian Anthropology', points out that the anthropology of Iran shares many of the same problems as the discipline in general, particularly the considerable difficulty in adapting its conceptual framework to the analysis of the present. In his view, contemporary anthropology in Iran has barely begun, and whole sectors of social and cultural experience have been neglected. To provide an example of new and innovative fields of activity for the discipline, he discusses his project to establish an open-air museum in Gilan. This endeavour is now continued by the Cultural Heritage Organization (Sāzimān-i Mirās-i Farhangī) in cooperation with French specialists, under the aegis of the United Nations Educational, Scientific and Cultural Organization.

Fariba Adelkhah discusses the characteristics of Iranian anthropology, and of Iranian social science more generally. In 'Islamophobia and Malaise in Anthropology', with reference to discussions of veiling (*hijab*) as practised in Iran, she critiques certain areas of research in the social sciences as tending to be fixed too strongly on ideological categories. She takes the view that research concerning changes in Iranian society following the Revolution tends to be dominated by political concerns. What results, then, is a highly dichotomous vision of the Revolution and the Islamic Republic.

Richard Tapper, in 'Personal Reflections on Anthropology of and in Iran', questions what anthropology of and in Iran has achieved so far and discusses the directions it might or should go in the future. To develop his ideas he refers to an unpublished paper, which he presented at an informal seminar in 1974 on 'ethical problems in fieldwork', that raises a number of issues of continuing relevance. He also refers more briefly to his subsequent fieldwork in Afghanistan, where he did research in 1968 and 1972. Finally, he reflects on the challenges to, but also the possible rewards of, a continuing anthropological engagement with Iranian culture and society.

Facing History

As for the history of Iranian anthropology, only a few studies have been carried out so far. Soheila Shahshahani (1986) gives an overview primarily of the inner-Iranian development, which is supplemented by two detailed review articles by Brian Spooner, 'Anthropology' (1987) and 'Ethnography' (1999), published in *Encyclopaedia Iranica*. Naraghi and Ayati (2000) more generally explain the development of the social sciences overall in Iran.[1]

Some Iranian scholars take the view that Persian ethnographic writing can be traced back to the early period of Islamic history, when writers and travellers wrote autobiographies and recorded their personal observations (Khaliqi 1975; Ruholamini 1975; Shahshahani 1986). The first ethnographic description of this kind is thus considered to have been the eleventh-century travel account by Nasser Khosrow, *Safarnameh*. Subsequent travel accounts go back to the period of the expansion of Iran's relationship with Europe (Wright 1977). During the Constitutional Revolution (1906–1911) and the beginning of the twentieth century nationalist discourses flourished, and both intellectuals and writers began to take interest in the everyday life of ordinary people, their language, customs and folk narratives. Outstanding among them are Jamalzadeh (1895–1997), Ali Akbar Dehkhoda (1879–1956) and Zeynul Abedin Maragheh'i (1838–1911). Later they were followed by Hedayat (1903–1951), Shamlu (1925–2000) and Jalal e Al-e Ahmad (1923–1969), who studied Iranian folklore and described the mores of the people. All of these thinkers and writers share a common project, that of literature as cultural critique.

A thorough study of the emergence of anthropology as a discipline was carried out for the first time by Nematollah Fazeli in *Politics of Culture in Iran: Anthropology, Politics and Society in the Twentieth Century* (2006). Here, he analyses the phases of the discipline as they were linked to political circumstances and ultimately asks 'how and to what extent has Iranian anthropology been involved in sociopolitical ideology' (2006: 4–5). According to the author, political and social factors have influenced the institutionalization and professionalization of the discipline. On the other hand, the discipline has influenced government authorities and been used by them as an 'ideological instrument, applied knowledge and cultural critique' (2006: 23). Nationalist ideology was reinforced and folklore studies were encouraged after Reza Shah (1925–1941) came to power. In 1937 Reza Shah ordered the establishment of the first anthropological museum in Iran. However, it was not until the mid 1950s that the discipline was institutionalized and professionalized.

In the present volume several contributors provide detailed consideration of the history of the discipline from very different perspectives. A prevalent concern that is taken up in several contributions relates to all those literary studies that were related to cultural phenomena, representing a kind of 'cultural critique' or 'folk studies'. Are they to be considered as the foundations of Iranian anthropology? Both Fazeli and Fakouhi refer in their contributions to the importance of this 'Literary Revolution' in the development of Iranian anthropology. Together with Shahshahani they assign a prominent role to Sadeq Hedayat as the Iranian who paved the way for modern anthropological research in Iran. Such discussions inevitably lead to further questions regarding what makes up the field of anthropology and how it is to be distinguished from both sociology and folk studies (Bulookbashi, Fakouhi, Marzolph, Shahshahani).

As for the presence of Western anthropologists in Iran, we agree with Jean Copans' statement of the early 1970s that the 'history of ethnology is also the history of the relations between European societies and non-European societies' (1974: 52). In the Iranian case many Western anthropologists were inspired by Fredric Barth, who came to Iran in 1959 under the aegis of a UNESCO sedentarization project and stayed with the Basseri nomads in the province of Fars in southern Iran. In this volume Bulookbashi delivers a detailed account of the history of the activities of Western anthropologists, their research topics and field sites, while Hegland traces the history of anthropology by presenting an extensive and highly useful list of references to anthropological works written and published in English, particularly from the 1960s through the revolutionary and postrevolutionary period up to the present.

The review of the history of anthropology in Iran presented by the contributors to this volume aptly reflects Iran's changing position in the modern world-system. There are two lines to be followed: one an 'inner circle', as I would call it, which is constituted by internal political and intellectual settings, starting with the Constitutional Revolution and the 'Literary Revolution' that led to the institutionalization of the discipline in the 1930s. This line of development made Iranian anthropology part of a greater nationalist project. Then there is an 'outer circle' shaped by the encounter between Western and Iranian anthropologists, leading to the academic establishment of the discipline. This line paved the way for Iranian anthropology to exceed national boundaries and join theoretical and methodological discussions put forward to conceptualize Middle Eastern societies. In both circles Iranian and European intellectuals took on the role of intermediaries providing data and interpreting and theorizing about the subjects of identity politics. The way these intellectuals responded to societal and political challenges in Iran during the different periods becomes an analytical and political question in its own right.

What is striking, however, in the encounter between Iranian and foreign anthropologists, is the fact that though their research interests overlapped closely during the 1970s, planned and systematic collaborative research was never carried out. The only exception to this was the ethnographic mapping project started by France's Centre National de Recherche Scientifique (CNRS) in cooperation with the Centre of Iranian Anthropology in 1972.[2] As for folk studies, Marzolph notes that folk narrative research in Iran has always been characterized by cooperation between foreigners and locals. However, it is also important to add that this cooperation always casts the foreigner as researcher and the local as informant.

Generally speaking, an immense amount of scholarly data has been collected since the beginning of anthropological research in Iran in the 1960s. Research has included national and cultural heritage, the documentation of material culture, nomadic and tribal studies, agrarian and rural change, family dynamics and the role of women, language, folk studies, ritual and performance and, more recently, issues of ethnicity, representation and cultural studies. However, it must be said that Iranian anthropology was never concerned with cross-cultural studies or studies abroad, but focused exclusively on national phenomena and developments, being primarily concerned

with the attainment of something like self-knowledge. The literature on regional relationships is closely tied to the ethnographic preoccupation with
local groups and villages, without much concern for comparative analysis
of indigenous discourses or the expression of ethnic identities. Rarely have
anthropologists aimed to achieve a grander scale of analysis that asks questions about the wider processes that unite or separate society. This preference for local particularities and case-by-case description makes it difficult
to conceive of Iranian anthropology as a unified field of ethnological study,
or to identify a distinctively Iranian theoretical and methodological approach
in sociocultural anthropology. This raises the question of whether there are
any fields at all that have been studied by means of anthropological assumptions and analytical categories. Some worthy topics have for the most part
been thoroughly ignored by scholarly attention.

Deficiencies, Shortcomings and Obstacles

Diverse reasons possibly hindering the successful formation of a body of anthropology in Iran are mentioned by the contributors. Fakouhi, Fazeli and
Shahshahani note the problematic state of affairs in teaching and training in
universities: the low number of qualified teaching staff and the absence of an
established Ph.D. programme or other professional training.

Substantial obstacles and deficiencies aside, further structural and sociopolitical causes are mentioned that have so far prevented the establishment
of anthropology as an independent and self-contained discipline. Fakouhi,
among others, attributes this to the long-standing and ongoing interlinking
of sociology and anthropology both in content and also with respect to institutions. Shahshahani and Bromberger attribute the difficulties of Iranian
anthropology at least in part to the exodus of Iranian specialists.

Finally, the absence of cooperation among anthropologists living in
Iran, and with those outside the country, is seen as one of the major causes
of the lack of development of Iranian anthropology. As one example of
the hindrance of cooperative projects, Tapper mentions his submission of
proposals for cooperation and the reaction of the authorities in declining
his suggestions. He also refers to governmental authorities and analyses the
reasons for their negative attitude towards anthropologists. For Hegland,
the lack of access to other anthropologists and publications and the obstacles to participation in conferences put Iranian students, professionals and
researchers at risk of isolation from the worldwide community.

These considerations lead us to a further point to be stressed: the failure
of Iranians to establish an indigenous anthropology. Ehsan Naraghi, one
of the founders of the Institute for Social Science Research (ISSR), showed

great concern for indigenizing the Iranian social sciences, arguing that Western methodology should not be applied but rather adapted to Iranian conditions of social research and that anthropology in particular should be involved in solving countries' problems, be problem-oriented and focus on presenting solutions. For Nadir Afshar-Naderi, the director of the anthropological department at the ISSR, indigenization meant applying anthropology for the benefit of the people studied (Fazeli 2006: 101). However, as the long and ongoing discussion about indigenization in other regions has shown (Atal 1981; Loubser 1988), application alone is not at issue. The question of indigenizing research is a matter of who participates in the construction of knowledge and who controls the process. This again presumes a guarantee of autonomy for universities, independent research institutes and encouragement of a spirit of fearless and impartial research. In this volume, Marzolph points out that Iranian researchers never took advantage of their familiarity with local folklore to develop an indigenous autonomy as was done other Asian, African or American cultures.

The Way Forward

Anthropology of Iran undoubtedly shares many of the same problems as the discipline in general. Despite the shortcomings and deficiencies in establishing the discipline, all of the present contributions agree that the rapid transformation of Iranian society and the changes that have taken place in Iran during the last century (revolution, urbanization, modernization of infrastructure, expansion of mass media) require Iranian anthropology to adjust to the present needs of society. As Tapper points out, anthropology has to engage in public and intellectual debates to show that it has something to offer to the central issues of contemporary society. A corollary question is how Iranian anthropology might most productively enact disciplinary self-criticism and redirection.

All contributors to this volume present suggestions, proposals and visions related to the position Iranian anthropology may take in future. A general view put forward by most of the contributors is the awareness that it is time to overcome the limited perspective of anthropological research that concentrates primarily on the internal dynamics of Iranian culture without questioning the global and historical context. There is an urgent need for research that offers theoretically and topically focused arguments connecting local ethnography with discipline-wide concerns. Beck, Bromberger, Tapper and others suggest that according more relevance to anthropological research in Iran calls for a readjustment of our methods. That ethnography is linked explicitly to and draws on larger disciplinary and interdisciplinary trends is nothing new. However, along these lines some conditions are necessary, foremost that we must grant that academic knowledge is relatively autonomous and capable of attaining desirable levels of communication. All contributors argue for a reflexive anthropology free of ideology, which may ultimately facilitate fruitful cooperation between Iranian and foreign anthropologists and strengthen the disciplinary consolidation and professionalization of anthropology within the Iranian academic context.

As mentioned above, the aim of such cooperation and dialogue would be the design and conceptualization of common research projects and exchange programmes. Fakouhi, Tapper and Beck advance concrete proposals that could constitute the basis for such cooperation. For Digard, one of the few anthropologists who, together with Bromberger, has experienced the conditions of cooperation in anthropological projects conducted with Iranian institutions, 'cooperation starts in the field and finishes with interpretation.' Further suggestions and proposals are specifically directed at the important contribution anthropology may make to a better understanding of processes of social and cultural transformation, which at the beginning of the twenty-first century impact not only Iranian communities but the entire Middle East.

Closing Remarks

In sketching the history and the actual state of Iranian anthropology, I am not arguing that it is unique but rather that it exhibits particularities that warrant critical reflection. Thus the collection of articles in this volume must be considered a starting point for acquiring a better understanding of these particularities. It should not be surprising that some of the contributions are rather tentative in conceptualizing the past and assessing various desirata for the future development of the discipline. Contrary to the usual concept of essays, the authors were asked not to focus on a particular issue related to their field of research, but to take a bird's-eye view in reflecting on the state of the discipline, with consideration of its past, its actual status and future development. While some of the authors take only the Iranian context to express their critical views (Buloukbashi, Fakouhi), there are others who refer to very particular topics in Iran (Adelkhah on *hijab*) and expand their views to the discipline in general (Beck, Digard and Tapper with respect to ethical topics, Mir-Hosseini referring to indigenous anthropology). The heterogeneous character of the contributions is due to differences in how the respective authors refer to the past and to the present, integrating their own experiences into the text, and in the way they see power relations operating in the process of research and teaching. Some therefore question the institutional settings, while others emphasize the importance of contextual relations in social and political configurations. The coherence of the contributions, however, lies in the fervour that the authors share with regard to their view that Iranian anthropology is an endeavour of central importance in and of itself. In this sense, the critiques expressed vis-à-vis the actual research opportunities and shortcomings in Iran do not mean that unfavourable judgment is being passed or that authors are engaging in wishful thinking. Rather they represent serious reflections and points of view that are fundamental to the advancement of the discipline and to the continued encouragement of its practitioners. But in order to understand the subtlety that is not accidental, one must often read between the lines.

With regard to the aims of 'world anthropologies' to make possible '[o]ther anthropologies and anthropology otherwise' (Restrepo and Escobar 2005), mentioned in the beginning, we have to admit that Iranian anthropology, as is the case with anthropologies elsewhere, is also affected by the spread of ideas from Europe and North America, where the discipline first was established and institutionalized in academic centres. However, the historical sketch of the field's development and institutionalization in Iran shows that this amounts to much more than simply the appropriation and reproduction of Western patterns, ideas and images. Iranian anthropology was cultivated and rooted in particular cultural, academic and practical circumstances, much like anthropology in other parts of the world. The various contributions in this volume show that to be aware of the particularities of Iranian anthropology we have to learn about the epistemic, economic and political contexts of the sites in which anthropology has developed, and about the way the geopolitics of knowledge contributes to structure the terms and conditions that govern the practice of the discipline.

With regard to the discipline's future prospects, the contributions also make clear that it is necessary to create networks of anthropologists and anthropological institutions to develop projects bridging gaps within national academic communities. This requires creation of a common space in which national and international anthropologists can meet, engage in dialogues and construct coalitions. Research projects must be planned cooperatively, in constant exchange and take into consideration their relevance to understanding contemporary Iranian life.[3] Once cooperative endeavours have been initiated, Iranian anthropologists must be empowered to go north to do fieldwork in the U.S. and Europe, so as to make their contributions to what Augé calls 'an anthropology of the contemporary world' (Augé 1994). Only then will the discipline finally achieve the balanced perspective necessary to make good on its claim to scientific universality.

For me, editing this volume was like a 'second socialization' in the discipline. The more I went back into history, the more I received insights into the close and complex connectedness of political transformations in Iran and the professionalization and establishment of the social sciences in academia. Moreover, I gained the firm conviction that certain individuals and socially and intellectually approved personalities, during specific periods and under certain conditions, played major roles in constructing anthropological knowledge in Iran by shaping its image and lending it a voice. Needless to say, I often regretted not having taken the opportunity to profit from chances I had to query the few Iranian and foreign anthropologists who played a decisive role in the establishment of the discipline in Iran. I am therefore all the more happy to have seized at least this occasion and now can offer the present publication, which contains valuable ideas and thoughts of many anthropologists who have been involved in the emergence and genesis of anthropological knowledge in Iran.

Last but not least I would like to acknowledge my debt to Birgit Reinel, who from the start contributed towards the making of this book. Later we were joined by Katja Riek, and I am deeply grateful to both of them for their criticism, comments and many suggestions. I would also like to express my gratitude to the Volkswagen Stiftung for their generous financial support for the organization of the first international conference on Anthropological Perspectives in Iran to be held since the Revolution of 1979 and for their encouragement and assistance in finalizing the present publication.

NOTES

1. In addition, the collection of articles on ethnographic fieldwork in Iran edited by Erika Friedl and Mary E. Hegland for a special issue of *Iranian Studies* in 2004 deserves particular mention. It provides very useful and representative insights into the range of ethnographic work done in Iran and the relevant methodological issues.
2. See Bromberger and Digard (1975) as well as Bulookbashi in this volume.
3. Fakouhi notes in his contribution that the current cooperation is unbalanced, i.e. it has been more advantageous to Western scholars than to anthropologists in Iran.

REFERENCES

Atal, Y. 1981. 'The Call for Indigenization'. *International Social Science Journal* 33(1): 189–97.

Augé, M. 1994. Pour une Anthropologie des mondes contemporain. Paris.

Bromberger, C. and J.-P. Digard. 1975. 'Pourquoi, comment des cartes ethnographiques de l'Iran ?', *Objets et Mondes*, 15, no 1: 7–24.

Copans, J. (ed.) 1975. Anthropologie et Impérialisme. Paris.

Fazeli, N. 2006. *Politics of Culture in Iran: Anthropology, Politics and Society in the Twentieth Century.* London.

Friedl, E. and M. E. Hegland (eds). 2004. *Iranian Studies: Special Issue on Ethnographic Fieldwork in Iran* 37(4).

Kuper, A. 1991. 'Anthropologists and the History of Anthropology', *Critique of Anthropology* 2: 125–42.

Khaliqi, M. 1975/1353. 'Fa'aliyat-haye Markaz-e Mardomshenasi Iran', *Mardomshenasi va farhang-e 'ammeh* 1: 2–21. (Activities of the Center for Iranian Anthropology)

Lem, W. and B. Leach 2002. *Culture, Economy, Power: Anthropology as Critique, Anthropology as Praxis.* Albany, NY.

Loubser, J. 1988. 'The Need for the Indigenization of the Social Sciences', *International Sociology* 3(2): 179–87.

Naraghi, E. and A. Ayati 2000/1379. *Nazari be tahghighat e ejtema'i dar Iran.* Tehran.

Patterson, T. 2001. *A Social History of Anthropology in the United States.* Oxford.

Restrepo, E. and A. Escobar 2005. 'Other Anthropologies and Anthropology Otherwise. Steps to a World Anthropologies Framework', *Critique of Anthropology* 25(2): 99–129.

Ruholamini, M. 1975/1354. 'Mardom-negari va naqhsh-e an dar tahqiqat-e mardomshenasi-ye Iran', *Majmu'eh-ye sokhanrani-haye nakhostin kongreh-ye tahqiqat-e Irani* (Proceedings of the First Congress of Iranology). Tehran: 402–8. Univ. Tehran.

Scholte, B. 1969. 'Toward a Reflexive and Critical Anthropology', D. Hymes (ed.), *Reinventing Anthropology.* Ann Arbor, MI.

Shahshahani, S. 1986. 'History of Anthropology in Iran', *Iranian Studies* 19: 65–87.

Spooner, B. 1987. 'Anthropology', *Encyclopædia Iranica* 2 New York: 107–15.

———. 1999. 'Ethnography', *Encyclopædia Iranica* 8 New York: 9–45.

Wright, D. 1977. *The English amongst the Persians: During the Qajar Period 1787–1921.* London.

PART I

From Folkore to Anthropology

The Passage

CHAPTER 1

The Contribution of Foreign Anthropologists to Iranology

Ali Bulookbashi

Historical Overview

The travel accounts of European travellers such as Adam Olearius (1603–1671), Jean Baptist Tavernier (1605–1689) and Jean Chardin (1643–1713), about characteristic manifestations of Iranian culture and ways of life in the seventeenth century, were what first attracted the attention of Europeans to this country.

At the beginning of the nineteenth century, Iran aroused particular interest among the two powerful governments of England and France. Subsequently Iran became a field of competition between these two powers in terms of their military, political and economic activities in the region. It was during that time that Sir John Malcolm (1769–1833), the orientalist and governmental representative of England and Eastern India, came to Iran. In 1815 he published the first well-known and comprehensive book about Iran, *Sketches of Persia*. James Morier (1780–1849), a British traveller and official, came to Iran as a member of a mission led by Sir Harford Jones, and a few years later, after he had become the secretary to Sir Gore Ouseley, the British ambassador in Tehran, he published three books (two travelogues), of which *The Adventures of Hajji Baba of Ispahan* (1824) became the most famous and familiar to European readers. The two other books were the accounts of his journeys to Iran and other countries in the years 1808–1809 and 1810–1816. In *Hajji Baba* Morier presented a picture of Iranian traditional life and conveyed a lively image of the social and cultural character of the people of Iran.[1] Ever since, an interest in acquiring knowledge about Iran and its people has been apparent among some scholars, who gradually began travelling to Iran to study the languages, religions, history, archaeology, literature and arts of a society different from their own. Later on, in the early 1920s, the term 'Iranology' came into use, designating a branch of oriental studies that focuses on systematic scientific Iranian studies.

Ethnological studies conducted by foreign anthropologists in Iran have been an outstanding branch of Iranian studies that has been ignored for quite a while and even despised by some scholars.[2] However, it was foreign anthropologists, particularly Henry Field, Carl Feilberg and Fredrik Barth, who were definitely the pioneers of modern *Iranshenâsi* (Iranology) in studying the cultures of Iranian societies. Among the first foreign ethnological researchers to come to Iran, they carried out fieldwork there long before anthropology gained a reputation for itself in Iran, and well before the first group of trained Iranian anthropology students began to conduct anthropological research in their society.

As anthropology became an established discipline within the social sciences in the Western world, European and North American anthropologists began studying 'other cultures' in non-Western societies, in particular in Africa, Australia, Asia and the Americas continent. During the first half of the twentieth century Western anthropologists directed their attention also to Iran and began travelling to this country to carry out ethnographical field research (Bulookbashi 2003). Providing detailed information about the sociocultural structure, systems of beliefs and religious practices of certain nomadic and settled tribal and rural peoples was the central outcome of their field research. This was the first time that foreign anthropologists reconstructed the past of nomads of nonliterate societies without any compiled written history, thus offering a real picture of the social and economic life of pastoral nomads and settled cultivators in Iran.

In 1934 Henry Field, a physical anthropologist from the United States, led an anthropological expedition of the Field Museum of Natural History in Chicago to carry out wide-ranging field research throughout Iran. His studies, published in *Contributions to the Anthropology of Iran* (1939), were mainly based on anthropometric data concerning the physical features of the inhabitants of Iran. In his book Field also provided some valuable information about the social, cultural, economic and religious organization of nomadic and settled tribal groups and rural societies in Iran.

In 1935 Carl Feilberg, a Danish ethnographer, carried out five months of fieldwork among the Pâpi, a Lor pastoralist tribe in Bâlâ Geriveh in Southern Lorestan. The results of his field research were published in two books: *La Tente Noire* (1944) and *Les Papis* (1952). Feilberg's research concerns the history of the Lor tribal nomads and certain aspects of their sociocultural and economic life. In *La Tente Noire* he also offers an analysis of the construction and distribution of the black tent (the nomadic Lori dwellings).

Fredrik Barth, a Norwegian anthropologist trained in Britain and writing in English, is an outstanding figure among anthropology's 'action theorists' (Kuper 1975: 229). He was the first anthropologist to conduct substantial fieldwork among the Iranian nomadic tribal population, in 1958. Barth – a methodological individualist and highly productive fieldworker – is known for his structural studies of pastoral nomads in the province of Fars in Iran. Today, his well-researched book *Nomads of South Persia: The Basseri Tribe of the Khamseh Confederacy* (1961) is a classic source in anthropological literature. Since then, Iranian societies without a written recorded history, particularly the pastoral nomadic groups, have fascinated foreign ethnographers and students of anthropology and attracted them to research in Iran (Bulookbashi 2003: 8).

Whereas the eighteenth century was a period of research on Iranian languages and religious ideas and practices, and the nineteenth century was the era of archaeological research and Iranian literary studies, the second half of the twentieth century was definitely the period of ethnological research in various societies of Iran. In this period, a great number of foreign ethnologists and anthropology graduate students from different universities around the world made visits to Iran. Some of them lived and worked for several years with different groups of tribal and rural peoples, learning their local languages in order to comprehend the constructions and categories of the sociocultural behaviours of these people.

At this point I would like to make some comments on folklore studies, an important locus of Iranological and anthropological activity that, however, in Iran is carried out independently of Iranology or anthropology proper. Part of the confusion is that in Iran, as in other countries of the world, there is no agreement among scholars about the definition of folklore and the field of its subject material. Some U.S. scholars, such as William R. Bascom, consider folklore to be an intrinsic part of anthropology.[3] The Iranian folklorists do not generally make any distinction between the two fields of ethnological and folkloric studies. A glance at the compilations of their collected folkloric subjects justifies this fact. Others draw a distinction between these two fields and regard folklore as an independent discipline.[4] In addition, as far as I know, anthropologists and folklorists have different definitions of folklore. For instance, there are more than twenty definitions of folklore in the *Standard Dictionary of Folklore and Mythology* (see Leach and Fried 1972: 398–403). William R. Bascom proposes an exact meaning of folklore from an anthropological point of view and defines it as 'verbal art', stating that '[i]n anthropological usage, the term folklore has come to mean myth, legends, folktales, proverbs, riddles, verse, and a variety of other forms of artistic expression whose medium is the spoken word' (Leach and Fried 1972: 398). Melville J. Herskovits gives the following definition: '[O]riginally the study of cultural curiosities, and held to be the survival of an earlier period in the history of "civilized" literate peoples, folklore has come more and more to denote the study of the unwritten literature of any group, whether having writing or being without it' (Leach and Fried 1972: 400).

In my understanding folklore means a common cultural product of illiterate people that is orally transmitted among them, from one group to
another group and one generation to another generation – in both traditional and advanced literate societies. These popular oral products include
all forms of folk literature, folk arts, folk sciences, customs, games, folk
religious beliefs and so on. These folkloric topics, like the religious beliefs
described by R. Loeffler in his book *Islam in Practice,* 'have always been
revised, replaced, and discarded in the face of confirming and disconfirming
evidence, in transmittance from group to group, generation to generation,
and within individuals' (1988: 266–67). Thus anthropology's view of folklore as a living, dynamic tradition and not simply a collection of cultural
'texts' has made an important contribution to the way in which Iranian
folklore is understood.

Current Research by Foreign Anthropologists

Nowadays, there are numerous foreign anthropologists who have based their
Ph.D. dissertations and the greater part of their publications on ethnographical materials collected through their fieldwork in Iran.[5] By publishing the
outcome of their field researches, these anthropologists have undoubtedly
opened up a new glorious chapter in the realm of Iranology and established
an anthropological school within the tradition of Iranian studies. In addition they have introduced a significant new field in ethnological studies to
scholars all around the world and have provided a new perspective in the
global understanding of Iranian cultures.

It is striking that foreign anthropologists have mostly focused their work
on specific areas of Iranian cultural geography. Each of them is specialized
and recognized, both inside and outside of Iran, in the specific nomadic or
settled groups of tribal and rural societies among whom they have done field
research. Thus for example, the following anthropologists are well known
for their treatment of particular ethnic groups in Iran: R. H. Loeffler and
Erika Friedl's among the settled people of the Boir Ahmad tribes in the Sisakht village of the province of Kohgiluyeh and Boir Ahmadi, in southern
Iran, since 1965; R. Tapper on the Shahsevan, who live on the frontier of
Azerbaijan, since the early 1960s; Lois Beck among the Qashqâi confederacy (see e.g. Beck 1991), a former nomadic pastoral people of the province
of Fars in southern Iran, since 1969; Jean-Pierre Digard and Gene R. Garthwaite among the nomadic peoples of the confederation of the Bakhtiâri (Bulookbashi 2003: 8–12); Philip Salzman and Brian Spooner on the Baluch;
William Irons on the Turkmen; and Christian Bromberger in the province of
Guilân, one of the northern provinces in Iran. Each of them has produced

a number of publications primarily based on profound systematic scientific studies in their own case research. Their works have acquired significance in Iranian studies and have helped to promote the global understanding of the lives of the peoples living in Iran. Moreover, they have provided precise and valuable information on the social, cultural, political, religious and economic organizations of the Iranian tribal and peasant societies.

It is important to point out that these foreign anthropologists specializing in Iran have themselves, and through their publications, had a more or less marked influence on Iranian ethnographers and folklorists and have transmitted to them the acquired experiences of their systematic methods of ethnographical fieldwork. Thus, to a considerable extent, they contributed to the Western approach and methodology in the field of anthropology and the richness of anthropological knowledge. They had weighty influence on the conceptions of Iranian ethnographic researcher and on the study of Iran in general. For example, the researchers of the Centre for Iranian Anthropology (Markaz-e Mardomshenâsi-ye Iran), who cooperated with foreign anthropologists while the latter were conducting their field research in Iran, have incorporated their anthropological experiences and their exposure to anthropological methods into their own field research and subject studies.[6]

Cooperation between Foreign and Iranian Anthropologists

In order to illustrate the cooperation between foreign ethnographers and Iranian researchers and to highlight the effects of the former on the latter, it is necessary to give an example. Before the Islamic Revolution, one of the activities of the Centre for Iranian Anthropology was to engage in cooperation with foreign researchers, especially ethnographers, who were carrying out field research in Iran and to support them in their research projects on different aspects of anthropology, folklore and sociohistorical studies in tribal, rural and urban societies.[7] In their research expeditions, they were mostly accompanied by Iranian researchers who were all university-educated, mostly in humanities, and employed at the Centre for Iranian Anthropology.

By sending its research staff to work together with the foreign ethnographers, the centre intended to equip its experts with information in the field of anthropology. The Iranian researchers offered valuable interpretation services to foreign ethnographers – who often spoke languages other than those of the people among whom they were working – helping them to communicate with the local people, to understand more clearly the features of the peoples' culture and to receive accurate information from the native informants. At the same time the foreign ethnographers familiarized their Iranian companions with the anthropological knowledge and methodology they had acquired through the academic courses of their anthropology education, and transferred their own experiences in anthropology and capabilities in collecting the materials in the field.

A few years later, the Centre for Iranian Anthropology dispatched fourteen members of its scientific personnel to universities and institutes in England, France, Italy and the U.S. The aim was to acquire academic training in social and cultural anthropology and other social science disciplines, such as rural sociology, linguistics, human ecology, demography, social psychology, folkloristics and material culture. The names of the fourteen expeditionary individuals have been listed in the 'Gozâreš-e Fa'âliyyathâ-ye Markaz-e Mardomšenâsi –ye Iran: From Autumn 1975 until Winter 1977', (Tayebâti 1977–78/1356: 113–14).

After the expeditionary members of the centre had completed their studies and returned home from abroad, some of them resumed anthropological research at the centre, whereas others joined Tehran University as members of the faculty. I was one of the graduates who was educated at the Institute of Social Anthropology in Oxford. After returning home, I rejoined the scientific board of the centre. Then, after early retirement in 1979–80, I joined the scientific boards of two nongovernmental organizations, namely the Cultural Research Bureau (Daftar-e pažuhešhâ-ye Farhangi) and the Centre of the Great Islamic Encyclopaedia (Markaz-e Dâyerat al-Ma'âref-e Bozorg-e Islami), where I am still working and heading their anthropology department. Today, we can proudly claim that there are several well-trained Iranian anthropologists who work as professors on the academic boards of different universities, and as active scholars in research groups of the anthropology departments of some governmental and nongovernmental organizations in Iran.

Unlike the foreign anthropologists, however, the majority of Iranian anthropologists apparently have not concentrated their attention on a specific geographical territory or a given ethnic tribal group. The scope of these anthropologists' studies has generally addressed various and extended subjects, and they have mostly oriented themselves towards the study of a multitude of fragmentary anthropological and folkloric themes.[8] Only a very few Iranian anthropologists have focused their research on a particular region or a group in tribal and rural society. One exception, so far as I know, is the Iranian anthropologist Sekandar Amanolahi-Baharvand, whose ethnological research is generally based on the Lor, in the province of Lorestan, in particular on the former pastoralist tribe of the Baharvand from which he originates.[9]

It should be noted that before and after trained Iranian anthropologists began their ethnographic studies in Iran, ethnographic and folkloric research was generally pursued by a large group of non-anthropologists from different disciplines, such as geography and literature. Most of them were attached to either governmental or nongovernmental centres and have to a certain extent played an effective role in advancing anthropological studies in Iran.[10]

Conclusion: Impediments to the Development of Anthropology in Iran

It is worth mentioning that the results of field studies of both Iranian and non-Iranian anthropologists and folklorists have contributed substantially to the recognition of the social and cultural identity of Iranians and a range of ethnic groups of nomadic and rural communities in Iran. They also represent an important written social history for each of these traditional societies that previously had only non-recorded history.

The point I would like to consider in my conclusion is that in Iran, for one reason or another, anthropology as a discipline has not developed to the same extent as other social scientific disciplines, like sociology, linguistics and social psychology. In my view a number of factors account for the relative backwardness of anthropology and the marginalization of anthropological studies in Iran. The first and most important factor, as Alexander Ervin puts it, is that 'anthropology sometimes seems an un-disciplined "discipline", because there are no clear-cut subject boundaries ... [O]ne thing that has always been notable about anthropology [is that] it cannot be purely an "ivory tower" subject; it operates with real people in real countries' (2000: 128).

Another problem is the popularization of ethnographic and folkloric research results by people who, though interested in such studies, mainly are not trained in anthropology and folklore and therefore are not well qualified to undertake such ethnological studies. Although these non-academic participants in the production of ethnographic knowledge may, through no fault of their own, find themselves doing ethnographic work without being qualified to do so, they are nevertheless active in conducting traditional ethnographic research in their own unique way and publishing the outcomes of their studies.

Thirdly, we are confronted with the variety of ideas arising in the absence of a common academic language or similar systematic method among the members of governmental and nongovernmental organizations engaged in anthropological studies in Iran, in conjunction with the lack of cooperation between these organizations and the departments of anthropology in universities of Iran.

It has not been long since anthropology has found, more or less, its own scientific status within academia and been established as an accredited academic discipline in Iranian universities. Up until a few decades ago, anthropology was not recognized as a science, but was regarded as 'the study of customs, mores and traditional ethics'. For instance, some Islamic governmental officials, politicians and even academics held a pessimistic view of anthropological studies and looked at anthropology as a sort of taboo, suspecting that some foreign anthropologists were spies. They strove to keep anthropology away from university spaces and to 'purge' student milieus of the presumably harmful impressions of anthropological theories and teachings (Bulookbashi 1999: 11–2).

Despite all the efforts that have been made during the last decades – for example to make clear the definition of anthropology and the boundaries of its subjects; to establish anthropology as a distinctive discipline; to indicate the usefulness of ethnographic fieldwork for the recognition of Iranian culture and society; and finally, to exploit the outcome of anthropological studies for the social and economic development of Iran – there are still no clear-cut subject boundaries of anthropology and no awareness of the significance of the discipline in our people's perception. Therefore, the situation of anthropology as a discipline and the methods of ethnographic fieldwork are not yet quite stable in Iran, and it is difficult to predict a well-defined perspective for anthropology in the future.

Finally, I wish to recall that anthropology is still in its beginnings in our country. It is regrettable that no figure has yet emerged as an outstanding theorist among the present generation of trained Iranian anthropologists with degrees from schools of anthropology all around the world. It seems to me that Iranian anthropology needs some active great thinkers to bring Iranian anthropological circles together and lead them to form a solid coalition of professionals in ethnographical research in Iran. Therefore, I believe it is essential both to establish scientific collaboration between all Iranian anthropological centres responsible for conducting anthropological affairs in Iran, and to set up a relationship between Iranian and Western anthropologists who specialize in Iranian anthropological studies, with aim of providing a new practical cooperation in expanding Iranian studies from an anthropological point of view.

NOTES

1. It has even been said that *The Adventures of Hajji Baba of Isfahan* has become the 'book about Persia' amongst Oriental experts (see Stewart's introduction in Morier 1974: vii).
2. Up until 1970, scientific meetings on Iranian studies held by Iranian and foreign orientalists in and outside Iran focused mostly on Iranian archaeology, history, languages, religion, literature, etc. Iranian ethnological and folkloric studies on

pastoral nomadic, rural and urban societies by Iranian and foreign researchers were unknown and not taken into consideration as part of the scientific field of Iranian studies. It was only in September 1970 that anthropology and folklore studies were included as scientific disciplines in one of the sections of the First Congress of Iranian Studies (Nakhostin Kongereh-ye Tahqiqât-e Irani), held at the University of Tehran. Since then we have witnessed the most important achievement in anthropology and folkloristics, which is their full inclusion in Iranian academic assemblies.

3. See his 'Folklore and Anthropology' (1965).

4. See the definitions of folklore given by leading folklorists and anthropological folklorists in Leach and Fried (1972: 398–403).

5. Some examples of these studies are: *The Turkic Peoples of South Iran* (1960) by P. Oberling; *Religious and Political Leadership in Persian Baluchistan* (1967) by B. Spooner; *The Yomut Turkmen: A Study of Social Organization Among a Central Asian Turkic Speaking Population* (1975) by W. G. Irons; *The Bakhtiyari Khans: Tribal Disunity in Iran, 1880–1915* (1969) by G.R. Garthwaite; *The Shahsevan of Azarbaijan: A Study of Political and Economic Change in a Middle Eastern Tribal Society* (1971) by R. Tapper; *Social Organization of a Nomadic Pastoral Nobility in Southern Iran: The Kashkuli Kuchek of the Qashqa'i* (1974) by R.E. Salzer; 'Aqha, Shaikh and State: On the Social and Political Organizations of Kurdistan' (1974) by M.M. van Bruinessen; 'Sedentarization, Change and Adaptation Among the Kordshuli Pastoral Nomads of Southwestern Iran' (1981) by G. Swee; 'Ziarat: Pilgrimage to the Shrines of Shiraz' (1985) by A. Betteridge; 'The Spatial Organization of Rural Settlement in Khar O Tauran, Iran: An Ethno-archaeological Case Study' (1988) by L. Horne; *Women of Deh koh: Lives in an Iranian Village* (1989) by E. Friedl; and so on.

6. Among the researchers who cooperated with foreign anthropologists and whose approach to research was affected by the experience were Asghar Karimi, who worked with Jean-Pierre Digard, and Asghar Askari Khaneghah, who worked with Christian Bromberger.

7. From 1973 to 1977, for instance, a total of sixty foreign investigators from various countries carried out fieldwork in different regions of Iran. Nineteen of them were from the U.S., including: Charlotte Farr, Judith Goldstein, William Beeman, June Star, Jain Bestor, Constance Cronin, Thomas Reckord, Mary Ellen Page, Carol Hamlin, Donald Stilo, Sara Shrill, Nikki R. (Anita) Keddie, Mark Howland, Geoffrey Hamada, Margaret Caton, Douglas Martin, Ann Marie Fioretta, Lois Beck and William Irons. Thirteen researchers came from Japan and can be divided into two groups, one directed by Akira Fujii and the other by Yoshi Fusa Seki. France is represented by seven ethnographers: Jean-Pierre Digard, Christian Bromberger, Anny Tual, Tresa Battesti, Helene Desmet, Lauren Lange and Patrice Fontaine. Six came from the U.K., including Peter Andrews, David Bradshaw, Robert Rice, Susan Rass, Jeremy Swift and Frances Oxford. A group of six ethnographers, directed by Shahnaz Razieh Nadjmabadi, came from Switzerland. Ura Shwartz coordinated a group of four researchers from Israel. Two researchers, Erika Friedl and Reinhold H. Loeffler (both resident in the U.S.), came from Austria. The following countries are

each represented by one ethnographer: Canada by Genevieve Turner; Sweden by Andres Lindstrom; Germany by Paul Lufft. Of these sixty ethnographers and other researchers twenty-four were women (Ministère de la Culture et des Arts, Centre Ethnologique d'Iran 1975(2): 102–3, 1977–78(3): 105–10).

8. For instance, I personally, and all trained ethnological researchers connected with the Centre for Iranian Anthropology (Markaz-e Mardomshenâsi-ye Iran), have done research on many different topics.
9. Amanolahi-Baharvand (1974, 1983, 1985).
10. There were and still are many active social and cultural researchers outside the anthropological discipline who have done much ethnographic and folkloristic work on Iranian subcultures and the daily life of the peoples. One need only note such eminent figures as: Jalal Al-e Ahmad (literature), Hushang Purkarim (rural sociology), Javad Safinejad (geography), Morteza Farhadi (sociology), Muhammad Ahmad Panahi (history), Ahmad Vakiliyan (culture and ancient languages), Muhammad Mirshokrai (ancient languages) and Abdullah Shabazi (history).

REFERENCES

Amanolahi-Baharvand, S. 1975. 'Baharvand: The Former Pastoralists of Iran', Ph.D. dissertation. Houston: Rice University.

———. 1983/1362. 'Nezam-e Ejtemai-Siyasi-ye Il-e Baharvand va Taghyier va Tahvvol-e ân', in (no editor), *Majmue-ye Kitâb Âgâh: Ilat va Ashayer.* Tehran: 102–29.

———. 1985. 'The Lors of Iran', *Cultural Survival Quarterly* 9(1): 65–69.

Barth, F. 1961. *Nomads of South Persia: The Basseri Tribe of the Khamseh Confederacy.* Oslo.

Bascom, W. R. 1965. 'Folklore and Anthropology', in A. Dundes (ed.), *The Study of Folklore.* Englewood Cliffs, NJ: 25–33.

Beck, L. 1991. *A Year in the Life of a Qashqa`i Tribesman in Iran.* London.

Betteridge, A. 1985. 'Ziarat: Pilgrimage to the Shrines of Shiraz', Ph.D. dissertation. University of Chicago.

Bruinessen, M.M. van. 1978. 'Aqha, Shaikh and State: On the Social and Political Organizations of Kurdistan', Ph.D. dissertation. University of Utrecht.

Bulookbashi, A. 1999/1377. *Naqd-o Nazar: Mo`arrefi va Naqd-e Âsâr-i dar Adbiyat-e Mardomshenâsi.* Tehran.

———. 2003/1382. *Jâmeh-ye Ili dar Iran.* Tehran.

Chardin, J. 1811. *Voyage du Chevalier Chardian en Perse, et autres lieux de L' Orient. Nouvelle ed.* Par L.Langles. Paris Le Normant, 10 vols.

Ervin, A.M. 2000. *Applied Anthropology: Tools and Perspectives for Contemporary Practice.* Boston.

Feilberg, C. 1944. *La Tente Noire.* Copenhagen.

———. 1952. *Les Papis.* Copenhagen.

Field, H. 1939. *Contributions to the Anthropology of Iran,* Anthropological Series, Field Museum of Natural History 29(1). Chicago.

Friedl, E. 1991. *Women of Deh koh: Lives in an Iranian Village*. New York

Garthwaite, G.R. 1969. *The Bakhtiyari Khans: Tribal Disunity in Iran, 1880–1915*. Los Angeles.

Horne, L. 1988. 'The Spatial Organization of Rural Settlement in Khar O Tauran, Iran: An Ethno-archaeological Case Study', Ph.D. dissertation. Pennsylvania: University of Pennsylvania.

Irons, W.G. 1975. *The Yomut Turkmen: A Study of Social Organization Among a Central Asian Turkic Speaking Population*. Ann Arbor: University of Michigan.

Kuper, A. 1975. *Anthropologists and Anthropology: The British School 1922–72*. London.

Leach, M. and J. Fried (eds). 1972. *Standard Dictionary of Mythology and Legend*. New York.

Loeffler, R.R. 1988. *Islam in Practice: Religious Beliefs in a Persian Village*. New York.

Malcolm, J. 1815. *Sketches of Persia*. Translated by Mirza Ismaiil Heyrat in the name of *Kitâb-i Târikh-i Îrân*, 1872. Bombay.

Ministère de la Culture et des Arts, Centre Ethnologique d' Iran. 1975/1354. *Mardomŝenâsi va Farhang-e Âmme-e Iran*, no. 2. Tehran.

———. 1977–78/1356. *Mardomŝenâsi va Farhang-e Âmme-e Iran*, no. 3. Tehran.

Morier, J. 1974. *The Adventures of Hajji Baba of Ispahan*, edited by C. W. Stewart. London.

Oberling, P. 1960. *The Turkic Peoples of South Iran*. New York.

Olearius, A. 1669. *The voyages and travells of the ambassadors sent ... to the Great Duke of Muscovy, and the King of Persia. Begun in the year 1633 and finished in 1639. Containing a complete history of Muscovy, Tartary, Persia ... Whereto are added The travels of John Albert de Mandelslo ... from Persia, into the East-Indies. Containing a particular description of Indosthan; the Mogul's empire, the oriental ilands, Japan, China, & c.*, trans. by John Davies. London.

Salzer, R.E. 1978. *Social Organization of a Nomadic Pastoral Nobility in Southern Iran: The Kashkuli Kuchek of the Qashqa'i*. Berkeley.

Spooner, B. 1969. 'Religious and Political Leadership in Persian Baluchistan', Ph.D. dissertation. Oxford: University of Oxford.

Swee, G. 1981. 'Sedentarization, Change and Adaptation Among the Kordshuli Pastoral Nomads of Southwestern Iran', Ph.D. dissertation. London: School of Oriental and African Studies.

Tapper, R. 1971. 'The Shahsevan of Azerbaijan: A Study of Political and Economic Change in a Middle Eastern Tribal Society', Ph.D. dissertation. London: University of London.

Tavernier, J.B. 1970. *Voyages en Perse*. Evreux.

Tayebâti, H. (ed.). 1977–1978/1356. 'Gozâreš-e Fa'âliyyathâ-ye Markaz-e Mardomŝenâsi –ye Iran: from Autumn 1975 until Winter 1977', in *Mardomŝenâsi va Farhang-e A'mme-ye Iran* (Ethnologie et Traditions Populaires de Ľ Iran). Tehran: Ministére de la culture et des Arts, Centre Ethnologique d' Iran, no. 3.

CHAPTER 2

Storytelling as a Constituent of Popular Culture

Folk Narrative Research in Contemporary Iran

Ulrich Marzolph

Introductory Note

The following essay draws on the author's personal experience as a folk narrative researcher over the past thirty years.[1] Since shortly before the Iranian Revolution of 1978–79, I have aimed to stay in close contact with Iranian colleagues active in the field of folk narrative research. The essay deals with four topics. First, it provides a short definition of folk narrative research as a discipline situated between the fields of folklore and anthropology. Second, it sketches the discipline's historical development in Iran. Third, it identifies the major issues in Iranian folk narrative research. In conclusion, it proposes a tentative assessment of current problems and their solutions.

Defining Folk Narrative Research

Folk narrative research deals with folk or popular literature – two terms I will be using indiscriminately (Cejpek 1968; Marzolph 1993, 1999a, forthcoming a and b; Bolukbâshi 2000; Rahmoni 2001). In terms of literary genres, popular literature in its traditional understanding designates a relatively fixed canon of genres, such as myths, historical, demonological and religious legends, heroic and romantic epics, narrative songs (ballads), fables, fairy tales, jokes and anecdotes as well as shorter forms of literature such as popular sayings and idioms, children's rhymes, lullabies and riddles.

At the beginning of the third millennium, international and particularly Western folkloristic research regards this restriction to a predefined and limited set of specific genres as reducing the creative and receptive constituents of popular imagination to an inadequate representation of the true circumstances and meanings of popular literature in its living context. Consequently, it strives to define popular literature in relation to the circumstances of its presentation or performance rather than its formal content. In this understanding, popular literature is conceived as the sum of all creative verbal activities, whether oral (in recent research often termed 'verbal art') or written (corresponding to the narrow definition of literature as a form of expression in writing).

Popular literature is distinguished from elite literature in that it is transmitted by other than the dominant elite channels of tradition, whether orally or in writing. The procedure of transmission does not, however, exclude formal or informal education of authors or performers. Though they are often illiterate, performers are required to possess special skills and training. Furthermore, popular literature is appreciated and/or practised through collective consent by a considerable number of people, conveniently termed the 'folk'. In this understanding, folk narrative research combines the approaches of both folklore and anthropology as a discipline focusing on storytelling as a pivotal constituent of human communication.

The History of Folk Narrative Research in Iran

While an early occupation with Persian folklore dates back as far as the Safavid period, the actual beginning of Persian folklore studies coincided with the keen interest taken in Iran by early Western travellers starting in the seventeenth century (Radhayrapetian 1990). Besides their curiosity, the main impetus for the developing field of Persian studies resulted from the strategic interests of the European powers. In India, where British rule was instituted in the mid eighteenth century, the Persian language maintained its position as the language of court and an intellectual lingua franca. Neighbouring Iran to the north, the Russian empire also held a vital interest in the region. Initially, and especially since the discovery and translation of the *Avesta*, Western scholars had focused on religious studies. But by way of linguistic interest in dialect specimens, they soon turned to collecting items of folklorist relevance, such as folktales, riddles, songs or narratives of everyday life. Pioneers in the field include Polish diplomat Alexander Chodzko (1804–1891),[2] Russian scholar Valentin Zhukovski (1858–1918),[3] British consuls D.C. Phillot (1860–1930)[4] and D. L. R. Lorimer (1876–1962),[5] Danish scholar Arthur Christensen (1875–1945)[6] and French scholar Henri Massé (1886–1969)[7]. For most of these authors, folklore and popular literature constituted a pleasant distraction from their 'serious' linguistic, religious or historical concern; folklore data were rarely studied in their own right.

The nineteenth century witnessed a strong orientation of the Iranian elite towards the scientific achievements of the West. At the beginning of the twentieth century folklore, owing to its quality of maintaining traditional ways of life, was regarded as anti-progressive and hence not deserving of serious study. Only in the constitutional period in the third decade of the twentieth century did Persian scholars begin to devote themselves to the study of folklore. It was then that strong patriotic feelings met with a growing awareness of the phenomenon of the 'common' ('âmme) people, mingled with a Romantic urge for unspoiled tradition. Iranian intellectuals such as Mohammad 'Ali Jamâlzâdeh ([1922] 1962), 'Ali-Akbar Dehkhodâ (1959–60; Sa'îdî Sîrjânî 1996), Sâdeq Hedâyat (1933, 1956, 1963; Katirâ'i 1971), and later Samad Behrangi (Behrangi 1970; Behrangi and Tabrizi 1978; and Jalâl Âl-e Ahmad (1958, 1960, 1973; Clinton 1985) began to prefer plain colloquial Persian to the previously practiced, refined and highly artificial language. Hedâyat also was the first Iranian to study folklore and outline the methods of scholarship in his Neirangestân (1933) and his essay 'Folklor yâ farhang-e tude', originally published in 1945 (1965).

As official institutions became interested in the preservation and study of folklore, the Iranian Academy (Farhangestân) in 1938 publicized its intention to collect regional (velâyati) words, expressions, poetry, proverbs, tales, stories, songs and melodies. Meanwhile, in the 1940s Fazlollâh Mohtadi, called Sobhi – probably by applying a method first attempted by the British journalist (and later Iranist scholar) L. P. Elwell-Sutton (1912–1984) – initiated a radio programme of folktales, asking his listeners to send in their tales and eventually publishing a series of booklets of Persian folktales (Rahgozar 1994; Pflaum 1993; Omidsâlâr 2002). Sobhi's prime concern, however, was to entertain. Accordingly, his publications (see also Sobhi 1947a, b, c), although still today constituting pleasant reading matter and even having been reprinted recently (Sobhi 1998, 2005) do not adhere to scientific standards.

At the same time leftist journals such as Payâm-e nou (The New Message, founded in 1944 by Sa'id Nafisi and later edited by Bozorg 'Alavi) started to publish short articles on various genres of popular literature (Amir-Ebrâhimi 1946a, 1946b, 1947; Keshâvarz 1944, 1945a, 1945b; Mir-Goli 1946). In 1958, the Office of Popular Culture (Edâre-ye Farhang-e 'âmme), aligned with the Ministry of Culture and Arts, was founded. In 1970 it was reorganized as the National Centre for Research in Ethnography and Popular Culture (Markaz-e melli-ye pazhuheshhâ-ye mardom-shenâsi va farhang-e 'âmme) and until the Revolution of 1978–79 continued to work under the name Markaz-e mardom-shenâsi-ye Irân (Centre of Iranian Ethnography). This institution and its team of researchers played a leading role in folklore research, above all through their series of monograph publications as well as the journal *Mardom-shenâsi va farhang-e 'âmme* (*Ethnography and Popular Culture*, founded in 1976).

Sobhi's method, as of the early 1960s, of utilizing radio broadcasts for collecting and propagating folktales was successfully taken up by Abu 'l Qâsem Enjavi Shirâzi, a close friend of the late Hedâyat (Marzolph 1994a). Enjavi installed the weekly radio programme 'Safine-ye farhang-e mardom' (The Ship of Popular Culture), educated a considerable number of assistants and founded an institution named Markaz-e farhang-e mardom (Centre for Popular Culture) within the National Broadcasting Company. In order to publish the collected texts, he established the series *Ganjine-ye farhang-e mardom* (*A Treasury of Popular Culture*), to which he himself contributed ten volumes of annotated texts. Not only was Enjavi a captivating orator, but he also had a great talent for organization. Along with a pencil, preprinted paper and envelope, his nationwide contributors also received his booklet *Tarz-e neveshtan-e farhang-e 'âmmiyâne* (*How to Document Popular Culture*, 1967), which contained general guidelines. Until the early 1980s, when his radio programme was discontinued, Enjavi succeeded in collecting an archive of several hundred thousands of manuscripts on numerous aspects of folklore, everyday life and popular literature in Iran. His archive is a mine of information on traditional language, customs, beliefs, tales, oral history and the like, unparalleled in any other Middle Eastern country.

Due to the strong national interest and considerable support of both official institutions and the imperial family, folklore studies were thriving in Iran during the 1970s. The International Congress of Iranian Popular Culture (Majma'-e beinolmellali-ye farhang-e 'âmme-ye Irân), organized in Isfahan in October 1977, was attended by a large number of qualified scholars from Iran and various Western countries. The Revolution of 1978–79, after a period of social and political upheaval, resulted in a complete rupture of contacts between Western scholars and Iranian publications in folklore, and many years passed before folklore and popular literature once again attracted major interest. An institutional result of the reassessment of cultural values after the Revolution was the foundation of the Organization for the Country's National Heritage (Sâzmân-e mirâs-e farhangi-ye keshvar) in 1986. The responsibility of this centralized institution today includes the supervision of all kinds of cultural activities, encompassing archaeology, anthropology and folklore. Its ethnographic department (Daftar-e pazhuheshhâ-ye mardom-shenâsi), which until 2007 had been headed for many years by Mohammad Mir-Shokraei, has not only educated junior folklorists (up to the MA level), but has also conducted various fieldwork research projects, including one on popular literature (*adabiyât-e 'âmme*) in 1994–95. Several monographs based on this research project have been

published (Beihaqi 2001; Jaktâji 2001; Nâderi and Movahhedi 2001; Vakiliyân 2000; Khazâ'i 2006; Rezavi 2006).

The Markaz-e farhang-e mardom, whose founder Enjavi died in 1993, is
at present aligned with the research department of the national radio institution Sedâ va simâ-ye Jomhuri-ye eslâmi-ye Irân (Islamic Republic Iran
Broadcasting [IRIB]). Enjavi's former house was acquired by this institution
in 2005 and has subsequently been turned into a research institute housing
the archive of textual data collected by Enjavi as well as a small but exqui-
site museum of artefacts of popular culture that his admirers had sent him.
The few major publications from the archive's materials since the Revolution
deal with popular sayings and proverbs and popular customs in the month
of Ramazân (Vakiliyân 1987, 1991). In spring 2002, a new scholarly Iranian
journal of folklore, the quarterly *Farhang-e mardom* (*Popular Culture*), was
initiated by the prominent Iranian folklorist Seyyid Ahmad Vakiliyân.[8]

Key Issues in Folk Narrative Research

As for folk narrative research in the Iranian context, several points bear
mentioning. First, cooperation and interaction between foreigners and locals has been a constant characteristic of folk narrative research in Iran.
The historical development suggests that this cooperation initially existed
between foreign researchers and local informants. Whereas the research
method was determined by the West, indigenous participants either supplied
material or applied methods developed in the West. It remains questionable,
or even dubious, to what extent the application of theoretical implications
and assumptions involved in this cooperation will succeed in understanding
the meaning of Iranian folk narrative in its living context. One of the many
reasons that Western researchers focus on Iranian folklore might be that
it appears easier to study than, say, Turkish or Arabic folklore. It is 'alien'
enough to be studied as the 'other', yet through its Indo-European backdrop
it is also attractively familiar, somewhat like an 'Oriental' cousin of Western
cultures. Considering ancient Iranian history as well as its aftermath in religious and cultural concepts, such as cosmic dualism, Iranian folklore was
regarded as preserving ancient customs and beliefs and hence mirroring the
roots of Western civilization. On the other hand, Iranian researchers have
never taken advantage of their superior familiarity with local folklore to
emphasize an indigenous autonomy similar to that stated by other Asian,
African or American cultures. As for theory, at least up to the Revolution,
Iranian researchers appeared to be quite content with developing their ideas
within the guidelines projected by Western research. After the Revolution
this strand of research continues, albeit in a certain competition with the

new ideological foundations – which themselves, at least to a certain extent, constitute a reaction to the previously experienced cultural transgression practised by the West. The implications of the new ideology for folklore and folkloristic research have been, to say the least, not very fruitful. A particularly devastating effect has been wrought by recent prepublication interference with texts that in a curious manner of ideological understatement is being labelled as 'editing' (*virâstâri*).[9]

Second, and closely related to the previous point, are questions concerning methods and texts. The published results of folk narrative research in Iran are restricted to texts. Even though some of these texts have been collected by fieldwork according to modern scientific standards, few collections mention any amount of contextual data (Hasanzâde 2002). Aspects of performance and interaction between the storytellers and their audience – brilliantly discussed for the case of prewar Afghanistan by U.S. scholar Margaret Mills (1990, 1992) – have so far been widely neglected. Even though Enjavi Shirâzi introduced in his publications the custom of mentioning at least some basic data about his informants (e.g. the storyteller's name, place of origin, age and profession), the first publication reproducing the storyteller's photograph and thus supplying an individual image to this collective tradition is the dissertation of Japanese scholar Shin Takehara (Takehara 2001, Takehara and Vakiliyân 2002).[10] Even the first-ever monograph presentation of a Persian storyteller, Elwell-Sutton's informant Mashdi Galin Khânom, a highly influential book that invigorated the publication of folktale and fairytale collections after the Revolution, lacks any substantial contextual data; however, in this case the lack results from the fact that both the researcher and the storyteller were long deceased at the time of publication.[11] The textual dominance of folk narrative research is further underlined by modern anthologies such as 'Ali-Asghar Darvishiyân's comprehensive *Farhang-e afsânehâ-ye mardom-e Irân* (1998–2005).[12]

Third, a point well known to social anthropology but rarely taken into account by folk narrative research concerns ethical problems relating to fieldwork, research questions and ensuing publications. Why document what, under which circumstances and for which purpose? How to elicit meaningful information from informants without exposing them to unwanted reactions resulting from the publication of their information? Even though folk narratives have often been, and sometimes still are, regarded as bespeaking simple minds, they are not at all meaningless, let alone insignificant. A telling contribution in this respect is Erika Friedl-Loeffler's publication (2006) of Luri folktales, which for the first time supplies the texts along with a thorough ethnographic (and sociological) analysis. At times, folk narratives might even constitute a powerful medium of expression for the popular mind, and the extent to which they may serve as an outlet of frustration on the one hand or as a medium of popular resistance and propaganda on the other may be closely connected. Furthermore: to whom do folktales belong? A recent competition between publications partly based on the very same fieldwork, one prepared by the former local organizer, the other published by a Western orientalist scholar, might serve to further the discussion as to the various sensibilities publications of folk narrative data will have to take into account in the future (Sâdât Eshkevâri 2007; Marzolph 2007).

Fourth, which directives are to be followed at present and in the near future? The state of folk narrative research in postrevolutionary Iran is closely connected with the presently propagated evaluation of folktales in general. Three points are important in this respect. As I have discussed elsewhere (Marzolph 1994c, 1995b, 1999a) folktales today are regarded with a certain amount of criticism and suspicion because of their affinities to the now-detested system of royal rule: folktales tell of kings and queens, rulers and princes. In addition, folk narrative research before the Revolution was propagated and sponsored by the Pahlavi monarch and his family. Also, folktales are distrusted because they deal with a fundamental pillar of national consciousness: folk narratives, especially hero tales, draw on the collective memory of Iran's imperial past. Folk narrative research therefore is seen as endorsing the previously ruling system. Finally, folk narratives are suspected to embody and encourage elements contradicting the presently defined Islamic values: folk narratives tell of love and hate, and of all kinds of illicit and morally objectionable acts such as extramarital sexual activities and the consumption of alcoholic beverages. In dealing with these issues, folk narrative research risks being understood as implicitly authorizing their actual performance. A case in point is the textual interference practised in editions of the *Arabian Nights* (*Hezâr-o yek shab*) published after the Revolution (Marzolph 2004: 286–90).

On the other hand, considering the general attitude in contemporary Iran that favours supervising all cultural activities in terms of their accordance with the presently propagated system of values, one should remember that the complexity of lived reality never corresponds to the theoretical assumptions of superimposed framing conditions. Researchers would learn a lot more from being able to study popular expression under unrestricted circumstances than from cooperating in the study and publication of folklore under restrictive regulations.

Contemporary Folk Narrative Research in Iran

As for an assessment of contemporary circumstances of folk narrative research in Iran, tendencies in research obviously can be encouraged or discouraged by official authorities according to desirable or undesirable results. Taking the religion of Islam as determining all fields of life also means propagating Islamic religion and the historical process of its spread as the major topic for research. Accordingly, after the Revolution, the number of collections of religious tales, of tales about venerated persons from Islamic history and of tales and research about religious duties and religious customs has considerably increased (Vakiliyân 1991; Vakiliyân and Sâlehi 2001). The 'revival' of scholarly interest in the dramatic art form *ta'ziye*, which has often been labelled the 'Persian passion play', may also be seen against this backdrop.[13] In this connection it is particularly revealing to witness the gradual changes in reading matter in Iranian primary schoolbooks since the Revolution, where national and international folktales have been eliminated in favour of tales of moral and religious concern (Marzolph 1994c, 1995a).

As for the actual telling of tales, it may be challenged whether folk narrative can be made to develop according to given directives (Marzolph 1998). Obviously, certain elements of traditional folk narrative today are judged as contradicting the officially propagated objectives, or, as I heard being voiced in a slightly rash judgment by one of the post-Revolution directors of the research department of the National Broadcasting Company, there exist certain components 'one ought to get rid of' (*'bâyad rikht dur'*). On the one hand, the future generation of children who have grown up internalizing the new conditions are bound to memorize the texts whose reading, listening and telling they have grown accustomed to. On the other hand, the interaction between literature and oral tradition is known to serve as a stabilizing factor in the growth and existence of collectively memorized narrative repertoires.

The cultural value of classical Persian literature is recognized beyond doubt by the present authorities, who have even come to peace with the Persian national epic, Ferdousi's *Shâhnâme*, a work that in the early years of the Revolution was heavily contested because of its 'nationalist' impact (Marzolph 1999b, 2001, 2002). It contains a large number of traditional narratives, which are bound to survive. Yet, if popular romance and jocular literature of the Mollâ Nasroddin kind, abundant before the Revolution, have meanwhile almost completely disappeared from the inventories of newspaper stands and sidewalk peddlers, the question arises: does this also imply that they are no longer appreciated, known and told orally any more (Marzolph 1995c, 1996, 2002)? Or, to voice just one suggestion, will the relegation of certain parts of narrative tradition to an underground atmosphere rather serve as a stabilizing, even invigorating, factor?

One would not render a faithful service to either folk narrative or folk narrative research if one were to judge the present situation in terms of good or bad, let alone suggest directives for what ought to be done in an extremely sensitive atmosphere such as prevails in Iran today. If there is any lesson international folk narrative research can learn from the contemporary situation, it is to watch, document and analyse whatever is happening. We all know that the Romantic lament for times and tales gone by does not correspond to contemporary requirements. Rather on the contrary, witnessing the societal developments in present-day Iran constitutes a unique opportunity for analysing and understanding the powerful dynamics of questions of sociological, political, religious and folklorist relevance.

NOTES

1. The present contribution draws heavily from several of the author's previous studies. As the published versions of those studies may not have reached the members of the ethnographic/anthropologist community to an extent promising a satisfactory discussion, it is here deemed permissible to practice an amount of self-referentiality higher than usual.
2. See Chodzko (1842).
3. See Zhukovski (1888–1922, 1902).
4. See Phillot (1905–07, 1906, 1907).
5. See Lorimer and Lorimer (1919) and Lorimer and Vahman (1974).
6. See Christensen (1918, 1923, 1930, 1936, 1958) and also Holbek (1979).
7. See Massé (1925, 1938) and also Omidsalar (1993).
8. Issues published so far include 1(1) (bahâr 1381); 1(2) (tâbestân 1381); 1(3–4) (pâyiz, zemestân 1381); 2(1) [2(5)] (bahâr 1382); 2(6–7) (tâbestân, pâyiz 1382); 3(8–9) (bahâr 1383); 3(10) (tâbestân 1383), 3(11–12) (pâyiz, zemestân 1383), 4(13) (bahâr 1384), 4(14–15) (tâbestân, pâyiz 1384), 4(16) (zemestân 1384), 5(17) (bahâr 1385), 5 (18) (tâbestân 1385), 5(19–20) (pâyiz, zemestân 1385), 6(21–22) (bahâr, tâbestân 1386), 6 (23) (pâyiz 1386), 7(24 25) (bahâr 1387), 7(26) (vizhe-ye Hamadân)
9. As a case in point, see for example the (unauthorized) 'publisher's remark' (yâddâsht-e nâsher) in Qessehâ-ye Mashdi Galin Khânom (Marzolph, Amirhosseini-Nithammer and Vakiliyân 1997: 7).
10. A Persian (selective) version was published by Takehara and Vakiliyân (2002); an extensive Japanese version was published by Takehara in 2001.
11. See Elwell-Sutton (1980); Marzolph and Amirhosseini-Nithammer (1994); Iranian (partial) edition Qessehâ-ye Mashdi Galin Khânom (Marzolph, Amirhosseini-Nithammer and Vakiliyân 1995) (second edition 1997 with an additional preface and the storyteller's photograph; third edition 2003; fourth edition 2006); German translations by Marzolph, Persische Märchen Miniaturen (1985), Persische Märchen (1990), revised and expanded in Wenn der Esel singt, tanzt das Kamel. Persische Märchen und Schwänke (1994b); see also Marzolph (2000, 2001).
12. Originally thirteen volumes were planned, but by 2008 the series had already published nineteen volumes. The texts include exclusively reprinted (and often bowdlerized) versions of earlier Persian publications.

13. Recent major publications include 'Anâsori (2003); Homâyuni (2001); Shahidi (2001).

REFERENCES

Âl-e Ahmad, J. 1958/1337. *Tâtneshinhâ-ye Boluke-Zahrâ*. Tehran.
———. 1960/1339. *Dorr-e yatim-e Khalij. Jazire-ye Khârg*. Tehran.
———. 1973/1352. *Ourazân. Vaz'-e mahall, âdâb va rosum, folklor, lahje*. 4th ed. Tehran.
Amir-Ebrâhimi, H. 1946a/1325. 'Mirzâ mast va Khammâr va Bibi Mehrnegâr', *Payâm-e nou* 3(2): 37–42.
———. 1946b/1325. 'Nei-ye sokhangu', *Payâm-e nou* 3(3): 49–53.
———. 1947/1326. 'Qesse-ye tambal', *Payâm-e nou* 3(6): 14–16.
'Anâsori, J. 2003/1382. *Sharh-e vâqe'e-ye 'Âshurâ*. Tehran.
Behrangi, S. 1970/1349. *Talkhun va chand qesse-ye digar*. Tehran.
Behrangi, S and Tabrizi, B. [Dehqâni, B.]. 1978/1357. *Afsânehâ-ye Âzarbâijan* 1–2. 4th ed. Tehran.
Beihaqi, J.-'A. 2001/1380. *Chehel afsâne-ye khorâsâni*. Tehran.
Bolukbâshi, 'A. 2000/1379. 'Nazari be adabiyât-e 'âmme-ye Irân', in M. 'A. Emâm Ahvâzi (ed.), *Chistân-nâme-ye dezfuli*. Tehran: 9–39.
Cejpek, J. 1968. 'Iranian Folk-Literature', in J. Rypka (ed.), *History of Iranian Literature*. Dordrecht: 607–709.
Chodzko, A. B. 1842. *Specimens of the Popular Poetry of Persia*. London.
Christensen, A. 1918. *Contes persans en langue populaire*. Copenhagen.
———. 1923. 'Les sonts dans la tradition populaire des Persans', *Acta Orientalia* 1: 43–75.
———. 1930. 'La Légende du sage Buzurjmihr', *Acta Orientalia* 8: 81–128.
———. 1936. 'La princesse sur la feuille de myrte et le princesse sur le pois', *Acta Orientalia* 14: 241–57.
———. 1958. *Persische Märchen*. Düsseldorf.
Clinton, J.W. 1985. 'Âl-e Ahmad, Jalâl', *Encyclopedia Iranica*, vol. 1. London: 745–47.
Darvishiyân, 'A.-A. 1998–2005/1377–84. *Farhang-e afsânehâ-ye mardom-e Irân*, vols. 1–18. Tehran.
Dehkhodâ, 'A.-A. 1959–60/1338–39. *Amsâl va hekam*, vols. 1–4. Tehran.
Friedl-Loeffler, Erika. 2006. *Folk Tales from a Persian Tribe: Forty-Five Tales from Sisakht in Kuri and English*. Dortmund.
Elwell-Sutton, L. P. 1980. 'A Narrator of Tales from Tehran', *Arv* 36: 201–8.
Hasanzâde, 'A.-R. 2002/1381. *Afsâne-ye zendegân*, vols. 1–2. Tehran.
Hedâyat, S. 1933/1312, 1956/1334, 1963/1342. *Neirangestân*. Tehran.
———. 1965/1344. 'Folklor yâ farhang-e tude', in S. Hedâyat, *Neveshtehâ-ye parâkande*. Tehran: 447–83.
Hillmann, M. C. 1990. 'Behrangi, Samad', *Encyclopaedia Iranica*, vol. 4. London: 110f.
Holbek, B. 1979. 'Christensen, Arthur Emmanuel', in *Enzyklopädie des Märchens*. Berlin: columns 1380–82.

Homâyuni, S. 2001/1380. *Ta'ziye dar Irân*, 2nd ed. Shirâz.

Jaktâji, M. T. A. 2001/1380. *Afsânehâ-ye Gilân*. Tehran.

Jamâlzâdeh. [1922] 1962/1341. *Yeki bud, yeki nabud*. Berlin.

Katirâ'i, M. 1971/1350. 'Sâdeq-e Hedâyat va folklor-e Irân', in H. Yaghmâ'i, I. Afshâr and M. Roushan (eds), *Nâme-ye Minovi*. Tehran: 368–55.

Keshâvarz, K. 1944/1323. 'Folklor. Qesse-ye rubâh va kalag', *Payâm-e nou* 1(7): 48–50.

———. 1945a/1324. 'Bozak-e zangule-pâ. Revâyat-e yazdi', *Payâm-e nou* 2(3): 51–53.

———. 1945b./1324. 'Folklor. Az qessehâ-ye yazdi. Raftam be-bâgh-e kâkâ', *Payâm-e nou* 2(11): 17.

Khazâ'i, 'Ali-Asghar. 2006/1385. *Afsânehâ-ye Quchân*. Mashhad.

Kreyenbroek, P. and U. Marzolph (eds). forthcoming. *History of Persian Literature*. vol. 18. *Companion Volume 2: Literature in Iranian Languages other than Persian (Kurdish, Pashto, Balochi, Ossetic) and Persian and Tajik Oral Literatures*

Lorimer, D. L. R. and E. S. Lorimer. 1919. *Persian Tales, Written down for the First Time in the Original Kermani and Bakhtiari*. London.

Lorimer, D. L. R. and Vahman, F. 1974/1353. *Farhang-e mardom-e Kermân*. Tehran.

Marzolph, U. 1993. 'Iran', *Enzyklopädie des Märchens*, vol. 7. Berlin: columns 248–70.

———. 1994a. 'Seyyid Abolqâsem Engavi Širâzi (1921–1993) und das iranische Volkskundearchiv', *Fabula* 35: 118–24.

———. 1994c. 'Die Revolution im Schulbuch. Die Grundschullehrbücher „Persisch" vor und nach 1979', *Spektrum Iran* 7(3–4): 36–56.

———. 1995a. 'Interkulturelles Erzählen. Der Transfer von Erzählgut in iranischen Grundschullehrbüchern', in C. Lipp (ed.), *Medien popularer Kultur. Erzählung, Bild und Objekt in der volkskundlichen Forschung. Festschrift Rolf Wilhelm Brednich*. Frankfurt am Main: 182–95.

———. 1995b. 'Zur Lage der Erzählforschung im nachrevolutionären Iran', *Spektrum Iran* 8(3): 39–51.

———. 1995c. 'Mollâ Nasroddîn in Persia', *Iranian Studies* 28: 157–74.

———. 1996. 'The UNESCO sponsored "International Nasreddin Hodja Year"', *Middle East & South Asia Folklore Bulletin* 13(3): 11–13.

———. 1998. 'What is Folklore Good for? On Eliminating Undesired Cultural Expressions', *Journal of Folklore Research* 35: 5–16.

———. 1999a. 'Folklore Studies in Persia', *Encyclopaedia Iranica* 10. New York: 71–5.

———. 1999b. 'Das persische Nationalepos im Spannungsfeld von Überlieferung und ideologischer Instrumentalisierung', *Lares* 65: 81–99.

———. 2000. 'Variation, Stability, and the Constitution of Meaning in the Narratives of a Persian Storyteller', in L. Honko (ed.), *Thick Corpus, Organic Variation and Textuality in Oral Tradition*. Helsinki: 435–52.

———. 2001. Ortsangaben in der persischen Volksliteratur', in R. Haag-Higuchi and C. Szyska (eds), *Erzählter Raum in Literaturen der islamischen Welt/Narrated Space in the Literature of the Islamic World*. Wiesbaden: 31–42.

————. 2002. 'Sanitizing Humor: Islamic Mediterranean Jocular Tradition in a Comparative Perspective', in M. Bernardini et al. (eds), *Europa e Islam tra i secoli XIV e XVI/Europe and Islam Between [the] 14th and 15th Centuries*, vol. 2. Naples: 757–82.

————. 2004. '*The Persian Nights:* Links between the *Arabian Nights* and Persian Culture', *Fabula* 45: 275–93.

————. forthcoming a. 'The Study of Popular Literature in the Persian Context', in Kreyenbroek and Marzolph.

————. forthcoming b. 'Persian Popular Literature', Kreyenbroek and Marzolph.

————. 2007/1386 (ed.). *Topuz-Qoli Mirzâ.* gerd-âvari: L. P. Elwell-Sutton, be-kushesh-e Ahmad Vakiliyân, Zohre Zangene. Tehran.

Marzolph, U. 1985 (transl.). *Persische Märchen Miniaturen.* Cologne.

————. 1990. *Persische Märchen.* Frankfurt am Main.

————. 1994b. *Wenn der Esel singt, tanzt das Kamel. Persische Märchen und Schwänke.* Munich.

Marzolph, U. and A. Amirhosseini-Nithammer (eds). 1994. *Die Erzählungen der Mashdi Galin Khânom/Qessehâ-ye Mashdi Galin Khânom.* Collected by L. P. Elwell-Sutton, parts 1–2. Wiesbaden.

Marzolph, U., A. Amirhosseini-Nithammer and A. Vakiliyân (eds). 1995/1374. *Qessehâ-ye Mashdi Galin Khânom.* Tehran.

Massé, H. 1925. 'Contes en persan populaire, recueillis et traduits', *Journal asiatique* 206: 71–157.

————. 1938. *Croyances et coutumes persanes.* 2 vols. Paris.

Mills, M. A. 1990. *Oral Narrative in Afghanistan: The Individual in Tradition.* New York.

————. 1992. *Rhetorics and Politics in Afghan Traditional Storytelling.* Philadelphia.

Mir-Goli, R. 1946/1325. 'Folklor. Afsâne', *Payâm-e nou* 2(6): 88–9.

Nâderi, A. and S. Movahhedi. 2001/1380. *Shouqân. matalhâ va qessehâ-ye mardom-e ostân-e markazi.* Tehran.

Omidsalar, M. 1993. 'Croyances et coutumes persanes', *Encyclopaedia Iranica,* vol. 6. Costa Mesa, CA: 432f.

————. 2002/1381. *Bachchehâ salâm (Sobhi va folklor-e Irân)* [1993/1372], in M. Omidsâlâr (ed.), *Jostârhâ-ye Shâhnâme-shenâsi va mabâhes-e digar.* Tehran: 358–76.

Pflaum, S. 1993. 'Subhî, ein persischer Märchenerzähler der Moderne', MA thesis. Freiburg: University of Freiburg i. Br.

Phillot, D.C. 1905–07. 'Some Current Persian Tales, Collected in the South of Persia from Professional Story-Tellers', *Memoirs of the Asiatic Society of Bengal* 1(18): 375–412.

————. 1906. 'Some Persian Riddles Collected from Dervishes in the South of Persia', *Journal of the Royal Asiatic Society* 2(4): 88–93.

————. 1907. 'A Note on Sign, Gesture, Code and Street-language, etc., among the Persians', *Journal of the Royal Asiatic Society* 3(9): 619–22.

Radhayrapetian, J. 1990. *Iranian Folk Narrative: A Survey of Scholarship.* New York.

Rahgozar, R. 1994/1373. *Fazl[ollâh] Mohtadi (Sobhi).* Tehran.

Rahmoni, R. 2001/1380. *Tarikh-e gerd-âvari, nashr va pazhuhesh-e afsânehâ-ye mardom-e fârsi zabân (Tâjikistân, Afghânestân, Irân)*. Tehran: 151–70 (*gerd-âvari va nashr*); 208–30 (*pazhuhesh*).

Rezavi, Sh. 2006/1385. *Afsânehâ-ye Kermân*. Tehran.

Sâdât Eshkevâri, K 2007/1386. *Afsânehâ-ye dahestân-e Barzrud*. Tehran.

Sa'îdî Sîrjânî, 'A.-A. 1996. 'Dehkodâ, Mîrzâ 'Alî-Akbar', *Encyclopaedia Iranica*, vol. 7. Costa Mesa, CA: 216–20.

Shahidi, 'E. 2001/1380. *Pazhuheshi dar ta'ziye va ta'ziye khvâni az âghâz tâ pâyân-e doure-ye Qâjâr dar Tehrân*. Tehran.

(Sobhi), Fazlollâh Mohtadi. 1947a/1326. 'Dom-duz', *Payâm-e nou* 3(12): 35–6.

———. 1947b/1326. 'Khâle-ye suske', *Payâm-e nou* 3(9): 56–58.

———. 1947c/1326. 'Kak be tanur-e murche-ye khâk be sar', *Payâm-e nou* 3(7–8): 52–3.

———. 1998/1377. *Afsânehâ*, vols. 1–2. Tehran.

———. 2005/1384. *Afsânehâ-ye kohan-e irâni*, ed. Mohammad Qâsemzâde. Tehran.

Takehara, S. 2001. *Adabiyât-e shafâhi-ye Irân. Hâsel-e bar-resi-ye meidâni va tahqiq*. Hiroshima.

Takehara, S. and A. Vakiliyân. 2002/1381. *Afsânehâ-ye irâni be-revâyat-e emruz va diruz*. Tehran.

Vakiliyân, A. 1987/1366. *Tamsil va masal*, vol. 2. Tehran.

———. 1991/1370. *Ramazân dar farhang-e mardom*. Tehran.

———. 1999/1378. *Matalhâ va afsânehâ-ye irâni*. Tehran.

———. (ed.). 2000/1379. *Qessehâ-ye mardom. gerd-âvarde-ye goruh-e pazhuhesh-garân-e pazhuheshkade-ye mardom-shenâsi*. Tehran.

Vakiliyân, A. and Sâlehi, K. 2001/1380. *Hazrat-e 'Ali dar qessehâ-ye 'âmmiyâne*. Tehran.

Zhukovski, V. 1888–1922. *Materialy dlya izuchenija persidskikh narechiy*, vols. 1–3. Petrograd.

———. 1902. *Obraztsy persidskogo narodnogo tvorchestva*. Petrograd.

CHAPTER 3

Iranian Anthropology – Crossing Boundaries

Influences of Modernization, Social Transformation and Globalization

Mary Elaine Hegland

Introduction

At its heart, anthropology endeavours to cross boundaries. Anthropologists attempt to cross the borders between their own society and culture and those of others to try to understand culture and worldviews elsewhere. Or else a student of anthropology may go far away to study, thereby crossing national or cultural boundaries. In Iran students must pass over the national boundary to become a trained anthropologist because there is no Ph.D. programme in anthropology in the country so far. Nader Afshar Naderi, for example, took this pioneering step: he travelled to France and earned a Ph.D. in anthropology from the Sorbonne and then returned to Iran for work and research.

During the 1950s and early 1960s, only a few Iranians left Iran for anthropological training, and obtaining research permits proved problematic for anthropologists coming from outside the country. During the 1970s, however, with the oil boom economy and the close cooperative relationship between Mohammad Reza Shah Pahlavi and the West, especially the United States, thousands of Iranian young people left for study abroad. Foreigners could relatively easily obtain research permits for anthropological fieldwork. This period marks the heyday of Iran anthropology.[1]

With the upsurge of the revolutionary movement during 1978 and 1979, Iran turned into a forbidding fieldwork country. During the Revolution several foreign anthropologists had to leave Iran. The university system in Iran was closed down for two years. The war with Iraq from 1980 to 1988 caused further disruptions and created barriers to studying anthropology at home or abroad for Iranians, and to doing fieldwork in Iran for foreign anthropologists. After the war, the isolationist policy of the Iranian government as well as the negative attitudes towards Iran on the part of Westerners prevented most border-crossing in pursuit of an anthropological enterprise. A few anthropologists, some with Iranian passports, and a few foreigners who managed to enter Iran provided a small number of exceptions.

In recent years, from about 1998 or 2000 on, however, some signs seem to indicate an upsurge in Iran anthropology. Mohammad Shahbazi, who left Iran to earn his Ph.D. in anthropology in the United States and then returned to conduct his dissertation research among his own cultural group, the Qashqa'i, provides a recent example of a trajectory wherein an Iranian crosses borders twice – first to go abroad for study and then to return to his home cultural group for anthropological field research (Shahbazi 1998, 2001, 2002, 2003, 2004, 2006). Several foreign anthropologists with previous experience in Iran as well as a number of Iranian anthropologists living outside the country have been able to return to Iran. A few Iranian anthropologists are working at universities or institutes in Iran, for example, Soheila Shahshahani, who has been particularly active in her profession. A very few intrepid foreign students have managed to get into Iran for dissertation research. One Iranian, Nematollah Fazeli, recently was able to go to England for his Ph.D. studies in anthropology and return to work in Iran. Most dramatically, quite a number of Iranian-born persons who moved abroad with their families during the Revolutionary period and received anthropological training in their new countries – the diaspora generation[2] – have been returning to their homeland for anthropological research or are working among Iranians abroad.

In the 1970s and 1980s, I remember hearing disparaging comments about the status of Iran anthropology. However, even earlier on, examples can be found of boundary crossings in terms of subject matter, fieldwork methodology or the research community/data collecting environment. During recent years, too, some of the more senior anthropologists and the young diaspora generation of Iran anthropologists are taking us in exciting new directions, and there are signs of a potentially dynamic revival in Iran anthropology. The dynamics of modernization, social transformation and globalization are providing impetus and opportunity for crossing and blurring boundaries.

As part of the regrouping effort, it might be useful to think about where we have been and what has been accomplished in Iran anthropology, and to give recognition to those who have practiced Iran anthropology. This article traces the history of anthropology in Iran[3] with emphasis on the recent examples of transgressing borders to move into new types of research arenas, fieldwork sites, methods of doing anthropology and presentation genres.[4] I focus on publications in English and hope others will provide retrospectives of Iran anthropology publications in other languages.

1832 through the 1950s and 1960s

I have not been able to find any Iranian anthropologists who conducted fieldwork in Iran earlier than the 1960s, when the founder of Iranian anthropology, Nader Afshar Naderi, came back from earning his anthropology Ph.D. in France and worked in Iran from the 1960s and 1970s until the Revolution of 1979.[5] Probably the first foreign ethnographer to work in Iran, James Atkinson, published his *Customs and Manners of the Women of Persia and Their Domestic Superstitions* in 1832. In 1902, Sir Peter Sykes published 'Anthropological Notes on Southern Persia', followed in 1921 by 'The Gypsies of Persia'. In 1939, Henry Field published *Contributions to the Anthropology of Iran*, and then in 1953, *The Track of Man: Adventures of an Anthropologist*, including materials from his travels in Iran. Paul Schumacher published a 'Report on the Second Iran Expedition: Ethnography' in 1950. Other than these, I have been able to find only two foreign anthropologists who worked in Iran during the 1950s: Robert Charles Alberts, who conducted in-depth ethnography of a village community for his dissertation (1963), and Fredrik Barth, who authored the classic study of the Basseri (1961).

Several more began field research in Iran in the 1960s: Lois Beck, David Brooks, Paula E. Drew (Ardehali), Erika Friedl, William Irons, Reinhold Loeffler, Paul Magnarella, David Marsden, Nancy Tapper (Lindisfarne), Richard Tapper, Elvia Testrepo and Brian Spooner. At that time, Iran was largely unknown territory for anthropologists, who had to meet numerous challenges in methodology as well as in everyday life, especially in tribal/rural areas. Most anthropologists conducted fieldwork among tribal/ethnic groups, joined by some anthropologists in the 1970s to produce outstanding studies of Iranian tribal groups – the Bakhtiyari, Baluch, Basseri, Lur, Mamasani, Qashqa'i, Shahsevan, Turkmen and others.

Iran Anthropology in the 1970s

The 1970s saw a flourishing of Iran anthropology. Iranians who received training abroad and conducted fieldwork in Iran during the 1970s included Sekandar Amanolahi, Mohammad Borghei, Ali Bulookbashi, Reza Fazel, Shahla Haeri, Nader Afshar Naderi, Rustam Pourzal, Shahnaz Nadjmabadi, Soraya Noland, Fereydoun Safizadeh, Soheila Shahshahani, Mehdi Soroya and Bahram Tavakoli. Even more non-Iranian anthropologists conducted fieldwork in Iran in the 1970s. They included Richard Antoun, Paula E. Ardehali (Drew), Daniel Bates, Mary Catherine Bateson, Janet Bauer, Lois Beck, William Beeman, Anne Betteridge, Daniel Bradburd, Christian Bromberger, David Brooks, Constance Cronin, Brian Good, Jean-Pierre Digard, Robert Joseph Dillon, Michael Fischer, Erika Friedl, Grace Goodell, John Gulick, Mary Elaine Hegland, Patricia Higgins, William Irons, Rafique Keshavjee, Janet Kestenberg Amighi (Janet Amighi), Lawrence Loeb, David Marsden, Mary Martin, Emily MacIntire (Gianfortoni), Sidney Mintz, Soraya Noland, Karen Pliskin, Howard Rotblatt, Kaveh Safa-Isfahani, Philip Salzman, Andre Singer, Brian Spooner, Brian Street, Gabrielle Tala-Minai, Nancy Tapper (Lindisfarne), Richard Tapper, Gustav Thaiss, Caroline Thompson, Thomas Thompson, Elvia Testrepo and Susan Wright.

1970s Boundary Crossings

In the 1970s, although Iran anthropology was at an early stage, anthropologists produced some boundary-crossing work, as the following examples show. The research experiences of Shahnaz Nadjmabadi provide an example of the challenges of the anthropological enterprise, even for an indigenous anthropologist. Although one might think Iranian anthropologists would find fieldwork in Iran to be relatively free of problems, Shahnaz Nadjmabadi's experiences show that even indigenous anthropologists may have to struggle against barriers (2004). For her, the self-other relationship is the crucial component of fieldwork, but few anthropologists write about these experiences and problems: we suppress or conceal much information through self-censorship, and tend to fashion ethnographies as perfect stories of success (2004: 604). Compared to native anthropologists, foreign researchers, Nadjmabadi suggests, can more easily distance themselves from, and be inaccessible to, local populations. People tend to associate Iranian-born researchers with government officials and either treat them with suspicion or make demands on them to interfere with government agents on their behalf. She uses her field experiences in three research locations to exemplify the challenges native ethnographers face and the wrong directions a fieldworker can take even while working in his/her own country of origin.

Retrospectively, she wondered if critical anthropology, exposing exploitative tactics to the oppressed, might not make matters worse at times, and might prevent one from looking at the exploiters' viewpoint, thus leading one to miss half the picture. In the Persian Gulf, she ran into problems when she tried to involve people in her research, as required by dialogical anthropology, by explaining her analyses to them. The people did not approve her conclusions, especially critical ones, even if they themselves freely talked about hopelessness and oppression. In order to cope with the mutual disillusionment, as well as with the strain of constant witnessing of injustice and harm and her inability to fulfil requests to help, she had to close down emotionally. Her fieldwork experiences painfully confronted Nadjmabadi with the discrepancy between her research interests and the interests and expectations of local people, and with the intellectual and emotional difficulties of straddling the boundary between outsider and insider.

In his classic study of peasant agency (1971), Reinhold Loeffler started to bridge the gap in our knowledge of the dynamic interaction between national politics and economy and local village communities (R. Loeffler 1971, 1973, 1976, 1978, 1986, 1988, 2004). Pioneering work among religious minorities, Laurence Loeb (1977, 1982) studied the Jews of Shiraz, and Michael Fischer (1973) and Janet Kestenberg Amighi (1990) conducted fieldwork among Zoroastrians. Rafique Keshavjee studied Ismailis in rural northeastern Iran, questioning whether Islamic mysticism necessarily requires retreat and whether a Muslim life requires adherence to any one monolithic structure of practices and beliefs (1989, 1998). Sekandar Amanolahi wrote about other minorities, the Baharvand (1975a), the Luti (1975b) and the Qashqa'i (2004b), and several other scholars made significant contributions to the anthropology of nomads and other minority groups. Crossing geographical boundaries in fieldwork, Robert Dillon, rather than working in one village or community, took a regional approach in his work on carpet economy (1976).

Byron Good pioneered the field of medical anthropology in Iran (1977a, 1977b; Good and Delvecchio Good 1982; DelVecchio Good and Good 1988; Good, Delvecchio Good and Moradi 1985). William Beeman started anthropological work on communication, focusing on Persian style, Iranian national character, humour and aspects of traditional theatre and popular performance (1976a, 1976b, 1977, 1979, 1981a, 1981b, 1984, 1986, 1992, 2001). Grace Goodell studied community effects of the World Bank Dezful dam project (1986), criticizing top-down development, and then crossed the boundary into development consulting and academic work. Patricia Higgins was one of the first to work on the anthropology of education in Iran (1976), and Brian Street pioneered the study of literacy in Iran (1995).

Gustav Thaiss conducted fieldwork among the Tehran *bazaaris,* focusing on the issues of Islam and political attitudes and rhetoric, including anti-government sermons by leading clerical figures. He broke the ground for investigation of the connections between Islam and politics, an area about which anyone who is anybody has something to say nowadays. Thaiss seems almost to have foretold the Iranian Revolution, with its Shi'a religious organization, metaphors, leaders and motivations (1972a, 1972b, 1973). Further, he pioneered the study of gender and sexual metaphors of nation and foreign incursion (1978) – themes that now are common in anthropology and other fields. Again, when few others assigned much salience to religion in Iran, Reinhold Loeffler (1988) undertook his detailed, longitudinal study of the religious worldviews of Iranian males in a Lurish village,

Along with Thaiss and Loeffler, Anne Betteridge also stepped over boundaries to undertake research on Shi'a Islam when few anthropologists, social scientists, historians or people in general ascribed much significance to Islam in the Middle East, and specifically in 'modern' Iran. Betteridge also initiated the study of women's religious activities, pilgrimage and rituals in Iran, and pioneered this work among Muslim societies in general (1983a, 1983b, 1985a, 1985b, 1989, 1992, 1993).

In the 1970s, Kaveh Safa-Isfahani conducted the research for his classic, pioneering publication on sexual innuendoes in wedding songs and performances (1980). Shahla Haeri conducted her innovative fieldwork on the Shi'a Muslim institution of temporary marriage, working in Qom and interviewing clerics, and also bringing anthropological attention to issues of sexuality in Iran (1983, 1986, 1989, 1994). Janet Bauer, working among rural to urban migrants in Tehran (1983, 1984, 1985), provided us with yet another pioneering work on issues of sexuality (1986). Also see Drew's work on sexuality (1997). These four anthropologists crossed high barriers; even today, little anthropological literature exists on issues of sexuality in Iran or the Middle East in general.

Because of the phenomenon of women entering educational and professional life in the West, and also entering the field of anthropology in large numbers, many females became involved in Iran anthropology, resulting in pioneering work and significant contributions to the field of feminist anthropology. At a point when feminist anthropology and the anthropological study of women was just beginning, Nancy Tapper (Lindisfarne) studied women and gender issues among the nomadic Shahsevan (1978, 1980). Soheila Shahshahani conducted research about the role of women among the Mamassani tribal groups (1982), and Lois Beck produced, together with Nikki Keddie (1978), a comprehensive volume of articles on women in the Muslim world that still stands unequalled, as well as other articles on nomadic Qashqa'i women (1978, 1980a, 1980b, 1980c). Susan Wright wrote about the verbal work of women in politics among the Doshman Ziari (1978, 1981). Working with village women in Iran during the Revolution, I was able to record women's numerous verbal and other contributions to local-level politics and also to the revolutionary movement (Hegland 1983c, 1986a, 1986b, 1991, 1998, 1999a, 1999b, 2003, 2006a, 2008).

Such efforts broke barriers in that they focused on women and gender in anthropological endeavours – a novel viewpoint in anthropology during the 1960s and 1970s. Further, their concentration on non-elite women's political influence and participation broke across a dual barrier – the separation between formal politics and informal, less visible, non-standardized political activity, such as movements, marches, demonstrations, communication and pressures; and the border constituted by the assumption, specifically in Muslim societies, that politics was a male realm. These anthropologists contributed to the feminist wave of anthropology by demonstrating that the less visible, announced, or even sometimes acknowledged work of women in politics, religion, economy, social organization, and creation and recreation of culture, although sometimes different from that of males, must be studied for a more comprehensive, undistorted understanding of society and culture and how individuals negotiate their social and cultural environments.

The Revolutionary Period and Its Aftermath

Karen Pliskin, who worked in Shiraz in 1978, wrote about the build-up to the Revolution (1980). The accident of timing for my dissertation research in 1978–79 allowed me the unusual opportunity to be a participant observer during the Revolution – mainly in Aliabad, a village near Shiraz – and to see the revolutionary experience through the eyes, emotions and analyses of village residents. This unique opportunity to observe actions and to listen to conversations regarding local-level politics and the revolutionary movement enabled me to cross into previously uncharted territory in a number of ways. I could observe at first hand village women's and men's participation in the Revolution; the interconnected dynamics of local politics and the Revolution; how people began to relate the martyrdom of Imam Hussein and the Karbala paradigm to the revolutionary movement; how people experienced the Revolution; and how, why and when people arrived at decisions about switching over to the side of the revolutionary forces. In addition, because I stayed until mid December 1979, I saw some of the early aftermath of the Revolution, such as the election supporting the formation of an Islamic Republic, the local-level revolt against the landlord and seizure of his land, and the telling commemoration of Taasua and Ashura by villagers in December 1979.[6]

In the 1950s, 1960s and 1970s, Iran anthropologists regularly pioneered and crossed boundaries: any topic we addressed was novel for Iran. We had to develop approaches and perspectives for our research, and often such efforts constituted early boundary crossing for Middle East anthropology and even initiating or sharing new initiatives in anthropology in general.

The Post-revolution Period

Working and Residing inside Iran

Very few Iranian anthropologists have been able to work and live inside of Iran. Those who have managed to do so include Sekandar Amanolahi of Shiraz University, Ali Bulookbashi and Nasser Fakouhi of Tehran University, Mohammad Mirshokraei of the Cultural Heritage Institute (*Mirath-e Farhangi*) and Soheila Shahshahani of Shahid Beheshti University in Tehran. Trying to work as an anthropologist inside the country presents severe challenges. Anthropological work is bounded in a number of ways.

Sekandar Amanolahi serves as an example because he has been stationed in Iran for the longest time of all in-country anthropologists. With a Ph.D. in anthropology from the U.S., he has taught and carried out field research projects in Iran while based at Shiraz University (formerly Pahlavi University) since 1974. Surely no other anthropologist has studied such variety of topics at so many research sites, resulting in numerous publications and reports in both Persian and English. He has been well aware of the dearth of anthropologists and ethnographic research in Iran, and has seen it as his mission to conduct as much research as possible, to record culture before it is lost.[7] Because of the great variety of topics, Amanolahi has had to be very flexible and eclectic with methodology, but he is careful to check the veracity of all information by comparing reports from different people against each other. Amanolahi sees his native/insider status as extremely helpful for his research: he does not need special permits, he enjoys the respect accorded to male professors in Iran, he commands languages and dialects and he has a home base near his research sites. Yet he too, like Nadjmabadi, has faced the problem of the recurrent expectation that his reports and publications should be positive and praising. Further, as he lives and works in Iran, he is vulnerable to political shifts. Lack of access to international contact due to Iran's isolation has also impinged on his work by keeping him (and other Iranian anthropologists) from participating in the wider scholarly community (Amanolahi 2004a: 621).

Iranian Anthropologists Educated Abroad Conducting Research in Iran in the 1980s and 1990s

Some Iranians, most in England but also in Norway, Germany and the U.S., were able thanks to their Iranian passports to begin or continue research in Iran. Fariba Adelkhah, Zahra Kamalkhani, Ziba Mir-Hosseini, Shahnaz Nadjmabadi, Ferydoun Safizadeh, Soraya Tremayne and Azam Torab conducted fieldwork in Iran during this period, continuing to expand themes and boundaries.

Longitudinal Anthropological Research in Iran

During and soon after the revolutionary period, anthropological fieldwork in Iran proved to be impossible for most people. However, Austrian citizens Erika Friedl (1983, 1989) and Reinhold Loeffler (1986) were able to go to

Iran again right after the Revolution. Lois Beck was able to write about the Qashqa'i during and following the Revolution (1980a, 1980b, 1980c, 1983, 1986, 1990, 1991, 1992, 1993, 1998 and 2000). Now Beck is preparing another book about the Qashqa'i, *Nomads Move On: Qashqa'i Tribespeople in Post-Revolutionary Iran* (forthcoming). These three senior foreign anthropologists, as well as Soheila Shahshahani (1984, 1995, 1997, 2000, 2003a, 2003b) working inside the country, have been able to return to the same research sites, publishing studies about the dynamics of change among groups, villages and women affected by the Revolution. Through their longitudinal research – itself rare in the world of anthropology – these four scholars have made significant new contributions to the field of socio-cultural anthropology.

Long before the astounding variety of Shi'a religious beliefs and practices became a hot topic, Reinhold Loeffler published the results of a decade (1965–1976) of research on the subject, conducted in a Boir Ahmad village, in a work that can be ranked as a classic in anthropology (1988). Loeffler's research and book broke through theoretical boundaries by showing how aspects of culture are developed and then modified through transmission and the dialectic between individual and structure (1978: 252), which has so confounded anthropologists. He further demonstrated the astounding variety of interpretations of Islam, even among men in one village, including such variegated perspectives as uncommitted formalism, religion of power, and virtuoso devotionalism. Finally, by presenting the religious worldviews of twenty-one different men instead of focusing on only one person or generalizing about a group of individuals, Loeffler invalidated the notion of Shi'a Islam as monolithic.

More recently (2004), Loeffler reflects on the insights his later fieldwork has provided. He feels that what made his sensitive fieldwork on religion possible were the hospitality, acceptance and helpfulness of the villagers. Men appreciated his companionship in isolated outposts and in the fields, and their discussions with him there on philosophies, theology and worldviews provided the bulk of the content of his book. On later visits, Loeffler found that his analyses of the religious worldviews of the twenty-one men featured in the book continued to ring true, proving good forecasts of the men's stances during and after the Iranian Revolution. However, such autochthonous religious worldviews as he studied in the 1970s are dying out, as official sources flood the younger generations with quite uniform religious teachings. He would not be able to replicate the earlier study now. Longitudinal anthropology dramatically confronts us with the dynamic quality of culture and society (2004).

Another highly significant contribution to Iran anthropology is Erika Friedl's book on women (1991). In this book, which is based on decades

of ethnographic research in Boir Ahmad, Friedl breaks down the boundary between anthropology and literature, developing the new genre of the
ethnographic short story. Her stories about Deh Koh women's agency and
struggles are based on insights about women's lives that could only be accumulated over a long time. Falling between literature and ethnography, the
book at first was difficult to publish, but it quickly gained popularity with
anthropologists and a general readership alike, and even was chosen among
the most notable books of 1989 by *The New York Times Book Review*.
Later (2004a), Friedl continued to think innovatively about stories by showing that over her thirty-seven years of involvement in village life local stories
took on lives of their own, and by suggesting that the lives of stories become
a new area of anthropological focus.

In 1997 Friedl broke through another boundary, into the worlds of village children. The ethnography of children is neglected in anthropology in
general, and thus no generally accepted appropriate ethnographic methodologies have been developed. For example, for several reasons children in
rural Iran are not easily accessible to ethnographic fieldworkers and are reluctant to talk freely (2004b). How, then, can the anthropologist get at how
children think of themselves and their place in the world, and at the categories they use to order their experiences? Friedl had to develop unorthodox
approaches, and could not have done this fieldwork without her longtime
familiarity with Persian culture, the villagers and government officials.

Through her numerous research stays with the nomadic Qashqa'i in
southwestern Iran, Lois Beck has been able to make significant contributions
to the study of the ethnography and history of this group, e.g. in her classic
book on the Qashqa'i (1986, 2000). She pioneered the study of women in
Iran (1978) and crossed the boundary into biography with a unique volume and an article documenting experiences of one Qashqa'i man respectively (1991, 1993). Beck's many publications follow the Qashqa'i through
decades of history, political disempowerment, confrontations with Iranian
governments, uprisings after the Iranian Revolution of 1978, with tragic
results, and entering the change and transformation of the twenty-first century. No other scholar has published so extensively about an Iranian tribal
group. Her work ranges from more wide-canvas discussions of Qashqa'i
(1986) to detailed presentation of individual lives (1991). She has focused
on such different but interrelated areas as the dynamics between herd owners
and hired shepherds (1980a); tribal peoples in revolutionary Iran (1980d);
the return from abroad of some Qashqa'i exiles and the subsequent fate of
Qashqa'i leaders and people; economic transformation among the Qashqa'i
nomads; the history of the Qashqa'i tribal confederacy (1983); nomadic
land use (1998); dynamics between the Islamic Republic government of Iran
and the Qashqa'i nomads (1992); and the history of a subtribe (2000). Beck

is currently preparing a book about the Qashqa'i since the 1979 Iranian Revolution for publication. Again, periodic visits and intensive fieldwork over a number of decades have allowed Beck to look holistically at Qashqa'i culture, society and individuals, as the tribal/ethnic group has faced the economic, political, social and religious transformations of the twentieth and twenty-first centuries.

Alternatives to Continuing Field Research in Iran

For those Iran anthropologists who did not live inside Iran, however, or were not able to continue to make research trips to Iran, lack of access to field research in Iran presented a professional dilemma. Some Iran anthropologists were not able to find jobs in academia, in an anti-Iran atmosphere in the West, and turned to other fields. Quite a few Iran anthropologists continued to write up their pre-1980 research in Iran, providing many new publications throughout the 1980s and 1990s.

Going Elsewhere for Anthropological Research

Some Iran scholars chose alternative research areas. For example, William Beeman has worked in Japan, Germany and Tajikistan. Michael Fischer has developed numerous projects in cultural and postmodern studies. Grace Goodell went on to study the Philippines and East Asia's 'four little dragons' (Hong Kong, Singapore, Taiwan and South Korea), worked as a consultant on numerous development projects and helped to reconceptualize the field of development anthropology. Shahla Haeri has worked in Pakistan, and I too went to Pakistan for several months in 1990–91. Homa Hoodfar went to Egypt, as did Nilufar Haeri. Nancy Lindisfarne (Tapper) has conducted fieldwork in Afghanistan, Turkey and Syria. Karen Pliskin conducted Ph.D. research among Iranians in Israel. Philip Salzman continued work on his theoretical interests in pastoral peoples in India and Italy. Richard Tapper has worked in Afghanistan and Turkey. Gustav Thaiss went to Trinidad to continue his study of Moharram rituals and politics. Brian Street and Sue Wright continued their respective research interests (literacy and community development) in England.

Conducting Research among Iranians Living outside Iran

The large diaspora communities of Iranians provided an accessible research population for anthropologists who could not go to Iran from the 1980s onward. Halleh Ghorashi has published on her work among Iranian women exiles in the Netherlands and the United States (2003), talking about all aspects of the diasporic experience. Diane Hoffman has written about 'Language and Culture Acquisition among Iranians in the United States' (1989). Mohsen Mobasher is writing about Iranian immigrants in Texas (2006). Other diaspora scholars include Sebnem Akcapar, Shirin Hakimzadeh, Lynn Harbottle, Mary Elaine Hegland, Patricia Higgins, Homa Hoodfar, Zahra Kamalkhani, Shahram Khosravi, Vida Nassehi-Behnam (1985, 2005), Karen Pliskin and Fereydoun Safizadeh. Shahram Khosravi is working with illegal immigrants in Sweden, breaking new ground in Iran anthropology.[8]

Of these, Higgins has provided the most detailed account of the challenges involved in diaspora research (2004). She found recruiting and accessing people a major challenge in urban research environments such as her own in Northern California. Higgins brought to her project the experience of conducting research about education in Iran during 1969–71, Persian language ability, knowledge of Persian culture and long-time friendship with Iranians in Northern California. She nevertheless faced a challenge in recruiting a sample of Iranian-American parents and adolescents to her research project. She mobilized school administrators and her network of Iranian friends and sent hundreds of letters to be able to include about one-third of the eligible families in her research. While Higgins found them to be welcoming families – warm, generous and very involved with their children's social and cultural development, academic success and overall well-being (2004: 702) – the participating parents considered their cooperation with her to be part of their support of their children's schooling, and even asked Higgins for advice in educational matters. Higgins thinks about what benefit her research brought to those families who participated. This is a question, usually highly abstract, that many of us ask ourselves in the course of our research. It seems that the people who talk to us appreciate the mere fact that we are interested in them, that we listen to them and patiently answer their questions and that, at times, we can offer useful advice (Higgins 2004: 706).

Public Anthropology and Journalism

In addition to carrying out research projects elsewhere, one Iran anthropologist, William Beeman, has become a public anthropologist. No other Iran anthropologist has done more to speak to the public about Iran and Middle East issues. Beeman works as a writer for Pacific News Service. He has published articles in a wide variety of newspapers, magazines and journals and has commented on politics in the Middle East and international relations on many television and radio programmes. In his recent book (2005), Beeman uses an anthropological framework to analyse how the Iranian and American governments conceptualize and behave towards each other.

1998–2000 and On: New Hopeful Developments in Iran Anthropology

Among other senior anthropologists presently working inside Iran, Sekandar Amanolahi, Nasser Fakouhi, Mohammad Mirshokra'i and Soheila Shahshahani have been struggling to develop Iranian anthropology. Shahshahani, for example, has founded two anthropological journals recently: *Ensanshenasi (Anthropology)* and *Anthropology of the Middle East*. In December 2005, she convened a double anthropology conference in Tehran, bringing many foreign fieldworkers as well as Iranian anthropology and sociology students together to learn about pilgrimage and the effects of globalization on Central Asian cities. Shahshahani also holds offices in international anthropology organizations, actively attends anthropology conferences outside of the country and has even developed an anthropology lecture series. Recently, Nematollah Fazeli, after earning his Ph.D. from the School of Oriental and African Studies, London, joined these four stalwart anthropologists to teach at Allameh Tabatabai University. His return to Iran and his book (2006) present highly encouraging developments in Iran anthropology.

Anthropologists Able to Return to Iran

The Iranian-American anthropologists Nilufar Haeri, Shahla Haeri, Homa Hoodfar and Fereydoun Safizadeh have been able to return to Iran for research. Non-Iranian anthropologists William Beeman, Anne Betteridge, Mary Elaine Hegland, Patricia Higgins, Nancy Lindisfarne, Richard Tapper and Sue Wright have been able to return to Iran since the 1979 Revolution, but for short trips only. The stringent time limits present great challenges to anthropological research based on participant observation, which usually requires a year or more of intense involvement.

Confronting this difficulty constituted another boundary-crossing of sorts, as I found through my own experience. After having not been able to return to Iran for twenty-five years, in 2003 I found myself back in Aliabad, where I had done fieldwork during the Revolution, but was able to stay only two weeks. Several factors helped me to make the utmost out of the limited time, most notably my previous stay in the village, which made it unnecessary to spend time introducing myself to the community; my long-standing friendship with several villagers and my familiarity with the village generally; the narrow research focus on issues of aging and the elderly; my willingness to use any situation as an opportunity to ask questions and conduct interviews about older people; the use of tape recorder, camera and the ever-present laptop computer as instant recording devices; and a daily 24-hour alertness. (Hegland 2004). With my direct approach and sharp focus on the task at hand, I was able to collect a great deal of information about change and transformation in Aliabad during the last twenty-five years (forthcoming 2008a), the meaning of Islam in the life of older village women (forthcoming 2008b) and aging and the elderly. Considering the time limitations posed on ethnographic research by non-Iranians at present, these methodological considerations will be relevant for other foreign ethnographers planning to work in Iran.

Foreign Anthropologists Turning to Iran

Marcia Inhorn has recently studied artificial insemination in the view of Sunni versus Shi'a Islam, including fieldwork in Iran (2006). Edward Simpson is including work in the earthquake-affected city of Bam in his comparative analysis of natural disaster in India, Iran and Indonesia. The medical anthropologist Diane Tober engaged in anthropological fieldwork in Iran in 2002. She worked on issues of health and family planning among Iranians and Afghan women near Isfahan, and with colleagues from Isfahan Medical School was able to develop a project about family planning among poorer Iranians and Afghan refugees. This collaborative process constitutes a crossing of the boundary between solitary research and cooperative research between Iranian and foreign scholars. Although it was logistically difficult in Tober's case (2004), it may provide an example for others to follow and shows how profitable collaboration can be for both partners.

New Foreign Ph.D. Researchers in Iran

A few hardy, tenacious foreign anthropologists have been able to conduct Ph.D. research in Iran recently, overcoming considerable resistance to do so. Yuko Suzuki, a Japanese scholar based in France, documents the difficulties she experienced with three different Iranian ministries and local authorities when applying for permits and conducting fieldwork among the Dushmanziari (2004). Furthermore, the research climate improved and worsened, Suzuki found, according to political developments. Anthropologists rarely talk about these important framework-conditions for research in Iran. Like Nadjmabadi and Amanolahi, Suzuki also describes the hardships involved in trying to comply with local people's expectations.

Sabine Kalinock provides a picture of the particular challenges of being a Christian European trying to learn about women's Shi'a rituals. The most important influence on her research was the relationship between herself and the women in her research population. At times, the desire to inform her, a European and potential convert, about correct interpretations of Islam brought out arguments among women, with the benefit of heated and relatively uncensored expressions of differences in religious opinions. Her long stay enabled her to understand the great diversity in women's ritual practices. The political sensitivity of women's religious beliefs and rituals also posed the challenge of how to determine to what extent religious representations and practices are based on personal beliefs and convictions and to what extent on dissimulation as a reaction to state control (2004: 673).

Agnes Loeffler, an Austrian who lives in the U.S., bridges the fields of medicine and anthropology with M.D. and Ph.D. degrees. Doing research in Iran on how Western (allopathic) medicine is understood and handled by Iranian medical personnel, and on how it is integrated into Iranian medical and health culture, she, too, faced nearly insurmountable practical, and considerable methodological, difficulties (1998, 2004, 2007a, 2007b). She found that any activity that is labelled *tahqiqat* or research can be seen as a critical and potentially subversive activity in Iran and brings increased surveillance of one's activities by government agents. At all times Loeffler felt the influence of the contradictory views of foreigners on her research: welcome and suspect, a source of pride and danger, someone to seek out and to avoid (2004: 642).

Recent Iran Anthropology Ph.D.s of the Diaspora Generation

Mohammad Shahbazi, based at Jackson State University, and Arzoo Osanloo, based at the University of Washington, Seattle, are writing about their research experiences in Iran. Shahbazi discusses the three main fieldwork methodology challenges that he faced, as an Iranian trained and working in the U.S., while studying Qashqa'i schoolteachers of a state educational programme specifically for nomads. One was dealing with the prejudices and lack of appreciation in Iran for the field of anthropology and social sciences in general, which, in fact, is a problem reported by Iranian scholars for the recruitment of good students into anthropology. Being Qashqa'i himself did not solve the trust problem. The second problem was dealing with bureaucratic difficulties. Although, as an Iranian, Shahbazi did not have an issue with visas, his dealings with the bureaucracy and officials were still problematic. His interest in working with the Qashqa'i – considered by the central government to be potentially politically dangerous – caused suspicions. He learned that he needed good working relationships not only with higher-level officials but also with local-level figures and networks in order to do his work.

Arzoo Osanloo, a lawyer, travelled to Iran in 1999 to conduct research for her Ph.D. in anthropology on women's perceptions of their rights in the Islamic Republic (2004, 2006a, 2006b). Like other young Iranian expatriates, she had relatives in Tehran who helped her, and she enjoyed the relatively liberal environment Tehran provides compared to other places in Iran.

Her main problem was methodological: nobody had done such research before, and no precedent existed for dealing with a drastically changing context for women's understanding of their rights in Iran or for collecting the relevant data. Her assumptions about what she would need to investigate, what kinds of data she would need to collect and the venues for collecting such data changed drastically during the fieldwork period.

Others from the diaspora generation have returned to Iran for research and Iran anthropology Ph.D.s. Yasmine Amir-Moez received a doctorate in 1985 from the Ecole des Hautes Etudes en Sciences Sociales in Paris; her thesis, based on fieldwork from 1979, was about the technology of the Qashqa'i pastoral nomads (see her 2002 article). Pardis Mahdavi, a medical anthropologist, earned a Ph.D. from Columbia University. With her work about sexuality and politics in post-Revolution Iran, she breaks through barriers that formerly prevented Iran anthropologists from focusing on sexuality. She joins a small group of insightful anthropologists of Iranian background focusing on the transgressing Iranian young people who are transforming Iranian society, in spite of their careful education under the aegis of the Islamic Republic of Iran (2008). Setrag Manoukian completed his Ph.D. about history and culture in Shiraz at the University of Michigan in 2001 and now teaches at McGill. Angela Sahraee-Smith completed her University of London Ph.D. on 'The Political Economy of Mourning: A Study of Practised Islam and Gender in Urban Iran' in 2001. Roxanne Varzi earned her Ph.D. at Columbia with a thesis on media and youth in Iran (2006) and now is based at the University of California, Irvine. Alireza Doostdar is working on his Ph.D. in anthropology at Harvard on the ethnographic study of blogging as an emergent speech genre (2004). Narges Erami has done field research on rug production and bazaari social networks for her Ph.D. dissertation at Columbia University. Navid Fozi has done fieldwork among the Ahl-e Haqq of Kermanshah for a Ph.D. at Boston University. Shokrullah Haidari studied among the Kalhor nomads (Wright and Haidari 2001) and is working on his dissertation. Pedram Khosronejad, who completed a dissertation about issues of death and mourning for the École des Hautes Etudes en Sciences Sociales in Paris (in French, thus not included in the bibliography), has actively promoted Iran anthropology by organizing conferences and workshops. Sholeh Shahrokhi has been conducting fieldwork in Iran for her Berkeley dissertation, 'Female Runaways: Gender Crossing, Teen Prostitution and Other Subversive Sexual Praxis' (forthcoming). Sima Shakhsari at Stanford University is working on a Ph.D. dissertation about gender, sexuality and nationalism in developing imaginations among the Iranian diaspora. Shahla Talebi recently completed her dissertation on 'Discourses of Self Sacrifice: State and Dissident Martyrs in Post-Revolutionary Iran' (2007) at Columbia University.

Some Foreign Students Pursuing Iran Anthropology

Satoshi Abe has begun working toward a dissertation for the University of Arizona, Tucson, about exchanges of technological expertise between the countries of Iran and Japan. Janne Bjerre Christensen conducted research in Iran about the marriage crisis in 1998 and 1999 and completed her MA in 2000. She returned to Iran for research on the involvement of local non-governmental organizations in drug-use issues in Tehran for her Ph.D. dissertation at Roskilde University, but has faced severe visa problems in Iran. Jason Price is studying anthropology at New York University with interests in Iranian film and poetry. Isabel Heck, University of Montreal, conducted fieldwork in Iran in 2005 and 2006 for her Ph.D. dissertation on community organizations for women in Iran. Rose Edith Wellman, granddaughter of Edith and Victor Turner, is at the University of Virginia, preparing for fieldwork in Iran. She wrote by email, 'I follow my grandparents in that I am interested in ritual, social drama, liminality' and also issues of globalization and gender.

Masters Degrees in Iran Anthropology

Ole Ramsing at the University of Copenhagen wrote an MA thesis titled, 'Uses of Rituals and Social Change in Tehran, Iran' (1995). Masoud Naseri wrote his MS thesis at the University of Wisconsin, Milwaukee, on 'Medical Pluralism among Iran's Nomadic Pastoralist Ethnic Minorities' (2003). Shirin Hakimzadeh earned an MA degree in social and cultural anthropology at Oxford University with the thesis 'Beyond Diasporic Generations: Transnational Identity and Integration of Second-Generation Iranians in London'. While interning at the Migration Policy Institute in Washington, D.C., she produced 'Iran: A Vast Diaspora Abroad and Millions of Refugees at Home' (2006) and, with David Dixon, 'Spotlight on the Iranian Foreign Born' (2006). Leila Pope earned an MA in film and anthropology from School of Oriental and Asian Studies in 2003. Parisa (Lisa) Yazdi is working on a master's degree at Simon Fraser University, focusing on Islamic democracy in Iran.

Concluding Comments

Anthropology as a conceptual framework has been made possible by boundary crossings and globalization. We can apply Fredrik's Barth's insight about 'ethnic groups and boundaries' and ethnic identity to the field of anthropology as well: lacking contact with or knowledge about people from different cultures, Barth concluded, one cannot be aware of one's own group as distinctive or conceptualize boundary markers. It is only contact with other cultural groups that enables imagining one's own ethnic group (1969). One also cannot, we might add, imagine the anthropological enterprise – looking at a culture not as the natural world, but as one among many, in comparative fashion. Initially, not surprisingly, those who enjoyed greatest access to global travel dominated the field of anthropology. In its earlier years, anthropological practitioners came from the colonizing countries, for example, the English anthropologists Bronislaw Malinowski, A. R. Radcliffe-Brown, S. F. Nadel, Max Gluckman and E. E. Evans-Pritchard, and might even have worked as colonial administrators. These men set the agenda for anthropological research, often taking into account the perceived needs of colonial administrations.

In Iran too, early anthropologists came from the West. Privileged with their greater resources, political capital, access to other countries and access to Western education and to anthropology – a field developed by Westerners – Westernizers dominated anthropological research in Iran. The first anthropologist to work in Iran was from the West. In the 1960s, and even more so in the 1970s, Western anthropologists (the great majority from the U.S.) far outnumbered Iranian anthropologists working in Iran.

The identity of those doing Iran anthropology and steering the field has changed over time, however. In the 1970s, through opportunities to travel abroad and gain access to education, enabled by oil revenues, some Iranians began to study anthropology. Then, because of the nativist movement in Iran in the form of the Revolution and the Islamic Republic, Western anthropologists' domination of fieldwork in Iran declined, and Iran anthropology and Iranian anthropology in general declined. For a couple of decades after the Revolution, Iranian anthropologists found it difficult to get out into the field, while non-Iranian anthropologists experienced great difficulty gaining access to research in Iran. For non-Iranian outsiders, it has been almost impossible to stay longer than three months at a time, if they are fortunate enough to gain entrance at all.

At the same time that the emergence of the Islamic Republic of Iran, and the relationship of enmity between the new Iranian government and Western governments, particularly the U.S., began to erect barriers to foreign anthropologists and even indigenous anthropologists wishing to conduct fieldwork in Iran, Iranian society broke over the boundary of Western consciousness onto the world stage. With the Revolution, the confounding turn to an Islamic government, the takeover of the American embassy and holding of hostages in Tehran, and subsequent incidents and accusations, Iran has drawn the attention – and fear – of the West. Anthropologists were well situated to try to provide some answers and insights regarding the revolutionary dynamics and the trajectory of the postrevolutionary government, as their long-term participant observation among 'ordinary' Iranians and their insights about Iranian culture shed light on happenings in Iran. Other anthropologists, scholars and the general public have drawn upon many anthropological publications about Iran, which still do not receive the attention they deserve, to try to make sense of these developments.

As the Iranian Revolution and subsequent Islamic Republic of Iran influenced religion and politics towards a resurgence of Islam in other societies, Iran anthropologists often led the way in discussions of Islam and politics; Islam, resistance, and revolution; Islam and gender; Islam and modifying meaning, and the role of religious symbolic complexes in political change and transformation. Other scholars often cite Iran anthropologists in their own work, and the works of Iran anthropologists are reprinted and translated for publication in other languages. Professors in various fields frequently use Iran anthropology publications for coursework. Some books by Iran anthropologists have become classics, for example Haeri's study of temporary marriage (1989). Some Iran anthropologists have used their Iran research as entries into becoming significant contributors in particular areas of anthropology, for example, Grace Goodell in development and Michael Fischer in postmodernism. Several books have even caught the attention of the educated public audience, such as Erika Friedl's book of short ethnographic stories set among the Boir Ahmad Lurs in southwestern Iran (1991), and the linguistic and public anthropologist William Beeman's study of the mutual demonization of the Iranian and American governments (2005). More recently, Iran anthropologists are again leading the way with the study of youth and resistance means and strategies and the rather ironic growth of secular tendencies in Iran (Doostdar 2004; Khosravi 2007; Mahdavi 2008; Varzi 2006).

In general, though, since anthropologists faced almost insurmountable obstacles to conducting fieldwork in Iran after the Revolution, most anthropologists were forced to work from a distance, become involved with emigrant Iranian groups or turn to research elsewhere. Yet today there are some indications that the anthropology of Iran appears to be reemerging. Influenced by the dynamism and diversification in topic and methodology that has developed in Western anthropology and by the influences of modernization and globalization on Iran and Iranians, a new group of Iran anthropologists are breaking barriers into new topics through new modes of research and analysis. Most of the current field researchers have come from abroad. However, many of those active in the field actually have Iranian backgrounds; they are from the diaspora generation. Only a very few English-speaking anthropologists have continued to make regular visits to Iran, outstanding among them Lois Beck, Erika Friedl and Reinhold Loeffler. Other than their work, that of Agnes Loeffler and my own few articles based on brief return visits to Iran in 2003, 2004, and 2005–6, anthropologists of Iranian background have provided the great majority of publications based on new research. These young anthropologists living in the West enjoy Western access to education, creative new anthropological approaches, research funding and travel opportunities. Because they hold Iranian passports they cannot be kept out of Iran, as can Westerners who lack Iranian background. Very likely, these anthropologists of Iranian background will dominate anthropological field research in Iran in the near future.

Certainly, young anthropologists of Iranian background can bring much to the field of Iran anthropology. But what will they contribute to the development of anthropology in Iran? They write in English, or other Western languages. They will work in the West, teaching students in the West rather than in Iran. They have become Westerners, on the whole, and like Western anthropologists they conduct their professional networking with other anthropologists in the West. In contrast to earlier generations of Iran anthropologists, they may not even maintain contact with their Iran anthropologist colleagues, but rather interact with other anthropologists at their own universities and in their respective theoretical fields. They have crossed over and are now of the West. Several of these young 'diaspora' Iran anthropologists, overwhelmed by the difficulties and dangers of participant observation in Iran or realizing they cannot return to Iran because of their publications, have now decided upon other field research sites.

Soheila Shahshahani and others inside Iran are making tremendous efforts to build Iranian anthropology. However, no Ph.D. programme in anthropology yet exists in Iran. Iranian anthropologists and students of anthropology remain isolated by lack of access to other anthropologists, anthropological publications, conferences and networking, and opportunities for travel, research and publication. If Iranian anthropologists inside the country cannot become a part of the worldwide community of anthropologists, they can neither profit from nor contribute to the globalized field of anthropology. If the field of Iranian anthropology does not advance to become a part of the worldwide field of anthropology, it will continue to be dominated by Western anthropologists, and by the new Western anthropologists – the diaspora generation of Iranians.

Efforts to bridge the barriers between Western anthropologists and Iranian anthropologists have been made. Shahnaz Nadjmabadi organized the September 2004 Frankfurt conference on Iranian anthropology, bringing Iranians together with Iran anthropologists based in the West. Soheila Shahshahani organized a double conference for the Urban Anthropology Commission of the International Union of Anthropological and Ethnological Societies in Tehran in December 2005, including participants from Iran, China, Japan and Uzbekistan as well as European countries. Mohammad Mirshokraei, director of the Anthropology Research Centre of Iran's Cultural Heritage and Tourism Organization (*Sâzemâan-e mirâs-e farhangi va gardeshgari*), organized an anthropology symposium in Kerman in February 2007, although Westerners were not able to obtain visas in order to attend.

We who care about both Iran anthropology and Iranian anthropology know we must work harder to find ways to coordinate efforts, to develop collaborative projects between anthropologists based in the West and those inside Iran and to create more opportunities for interacting and sharing perspectives and research. Another boundary must be bridged: anthropologists must cross over the border between Iranian anthropology and the world of global anthropology.

NOTES

1. In this chapter, I use 'Iran anthropology' to connote all anthropological work based on research in Iran or with Iranians abroad, in other words, the anthropology of Iran and/or Iranians abroad. By 'Iranian anthropology' I mean anthropology as it has been developed in Iran, by Iranians, in other words, anthropology of Iran as it is viewed and practiced by Iranian anthropologists living and working inside Iran.
2. I heard the term 'diaspora generation' for the first time at the International Society of Iranian Studies conference in London, 2–5 August 2006, as applied to the group of Iran scholars with such backgrounds.
3. For more about anthropology, methods and fieldwork in Iran, see not only the 2004 special issue of *Iranian Studies* (edited by Friedl and Hegland), but also Hegland and Friedl 2007, Mir-Hosseini 2002, Naderi 1982, Razavi 1993, Shahbazi 2003, Shahshahani 1986 and Spooner 1971, 1987, 1997. In his recently published book (2006), Fazeli documents and analyses the history of anthropology within Iranian society.
4. Many thanks to those who offered leads and information, to Erika Friedl, Shahnaz Nadjmabadi and Birgit Reinel, and anonymous reviewers for suggestions and editing assistance.
5. See Fazeli's (2006) discussion of Dr. Nader Afshar Naderi's crucial contributions to Iranian anthropology.
6. See Hegland 1980 through 1998. The dissertation material has not yet been published as a book but is expected to be available soon (1986b, forthcoming b).
7. For a description of seventeen of his projects, see Amanolahi (2004a).
8. For some of their other publications see in particular: Akcapar 2006; Bauer 1991, 2000; Harbottle 2000; Hegland 2006a, 2006b; Hegland and Zahedi 1998; Higgins 1997a, 1997b, 2004; Kamalkhani 1988; Khosravi 1999; Mobasher 2006.

REFERENCES

Akcapar, S. K. 2006. 'Iranian Transit Migrants in Turkey', Ph.D. thesis. Catholic University of Leuven (Belgium).

Alberts, R. C. 1963. 'Social Structure and Culture Change in an Iranian Village', Ph.D. thesis. University of Wisconsin. Madison.

Amanolahi, S. 1975a. 'The Baharvand: Former Pastoralists of Iran', Ph.D. dissertation. Rice University. Houston, Texas.

———. 1975b. 'Luti, an Outcaste Group of Iran', *Rice University Studies* 61(2): 1–12.

———. 2004a. 'Fieldwork Among Pastoral Nomads and in Sedentary Communities of Iran', *Iranian Studies: Special Issue: Ethnographic Fieldwork in Iran* 37(4): 613–21.

———. 2004b. 'The Status of Women among the Qashqai of South Iran', *Iran and the Caucasus* 8(1): 131–40.

Amir-Moez, Y. 2002. 'The Qashqa'i', in R. Tapper and J. Thompson (eds), *The Nomadic Peoples of Iran*. London: 190–251.

Atkinson, J. 1832. *Customs and Manners of the Women of Persia and Their Domestic Superstitions*. London.

Barth, F. 1961. *Nomads of South Persia: The Basseri Tribe of the Khamseh Confederacy*. Oslo: Universitetsvorlaget.

———. 1969. 'Introduction', in F. Barth (ed.), *Ethnic Groups and Boundaries: The Social Organization of Culture Difference*. Long Grove, IL: 9–38.

Bauer, J. 1983. 'Women, the Veil, and the Islamic Revolution in Iran', *Sacramento Anthropological Society, California State University, Sacramento* 16: 120–27.

———. 1984. 'New Models and Traditional Networks: Migrant Women in Tehran', in J. T. Fawcett, S.-E. Khoo, and P. C. Smith (eds), *Women in the Cities of Asia*. Boulder: 269–93.

———. 1985. 'Demographical Change, Women and Family in Migrant Neighbourhood of Tehran', in A. Fathi (ed.), *Women and Family in Iran*. Leiden: 158–186.

———. 1986. 'Sexuality and the Moral "Construction" of Women in an Islamic Society', *Anthropological Quarterly* 58(3): 120–29.

———. 1991. 'A Long Way Home: Islam in the Adaptation of Iranian Women Refugees in Turkey and West Germany', in A. Fathi (ed.), *Iranian Refugees and Exiles Since Khomeini*. Costa Mesa, CA: 102–19.

———. 2000. 'Desiring Place: Iranian "Refugee" Women and the Cultural Politics of Self and Community in the Diaspora', *Comparative Studies of South Asia, Africa, and the Middle East* 10(1–2): 180–97.

Beck, L. 1978. 'Women among Qashqa'i Nomadic Pastoralists in Iran', in L. Beck and N. Keddie (eds), *Women in the Muslim World*. Cambridge: 351–373.

———. 1980a. 'Herd Owners and Hired Shepherds: The Qashqa'i of Iran', *Ethnology* 19(3): 327–51.

———. 1980b. 'Tribe and State in Revolutionary Iran: The Return of the Qashqa'i Khans', *Iranian Studies* 13(1–4): 215–55.

———. 1980c. 'The Religious Lives of Muslim Women', in J. Smith (ed.), *Women in Contemporary Muslim Societies*. Lewisburg, PA: 27–60.

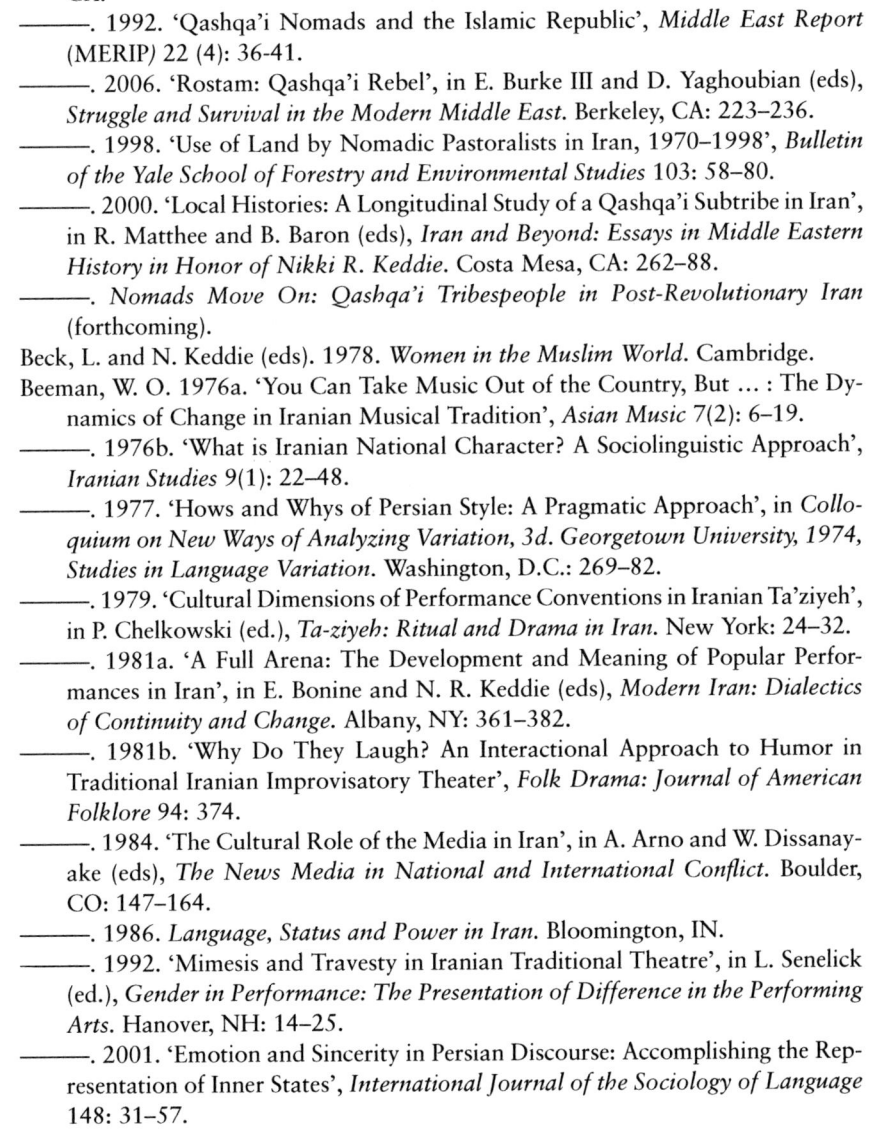

―――. 1980d. 'Revolutionary Iran and Its Tribal Peoples', *Middle East Report (MERIP Report)*, 10(4):14–20.

―――. 1983. 'Iran and the Qashqai Tribal Confederacy', in R. Tapper (ed.), *The Conflict of Tribe and State in Iran and Afghanistan*. London: 284–313.

―――. 1986. *The Qashqa'i of Iran*. New Haven, CT.

―――. 1990. 'Tribes and the State in Nineteenth and Twentieth-Century Iran', in P. Khoury and J. Kostiner (eds), *Tribes and State Formation in the Middle East*. Berkeley, CA.

―――. 1991. *Nomad: A Year in the Life of a Qashqa'i Tribesman in Iran*. Berkeley, CA.

―――. 1992. 'Qashqa'i Nomads and the Islamic Republic', *Middle East Report (MERIP)* 22 (4): 36–41.

―――. 2006. 'Rostam: Qashqa'i Rebel', in E. Burke III and D. Yaghoubian (eds), *Struggle and Survival in the Modern Middle East*. Berkeley, CA: 223–236.

―――. 1998. 'Use of Land by Nomadic Pastoralists in Iran, 1970–1998', *Bulletin of the Yale School of Forestry and Environmental Studies* 103: 58–80.

―――. 2000. 'Local Histories: A Longitudinal Study of a Qashqa'i Subtribe in Iran', in R. Matthee and B. Baron (eds), *Iran and Beyond: Essays in Middle Eastern History in Honor of Nikki R. Keddie*. Costa Mesa, CA: 262–88.

―――. *Nomads Move On: Qashqa'i Tribespeople in Post-Revolutionary Iran* (forthcoming).

Beck, L. and N. Keddie (eds). 1978. *Women in the Muslim World*. Cambridge.

Beeman, W. O. 1976a. 'You Can Take Music Out of the Country, But … : The Dynamics of Change in Iranian Musical Tradition', *Asian Music* 7(2): 6–19.

―――. 1976b. 'What is Iranian National Character? A Sociolinguistic Approach', *Iranian Studies* 9(1): 22–48.

―――. 1977. 'Hows and Whys of Persian Style: A Pragmatic Approach', in *Colloquium on New Ways of Analyzing Variation, 3d. Georgetown University, 1974, Studies in Language Variation*. Washington, D.C.: 269–82.

―――. 1979. 'Cultural Dimensions of Performance Conventions in Iranian Ta'ziyeh', in P. Chelkowski (ed.), *Ta-ziyeh: Ritual and Drama in Iran*. New York: 24–32.

―――. 1981a. 'A Full Arena: The Development and Meaning of Popular Performances in Iran', in E. Bonine and N. R. Keddie (eds), *Modern Iran: Dialectics of Continuity and Change*. Albany, NY: 361–382.

―――. 1981b. 'Why Do They Laugh? An Interactional Approach to Humor in Traditional Iranian Improvisatory Theater', *Folk Drama: Journal of American Folklore* 94: 374.

―――. 1984. 'The Cultural Role of the Media in Iran', in A. Arno and W. Dissanayake (eds), *The News Media in National and International Conflict*. Boulder, CO: 147–164.

―――. 1986. *Language, Status and Power in Iran*. Bloomington, IN.

―――. 1992. 'Mimesis and Travesty in Iranian Traditional Theatre', in L. Senelick (ed.), *Gender in Performance: The Presentation of Difference in the Performing Arts*. Hanover, NH: 14–25.

―――. 2001. 'Emotion and Sincerity in Persian Discourse: Accomplishing the Representation of Inner States', *International Journal of the Sociology of Language* 148: 31–57.

————. 2005. *The 'Great Satan' vs. the 'Mad Mullahs': How the United States and Iran Demonize Each Other.* Westport, CT.

Betteridge, A. 1983a. 'Muslim Women and Shrines in Shiraz', in S. J. Palmer (ed.), *Mormons and Muslims.* Provo, UT: 127–38.

————. 1983b. 'To Veil or Not to Veil: A Matter of Protest or Policy', in G. Nashat (ed.), *Women and Revolution in Iran.* Boulder, CO: 109–28.

————. 1985a. 'Gift Exchange in Iran: The Locus of Self-Identity in Social Interaction', *Anthropological Quarterly* 58(4): 190–202.

————. 1985b. 'Ziarat: Pilgrimage to the Shrines of Shiraz', Ph.D. dissertation. University of Chicago.

————. 1989. 'The Controversial Vows of Urban Muslim Women in Iran', in N. A. Falk and R. M. Gross (eds), *Unspoken Worlds: Women's Religious Lives in Non-Western Culture.* San Francisco, CA: 102–11.

————. 1992. 'Specialists in Miraculous Action: Some Shrines in Shiraz', in A. Morinis (ed.), *Sacred Journeys: The Anthropology of Pilgrimage.* Westport, CT: 189–209.

————. 1993. 'Women and Shrines in Shiraz', in D. Bowen and E. Early (eds), *Everyday Life in the Muslim Middle East.* Bloomington, IN: 239–47.

Dillon, R. 1976. *Carpet Capitalism and Craft Involution in Kirman, Iran: A Study in Economic Anthropology.* Ph.D. diss., Department of Anthropology, Columbia University, New York.

Doostdar, A. 2004. '"The Vulgar Spirit of Blogging": On Language, Culture, and Power in Persian Weblogestan', *American Anthropologist* 106(4), 651–662.

Drew, P. E. 1997. 'Sexuality', in R. T. Francoeur (ed.), *The International Encyclopaedia of Sexuality*, vol. 2. New York: 620–49.

Fazeli, N. 2006. *Politics of Culture in Iran: Anthropology, Politics and Society in the Twentieth Century.* New York.

Field, H. 1939. *Contributions to the Anthropology of Iran*, Anthropological Series, Field Museum of Natural History 29(1), Chicago.

————. 1953. *The Track of Man; Adventures of an Anthropologist.* Garden City, NY.

Fischer, M. 1973. 'Zoroastrian Iran Between Myth and Praxis', Ph.D. thesis. University of Chicago.

Friedl, E. 1983. 'State Ideology and Village Women', in G. Nashat (ed.), *Women and Revolution in Iran.* Boulder, CO: 217–30.

————. 1989. 'Islam and Tribal Women in a Village in Iran', in N. A. Falk and R. M. Gross (eds), *Unspoken Worlds: Women's Religious Lives.* Belmont, CA: 125–33.

————. 1991. *Women of Deh Koh: Lives in an Iranian Village.* New York.

————. 1997. *Children of Deh Koh: Young Life in an Iranian Village.* Syracuse.

————. 2004a. 'Stories as Ethnographic Dilemma in Longitudinal Research', *Anthropology and Humanism* 29(1): 5–21.

————. 2004b. 'The Ethnography of Children', *Iranian Studies* 37(4): 655–63.

Friedl, E. and M. E. Hegland (eds). 2004. *Journal of Iranian Studies: Special Issue on Ethnography in Iran* 37(4).

Ghorashi, H. 2003. *Ways to Survive, Battles to Win: Iranian Women Exiles in the Netherlands and the United States.* New York.

Good, B. 1977a. 'The Heart of What's the Matter: The Structure of Medical Discourse in a Provincial Iranian Town', Ph.D. thesis. University of Chicago.

———. 1977b. 'The Heart of What's the Matter: The Semantics of Illness in Iran', *Culture, Medicine and Psychiatry* 1(1): 25–58.

Good, B. and M.-J. Delvecchio Good. 1982. 'Toward a Meaning-Centered Analysis of Popular Illness Categories: "Fright Illness" and "Heart Distress" in Iran', in *Cultural Conceptions of Mental Health and Therapy*. Dordrecht: D. Reidel Publishing 141–66.

Good, M.-J. DelVecchio and B. Good. 1988. 'Ritual, the State, and the Transformation of Emotional Discourse in Iranian Society', *Culture, Medicine & Psychiatry* 12: 43–63.

Good, B., M.-J. DelVecchio Good and R. Moradi. 1985. 'The Interpretation of Iranian Depressive Illness and Dysphoric Affect', in A. Kleinman and B. Good (eds), *Culture and Depression: Studies in the Anthropology and Cross-Cultural Psychiatry of Affect and Disorder*. Berkeley, CA: 369–428.

Goodell, G. 1986. *The Elementary Structures of Political Life: Rural Development in Pahlavi Iran*. New York and Oxford.

Haeri, S. 1983. 'The Institution of *Mut'a* Marriage in Iran: A Formal and Historical Perspective', in G. Nashat (ed.), *Women and Revolution in Iran*. Boulder, CO: 231–52.

———. 1986. 'Power of Ambiguity: Cultural Improvisations on the Theme of Temporary Marriage', *Iranian Studies* 19(2): 123–54.

———. 1989. *Law of Desire: Temporary Marriage in Shi'i Iran*. Syracuse, NY.

———. 1994. 'Temporary Marriage: An Islamic Discourse on Female Sexuality in Iran', in M. Afkhami and E. Friedl (eds), *In the Eye of the Storm: Women in Post-revolutionary Iran*, Syracuse, NY: 98–114.

Hakimzadeh, S. 2006. 'Iran: A Vast Diaspora Abroad and Millions of Refugees at Home', *Migration Information Source*. Retrieved in September 2006 from http://www.migrationinformation.org/Profiles/display.cfm?ID=424.

Hakimzadeh, S. and D. Dixon. 2006. 'Spotlight on the Iranian Foreign Born', *Migration Information Source*. Retrieved 1 June 2006 from http://www.migrationinformation.org/USfocus/print.cfm?ID=404.

Harbottle, L. 2000. *Food for Health, Food for Wealth: The Performance of Ethnic and Gender Identities by Iranian Settlers in Britain*. Oxford and London.

Hegland, M.E. 1980. 'One Village in the Revolution', Middle East Report (MERIP) 10(4): 7–12.

———. 1982a. 'Religious Ritual and Political Struggle in an Iranian Village', *Middle East Report* (MERIP) 12(1): 10–17, 23.

———. 1982b. '"Traditional" Iranian Women: How They Cope', *The Middle East Journal* 36(4): 483–501.

———. 1983a. 'Two Images of Husain: Accommodation and Revolution in an Iranian Village', in N. R. Keddie (ed.), *Religion and Politics in Iran: Shi'ism from Quietism to Revolution*. New Haven, CT: 218–36.

———. 1983b. 'Ritual and Revolution in Iran', in M. J. Aronoff (ed.), *Political Anthropology: Culture and Political Change*, vol. 2. New Brunswick, NJ: 75–100.

———. 1983c. 'Aliabad Women: Revolution as Religious Activity', in G. Nashat (ed.), *Women and Revolution in Iran*. Boulder, CO: 171–94.

———. 1986a. 'Political Roles of Iranian Village Women', *Middle East Report* (MERIP) 16(10): 14–9.

———. 1986b. 'Imam Khomaini's Village: Recruitment to Revolution', Ph.D. thesis. Binghamton: State University of New York.

———. 1991. 'Political Roles of Aliabad Women: The Public/Private Dichotomy Transcended', in N. R. Keddie and B. Baron (eds), *Shifting Boundaries: Gender Roles in the Middle East, Past and Present*. New Haven, CT: 215–30.

———. 1998. 'Women and the Iranian Revolution: A Village Case Study', in M.J. Diamond (ed.), *Women and Revolution: Global Expressions*. Dordrecht, Netherlands: Kluwer Academic Publishers: 211–25.

———. 1999a. 'Gender and Religion in the Middle East and South Asia: Women's Voices Rising', in J. Tucker and M. Meriwether (eds), *Social History of Women and Gender in the Modern Middle East*. Boulder, CO: 177–212.

———. 1999b. 'Wife Abuse and the Political System: A Middle Eastern Case Study', in D. Counts, J. Brown, and J. Campbell (eds), *To Have and to Hit: Cultural Perspective on Wife Beating*. Urbana, IL: 234–51.

———. 2003. 'Talking Politics: A Village Widow in Iran', in L. S. Walbridge and A. K. Sievert (eds), *Personal Encounters: A Reader in Cultural Anthropology*. Boston, MA: 53–59.

———. 2004. 'Zip In and Zip Out Fieldwork', *Iranian Studies* 37(4): 575–583.

———. 2006a. 'Women of Karbala: Moving to America', in K. S. Aghai (ed.), *Women of Karbala: Ritual Performance and Symbolic discourses in Modern Shi'i Islam*. Austin, TX: 199–227.

———. 2006b. 'Iranian-American Elderly in California's Santa Clara Valley: Crafting Selves and Composing Lives', in H. Moghissi (ed.), *Muslim Diaspora: Gender, Culture and Identity*. London: 205–19.

———. 2008. 'Esmat Khanum and a Life of Travail: "You Yourself Help Me, God"', in F. Trix and J. Walbridge (eds), *Muslims Around the World*. New York: 57–68.

———. forthcoming a. 'Aliabad of Shiraz: From Village to Suburb', *Iran Nameh*.

———. forthcoming b. *Imam Khomeini's Village: Recruitment to Revolution*.

Hegland, M. and E. Friedl. 2007. 'Methods Applied: Political Transformation and Recent Ethnographic Fieldwork in Iran', *Anthropology in the Middle East, Special Issue: Methodology* 1(2): 1–19. Oxford, New York. Berghahn Journals.

Hegland, M.E. and A. Zahedi. 1998. Payvand and IFWC: Maintaining Iranian Identity in California's Bay Area', *DANESH Bulletin* 3(1): 12–17.

Higgins, P. 1976. 'The Conflict of Acculturation and Enculturation in Suburban Elementary Schools of Tehran', *Journal of Research and Development in Education* 9(4): 102–12.

———. 1997a. 'Intergenerational Stress: Parents and Adolescents in Iranian Immigrant Families', in D. Baxter and R. Krulfeld (eds), *Beyond Boundaries: Selected Papers on Refugees and Immigrants 5*. Arlington, VA: 189–213.

———. 1997b. 'Adolescent Ethnic Identities: Iranians in the U.S.', *DANESH Bulletin* 1(2): 10–14.

———. 2004. 'Interviewing Iranian Immigrant Parents and Adolescents', *Iranian Studies* 37(4): 706.

Hoffman, D.M. 1989. 'Language and Culture Acquisition among Iranians in the United States', *Anthropology and Education Quarterly* 20: 118–132.

Inhorn, M.C. 2006. 'Islam, IVF and Everyday Life in the Middle East: The Making of Sunni versus Shi'ite Test-Tube Babies', *Anthropology in the Middle East* 1(1): 42–50.

Kalinock, S. 2004. 'Touching a Sensitive Topic: Research on Shiite Rituals of Women in Tehran', *Iranian Studies* 37(4): 665–74.

Kamalkhani, Z. 1988. *Iranian Immigrants and Refugees in Norway.* Bergen.

Keshavjee, R. 1989. 'Power of Games and the Games of Power in Rural Iran', *Iranian Studies* 22(2–3): 87–97.

———. 1998. *Mysticism and the Plurality of Meaning: The Case of the Ismailis of Rural Iran.* London.

Kestenberg Amighi, J. 1990. *The Zoroastrians of Iran: Conversion, Assimilation, or Persistence.* New York.

Khosravi, S. 1999. 'Displacement and Entrepreneurship: Iranian Small Businesses in Stockholm', *Journal of Ethnic and Migration Studies* 25(3): 493–508.

———. 2007. *Young and Defiant in Tehran.* Philadelphia.

Loeb, L. 1977. *Out caste: Jewish Life in Southern Iran.* New York.

———. 1982. 'Prestige and Piety in the Iranian Synagogue', in S. Deshen, W. P. Zenner (eds) *Jewish Societies in the Middle East: . community, culture, and authority .* Washington, D.C.: University Press of America: 285–97.

Loeffler, A. 1998. 'Memories of Difference: From Lur to Anthropologist', *Anthropology and Humanism* 23(2): 146–56.

———. 2004. 'The Double-edged Foreign Connection', *Iranian Studies* 37(4): 633–42.

———. 2007a. 'Individual Constitutions vs Universal Physiology: Iranian Responses to Allopathic Medicine', *Body & Society* 13(3): 103–23.

———. 2007b. *Allopathy Goes Native: Traditional Versus Modern Medicine in Iran.* London.

Loeffler, R. 1971. 'The Representative Mediator and the New Peasant', *American Anthropologist* 73(2): 1077–91.

———. 1973. 'The National Integration of Boir Ahmad', *Iranian Studies* 6(2–3): 127–35.

———. 1976. 'Recent Economic Changes in Boir Ahmad: Regional Growth without Development', *Iranian Studies* 9(4): 266–87.

———. 1978. 'Tribal Order and the State: The Political Organization of Boir Ahmad', in A. Banani (ed.) *Iranian Studies, Special Volume, State and Society in Iran* 11: 145–71.

———. 1986. 'Economic Changes in a Rural Area Since 1979', in N. R. Keddie and E. Hooglund (eds), *The Iranian Revolution and the Islamic Republic.* Syracuse, NY: 93–109.

———. 1988. *Islam in Practice: Religious Beliefs in a Persian Village.* Albany, NY.

———. 2004. 'The Making of a Historical Document', *Iranian Studies* 37(4): 585–93.

Mahdavi, P. 2008. *Passionate Uprisings: Iran's Sexual Revolution*. Palo Alto, CA.

Mir-Hosseini, Z. 2002. 'Negotiating the Politics of Gender in Iran: An Ethnography of a Documentary', in R. Tapper (ed.), *The New Iranian Cinema: Politics, Representation and Identity*. London: 167–99.

Mobasher, M. 2006. 'Cultural Trauma and Ethnic Identity Formation among Iranian Immigrants in the United States', *American Behavioral Scientist* 50(1): 100–17.

Naderi, N.A. 1982. 'Some Considerations Regarding Anthropological Dilemmas', in H. Fahim (ed.) *Indigenous anthropology in non-western countries*. Proceedings of a Burg Wartenstein symposium. Durham, NC: 242–49.

Nadjmabadi, S. 2004. 'From "Alien" to "One of Us" and Back: Field Experiences in Iran', *Iranian Studies* 37(4): 603–12.

Naseri, M. 2003. 'Medical Pluralism among Iran's Nomadic Pastoralist Ethnic Minorities', MA thesis. Milwaukee: University of Wisconsin.

Nassehi-Behnam, V. 1985. 'Change and the Iranian Family', *Current Anthropology* 26(5): 557–62.

———. 2005. 'Transnational Identities: A Generational Study of Iranian Immigrants in France', The Japan Center for Area Studies (JCAS) Symposium Series 17, Osaka: 251–268.

Osanloo, A. 2004. 'Doing the "Rights" Thing: Methods and Challenges of Fieldwork in Iran', *Iranian Studies* 37(4): 675–84.

———. 2006a. 'Islamico-civil "Rights Talk": Women, Subjectivity, and Law in Iranian Family Court', *American Ethnologist* 33(2): 191–209.

———. 2006b. 'The Measure of Mercy: Islamic Justice, Sovereign Power, and Human Rights in Iran', *Cultural Anthropology* 21(4): 570-602.

Pliskin, K. 1980. 'Camouflage, Conspiracy, and Collaborators: Rumors of the Revolution', *Iranian Studies* 13(1–4): 55–81.

Razavi, S. 1993. 'Fieldwork in a Familiar Setting: The Role of Politics at the National, Community and Household Levels', in S. Devereux and J. Hoddinott (eds.), Fieldwork in Developing Countries. Boulder, CO: 152–163.

Safa-Isfahani, K. 1980. 'Female Centered World Views in Iranian Culture: Symbolic Representations of Sexuality in Dramatic Games', *SIGNS: Journal of Women in Society* 6(1): 33–53.

Sahraee-Smith, A. 2001. 'The Political Economy of Mourning: A Study of Practised Islam and Gender in Urban Iran', Ph.D. thesis. London: University of London.

Schumacher, P. 1950. 'Report on the Second Iran Expedition: Ethnography', *Philadelphia Anthropological Society Bulletin* 4(2): 3–4.

Shahbazi, M. 1998. 'Formal Education, Schoolteachers, and Ethnic Identity among the Qashqa'i of Iran', Ph.D. thesis. Washington University. St. Louis.

———. 2001. 'Qashqa'i Nomads of Iran (Part I): Formal Education', *Nomadic Peoples* 5(1): 37–64.

———. 2002. 'The Qashqa'i Nomads of Iran (Part II): State-Supported Literacy and Ethnic Identity', *Nomadic Peoples* 6(1): 95–123.

———. 2003. 'Anthropological Fieldwork Endeavour and Indigenous Researchers', *Nomadic Peoples* 7(2): 98–107.

———. 2004. 'Insider/Outsider: An Indigenous Anthropologist Bridges a Gap', *Iranian Studies* 37(4): 593–602.

———. 2006. 'Editorial: Everyday Life in the Middle East', *Anthropology in the Middle East* 1(1): v–vi.

Shahrokhi, S. forthcoming. 'Female Runaways: Gender Crossing, Teen Prostitution, and Other Subversive Sexual Praxis', Ph.D. thesis. Berkeley: University of California.

Shahshahani, S. 1981. 'The Four Seasons of the Sun: An Ethnography of the Sedentarized Village of the Mamassani Pastoral Nomads of Iran', Ph.D. thesis. Graduate Faculty of the New School for Social Research, New York.

———. 1984. 'Religion, Politics and Society: A Historical Perspective on the Women's Movement in Iran', *Samya Shakti* 1(2): 100–20.

———. 1986. 'History of Anthropology in Iran', *Iranian Studies* 19(1): 65–86.

———. 1995. 'Tribal Schools in Iran: Sedentarization through Education', *Nomadic Peoples*: 145–55.

———. 2000. 'Ambiguity in Law and the Marginalization of Sedentarized Nomads of the Southern Zagros Mountains of Iran', *Nomadic Peoples* 4(1): 23–36.

———. 2003a. Guest Editor *Nomadic Peoples* 7(2), special issue on Nomads and Nomadism in Post-revolutionary Iran.

———. 2003b. 'The Mamassani of Iran: At the Juncture of Two Modes of Subsistence', *Nomadic Peoples* 7(2): 87–97.

Spooner, B. 1971. 'Cultural Anthropology in Iran: Beginnings and Prospects', *Expedition* 13(3–4): 66–71.

———. 1987. 'Anthropology, social and cultural, in Iran', In Encyclopaedia Iranica 2: 107–16.

———. 1998 'Ethnography', Encyclopaedia Iranica 9: 9–45.

Street, B. 1995. *Social Literacies: Critical Approaches to Literacy in Development, Ethnography, and Education*. London.

Suzuki, Y. 2004. 'Negotiations, Concessions, and Adaptations During Fieldwork in a Tribal Society', *Iranian Studies* 37(4): 623–32.

Sykes, Sir P. 1902. 'Anthropological Notes on Southern Persia', *Journal of the Anthropological Institute* 32: 339–49.

———. 1921. 'The Gypsies of Persia', *Journal of the Anthropological Institute* 36: 302–11.

Talebi, S. 2007. 'Discourses of Self Sacrifice: State and Dissident Martyrs in Post-Revolutionary Iran', unpub. Ph.D. dissertation. Columbia University. St. Louis.

Tapper (Lindisfarne), N. 1978. 'The Women's Subsociety Among the Shahsevan Nomads of Iran', in L. Beck and N. R. Keddie (eds), *Women in the Muslim World*. Cambridge, MA: 374–98.

———. 1980. 'Matrons and Mistresses: Women and Boundaries in Two Middle Eastern Tribal Societies', *European Journal of Sociology* 21: 374–98.

———. 1972a. 'Unity and Discord: The Symbol of Husayn in Iran', in C. J. Adams (ed.) *Iranian Civilization and Culture*. Montreal: 111–19.

———. 1972b. 'Religious Symbolism and Social Change: The Drama of Husain', in N. R. Keddie (ed.), *Scholars, Saints and Sufis: Muslim Religious Institutions since 1500*. Berkeley, CA: 349–66.

———. 1973. 'Religious Symbolism and Social Change: The Drama of Husain', Ph.D. thesis. Washington University.

———. 1978. 'The Conceptualization of Social Change through Metaphor', *Journal of Asian and African Studies* 13(1–2): 1–13.

Tober, D. 2004. 'Children in the Field and Methodological Challenges of Research in Iran', *Iranian Studies* 37(4): 643–54.

Varzi, R. 2006. *Warring Souls: Youth, Media, and Martyrdom in Post-Revolution Iran.* Durham, NC.

Wright, S. 1978. 'Prattle and Politics: The Position of Women in Dushman-Ziari', *Anthropological Society of Oxford Journal* 9: 98–112.

———. 1981. 'Place and Face: Of Women in Doshman Ziari, Iran', in S. Ardener (ed.), *Women and Space.* New York: 136–57.

Wright, S. and S.H. Haidari. 2001. 'Participation and Participatory Development among the Kalhor Nomads of Iran', *Community Development Journal* 36(1): 53–62.

PART II

Voices from Within
Institutions and Professions

CHAPTER 4

Anthropology in Post-Revolution Iran

Nematollah Fazeli

Introduction

This chapter examines the development of anthropology as an academic and intellectual discipline in Iran from the 1979 Revolution till the present day. I intend to explore the political and ideological nature of anthropology as an academic discipline in Iran. My major argument is that anthropology in Iran was established in the early twentieth century in the Constitutional period (1906–11) and developed in the Pahlavi era (1941–78). With the advent of the Islamic Revolution it was then faced with some harsh political encounters, but later, with the emergence of new nationalist and reformist ideologies, the discipline began to develop.

This article is based on an ethnographic study of Iranian anthropology. It is ethnographic in the Geertzian sense, conceiving ethnography as 'an enterprise ... whose aim is to render obscure matters intelligible by providing them with an informing context' (Geertz 1983: 152). In the same way, this research is intended to contextualize modern anthropology in Iran within its pertinent sociopolitical context. I believe that 'intellectual paradigms, including anthropological traditions, are culturally mediated, that is they are contextually mediated and relative; and if anthropological activities are culturally mediated, they are in turn subject to ethnographic description and ethnological analysis' (Scholte 1969: 431).

I have organized the article in three parts. The first provides a brief history of anthropology in Iran. The second focuses on the ideological impact of the advent of the Islamic Revolution on the discipline. The final part is devoted to the impact of the recent Reformist movement on the discipline. Since my focus here is to explain the state of anthropology after the Revolution, I do not examine prerevolutionary developments in detail.

An Overview of the History of Anthropology in Iran

With the turn of the twentieth century, Iran witnessed major historical changes. In the first decade, the Constitutional Revolution (1906–11) took shape, changing certain structural bases of society including the elites' attitudes towards culture. During the Constitutional Revolution era, a group of prominent literati, such as Mohammad Ali Jamalzadeh (1922, 1962), Ali Akbar Dehkhoda (1983) and Zeynul 'Abedin Maragheh'i (1965), approached culture from the viewpoint of ordinary people, not that of the ruler and court, which had been predominant for centuries. They sought to reform society and purify traditional culture of superstitions and obstacles, and to pave the way for modernization and rationalization. They adopted a 'critical approach' towards culture that was unprecedented in Persian literature and Iranian intellectual history. They began with the simplification of the Persian language and popularization of Persian folk literature. Called a literary revolution (*Enqelab Adabi*), this movement aimed to democratize Persian literature and language. This literary revolution was mainly carried out through folklore studies, and also developed the foundations of Iranian folkloristics (folklore studies).

Then, in the 1910s and 1920s, the idea of an Iranian anthropology was further popularized by Sadeq Hedayat and his followers (Shahshahani 1986: 106). Hedayat approached Iranian culture and folklore from nationalist and modernist perspectives. In his view, Iranian culture comprised two distinctive elements: non-Iranian and Iranian. Islamic cultural elements were treated as 'alien' (Hedayat calls them *biganeh*), irrational and anti-modern, whereas cultural elements from the pre-Islamic period were taken as 'genuine culture' (Hedayat calls them *eteqadat boomi*), suited to a modern society based on European civilization. Hedayat's approach towards Iranian culture became the guideline for all nationalist folklorists and paved the way for the distinctively secular tone for modern folklore studies in Iran. It should be noted here that Hedayat established a tradition that became, as we will see, the cornerstone and basis of Iranian anthropology for the next generations of Iranian cultural scholars, though academic anthropology was established later. As we will see, this academic trend has not been influential so far. Since most of the scholars of folklore studies were writers and literati, they mainly focused on issues that could be used as literary material. Examples of this are the works of Amini (1944) and Enjavi-Shirazi (1975).

This folklore tradition was characterized primarily by an emphasis and focus on oral traditions such as national folk narratives, folk songs, proverbs, ballads and national customs such as *Norooz* (Iranian New Year celebrations). Meanwhile, the folklore scholars did not analyse collected materials; rather, they provided only descriptive accounts of Persian folklore without any serious analytical and critical approach. Hedayat himself collected a bulk of Iranian folklore that has been printed repeatedly.[1] Another point that might be considered here is the significant impact of this folklore studies tradition on the formation of Iranians' concept of anthropology. Anthropology in Iran is mainly recognized as the science and study of tradition, in particular folklore. As will be discussed here, the first and main anthropological research institution of Iran was established to collect material and folk culture.

During the reign of Reza Shah (1925–41) folklore studies were actively encouraged by the government and used to support and popularize the nationalist ideology of the state. The nationalization of the Persian language, the invention of national traditions and symbols, and other state policies created a need for an anthropological enterprise. In 1938 the Centre for Iranian Anthropology (Markaz-e Mardomshanasi-ye Iran) was founded. As the first Iranian institution for studying anthropological themes, and the first cultural and social research centre in Iran, the centre was commissioned to document historical and existing Iranian cultural traits, in particular folklore. Soon after its formation, the centre established the Museum of Iranian Anthropology (Muzeh Mardomshenasi Iran) and the Museum of Ancient Iran (Muzeh Iran Bastan). Later, during Mohammad Reza Shah's reign (1941–79), the centre was considerably extended, and from the 1960s on it produced a vast corpus of folkloric and ethnographic materials (Khaliqi 1974: 5).

From the 1960s until the 1970s, Iranian folklore studies attracted further attention from both government and independent scholars. In 1965 the government established the Centre for Iranian Folklore (CIF; Markaz Farhange Mardom) (Enjavi-Shirazi 1992: 17) under the auspices of the Iranian National Broadcasting Company (Sazman Radio va Televezion Meli Iran). The CIF played a highly significant role in popularizing and spreading folklore studies around the country. At that time an intellectual movement had emerged against the Westernization of the society in the name of modernization and development. This anti-Western movement aimed to preserve traditional culture and focused on folklore studies, the revitalization of peasant culture, the extension of rural and nomadic studies and an emphasis on religious and Islamic culture.

Iranian anthropology evolved into an academic and professional discipline in the 1960s with the formation of the Institute for Social Studies and Research (ISSR; Mo'asseseh Motale'at va Tahqiqat Ejtema'i), and the Department of Anthropology of Tehran University (1971) (Markaz Farhang-e Mardom-e Iran). In the 1960s and 1970s Iranian anthropology changed its focus to applied research to provide basic data for implementing government development programmes (Enayat 1973: 10; Zahedi-Mazandarani 1996:

18). At that time, Iranian researchers published a host of ethnographic accounts of nomadic and rural communities (Afshar-Naderi 1968; Amanollahi-Baharvand 1975; Sa'edi 1963, 1965; Varjavand et al. 1967). Those studies mainly served the state policy of modernization.

Meanwhile, a large number of non-Iranian, mainly European and North American, anthropologists came to Iran to do ethnographic fieldwork. Overall, by 1979, Iranian culture and society had attracted a large number of non-Iranian ethnographers (Larijani 1991; Safinezhad 1997; Spooner 1999), and Iran had become the second-favourite ethnographic site in the Middle East for anthropologists (Antoun with Hart and Redman 1976: 181).

Anthropology and the Islamic Revolution

With the advent of the newly established Islamic government, the revolutionaries began to challenge the core ideological nature of all the social and human sciences, in particular anthropology. From their ideological point of view, social science disciplines by nature were secular, Western, nationalist and colonialist, all features contrary to the ideals of the Revolution. Accordingly, in the so-called Cultural Revolution (*Enqelab Farhangi*) the universities were closed and the human sciences were put under ideological pressure. The government began to oust academic staff, and many faculty members of the Department of Anthropology of Tehran University and the ISSR lost their positions. Other anthropological activities decreased, and for about a decade the discipline was treated as illegitimate. Yet, because there was a need to revitalize Shiite culture and identity, the revolutionaries began to produce some kinds of ethnographic texts. In what follows I shall explain these developments.

The decline of anthropology after the Revolution can be attributed to various academic, political and social factors. Some authors emphasize the academic factors. They point to a range of shortcomings, including the absence of educational facilities such as a professional society, the lack of experienced and trained anthropologists, the lack of resources, unawareness of the latest theoretical developments (Amanollahi-Baharvand 1996: 38–48), the theoretical immaturity of anthropology (Kousari 1998: 137–50), the restriction of research topics, the lack of relationships between Iranian anthropologists and those in other developing countries, the absence of government support (Farhadi 1994: 85), the ambiguity of theoretical concepts in Iranian anthropology, the lack of practical uses for anthropology (Maqsoudi 1998: 151–60), the general epistemological crisis of legitimacy in anthropology (Azad-Armaki 1999; Mahdi and Lahsaizadeh 1996; Tehranian et al. 1987) and the theoretical inability of anthropology to deal with Iranian sociocultural questions (Azad-Armaki 1999: 123).

Undoubtedly, each of these explanations has some merit in that each demonstrates the existence of a critical state. Yet none of them takes full account of the role of sociopolitical and cultural change in society since the Revolution. In my opinion, to explain the crisis one needs to study the nature of anthropological concepts and discourses and their relevance to recent sociopolitical changes, in particular how they conflicted with the discourse of the Islamic Revolution. This conflict limited the expansion of anthropology, but has meanwhile, in one way or another, provided a new basis for Iranian anthropology and extended its horizons. In this regard two main sites of conflict between anthropology and the Revolution might be identified. First, the revolutionary discourse was, at its inception, non-nationalist, even anti-nationalist, in that it sought to revitalize and invigorate the Shiite identity of Iran as an alternative to the nationalist pre-Islamic identity promoted by the Pahlavi regime. Here we shall examine the role of anthropology in the conflict between Islamic and nationalist identities. Second, with the 'traditionalist' orientation of the Revolution, both the notion of tradition and its elements have become strongly politicized, and the core concepts of Iranian anthropology have become a sensitive political domain. Over the last two decades, as most intellectuals, elites, students and youth have increasingly adopted a critical attitude towards the revolutionaries, so religious traditions, seen as markers of loyalty to the ideology of the Revolution, have become a less attractive topic for study. Anthropology, as the study of tradition, lost its social legitimacy and popularity. Here, we shall examine the role of anthropology in the conflict between tradition and modernity.

Anthropology and the Conflict between Islamic and National Identity

In the late nineteenth century and the beginning of the twentieth, as an alternative ideology to Islam, intellectuals disseminated a Romantic nationalism that was used by the Pahlavi dynasty as a source of their political legitimacy (Gheissari 1998). The Islamic Revolution was, in a sense, a reaction to that nationalism. However, the Revolution was intrinsically anti-nationalist not only because nationalism was the political ideology of the Pahlavis, but also because of the many philosophical challenges it posed to Islam.[2]

Before the Revolution, Ali Shariati (1979) criticized nationalism and addressed the conflict between Shiism and nationalism from an Islamic and religious point of view. The Safavid dynasty (sixteenth to eighteenth centuries) adopted Shiism as the official religion of Iran, and blended nationalism with Shiism in the establishment of the Safavid state. In Shariati's view, nationalist ideas polluted Shiism, and Islam did not need to be justified by love of land and history. This was the background to the anti-nationalist policy of the Revolution.

In the 1980s, any notion of nationalism was seen as contrary to Islam and the Revolution. This is best reflected in Reza Davari's book *Nasionalizm va Enqelab-e Eslami* (*Nationalism and the Islamic Revolution*, 1980), which also represents the official attitude towards the social sciences. The author, a renowned Islamic philosopher, has since 1980 been a key member of the Supreme Council for Cultural Revolution (Shura-ye 'Ali-ye Enqelab Farhangi)[3] and is now president of the Islamic Republic's Academy of Sciences (Farhangestan 'Olum). Davari states that the purpose of his study is to approach nationalism from a revolutionary and Islamic perspective, with the ultimate goal of addressing the problem of the humanities after the Revolution. In the introduction, he argues that, for a profound insight into the ideological nature of contemporary humanities, we must study nationalism because it is one of the basic ideologies of the humanities. He insists that nationalism is a modern phenomenon, different from the traditional and conventional concept of *hobb-e vatan* (patriotism) prescribed by Islam.

Davari discusses nationalism in its various forms, arguing that in Iran it was a blind imitation of European orientalism: 'It was a form of *melligara'i farhangi* (cultural nationalism) that atheist Iranian intellectuals and scholars, not the masses, believed in and tried to spread throughout the country' (1980: 56). He argues that nationalism was a cultural phenomenon: a group of intellectuals wanted to divert Iranians from their Islamic identity and replace it with secular and liberal values and beliefs. An important point of Davari's thesis is that he takes nationalism as a branch of the humanities and social sciences, which, he maintains, 'has been a predominant trend in Iranian academia'. He criticizes scholars for corrupting their objectivity with an ideological commitment to nationalism (1980: 210). Davari's view epitomizes the official attitude and policy towards nationalism and the social sciences in the 1980s. What is relevant to our discussion is that this issue strongly affected anthropological activities, and this anti-nationalist and anti–social science view provided a strong ideological and theoretical background from which to challenge and criticize social science disciplines and their research institutions, including the Centre for Iranian Anthropology.

The Religious-Secular Conflict

Although the concept of an Islamic social science is a polemical issue in Iranian academia on which no consensus has been reached (Tabatabai 1995), its proponents enjoy government support and have produced a considerable literature. The concept has two different roots: first, a theoretical and philosophical conflict between social sciences and Islamic ideology, and second, an actual conflict between two groups: dissident intellectuals and the clergy. From a practical viewpoint, the Islamization of knowledge has been an ideological tool. This point becomes clearer when we see how in recent years the Islamization of knowledge has turned into the Islamization of the universities and the project of establishing an Islamic university.

The Islamicists follow two lines of argument to establish an Islamic anthropology. First, they try to extract the idea of anthropology from Islamic texts and traditions. Secondly, they evoke the intellectual history of Muslim societies. They argue that the study of culture – the subject of anthropology – is not limited to modern European academic disciplines, because Islamic sources (the Qur'an, Hadith, Sunna, Islamic sciences such as jurisprudence, theology and mysticism) are full of anthropological ideas and theories, and Muslim scholars throughout history have produced a vast literature on culture. They argue that Islam has its own humanities.[4]

Islamic anthropology and social sciences are not compatible with modern anthropology. Anthropologists are unanimous in claiming that theirs is a liberal, secular and, to some extent, objective discipline. These characteristics are antithetical to the Islamic Revolution's ideology and the Islamic education system of Iran.

Reformist Movement and Anthropology

Despite all the above-mentioned ideological and theoretical conflicts, Iranian anthropology found new ground on which to be reborn in the 1990s. The period of the end of the Iran-Iraq War, from 1988 through to 2003, featured a revival and expansion of academic activity, higher education and academic disciplines in Iran. Therefore anthropology, like many other disciplines, found a new basis for institutional development. The following aspects illustrate this development:

- Government policy in rural and agricultural development became more participatory in nature, a change that also provided new grounds for anthropological studies of local knowledge (Fazeli 2006; Shakoori 2001).
- During this period, undergraduate and research degrees were added to already established graduate degree programmes. Apart from Tehran University, other universities, including those of Mazandaran, Sistan Baluchestan, Yazd, Garmsar and Rudehen, as well as Tehran

Islamic Azad University (with its three separate parts in central, south and north Tehran) and the Centre for Higher Training of the Organization for Cultural Heritage (Daneshsaraye Alye Tarbiyat Moallem), began to offer diploma, undergraduate and graduate degrees in anthropology (see Fakouhi in this volume).

- A new wave of cultural heritage studies emerged, giving prominence to folklore, archaeology and ethnography. In the 1990s, the government established several anthropological museums, and the Centre for Iranian Anthropology carried out several national ethnographic projects. My examination of the centre's recent activities suggests that its research projects and activities can be classified into four categories: (1) religious research, (2) development studies, (3) nationalist and historical studies and (4) studies of cultural change.

- As part of its campaign against Westernization and what the Leader of the Revolution called *tahajom-e farhangi* (cultural invasion), the state decided to reinforce native, local and national cultures, giving further scope for ethnological studies and enterprises. In recent years too, secularist scholars and members of ethnic minorities have begun to produce and publish a series of secular and local folklore studies (for example, Ahmade Shamlo's *Ketabe kucheh: farhang-e loghat, estelahat, ta'birat, zarbolmasa-haye Farsi* (Shamlo 1357/1978) and Darvishiân's *Afsaneha va masal-haye Kurdi*) (Darvishiyân, 'A.-A. 1998–05/1377–84)

- Several new anthropological institutions were established, including the Iranian Anthropological Association (Anjoman Ensanshenasi Iran) in 2001, the Centre for Iranian Anthropology (Markaz Madoshenasi Iranian) and the Iranian Centre for Local Knowledge Studies (Markaz Motaleat Daneshe Bumi). I have discussed and introduced these developments elsewhere (Fazeli 2006).

- In addition, in recent years, the Centre for Iranian Anthropology has become very active and has held several anthropological conferences and carried out national research projects (see Fazeli 2006).[5]

- In addition, a number of new research centres for applied anthropology have been established.

Teaching and academic activity in anthropology have thus increased since the early 1990s, in line with the massive expansion of higher education in general and of the social sciences in particular. Several new academic anthropological journals were established, such as *Ensanshenasi* (published by Markaz Nashr-e Daneshgahi), *Nameh Ensanshenasi* (published by the Iranian Anthropological Association), *Faslnameh Farhang Mardom* (published by Seyyed Ahmad Vakilian) and *Faslnameh Ensanshenasi* (published by Jahad Daneshgahi of the Social Science Faculty of Tehran University).

Alongside these institutional developments, the anthropological literature has been proliferating. According to statistics provided by the Iranian
Book Society (Khaneh Ketab Iran) on the period between 1989 and 2002,
a total of 5,529 books were published in different anthropological fields
such as folklore, archaeology, mythology, ethnography, social and cultural
anthropology, ethnology and cultural studies.[6] In this connection it should
be noted that more than 80 per cent of anthropological books were published by nongovernmental organizations. This shows that anthropological
knowledge has attracted public attention and therefore more intellectuals
are working in this field.

Conclusion

Despite certain positive developments outlined above, anthropology in Iran
has been faced with many impediments. Increases in student and academic
staff numbers do not always indicate development in academic knowledge
and in the discipline. The government has regarded an advanced higher education system as an indication of development. It has treated the expansion
of higher education as an end in itself and at the same time as a means of
educating a skilled workforce to implement socioeconomic and development plans. The recent development of higher education generally and anthropology in particular can be seen as the consequence of the expansion
of a bureaucratic system rather than of any structural development in academic disciplines.

Meanwhile, the discipline has faced many political and institutional
problems. Ethnographic studies of the nomadic tribes lost their position
on the map of Iranian anthropology and were replaced by quantitative sociological studies. Moreover, the universities have been unable to satisfy
student expectations, and the available literature on anthropological theory
and method is far from adequate, though the discipline has been developed
institutionally. From a political standpoint, however, the growth of social
science disciplines and the universities in general have been very important
elements in the political changes of the last decade. The university is a modern institution that disseminates modern knowledge, ideas and perspectives,
and functions as a modernization machine. Thus it has a deep impact on
people's attitudes, and students learn a more critical and modern view of
their culture and society.

The developments and constraints mentioned above are mainly rooted
in contemporary sociopolitical changes in Iran. This period has seen fundamental political, cultural and economic changes in Iranian society. The
war with Iraq ended, Ayatollah Khomeini died, revolutionary anti-nation-
alism declined and a new Islamic nationalism was born. The demographic

structure of society changed with an explosion of youth, and as a corollary, the social demand for higher education dramatically increased. New communication technologies arrived and society was opened to a global culture. Meanwhile, the government's postwar reconstruction plans failed to meet the people's social, political and economic expectations; policies for nomads and rural areas changed; the conservative, totalitarian and traditional nature of the state was challenged and, in due course, a Reformist movement has made significant advances over fundamentalist readings of the revolutionary ideology and Islam. With all these societal changes, the universities, scholars, media and people have become freer to express their culture and desires.

The 1990s saw rapid developments in anthropology in Iran involving all elements of the discipline: institutions, numbers of practitioners and students, research, teaching, books, journals, museums and, finally, epistemological and methodological issues. Generally, anthropology in Iran is conceived as the scientific study of tradition and cultural identity, and in this sense anthropology is potentially in line with the ideology of the Revolution and the political culture of the Islamic Republic. The Revolution's major aim in the 1990s – to maintain Irano-Islamic identity and culture against processes of globalization and Westernization – was the basis on which the state and society tried to develop anthropology. Indeed, this political logic has been visible in all anthropological activities.

NOTES

1. All of Hedayat's folklore studies were recently published in a book called *Farhange Mardome Iran* (Folklore of Iranian People) (1999).
2. The difficult relationship between Islam and nationalism has been much studied. See, for example, Ernest Gellner's *Nationalism* (1997).
3. The council is the highest authority of the higher education system.
4. I have presented some examples of Islamic anthropological texts elsewhere (Fazeli 2006).
5. All information about the centre is based on an interview I held with Dr. Mohammad Mirshokrai, the director of the centre, in the summer of 2000.
6. This statistical information is extracted from the *Khaneh Ketab* database information, and I received it personally from the authorities at the centre.

REFERENCES

Afshar-Naderi, N. 1968/1347. *Monografi-ye il-e Bahme'i*. Tehran.
Amanollahi-Baharvand, S. 1975/1354. *Manzelat-e zan dar ejtema'-e 'ashayeri: tayefeh Dareh-shuri*. (The status of woman in tribal society: the Dareh-shuri tribe). Sazman Zanan Iran. Tehran.

————. 1996/1375. 'Masa'el va moshkelat-e ensanshenasi dar Iran', in *Seminar-e Barresi-ye ravesh va teknuluzhi-ye amuzeshi*. Tehran: 35–51.

Amini, A. Q. 1944/1323. *Farhang avam ya tafsir-e amsal va estelahate zaban-e farsi*. Esfahan.

Antoun, R. T., with D. M. Hart and C. L. Redman. 1976. 'Anthropology', in L. Binder (ed.), *The Study of the Middle East*. New York: 451–560.

Azad-Armaki, T. 1999/1378. *Jame'eh-shenasi-ye jame'eh-shenasi dar Iran*. Tehran.

————. 1969/1348. *Bavar-ha va danesteh-ha dar Lurestan va Ilam*. Tehran.

Darvishiyân, 'A.-A. 1998–05/1377–84. *Farhang-e afsânehâ-ye mardom-e Irân* 1–18. Tehran.

Davari, R. 1980/1359. *Nasionalizm va enqelab-e eslami*. Tehran.

————. 1984/1363. *Enqelab-e Eslami va va'z-e konuni-ye 'alam*. Tehran.

Dehkhoda, A.-A. 1983/1362. *Maqalat-e dehkhoda*, edited by M. Darbirsiyaqi. Tehran.

Enayat, H. 1973. 'The Politics of Iranology', *Iranian Studies* 1: 2–20.

Enjavi-Shirazi, S.A. 1975/1354. *Qesehaye Irani*, 3 vols. Tehran.

————. 1992/1371. *Gozari va nazari be farhang mardom*. Tehran.

Farhadi, M. 1994/1373. 'Asib-shenasi-ye pazhuhesh-haye farhang-e 'amiyaneh', *Nameh 'olum-e ejtema'i* 6: 85–115.

Fazeli, N. 2006. *Politics of Culture in Iran: Anthropology, Politics and Society in the Twentieth Century*. London.

Geertz, C. 1983. 'The Way We Think Now: Toward an Ethnography of Modern Thought', in C. Geertz, *Local Knowledge: Further Essays in Interpretive Anthropology*. New York: 147–167.

Gellner, E. 1997. *Nationalism*. New York.

Gheissari, A. 1998. *Iranian Intellectuals in the 20th Century*. TX: Univ. of Texas Press. Austin.

Hedayat, S. 1999/1378. *Farhange Mardome Iran* (Folklore of Iranian People) (collected by J. Hedayat). Tehran.

Jamalzadeh, M.A. 1962/1341. *Farhang-i lughat-i `amiyanah*. Tehran.

————. 1985 [1922/1301]. *Yaki bud yaki nabud*, trans. H. Moayyad and P. Sprachman. New York.

Kousari, M. 1998/1377. 'Kefayat-e nazariyeh-e mafahim dar ensanshenasi Iran', *Nameh 'olum-e ejtema'i* 11: 137–50.

Khaliqi, M. 1974/1353. 'Fa'aliyat-haye Markaz-e Mardomshenasi Iran', *Mardomshenasi va farhang-e 'ammeh* 1: 2–21.

Larijani, H.H. 1991/1370. *Ketab-nameh-ye 'ashayer Iran*. Tehran.

Mahdi, A.A. and A. Lahsaizadeh. 1996/1375. *Sociology in Iran*, trans. N. Ahmadi-Khorasani. Tehran.

Maqsoudi, M. 1998/1377. 'Arzyabi-ye Vaz'iyat-e konuni-ye mardomshenasi dar Iran', *Nameh 'olum-e ejtema'i* 11: 151–61.

Maraghei, Z. 1965/1344. *Syahatnameh Ebrahim Beg*, 2 vols. Tehran.

Sa'edi, G.H. 1963/1342. *Ilkhchi*. Tehran.

————. 1965/1344. *Khiyav ya Meshkin-shahr*. Tehran.

————. 1989/1368. *'Ashayer-e markazi-ye Iran*. Tehran.

Safinezhad, J. 1997/1376. *Majmu'eh-ye tafsiri ma'akhez-e 'ashayer-e Iran*. Tehran.

Scholte, B. 1969. 'Toward a Reflexive and Critical Anthropology', in D. Hymes (ed.), *Reinventing Anthropology*. Ann Arbor, MI: 430–59.

Shahshahani, S. 1986. 'History of Anthropology in Iran', *Iranian Studies* 19: 65–87.

Shakoori, A. 2001. *The State and Rural Development in Post-revolutionary Iran*. London.

Shamlo, A. 1357/1978. *Ketab-e koche: farhang loghat, estelahat, ta'birat, zarbol-masl-haye, Farsi*. (Book of the street: dictionary of Persian words, idioms, sayings and proverbs). Tehran.

Shariati, A. 1979. *On the Sociology of Islam*, trans. H. Algar. CA: Mizan. Berkley.

Spooner, B. 1999. 'Ethnography', *Encyclopaedia Iranica* 8: 9–45.

_____. 1987. 'Anthropology', *Encyclopaedia Iranica* 2: 107–15.

Tabatabai, J. S. 1995/1374. *Ebn Khaldun va 'olum-e ejtema'i: vaz'iyat-e 'olum-e ejtema'i dar tamaddon-e eslami*. Tehran.

Tehranian, M., H. Aflaton, E. Terry, A. Dallalfar and T.J. Rudolph. 1987. 'Social Science Research in Iran: Origins, Development, Problems, and Prospects', *International Review of Modern Sociology* 1: 181–97.

Varjavand, P., A. Rakhsh-Khorshid, H. Keshavarz, H. Golesorkhi and M. Rahimi. 1967/1346. *Bamedi: tayfe'i az Bakhtiyari*. Tehran.

Zahedi-Mazandarani, M. 1996/1375. 'Moruri-ye tahlili bar motale'at-e rusta'i va 'ashayeri dar Iran', *Eqtesad-e keshavarzi va towse'eh* 6: 151–78.

CHAPTER 5

Making and Remaking an Academic Tradition

Towards an Indigenous Anthropology in Iran

Nasser Fakouhi 🖋

Introduction

Within the Iranian academic structure, anthropology can be considered as both an established and a new discipline. This is due to a paradoxical condition that has governed the difficult process that the discipline has been through to attain its present-day position. In the 1950s, during the early stages of the formation of modern social sciences in Iran, anthropologists had 'authorized' and 'legitimate' social fields, i.e. rural and tribal studies, that not only were recognized by their sociologist counterparts, but also were supported financially and politically by the state.[1] Within the framework of Iranian social research, these fields largely corresponded to those that were supposed to be 'naturally' the field of study for European anthropologists in the nineteenth century, namely 'primitive societies'.[2] Even for Iranian anthropologists these rural and tribal societies were, and to some extent still are, deemed to be at least in certain respects 'traditional' or even 'primitive' (for example, regarding their ways of life and modes of subsistence). In this 'sharing' of the social field, Iranian sociologists had their 'part', i.e. 'urban societies'.

One consequence of this 'distribution' was the domination of theoretical and methodological concepts in Iranian sociology, whereas anthropology was put aside and left with monographic experimentations. In the academic realm, students of anthropology were not pressured to acquire or present serious analytical efforts to conceptualize their field of research, but were expected to engage primarily with the field. This is why the main focus of interest was on the composition of monographs rather than the production of theoretical discourses.[3]

The results of this analytically impoverished approach are quite palpable in the period from 1970 to 2000 in Iranian anthropology and have been documented by numerous major publications and research papers. Tribal, rural and folkloric studies have been the classical fields of the discipline. These studies were supported and in many cases even initiated by various anthropological institutions. Non-Iranian anthropologists did most research before the 1979 Islamic Revolution. Among the first generation of foreign researchers working in Iran before the Revolution, the most important are: Bacon on the east of Iran and Afghanistan (1946, 1954); Feilberg on the Lors (1944, 1952); Barth on Kurdistan and southern Iran (1953, 1959, 1961). Among the second generation we should mention: Beck on the Qashqa'i (1980, 1983); Black-Michaud on the Lors (1974); Bromberger on the Gilaks (1974, 1982); Digard on the Bakhtiaris (1979, 1981); Fischer on Islam (1980); Irons on the Turkmen (1971, 1974); Loeffler on Boir Ahmads (1971, 1973, 1978); Salzman on Balutchs (1971, 1979); Spooner on eastern and southeastern Iran (1965, 1969, 1974); Tapper on the Shâhsavans (1979, 1983). The majority of these anthropologists had to interrupt their fieldwork after the Revolution; however, some of them had the chance to return to Iran in recent years to continue their studies.

Anthropology and Sociology

This 'scientific heritage', particularly defined by the relations between sociologists and anthropologists, placed our discipline in a rather uncomfortable position, embarrassingly labelled 'second-hand', 'marginal' or 'pseudo-scientific'. This negative image was held not only by many of its practitioners but also by other professional social scientists and even by ordinary people. As far as academic contests on the one hand, and the restrictions on research budgets on the other hand are concerned, this position designated to anthropology has been quite favourable for sociologists since it has allowed them to reap the biggest share of the budget.

Yet it should be noted that this marginalization of anthropology in relation to sociology is not just an Iranian but almost a global phenomenon. This certainly applies to many countries where anthropology has not been able to prove its relevance to social and cultural problems. The particularity of Iran is perhaps that whereas the primarily social and cultural problems of tribal and ethnic life can be classified as the main field of anthropology, many studies have nevertheless been conducted by sociologists using mostly positivist and quantitative research methods, thus defining and furthering the knowledge of their discipline. This competition between the two disciplines has been far from fair: sociology has been introduced as a basic study in nearly all disciplines (even in engineering and the natural sciences), while anthropology has not been properly established, even just within the social sciences.

Throughout the years of the Revolution and the Iran-Iraq War, there existed no significant research and, of course, no substantial budget. Along with the later expansion of academia and the increase in research allocations, a fresh course of dispute emerged between sociologists and anthropologists. During this new period sociologists not only wanted to preserve their conventional urban fields of research, but they also became increasingly interested in getting involved in tribal and rural studies. In university courses there was a common preference for the 'sociology of tribal life' or 'rural sociology' rather than for anthropological courses in the same fields. The main argument put forward by Iranian sociologists was that the primary problem of Iranian society should be defined as the 'successful passage' from tribal and rural modes of life to the urban mode: 'applied studies' was the keyword. Anthropology, in turn, was classified as a 'non-applied descriptive discipline' not concerned with 'changing' but particularly with 'preserving' current conditions. As a result 'cultural heritage' (mirâs-e farhangi) was defined as the primary area of anthropology and 'cultural studies' (motâl'ât-e farhangi) as that of sociology. Thus anthropologists were assigned to deal with 'preservation', whereas sociologists showed their ability to resolve problems. This has led to the extension of cultural studies courses and even the establishment of Ph.D. degrees in the field of sociology, whereas anthropology has been deprived of the right to organize courses leading to this degree.

This is not to say that the problems of Iranian anthropology are all rooted in sociology. No doubt Iranian anthropologists themselves preferred to confine their studies to subjects such as folklore and traditional ways/objects of life for a very long time, that is, from 1960 to 1990. Further contributing factors have been: the lack of theoretical and practical perspectives proving to be sufficiently relevant, skilled and efficient in the face of the social and cultural problems of Iranian society; weak analytical instruments and methodology; the paucity of scientifically rigorous literature; the absence of professional collective bodies; the lack of common approaches to the discipline.

Anthropology, Ethnic Studies and Folklore Studies

Another field occupied by sociologists and political scientists at the expense of anthropology has been ethnic studies (motâl'ât-e ghomi). The primary challenge in this connection is that the subject is regarded as politically sensitive in Iran (i.e. Ahmadi 1378; Maghsoudi 1383; Mirmohammadi 1383). Limiting ethnic studies to political aspects has had a profoundly negative effect on anthropological studies in this field by trying to push them towards addressing only the folkloristic and historical dimensions of any ethnic entities, thus ignoring their actual problems and situation. For this reason only a small number of studies are available on this domain (for example, Digard 1988; Tapper 1983).

In recent decades folklore studies have gained importance among scholars as a highly significant branch of anthropology and an independent academic discipline. Folklore studies principally refer to the study and analysis of popular beliefs and practices, popular art, knowledge and all sorts of skills in a defined society. This can and must improve the condition of the discipline in Iran. However, limiting anthropology in any way to folklore studies or exaggerating the importance of this field in relation to other social and cultural problems of our society may have negative effects on the development of anthropological studies in this country. In addition it seems that folklore studies need to be improved methodologically and theoretically in order to meet global scientific standards. Despite these caveats, folklore studies seem to be the only intentionally 'suggested' and properly 'authorized' field for anthropological research in Iran. Considering the history of Iranian anthropology, folklore studies might be respected as a founding part (Fazeli 1376; Fakouhi 1380; Shahshahani 1986; Spooner 2005). Some Iranian authors, such as Sâdeq Hedâyat (1381) and Mohamad Ali Jamâl-Zâdeh in the first generation, Gholâmhossein Sâ'edi (1355) and Jalâl Al-e Ahmad (1378), and more recently Ahmad Shâmlou can be quoted among the non-academic people contributing enormously to this discipline, especially with their folkloristic studies.

Some academics and folkloristic specialists such as Enjavi Shirâzi were involved from the very beginning in Iranian anthropological institutions. In this field, non-academic and academic literature, based on all sorts of data gathering of ethnographical material, has been published in a rather haphazard and disorganized way. Many ethnographic texts and monographs, ethnographic films and photos are still unpublished and even lie forgotten in certain state archives, such as the Bureau of Ethnological Studies of Iranian TV or the Cultural Heritage and Tourism Organization (CHTO, Sâzemâan-e Mirâs-e Farhangi va Gardeshgari). Nevertheless, during recent years this field has been reapproached by some Iranian anthropologists, such as Hassanzâdeh (1381). In addition, new studies by non-Iranians have made a real impact in Iran, such as those by Marzolph (2001).

Anthropology and Iranology

Certain studies known in Iran under the term Iranology (*Irânshenâsi*), or more precisely regional studies (*motâl'ât-e mantagheii*), such as Kermanology, Gilanology, Farsology and Kurdology, often define themselves as too particular and different from each other to be lumped together in a discipline such as Iranology. These studies, which have been carried out primarily by the CHTO, are a constitutive part of Iranian anthropology.[4] The recent initiation of a large institution called the Iranology Foundation (IF, Bonyâd-e Irânshenâssi) is seen as an attempt to congregate and to bureaucratically direct the small organizations active in this field all over the country. Regional studies, most of which were started after the 1979 Revolution, have undoubtedly been crucial for a country as culturally and ethnically diversified as Iran. However, they suffer seriously from a lack of analytical instruments and theoretical approaches, as well as the absence of rigorous methodology in their ethnographic data gathering.

It should be noted that while academic anthropologists are often in competition with public or private research institutes, relationships with these institutes are quite acceptable as they recruit many postgraduates who are well informed about the discipline. The most notable public institutions are: the Iran Heritage Organization (IHO, Sazemân-e Mirâs-e Farhangi); the Institute of National Studies (Moassesse-ye Motâle'ât-e Melli), which specializes in ethnic studies; the Culture, Art and Communication Research Centre (Pajuheshgâh-e Farhang, Honar va Ertebâtât) affiliated with the Ministry of Culture and Islamic Guidance (MCIG, Vezârat-e Farhang va Ershâd-e Eslâmi). In the private sector the most significant institutions are the Bureau of Cultural Studies (Daftar-e Pajuheshhâ-ye Farhangi) and the Foundation of the Great Islamic Encyclopedia (Bonyâd-e Dâeratolmo'âref-e Bozorg-e Eslâmi).

In recent years, Iranian anthropology has been in contact with different national institutions of Iranology more than with any others. The reason for this is obviously their rich and vast diversity of historical, ethnic and linguistic material – in brief, the Iranian cultural heritage. Some of these institutions are the regional institutes of Iranology mentioned above, the central IF and the CHTO. In this context two tendencies have prevailed. On the one hand there is the will 'to know and to analyse', and on the other hand the will 'to manage and to exploit' this heritage. This has resulted in a sort of spontaneous division of responsibility in which the first task is ascribed to the academic sphere and the second to the Iranology institutions (such as the CHTO). Nevertheless, this division is far from absolute. The CHTO, for example, is an executive office working directly under the Iranian presidency with the main task of preserving and promoting different aspects of Iranian culture in the widest sense of the term. Meanwhile, this organization has also trained numerous students, for instance, in cultural anthropology. In recent decades the Centre of Ethnological Studies (Pajouheshkade-ye Mardomshenâsi) and the Centre of Archaeological Studies (Pajouheshkade-ye

Bâstânshenâsi), both within the CHTO, have run different educational and research programmes at the BA and MA levels and have even directed national and international research programmes in collaboration with some state universities (for example the University of Tehran and University of Sistan and Baluchistan). At the same time Iranian universities have not confined themselves to educational tasks and have conducted numerous research programmes. However, the real discrepancy between these two institutions consists in the financial and other material advantages they hold. Iranological institutions such as the CHTO, IF and various organizations in the MCIG have been the main benefactors, whereas academic faculties have had to content themselves with narrow budgets that are absorbed almost completely by current educational assignments.[5]

Having a powerful and large realm of Iranology is likely to influence anthropology in two opposite ways: negatively, if it marginalizes anthropologists, constrains their field to teaching tasks and excludes them from important cultural research and applied projects; and positively, if it permits professional anthropologists to actively participate in these endeavours. To realize this second option, universities need to have the confidence of executive officers and the material means to achieve their goals. So far we are still a long way from this. Non-academic state institutions[6] prefer to bring into play and employ their internal resources and even train their future 'researchers' at their own centres. This trend will surely have a real negative impact on the future of anthropology in Iran.

The creation of the Iranology Foundation in 2001 raised hopes for change in this situation and for positive regulation of the difficult relationships between executive officers and academics. Unfortunately, developments during the past years have not validated this hope. Hence, the IF is still preoccupied with putting some order in its relationships with different regional Iranological foundations and rebuilding the damaged relations with foreign Iranologists who had to abandon the country (if not their studies) after the 1979 Revolution.

'Popular'/'Non-academic' Anthropology

Apart from governmental organizations and institutions, Iranian anthropology has had to encounter another important and analogous actor on the cultural scene. What might be denominated as 'popular' or 'non-academic'[7] comprises many different individuals, groups, communities, associations and NGOs that for various (personal, ethnic, corporational, local, etc.) reasons have been interested in doing some sort of anthropological research and publishing, particularly on folkloristic and ethnic subjects.[8] To use the adjective 'popular' is not to disregard or diminish the contribution of this domain to the general knowledge about Iranian culture, but to bear in mind that there is almost no scientific control over the use of methods, nor any generally accepted standards regarding the intellectual production in this field. Thus both the best and the worst contributions on the same subjects can be found among 'popular' publications. Indeed, some of the work in this realm has even exceeded the quality of that produced by academia.

Cultural NGOs have played a considerable role in promoting anthropological interests among the non-academic elite. Most of them are small organizations with young members (many of them students or graduates) who are very active on the local level. Their aims frequently consist of helping ordinary people to improve their everyday life situation by utilizing their cultural resources or animating cultural activities within the framework of ethnic and local identities. However, the fact that there is little or no reference to scientific authority has led to some unqualified and incompetent pieces of work. Looking at different books and magazines published recently, especially in various Iranian provinces, highlights this lack of scientific rigour. During the last decades this has contributed to the miserable image of anthropology within the scientific elite as well as among ordinary educated people – an image that is extremely harmful to the present and future of the discipline in Iran.

Promoting scientific NGOs may be considered as an alternative, with official organizations (including academic ones) being able offer orientation and support for the popularization of scientific findings. NGOs such as the Anthropological Society of Iran (ASI, Anjoman-e Ensânshenâsi-ye Irân) and the Sociological Society of Iran (Anjoman-e Jâm'eh shenâsi-ye Irân) may tackle this task by assisting, or even replacing, the state organizations and cultural NGOs in meeting both amateur and professional demands for anthropological knowledge and cultural activities. In recent years the Ministry of Sciences has endorsed this approach and supported scientific NGOs financially, albeit weakly. The ASI represents a telling example in this respect, and shall therefore be addressed in more detail now.

The Anthropological Society of Iran (ASI)

In October 2000, three different new scientific, nationwide NGOs were created in Iran: the Iranian Society of Social Psychology (Anjoman-e Irâi Ravânshenâssi-ye Ejtemâi), the Iranian Society of Demography (Anjoman-e Jamiatshenâssi-ye Irân) and the ASI. Previously the only scientific association in the social sciences was the Iranian Sociological Association (ISA, Anjoman-e Jâm'eshenâssi-ye Irân), which had been established in the 1980s without being active and effectively started its activities in the late 1990s. Today the ASI is an authoritative and weighty association with more than 600 members and many regional sections (in Khuzistan, Mashhad, Ilam, Arak, Ghazvin, etc.). In addition, postgraduate students have made important and effective contributions.

During the ASI's first period of assignment (from 2001 to 2003), equipped with a pocket-sized annual budget of approximately 30 million Rials (3,000 Euros) financed by the Ministry of Sciences, the ASI succeeded in carrying out some important tasks such as enrolling 130 affiliated members, publishing three issues of a trilingual scientific journal called the *Iranian Journal of Anthropology* (*Nâme-ye Ensâshenâssi*), creating a website and organizing three national conferences on Turkmen, Gilak and Lor culture and more than thirty sessions of lectures and ethnographic film projections. The ASI's main difficulties, however, have been rooted in the lack of the financial resources it needs to expand its activities, especially outside of Tehran and in cooperation with international partners. The attitudes of the Ministry of Sciences and other state institutions have not been very encouraging, as there has been no particular willingness to allocate research projects and budgets to the ASI and no sign of real interest in cooperating. Another impediment has been the small number of anthropological faculty members in Iran who lead the ASI to invite and collaborate with academics from neighbouring disciplines, such as sociology, cultural studies, mythology, history and linguistics, who are interested in anthropological work.

Anthropology in the Academic Domain

The future of Iranian anthropology seems to be largely dependent on its expansion within the academic domain, especially the proliferation of anthropological departments in Iranian faculties. Yet in this process qualitative improvements are definitely even more important than quantitative aspects. The Iranian academic system comprises two almost equal parts, each of which includes nearly 1.5 million students. Firstly, there are more than thirty state colleges and universities, which are largely autonomous in their current management. Secondly, there exists a vast and fragmented web of private faculties under a central administrative authority constituting the Free Islamic University (FIU, Dâneshgâh-e Azâd-e Eslâmi). In addition there are some other, private institutes and colleges, which are, however, not very significant. The following analysis is based almost entirely on data about the state universities, because it is extremely difficult to access FIU data.

At present, the only department of anthropology in the state universities is the Department of Anthropology of the Faculty of Social Sciences (DAFSS) at the University of Tehran. This department has eight members – three women, five men: two full professors, one associate professor and five assistant professors. In addition, the department has more than ten external collaborators for certain specialist courses. The department annually enrols about forty students in graduate courses and fifteen students at postgraduate levels. Currently there are approximately 250 graduate students and twenty postgraduate students. At the moment the department is preparing two new programmes for postgraduate studies in biological anthropology and urban anthropology. Besides this, the department has already completed and presented to the central authorities a programme for a Ph.D. in anthropology.

The first generation of anthropologists in the DAFSS – its founders – were all trained in France: Nâder Afshâr-Nâderi, Mahmoud Rouhalamini, Asghar Asgari-Khâneghâh and Mohammad-Ali Youssefi. During the last ten years the DAFSS has changed radically, having lost two of its members and seen four others retire. The majority of the current four members were trained in France. Since 1996 three new members have been appointed, and within the next five years there is room for five or six new members. The new generation of faculty members, like Jalâaleddin Rafifar, Manigeh Maghsoudi and Nasser Fakouhi, have also been educated at French universities. Collaboration between institutions such as the Centre Nationale de la Recherche Scientifique (CNRS) in Paris and the Faculty of Social Sciences of Tehran University began in the1960s and was particularly intense in the1970s until the 1979 Revolution, which brought it to a halt. During the 1970s researchers such as Jean-Pierre Digard, Christian Bromberger and Michel Bazin worked together with Iranian anthropologists such as Asghar Karimi, Houchang Pourkarim, Ali Bulookbashi, Javad Safinejad and many others to produce some of the most interesting monographs and scientific papers. Since the 1990s a new wave of collaboration, although on a smaller scale, has been emerging between these same institutions.

Until 1999 the department only offered postgraduate studies, but since then graduate studies have been introduced too. Since 1978 more than ninety students have attained their MA degrees by conducting and presenting fieldwork in the form of a final dissertation. During the last five years alongside classical subjects, such as tribal, rural and folklore studies, new ones have been addressed, such as urban, cyber, ethnic and political anthropology.[9] One of the most significant successes of the DAFSS has been the achievement of a national project to revise all BA level courses in anthropology, which were thirty years old. In the course of this project more than 80 per cent of courses have been transformed and many new courses established, including urban anthropology, political anthropology, culture and development, anthropology of gender, anthropology of leisure, anthropology of communication, ethnomusicology, visual anthropology, history of anthropology, applied anthropology, anthropology of Europe, anthropology of the Middle East and North Africa and anthropology of pre-Columbian America. The DAFSS currently is involved in a similar project to update MA courses. Meanwhile, the department is also trying to organize a Ph.D. programme in anthropology and to this end is negotiating with the Ministry of Sciences, which so far has not accepted this.

There are multiple reasons for these radical changes: hiring of new academic staff; rising numbers of students, levels and institutions; new academic and non-academic literature. All of these have created new, dynamic incentives among young people to choose anthropology as their main subject of study. In order to analyse the present situation of anthropology at Iranian universities, three different levels need to be addressed: the situation of faculty members, the state of students and the situation in terms of the available literature. Regarding the first two levels I will base my arguments on data from the Ministry of Sciences, Technology and Research. In order to assess the situation regarding anthropological literature, I will draw on my own sampling survey based on data collected in 2004.

Faculty Members

During the past twenty years, the number of faculty members in the social sciences has increased at almost the same rate as the number of students. However, this quantitative growth has rarely been accompanied by an improvement in the quality of teaching and research at universities. This is why even high-ranking authorities are rather critical of the production of knowledge and the level of scientific results in Iran compared with other developing countries. The problem is basically grounded in the low level of academic competence of many faculty members. This is one reason why some students hold public intellectuals outside the academy in higher regard, often contrasting them to their own teachers at university, whom they call 'incompetent professors'. In addition there are prestigious private, non-academic, scientific publishing houses that stand in stark contrast to hopelessly inefficient academic editors.

Let us now turn to the data concerning faculty members. Table 5.1 shows the number of faculty members in anthropology during the period from 1975 to 2003. The figure in brackets indicates corresponding data concerning the discipline of sociology. The table shows that the number of sociologists is almost ten times higher than the number of anthropologists.

TABLE 5.1 • Full-time Anthropology Faculty Members (1975–2003)

Retired	6
Deceased	2
Active	24
Total	32 (216)

Source: Ministry of Sciences, Technology and Research (2004).

Table 5.2 indicates the distribution by sex and shows that the presence of women anthropologists is more substantial in anthropology than in sociology. In this connection it should be noted that in recent years the number of female students in universities (especially in the human and social sciences) has increased dramatically, and women today constitute an average majority of about 70 per cent. This trend is likely to influence the number of female faculty members in future years.

TABLE 5.2 • Full-time Anthropology Faculty Members: Distribution by Sex

	Number		Percentage	
Sex	*Anthropology*	*Sociology*	*Anthropology*	*Sociology*
Male	20	185	83.3	85.6
Female	4	31	17.7	14.3
Total	24	216	100	100

Source: Ministry of Sciences, Technology and Research (2004).

Table 5.3 shows the distribution of faculty members in terms of the place where they completed their Ph.D. studies. It illustrates that Iranian anthropologists have been trained primarily in the European and especially the French tradition of anthropology. Compared to sociologists, anthropologists are educated in fewer countries (i.e. France, the U.S., the U.K. and India). An increasing number of faculty members (especially in sociology) have issued from Iranian universities, which will change radically the general situation in future years. By contrast the lack of a Ph.D. level in Iranian anthropology has put the discipline in a weaker position.

Table 5.4 indicates the distribution by academic grade. In sociology the main concentration of faculty members is at the assistant professor level, whereas in anthropology there is a higher presence of instructors. Besides, there are proportionally more associate and full professors in anthropology than in sociology.

Table 5.3 • Full-Time Anthropology Faculty Members: Distribution by Place of
       Ph.D. Studies

	Number		Percentage	
Country	Anthropology	Sociology	Anthropology	Sociology
U.K.	1	11	4.1	5.1
France	7	27	29.1	12.5
India	2	11	8.3	5.1
Iran	10	120	45.8	55.3
U.S.	4	25	16.6	11.6
Canada	—	3	—	1.3
Austria	—	2	—	0.9
Malaysia	—	1	—	0.4
Colombia	—	1	—	0.4
Switzerland	—	1	—	0.4
Germany	—	7	—	3.2
Australia	—	5	—	2.3
Turkey	—	1	—	0.4
Belgium	—	1	—	0.4

Source: Ministry of Sciences, Technology and Research (2004).

Table 5.4 • Full-time Anthropology Faculty Members: Distribution by
       Academic Grade

	Number		Percentage	
Academic Grade	Anthropology	Sociology	Anthropology	Sociology
Instructor	11	88	45.8	40.7
Assistant Professor	7	99	29.1	45.8
Associate Professor	3	20	12.5	9.2
Full Professor	3	9	12.5	4.1
Total	24	216	100.0	100.0

Source: Ministry of Sciences, Technology and Research (2004).

Table 5.5 shows the geographical location of faculty members. Among
twenty-nine different academies, anthropologists are present in four, with
two members each (University of Tehran, University of 'Allameh, University of Bu'Ali-Sina of Hamedan, University of Sistan and Baluchistan). Two
other academic institutions of Tehran and three other faculties in the provinces (Babolsar, Shiraz and Yazd) each have a single anthropologist.

TABLE 5.5 • Anthropology and Sociology Full-Time Faculty Members –
Distribution by Academy

Academy	Anthropology	Sociology
'Allameh	2	18
Alzahra	1	8
Babolsar	1	8
Beheshti	1	7
Bu 'Alisina (Hamedan)	2	3
Shiraz	1	10
Sistan and Baluchistan	2	—
Tehran	8	30
Yazd	1	2
Payaam Nour	1	13
Honar (Arts)	—	1
Imam Hussein	—	4
Esfahan	1	13
Ahwaz	—	6
Tarbiat Modares	—	4
Tarbiat Mo'alem	—	9
Tabriz	—	6
Mashhad	—	8
Imam Khomeini	1	2
Sazeman Sanjesh	—	1
Oloum Behzisti	—	1
Imam 'Ali	—	1
Oloum Pezeshki	—	1
Kurdestan	—	2
Pajouheshgah Oloum Ensani	—	2
Mohades Nouri	—	1
Gilan	2	1
Zanjan	—	1
Naja	—	6
Total	24	169

Source: Ministry of Sciences, Technology and Research (2004).

Table 5.6 shows the distribution by anthropological specialty. Evidently the majority of Iranian anthropologists are in some way 'generalists', though there are a few specialists in domains such as urban, tribal, archaeological, biological and rural anthropology.

Table 5.6 • Full-time Anthropology Faculty Members: Distribution by Anthropological Specialty

Specialty	Number
Urban and Development	2
Cultural Anthropology	12
Biological Anthropology	2
Archaeological and Tribal Anthropology	2
Kinship and Family	1
Linguistics Anthropology	1
Anthropology of Religion	1
Anthropology of Gender	1
Rural Anthropology	2
Total	24

Source: Ministry of Sciences, Technology and Research (2004).

Students

The existence of an admission competition (*konkur*) as the only way to enter the Iranian academic system (state and private) and its specific mechanisms account for the fact that a large number of students consider the discipline in which they are admitted as an enforced choice and therefore lack enthusiasm to study seriously. The low standard of many faculty members further intensifies this sentiment and deteriorates the general conditions of teaching and research, diminishing the level of scientific production. On the MA and Ph.D. levels this situation is slightly better. Measuring the quality and scientific standard of students is hard work and has not been the purpose of the present survey. Therefore the following tables only say something about the quantitative conditions.

Table 5.7 indicates the number of students at three levels: college degree (the first two years of studies), BA and MA degrees. The first level exists only at Sistan and Baluchistan University, while BA courses are offered at three universities (Babolsar, Tehran and Yazd). It is striking that the University of Tehran has two times more students than the total of the two others. MA courses exist at only two universities (Tehran and Hamedan). In this connection it should be noted that the latter seriously lacks faculty members in anthropology and has been criticized for this by students and other professional anthropologists.

TABLE 5.7 • Anthropology Students (2003)

| Academy | College Degree | Present Students | | Total |
		BA	MA	
Babolsar	—	89	—	89
Bu 'Alisina	—	—	5	5
Sistan and Baluchistan	107	—	—	107
Tehran	—	241	30	271
Yazd	—	112	—	112
Total	107	442	35	584

Source: Ministry of Sciences, Technology and Research (2004).

Table 5.8 shows the approximate number of graduates in anthropology. About 30 per cent of these students hold an MA degree, which indicates a real potential and persistent need for a Ph.D. programme.

TABLE 5.8 • Graduate and Postgraduate Anthropology Students (1958–2000) (Approximate Numbers)

Academy	BA	MA	Total
Babolsar	30	—	30
Tehran	150	120	270
Yazd	30	—	30
Total	210	120	330

Source: Ministry of Sciences, Technology and Research (2004).

Table 5.9 illustrates that, compared with state universities, the number of students in anthropology at the Free Islamic University has risen dramatically in recent years and currently comprises ten times more students.

TABLE 5.9 • Free Islamic University: Present Students in Anthropology (Approximate Numbers)

College Degree	BA	MA	Total
340	2500	200	3040

Source: Official Guide for Admission Examination, Islamic Free University (2005).

Table 5.10 illustrates that whereas BA students are geographically dispersed, on the MA level they are concentrated in the cities of Tehran and Arak.

TABLE 5.10 • Free Islamic University: Present Students in Anthropology, Distribution by Academy (Approximate Numbers)

Academy	College Degree	BA	MA
Ashtian	—	50	—
Ilam	60	60	—
Arak	—	—	25
Bardsir	—	60	—
Tabriz	—	60	—
Jahrom	50	—	—
Tehran Research Dep.	—	60	—
Tehran Central	—	—	25
Zarand	—	60	—
Shirvan	—	50	—
Khoramabad	60	—	—
Darab	50	—	—
Shoushtar	60	—	—
Ghouchan	—	50	—
Garmsar	—	100	—
Neyriz	60	—	—
Total	340	550	50

Source: Official Guide for Admission Examination, Islamic Free University (2004).

Anthropological Literature

To present the situation in this domain, three types of documents were considered: MA dissertations at the DAFSS from 1978 to 2003; final reports of the Social Studies and Research Institute (SSRI, Moassesse-ye Tahghighât va Motâl'ât-e Ejtemâaii) of the University of Tehran from 1958 to 2003; and finally, a sample of 350 anthropological books published in the last twenty years.

Table 5.11 shows the trends in MA dissertations over the past two decades. Whereas earlier there was a real concentration of research in the area of rural and religious studies, during the last ten years urban anthropology has progressed in obvious ways. In addition there has been a growing interest in new subjects such as cyber anthropology and lifestyles.

TABLE 5.11 • MA Dissertations, DAFSS, University of Tehran, Distribution by Subject (1978–2003)

Subject	Number	Percentage
Communication	1	1.1
Cyber Anthropology	1	1.1
Economics	5	5.7
Ethnicity	1	1.1
Ethnomusicology	3	3.4
Folkloristic Studies	6	6.8
Gender	3	3.4
Kinship	5	5.7
Lifestyles	3	3.4
Nutrition	3	3.4
Religion	14	16.0
Rural Anthropology	17	19.5
Technology and Culture	4	4.5
Theoretical Anthropology	6	6.8
Tribal Studies	6	6.8
Urban Anthropology	11	12.6
Total	89	100

Source: Faculty of Social Sciences, Library (2005).

Table 5.12 shows the distribution of theses dissertations by sex. About two-thirds of the research has been conducted by male students in the total period, however the composition has been changing during the last ten years, and at the moment females comprise the majority of postgraduate students at the DAFSS.

TABLE 5.12 • MA Dissertations, DAFSS, University of Tehran, Distribution by Sex (1978–2003)

	Number	Percentage of total
Male	66	74.1
Female	23	25.9

Source: Faculty of Social Sciences, Library (2005).

Table 5.13 indicates the number and subjects of research projects that have been conducted over a period of forty years (1958 to 2000) under the

SSRI at the University of Tehran. Among theses projects, studies in rural, urban and cooperation sections are closely related to subjects and methods of anthropology. This institution's approach to social problems before the Revolution was generally influenced by French sociology and qualitative methods. The presence of scholars such as Nâder Afshâr-Nâderi, Houshang Keshâvarz and Javâd Safi Nejâd was a determining factor in this state of affairs. After the Revolution the institute has been more under the influence of North Amerian sociology and quantitative methods and thus has become increasingly removed from an anthropological approach.

TABLE 5.13 • Part of Anthropology in Research Projects of the SSRI (1958 to 2000)

Section	Number	Percentage
Rural Studies	112	22.7
Urban Sociology	150	30.4
Tribal Studies	79	16.0
Demographic Studies	59	11.9
Cooperation	40	8.1
Socio-Psychological Studies	29	5.8
Comparative Sociology	19	3.8
Sociology of Islamic Countries	4	0.8
Total	492	100.0

Source: Faculty of Social Sciences (2003).

Table 5.14 shows the distribution of research subjects before and after the Revolution. The fact that the number of comparative sociological studies has increased might be positive in terms of a certain anthropological impact on the Iranian social sciences in this period.

TABLE 5.14 • Comparison of Research Projects of the SSRI before and after the Revolution (Percentage of Total)

	Rural	Urban Sociology	Tribal Studies	Demo-graphic Studies	Coop-eration	Social Psycho-logical Studies	Compar-ative Sociology	Sociology of Islamic Countries
1958–1978	27/2	22/7	16/3	13/5	8/8	6/3	5/2	—
1979–2000	11/9	49/7	15/4	8/4	6/3	4/9	0/6	2/8

Source: Faculty of Social Sciences (2003).

As indicated earlier, the general trend concerning anthropological books during the last twenty years demonstrates a predominance of folkloristic publications. One characteristic of many publications in folklore studies is that they include in their titles words such as 'folktales' (*ghesehâ*), 'sayings' (*zarbolmasalhâ*), 'beliefs' (*bâvarhâ*) and 'ceremonies' (*marâsem va âi-inhâ*). Many of these non-academic publications on folklore include only the raw data without any defined methodology or analysis of the gathered material.

Another development in this realm is that new and modern anthropological subjects have increased both in quantity and in quality. A survey of 177 books published between 1983 and 2003 (excluding publications on folkloristic subjects) shows that more than half of these books have been translated into Persian, primarily from French and English (see Table 5.15). If we add publications of folklore studies to this number, the percentage surges to 72 per cent (see Table 5.16). It should be noted that the real number of what are classified in Iran as anthropological or ethnological books (*ketâbhâ-ye ensânshenâssi va mardomshenâssi*) is at least ten times higher than our figure. However, we corrected this 'inflation' to account for so-called textbooks and study guides (*ketâbhâ-ye darsi va komakdarsi*), which are really nothing more than collections of questions and tests for different exams. For this reason we decided to choose a sample of 350 books (including folkloristic publications) that had a minimum of scientific characteristics.

TABLE 5.15 • **Anthropological Books (Excluding Folkloristic) (1983–2003)**

	Number	*Percentage of total*
Books Originally in Persian	84	47.5
Books Translated into Persian	93	52.6
Total	177	100

Source: Ministry of Culture and Islamic Guidance, Khâne-ye Ketâb, Library of Faculty of Social Sciences, University of Tehran (2005).

TABLE 5.16 • **Anthropological Books (Including Folkloristic) (1983–2003)**

	Number	*Percentage of total*
Books Originally in Persian	252	72.0
Books Translated into Persian	98	28.0
Total	350	100

Source: Ministry of Culture and Islamic Guidance, Khâne-ye Ketâb, Library of Faculty of Social Sciences, University of Tehran (2005).

Regarding translated anthropological books, it is telling that only a tiny number of classics have been translated into Persian (for example, Ballendier, Lewis, Morgan, Benedict). Some authors, such as Margaret Mead (three titles) and Levi-Strauss (four titles), have had more presence, but even in their case none of their important work has been translated. Frazer's classic *The Golden Bough* and Durkheim's *The Elementary Forms of Religious Life* were published only in recent years.

Table 5.17 shows the distribution of academic and non-academic books (including folkloristic). We have defined academic books as works written or accepted by an academic scholar or published by an academic editor. The table illustrates that only a small portion of these books (16 per cent) may be considered academic. If we exclude the folkloristic publications, as is done in Table 5.18, the figure surges to 31.6 per cent. It also shows that most folkloristic books are written by non-professionals/amateurs.

TABLE 5.17 • Anthropological Books (including Folkloristic) (1983–2003): Distribution by Academic and Non-academic Books

	Number	Percentage of total
Academic	61	17.4
Non-academic	289	82.6
Total	350	100

Source: Ministry of Culture and Islamic Guidance, Khâne-ye Ketâb, Library of Faculty of Social Sciences, University of Tehran (2005).

TABLE 5.18 • Anthropological Books (excluding Folkloristic) (1983–2003): Distribution by Academic and Non-academic Books

	Number	Percentage of total
Academic	56	31.6
Non-academic	121	68.4
Total	177	100

Source: Ministry of Culture and Islamic Guidance, Khâne-ye Ketâb, Library of Faculty of Social Sciences, University of Tehran (2005).

Table 5.19 indicates the distribution of books by subjects. It shows that almost all of these books are in cultural anthropology (44.5 per cent) and folklore studies (49.4 per cent), whereas specialist fields comprise only a tiny part.

TABLE 5.19 • Distribution of Books by Subdiscipline

	Number	Percentage of total
Cultural Anthropology	156	44.5
Archaeological Anthropology	14	4.0
Linguistic Anthropology	5	1.4
Biological Anthropology	2	0.5
Folkloristic	173	49.4
Total	350	100

Source: Ministry of Culture and Islamic Guidance, Khâne-ye Ketâb, Library of Faculty of Social Sciences, University of Tehran (2005).

Table 5.20 illustrates that the dominant subject in cultural anthropology is culture in a very general sense (61.5 per cent). Among the other subjects we find certain concentrations in tribal studies (23.0 per cent), mythology (7.0 per cent) and religion (3.2 per cent).

TABLE 5.20 • Cultural Anthropology Books: Distribution by Themes

	Number	Percentage of total
General (on Culture)	96	61.5
Religion	5	3.2
Tribal	36	23.0
Kinship	3	1.9
Economic Anthropology	1	0.6
Urban Anthropology	1	0.6
Political Anthropology	2	1.2
Mythology	11	7.0
Total	156	100

Source: Ministry of Culture and Islamic Guidance, Khâne-ye Ketâb, Library of Faculty of Social Sciences, University of Tehran (2005).

Tables 5.21 and 5.22 show some general characteristics of folkloristic books. The majority of these books address different aspects of Iranian Persian-speaking peoples (51.9 per cent). There is also a considerable literature on Azeris (23.1 per cent), and a small portion is devoted to other ethnic groups. Table 5.22 shows that only Azeris (77.5 per cent) and Turkmen have an important part of their books written in their own language, whereas for other ethnic groups this advantage is either negligible or nonexistent. It should be mentioned, however, that some local and often unofficial literature in ethnic languages does exist and has been growing in recent years.

TABLE 5.21 • Folkloristic Books: Distribution by Ethnic Groups

	Number	% of total
Persian	89	51.4
Azeri	40	23.1
Lor	14	8.0
Gilan and Mazandaran	13	7.5
Kurd	12	6.9
Turkmen	5	2.8
Total	173	100

Source: Ministry of Culture and Islamic Guidance, Khâne-ye Ketâb, Library of Faculty of Social Sciences, University of Tehran (2005).

TABLE 5.22. • Folkloristic Books: Distribution by Ethnic or Persian Languages

	Ethnic Language Percentage of total	Persian Language Percentage of total
Persian		100
Azeri	77.5	22.5
Lor		100
Gilân and Mâzandarâni	15.0	85.0
Kurd	8.3	91.7
Turkmen	40.0	60.0
Total	—	—

Source: Ministry of Culture and Islamic Guidance, Khâne-ye Ketâb, Library of Faculty of Social Sciences, University of Tehran (2005).

Conclusion

The situation of Iranian indigenous anthropology today is very far from an ideal, suitable or desirable state. Nonetheless, in the past ten years there have been obvious changes in these conditions, which have been surprisingly effective. In both state and private universities we now have graduates in anthropology by the hundreds nearly everywhere in the country, as well as postgraduate students in a few academic institutions. A change in curriculum has been completed at Tehran University and will soon be applied in all Iranian academies. In the research sphere, the budget devoted to anthropological projects is steadily increasing. Although no precise data are available, the fact that nowadays anthropological projects are accepted on subjects such as urban and industrial issues means more allocation in funds. For the same reasons anthropological projects are becoming more 'applied', in the sense that they comprise developmental aims such as empowerment and social impact assessments and as such are accepted by central and local authorities. Finally, both public and private publishers have been producing a new wave of academic anthropological literature.

The main difficulty however, remains: lack of human resources. In many of our universities today, postgraduate students and/or specialists from fields other than anthropology are in charge of teaching anthropological courses. Most of these non-anthropologists are not willingly teaching anthropology, but are 'constrained' to do so because there are not enough academic positions in their fields of interest. One result is the dissatisfaction of graduate students, who frequently claim that non-anthropologist professors have no real understanding of what they are teaching and therefore have no specific approach to the subject. Hence, undergraduate students often prefer to have postgraduate anthropological tutors, though this usually causes administrative problems. For this and many other reasons the lack of a Ph.D. degree in this discipline is ever more serious.

Both Iranian anthropologists and their non-Iranian peers who work in Iran know better than anyone else that there is real potential and crucial necessity for the development of this academic discipline in Iran. For this reason I have attempted to provide an initial, rough depiction of the current state of anthropology in Iran, especially in the academic sphere. This might offer a point of departure for a real collaboration on national and international levels to define an effective programme to revive the discipline in the short and long term.

Iranian anthropology has two main advantages. First there is the very rich diversity of Iranian culture, which has drawn numerous non-Iranian scholars to choose Iran as their field of research. Second there is the large Iranian academic diaspora, among whom a significant number of anthropologists enjoy good positions and reputations. Currently, the most important task is to draw together these specialists in a systematic way. This might be achieved by annual scientific conferences like the one in Frankfurt in 2004 and through the founding of international NGOs, scientific journals, websites and any other means that can be employed on a common basis.

In recent years some efforts have been made in this regard. The question, however, remains as to what is the best strategic approach for pulling together Iranian anthropologists in Iran, Iranian anthropologists living abroad and non-Iranian anthropologists specializing in peoples of Iran. One institutional venue towards reaching this objective is the academic protocol signed between Iranian universities and institutes and their foreign counterparts. Such protocols already exist, allowing many universities to develop exchange programmes and organize scientific trips and fieldwork. Nevertheless, these exchanges so far have been more beneficial for the Western side, as they enable researchers to restore their traditional fields of research (often lost after the Revolution), rather than for indigenous Iranian anthropology. This is partly due the fact that the Iranian side of this relationship has mostly consisted of bureaucrats and government agents (customarily without any scientific concerns) instead of independent academics and scientists. For this reason, collaboration or institutional pacts in the form of international NGOs might be much more beneficial for indigenous anthropology than government-supported protocols that are not being executed by competent and independent scientists. Indeed, the existence of such strong and efficient NGOs could offer a real possibility to use these official protocols more effectively. Moreover, this might compel the officials to cease marginalizing independent scientists and allow them to organize their discipline and pursue their academic goals as they wish.

Unfortunately for many expatriate Iranian anthropologists and especially for most non-Iranians, this represents a long and difficult journey to the pursuit and accomplishment of their tasks. Currently, the easiest and most effective way to do research in Iran is either, for non-Iranians, to compromise with official authorities by making certain concessions, or, for the Iranians of the diaspora, to conduct their work individually with little or no contact with their native fellow scholars.

The academic development of anthropology in Iran would be the first step towards shaping an indigenous version of this discipline. Finding ways to overcome the shortage of specialists in academia; creating new departments of anthropology and Ph.D. degrees; extending and rationally organizing more anthropological societies; producing literature more relevant to the discipline; reestablishing authority in rural, tribal and ethnic studies; achieving a significant role in development and applied research projects; and last but not least, enhancing and creating bona fide ways to convene all anthropologists working on Iran: these are among the most important tasks to be fulfilled in future years.

Notes

1. The most important institutions in this era were the ethnological section named the Office of Popular Culture (Edâre-ye Farhang-e'Âmme) in the Ministry of Culture and the ethnological and tribal section in the Social Research and Studies Institute (Mo'assesse-ye Motâl'ât va Tahghighât-e Ejtemâi). State support basically took the form of allocating research funds to these institutions.

2. In this article I use the terms 'anthropology' and 'anthropologist' as the most common words designating the discipline. In some countries like France the cor-

responding terms are 'ethnology' and 'ethnologist'. In Iran we use 'ethnology' and 'ethnologist' to refer to *mardomshenâsi* and *mardomshenâs*, and we use 'anthropology' and 'anthropologist' for *ensânshenâsi* and *ensânshenâs*. Iranian anthropologists (and other social science scholars) have not reached any agreement about which term should designate the discipline. Thus, the University of Tehran, for example, prefers *ensânshenâsi*, whereas the Ministry of Culture tends to use *mardomshenâsi*.

3. Some of the works conducted in the period from 1945 to 1975 (1320 to 1350) are: 'Anâsori (1345); Ghâemmaghâmi (1324a, 1324b, 1324c, 1325); Derakhshân (1337); Kalântari (1350); Karimi (1350); Kasbiân (1341); Lam'eh (1346, 1367, 1348); Majidzâdeh (1342); Nâseh (1337); Pourkarim (1343, 1345, 1346); Shahriâr-Afshâr (1345); Vadii (1349); Younesi (1324, 1325); Zarâbi (1340, 1341); etc. The complete list of these works is very long and can be found in *Fehrest-e Maghâlât-e Mardomshenâsi* (2536).

4. Examples of such regional studies are 'Abbâssi (1378), 'Allâmeh (1378), Dâdmehr (1378), Hosseini-Khâh (1378), Nâderi (1378), Pâpi (1378) and Assadiân (1383).

5. Some estimated figures concerning the research budget for 2006–07 are as follows: Iranology Foundation: 2,9,037 million Rials (2.4 million Euros); University of Tehran: 6,8,613 million Rials (5.6 million Euros); CHTO: 9,9,000 million Rials (8.2 million Euros); Ministry of Science, Research and Technology: 5,0,068 million Rials (4.1 million Euros); Ministry of Culture and Islamic Guidance: 5,3,034 million Rials (4.4 million Euros).

6. In Iran theses institutions are basically known under the name *pajouheshkadeh* or *pajouheshgâh*, meaning simply research centre. Most of them are independent from the universities.

7. In Persian we use *mardomi* for 'popular' and *ghayre daneshgâhi* for 'non-academic'.

8. E.g. the regional studies mentioned above. See also, for example, 'Azizi (1378), Afshâr-Sistâni (1378a, 1378b), Hâtami (1378), Khânsâri Abiyâneh (1378), Khastou (1378), Rafiipour-Lâhiji (1378) and Sâleh-Tabari (1378).

9. Among some of the most recent MA theses (supervised by the author) have been, for example: "Iranian Ethnics on Cyberspace" (2005), "Comparative Study on Ethnic Identity of Two Groups of Students in Tehran" (2005), "National and Ethnic Identities among Youth in an Iranian Kurd Town" (2005), "Comparative Study of Two Ethnic Group NGOs" (2006), "Anthropological Study of Afghans in the City of Ghom" (2006), "Poser Strategy among Women in a Kurd City" (2006).

REFERENCES

'Abbâssi, H. 1378. *Lasht-e Nashâ, Rasht, Gilkân*.

Afshâr-Nâderi, N. 1345. *Gozâresh-e Barress-ye Moghadamâti-ye Tarh-e Motâl'e-ye Âyandeh dar Kohgiluyeh va Boyer Armadi*. Tehran.

———. 1347. *Monogrâfi-ye Sugh-e Tayebi*, Gozâresh-e no. 6. Tehran.

————. 1362. 'Eskân-e 'ashâyer va assar-e ejtemâ'i va eghtesâdi-ye ân', Ilât va 'Ashâyer, Ketâb-e Agâh. Tehran.

Afshâr-Sistâni, I. 1378a. Shenâxt-e Ostân-e Khorâsân (Introduction to Khorasan Province). Tehran.

————. 1378b. Shenâxt-e Ostân-e Yazd (Introduction to Yazd Province). Tehran.

Ahmadi, H. 1378. Ghomiyat va Ghomgerâi dar Irân, az Afsâneh tâ Vâgh'iyat. Tehran.

Al-e Ahmad, J. 1378. Orâzan. Tehran.

'Allâmeh, S. 1378. Târix-e Jâmeh-ye Tonkâbon. Tonkâbon.

Âmâr-e Âmouzeshe 'Âli. 1382. Grouhe Pajouheshhâ-ye Âmâri va Informâtik. Tehran.

Ammanolahi, S. 1360. Kuchneshini Dar Irân. Tehran.

Anâsori, J. 1345. 'Dehkadeye Jajin', Honar va Mardom 52 (Bahman): 26–36.

'Askari-Khâneghâh, A. and M.S. Kamâli. 1373. Ensânshenâssi-ye Zisti. Tehran.

————. 1374. Irâniân-e Torkamân. Tehran.

Assadi, N. 1378. Negâhi be Garmsâr. Tehran.

Assadiân, M. 1383. Gushei az Dâneshhâ va Bâvarhâ-ye 'Âmmeh dar Shahr-e Gheshm. Tehran.

Azizi, M. 1378. Diyâr-e Âftâb (Xorâsânshenâssi). Tehran.

Bacon, E. 1946. 'A Preliminary Attempt to Determine the Culture Areas of Asia', Southwestern Journal of Anthropology 2: 117–32.

————. 1954. 'Types of Pastoral Nomadism in Central and Southwest Asia', Southwestern Journal of Anthropology 10: 44–68.

Bahar, M. 1362. Pajouheshi dar Assâtir-e Irân. Tehran.

Barth, F.1953. Principles of Social Organization in Southern Kurdistan. Oslo.

————. 1959. 'The Land use Pattern of Migration Tribes of South Persia', Norsk Geografisk Tidsskrift 17: 1–11.

————. 1961. Nomads of South Persia: The Basseri Tribe of the Khamseh Confederacy. Boston, MA.

Bazin, M. 1978: "Le culte des arbres et des montagnes dans le Tâlesh (Iran du nord-ouest) in Quand le crible était dans la paille ... hommage à P.N. Boratav, Paris, G.P. Maisonneuve et Larose: 95–104.

Bazin, M. et Ch. Bromberger, 1982. Gilân et Âzarbâyjân oriental. Cartes et documents ethnographiques. Paris, Éditions Recherche sur les civilisations.

Beck, L. 1980. 'Tribe and State in Revolutionary Iran: The Return of the Qashqa'i Khans', Iranian Studies 13(1–4): 215–55.

————. 1983. 'Iran and Qashqa'i Tribal Confederacy', in R. Tapper (ed.), The Conflict of Tribe and State in Iran and Afghanistan. London: 284–313.

Black-Michaud, J. 1974. 'An Ethnographic and Ecological Survey of Luristan, Western Persia: Modernization in a Nomadic Pastoral Society', Middle Eastern Studies 10: 209–28.

Bromberger, Ch. 1974 . 'Habitations du Gilân', Objets et Mondes 14(1): 3–56.

Bulookbashi, A. 1356. Farhange 'Âmmeh. Tehran.

————. 1377. Naghd va Nazar. Tehran.

————. 1381. Ilât va 'Ashâyer-e Irân. Tehran.

Dâdmehr, M. 1378. *Pajouheshi Darbâre-ye Saghâxânehhâ va Sangâbhâ-ye Esfehân.* Esfahan.

Dâneshgâhe Âzad Eslâmi. 1383. (Official Guide of Admission Examination). Tehran.

Dâneshkade-ye 'Ouloume Ejtemâi. 1381 (Mehr). *Seyre 'Ouloume Ejtemâi dar Irân.* Tehran.

Dâneshkadeye 'Oulume ejtemâ'i va T'âvon (eds). *Fehrest-e Maghâlât-e Mardomshenâsi* 1(85): 2536(1979).

Derakhshân, H. 1337. 'Ashâyere Jabale Bârez', *Mardomshenâsi* 2 (Farvardin, Ordibehesht and Khordâd): 16–25.

Digard, J.P.1979. 'De La Nécessité et des inconvenients pour un baxtyari d'être baxtiyari: communauté, territoire et inégalité chez les pasteurs nomads d'iran', in L'Equipe Ecologie et Anthropologie des Sociétés Pastorales (ed.), *Pastoral Production and Society.* Cambridge: 127–40.

———. 1981. *Techniques des nomads Baxtyari d'Iran.* Cambridge.

———. (ed.). 1988. *Le fait Éthnique en Iran et en Afghanistan.* Paris.

Faculty of Social Sciences, Library, University of Tehran. 2003.

Faculty of Social Sciences, Library, University of Tehran. 2005.

Fakouhi, N. 1378a. *Khoshounat-e Siyâsi.* Tehran.

———. 1378b. *Ostourehshenâssi-ye Siyâssi.* Tehran.

———. 1379. *Az Farhang tâ Toss'eh.* Tehran.

———. 1380. 'Mardomshenâssi dar Irân, Pishineye Târixi va Cheshmandâzhâ', in C. Rivière (ed.), *Darâmadi bar Ensânshenâssi.* Tehran.

Farhâdi, M. 1373. *Farhang-e Yârigari.* Tehran.

———. 1380. *Vâreh, No'i T'aâvoni-ye Sonati Kohan va Zanâneh dar Irân.* Tehran.

Fazeli, N. 1376. 'Morouri bar Seyr-e Mardomshenâssi dar Irân', *Faslnâme-ye 'Ulume Ejtemâii* 9 : 117–142.

Feilberg, C. 1944. *La Tente Noire.* Copenhagen.

———. 1952. *Les Papis.* Copenhagen.

Fischer, M. 1980. *Iran: From Religious Dispute to Revolution.* Cambridge, MA.

Ghâemmaghâmi, J. 1324a. 'Ashâyere Khouzestân, Tavâyefe Shoush' (Khouzestan Tribes, Shoush Clans), *Yâdegâr* 1(10) (Khordâd): 19–26.

———. 1324b. Ashâyere Khouzestân, Tavâyefe Miyânâb', *Yadegâr* 2(4) (Azar): 58–68.

———. 1324c. 'Ashâyere Khouzestân, Tavâyefe Miyânâb', *Yadegâr* 2(8) (Favardin): 22–28.

———. 1325. 'Ashâyere Khouzestân, Larkihâ', *Yadegâr* 3(1) (Shahrivar): 71–74.

Hassanzâdeh, 'A. 1381. *Afsââne-ye Zendegân.* Tehran.

Hâtami, H. 1378. *Moharram dar Kâzeroun.* Tehran.

Hedayat, S. 1381. *Farhang-e 'Âmmiyâne-ye Mardom-e Irân.* Tehran.

Hosseini-Khâh, J. 1378. *Boir-Ahmad va Rostam Gahvâre-ye Târix.* Esfahan.

Irons, W. 1971. 'Variation in Political Stratification among the Yamout Turkmen', *Anthropological Quarterly* 44: 143–56.

———. 1974. 'Nomadism as a Political Adaptation: The Case of the Yomut Turkmen', *American Ethnologist* 1(4): 635–58.

Kalântari M. 1350. 'Dehkadeye Anbi', *Honar va Mardom* 109 (Aban): 36–45.

Karimi, A. 1350. 'Negâhi be Zendegi va Âdâb va Sonan dar Ilâte Haftlang va Châharlang', *Honar va Mardom* 111 (Dey): 34–47.

Kasbiân, H. 1341. 'Zendegiye Qashqâihâ' (The Life of the Qashqa'i), *Honar va Mardom* 4 (Bahman): 19–27.

Katiraii, M. 1357. *Zabân va Farhang-e Mardom*. Tehran.

Khânsari Abiyâneh, Z. 1378. *Abiyâneh va Farhang Mardom-e Ân*. Tehran.

Khastou, B. 1378. *Târixche-ye Roustâ-ye 'Mir' Taleghân*. Tehran.

Kia, M. 1354. *Mardomshenâssi-ye Eghtesâdi*. Tehran.

Lam'eh, M. 1346–1347. 'Kohgiluyeh va Boyehahmad', *Khousheh*, 12(34) (Mehr): 14–16; 12(37) (Âban): 20–21; 12(39) (Âban): 47–49; 12(42) (Âzar): 36–37; 12(44–45) (Dey): 43–45; 13(10) (Ordibehesht): 42.

———. 1348. 'Kohgiluyeh va Boyerahmad', *Talâsh* 17 (Tir and Mordâd): 41–44.

Loeffler, R. 1971. 'The Representative Mediator and the New Peasant', *American Anthropologist* 73(2): 1077–91.

———. 1973. 'The National Integration of the Boir Ahmad', *Iranian Studies* 6(2–3): 127–35.

———. 1978. 'Tribal Order and the State: The Political Organization of Boir Ahmad', in A. Banani (ed.), State and Society in Iran, *Iranian Studies* 11: 145–71.

Maghsoudi, M. 1383. *Tahavolât-e Ghomi dar Irân*. Tehran.

Majidzâdeh, Y. 1342. 'Ile Zarzâ', *Honar va Mardom* 8 (Khordâd):11–17; 11 (Sharivar): 11–15; 24 (Mehr): 25–31.

Mardomshenâssi va Farhang-e 'Ammeh. 1354–1356. Ministry of Culture, Markaz-e Mardomshenâssi-ye Irân.

Marzolph, U. 2001. *Narrative Illustration in Persian, Lithographed Books*. Leiden.

Ministry of Culture and Islamic Guidance, Khâne-ye Ketâb, Library of Faculty of Social Sciences, University of Tehran. 2005. Tehran.

Ministry of Sciences, Technology and Research. 2004. Tehran.

Mirmohammadi, D. 1383. *Goftehâyi Darbâre-ye Hoviyat-e Melli dar Irân*. Tehran.

Mohammadi, 'A. 1378. *Shirâz, Shahr-e Gol va Bolbol*. Shiraz.

Naderi, T., 'A. Chegini and 'A. Bouchaloufard. 1378. *Simâ-ye Boin-Zahrâ, Ghazvin, Bahr al-ulum*.

Nâseh, M. 1337. 'Khâsh-Balouch', *Yaghmâ* 11(9) (Âzar): 424–27; 11(10) (Dey): 472–74; 11(11) (Bahman): 522–24.

Official Guide for Admission Examination, Islamic Free University. 2005. Tehran.

Official Guide for Admission Examination, Islamic Free University (2004)

Papi, M.H. 1378. *Shenaxt-e Il-e Papi*, 2. vols. Ghom.

Pourafkâari, N. 1354. *Jâme'ehshenâssi-ye 'Avâam*. Isfahan.

Pourkarim, H. 1343. 'Pâkdeh', *Honar va Mardom* 27 (Dey): 9–18.

———. 1344a. 'Torkamanha-ye Irân', *Honar va Mardom* 41(Esfand): 42–4.

———. 1344b. 'Pâveh', *Honar va Mardom* 32–3 (Khordâd and Tir): 8–12.

———. 1345. 'Dehkadeye Jahij', *Honar va Mardom* 47 (Sharivar): 34–46.

———. 1346. 'Dehkadeye Pâghaleh', *Honar va Mardom* 58 (Mordad): 24–46.

Rafiipour-Lâhiji, 'A. 1378. *Simâ-ye Shahrestân-e Langaroud*. Ghom.

Rouhalamini, M. 1368. *Zamine-ye Farhangshenâssi*. Tehran.

———. 1378. *Nemoudhâ-ye Farhangi va Ejtemâi dar Adabiyât-e Fârsi*. Tehran.

Sâ'edi, G. 1355. *Ahl-e Hava*. Tehran.

Safi Nejâd, J. 1347. *Atlas-e Ilât Kohgiluye*. Tehran.

―――. 1366. *Mabâni-ye Joghrâfiyâ-ye Ensâni*. Tehran.

―――. 1368. *Boneh: Nezâmhâ-ye Zerâ'ati-ye Sonati dar Irân*. Tehran.

―――. 1375. '*Ashâyer-e Markazi-ye Irân*. Tehran.

―――. 2535. *Taleb-âbâd, Nemune-ye Jâm'ei az Barresi yek Deh*. Tehran.

Sâleh-Tabari, S. 1378. *Bâbol, Sarzamin-e Tâla-ye Sabz*. Tehran.

Salzman, P. 1971. 'Adaptation and Political Organization in Iranian Baluchistan', *Ethnology* 10: 433–44.

―――. 1979. 'Inequality and Oppression in Nomadic Society', in Equipe écologie et anthropologie des sociétés pastorales (eds), *Pastoral Production and Society*. Cambridge, Cambridge University Press/Paris, Maison des Sciences de l'Homme : Cambridge: 429–46.

Shahbazi, 'A. 1368. *Moghadamei bar Shenâxt Ilât va 'Ashâyer*. Tehran.

Shahhosseini, 'A. 1376. 'Fehrest-e Maghâlât-e 'Ashâyeri b'ad az Enghelâb-e Eslâmi', *Faslnâme-ye 'Ulum-e Ejtemâi* (9).

Shahriâr-Afshâr, B. 1345. 'Ile Shakâk', *Honar va Mardom* 44 (Khordâd): 38–46.

Shahshahâni, S. 1986. 'History of Anthropology in Iran', *Iranian Studies* 19(1): 65–87.

Spooner, B. 1965. 'Kinship and Marriage in Eastern Persia', *Sociologus* 15(1): 22–31.

―――. 1969. 'Politics, Kinship and Ecology in Southeast Persia', *Ethnology* 8(2): 139–52.

―――. 1974. 'City and River in Iran: Urbanization and Irrigation on the Iranian Plateau', *Iranian Studies* 7(3–4): 681–713.

―――. 2005. 'Anthropology', *Encyclopedia Iranica*. Retrieved on 10 June 1006 from: http://www.Fgjsljls.org.

Tabibi, H. 1371. *Jâm'ehshenâssi va Mardomshenâssi-ye Ilât va 'Ashâyer*. Tehran.

Tapper, R. 1979. '"Individuated grazing rights and social organization among the Shahsevan nomads of Azarbayjan." in Equipe écologie et anthropologie des sociétés pastorales (eds), *Pastoral Production and Society*. Cambridge, Cambridge University Press/Paris, Maison des Sciences de l'Homme: 95- 114.

―――. (ed.). 1983. *The Conflict of Tribe and State in Iran and Afghanistan*. London.

Vadii, J. 1349. 'Bakhshe Ilât va 'Ashâyere Lor', *Honar va Mardom* 101 (Esfand): 24–25.

Younesi, S. 1324. 'Sanjâbi', *Kouhestân* 48(1) (Esfand): 6.

―――. 1325. 'Sanjâbi', *Kouhestân* 55(2) (Esfand): 3.

Zarâbi, M. 1340. 'Tavâyefe Kogilouyeh', *Farhange Irân Zamin* 9: 278–302.

―――. 1341. 'Tavâyefe Miyânâb', *Farhange Irân Zamin* 10(1–4): 394–407.

CHAPTER 6

Iranian Anthropologists Are Women

Soheila Shahshahani

Introduction

Iranian anthropology is like an orchestra trying to perform in the middle of a highway. Pressured by the police, heavy traffic and people all around, the orchestra tries to hold its concert, but there are many conductors and each instrument is tuned differently. The emanating music, if not worse, is no better than the noise pollution it is trying to overcome.

One of the most unique characteristics of anthropology compared to other social and human sciences has been its reflexive quality. Having integrated self-criticism as one of its pillars, it has been able to continue its precious existence and make valuable contributions to other fields ranging from medicine and genetics to literature, sociology and history. However, anthropology is practised as a third-rate field in Iran and leads a suffering existence. It is trapped in a vicious circle of scarcity of experts and intelligent students alike, plagued by insufficiency of funds, books and research centres. As a researcher who has lived and taught in Iran, I have been looking for the causes of this lamentable situation (Shahshahani 1986). The first generation of Iranian so-called anthropologists have now practically disappeared, the second generation are women, and the third generation, formed partially by the first generation and partially by those working outside of Iran, are going their diverse ways. My concentration in this article is on the second generation, where I find women dominating as far as the number of scholars and quality of work is concerned. My claim is that their absence from Iran, for whatever reason, has contributed greatly to this actual situation. Self-reflection and auto-criticism become extremely helpful at this juncture, for we are facing the making of the future of anthropology in Iran.

'Anthropological Perspectives on Iran' is a nebulous topic, but the particular aim to gain a sum of assessments on present anthropological research in order to find future directions can provide a clearer focus. However, we should bear in mind that 'anthropological insights have only played a minor role in the current debates'[1] on Middle Eastern societies. In what follows I shall concentrate on these particular problems, as I think they are urgent for the field of anthropology in Iran.

As the editor of a special issue of *Iranian Studies* on the 'History of Anthropology in Iran' (1986), I wrote at the beginning: 'This article is actually an outline of the history of anthropology in Iran. In part, it traces the development of the field and the problems that some of its practitioners have been endeavoring to overcome. In part, it recounts some of the experiences of the author and the frustrations she and others encountered in trying to broaden the scope of the permissible range of study of anthropology' (1986: 65). I shall not repeat the same outline, but my questions and frustrations continue to exist as I have experienced them in the period after the above article was written. Here I shall broaden my perspective to include some comparisons with other Middle Eastern countries, so that the problem of establishing this field can be viewed both from above, and institutionally and culturally from within.

Today I still hold my earlier position that the foundation of anthropology laid by Sadeq Hedayat was taken astray by the Institute of Ethnology (Edar-e ye Mardomshenassi), which was established in 1937. Let me take a poem by one of the members of its scientific council, Mr Shafaq, to reflect this problem succinctly:

> The ministry of public instructions has made its basis principleless.
> It propagates in all ways ignorance and ingratitude.
> On the one hand it does not appreciate the knowledge of those who know,
> on the other it builds the museum of ethnology. (1335: 7)

Mr Shafaq is clearly separating culture into one part belonging to the elite and the learned, and another part belonging to the illiterate and the ethnological museum, which to him seems the opposite of respecting the erudite and the knowledgeable of the country. Whereas I share his view in regard to disrespect for the erudite, I am questioning the appropriateness of his view on an institution for which he neither had any scientific training nor any appreciation. In fact this applies to all members of the scientific committee of the Institute of Ethnology: none of them was a specialist in the field that they were supposed to promote.

There is an old story in Iran that when Alexander came to Iran and found so many learned people he was perplexed as to how he could rule such a country. He was told to appoint the unlearned to positions of power – this would alienate the learned and he could thus continue his rule. This principle has been remembered for good reasons. In relation to our present concern, it was arguably a political act to establish an institution, but it was a negative political act for the field to appoint such a committee, meanwhile alienating Sadeq Hedayat by denying him membership (Hedayat 1310, 1312, 1323–2). This hindered a solid foundation for the field and made the field incapable of responding to the local need to gather and classify information with some methodology. Why was this done? I think the basic problem is that it a general trend for the government at that time to institutionalize and thus dominate any local intellectual search. Many problems come to mind concerning the relationship between the government and anthropology. What was the government's view of this field? Where did this view come from? Did it like or dislike anthropology? Did it consider this field a threat to its own existence? Why did it direct it in one way or the other? What were its criteria for the inclusion or exclusion of specialists and topics of interest, and did these affect the field's continued existence? If the field lacked importance, why was the government keen to form an institution and appoint specific persons to direct it? Was this its cunning way of misdirecting and derailing it?

Anthropology in the Middle East: Academia and Research

Let us look sideways and broaden our perspective by considering the situation of anthropology in other Middle Eastern countries. Sholkamy (2001) identifies many hindrances in the establishment of anthropology in Egypt. She finds two approaches in the social sciences are accepted: one is the statistical approach practised by sociologists; the other the descriptive approach to unimportant topics without analysis by ethnologists. Any serious analytical work by anthropologists that also uses statistics would fall outside what was permissible. The history of anthropology in Egypt goes back to the 1930s, when Evans-Pritchard taught at the American University in Cairo, and to the 1940s, when Radcliff Brown taught there, and there have been many prominent Egyptian anthropologists, yet: 'Anthropology is poorly institutionalized in Egypt ... It is possible to become an anthropologist in Egypt but harder to remain one because of scarcity of teaching and research positions' (Hopkins 1998: 3). Furthermore, fieldwork can be problematic in Egypt, especially from the point of view of authorities (Sholkamy 2001: 9). In an article on Iran entitled 'Xatare ensanshenasi va ensanshenasi dar xatar' (The Danger of Anthropology and Anthropology in Danger), similar points were made (Shahshahani 1360: 100).

Anthropology in Turkey, as reported by Ayfer Bartu from the University of California in Berkeley, is definitely dominated by American scholarship, which collaborates to some degree with Bosporus and Istanbul Universities. The Institute of Turkish Studies in Istanbul, for example, awards grants exclusively to United States citizens. I recall how, when I went to Iran in 1977, I was approached by an anthropologist who was an American citizen, offering me a position teaching at Reza Shah University (today Babolsar University). Later, in December 1978 in Delhi, right before the Revolution, I met an anthropologist, an Israeli citizen, who had been approached by the same person for the same reason. William Beeman's article 'Anthropological Research in Tajikistan' (1999) almost reads like a tourist guide for anthropologists going to the country. Huxley (1998), writing on practising anthropology in the Middle East, says the emphasis on holism and close contact 'may give an edge' to consulting anthropologists over specialists from other disciplines, but given time and budget limits, he finds anthropologists 'have no corner on such abilities' (1998: 2).

In a personal communication, Professor of Anthropology Ghaus Ansari, who taught in Baghdad from 1958 to 1963 and in Kuwait from 1967 to 1989, states that in the Middle East there is anthropology only in Alexandria in Egypt, where there is an independent anthropology department with good scholarship. He says that during his stay in these countries, he felt most opposition came from sociologists. The situation in Kuwait was very clear. In 1967, when he started to teach at the university, there were two anthropologists and no sociologists. When he left Kuwait in 1989 there were four anthropologists and twelve sociologists. In 2004 there were two anthropologists, one of whom had been having great problems with promotion, and sixteen sociologists. This trend was due partly to the increasing number of Kuwaiti sociologists who had come back from American universities. A similarly competitive, if not destructive attitude by sociologists towards anthropologists is reported for Egypt by Sholkamy, who writes about 'the reign of modernist "scientific" thinking that finds strength and meaning in lots of numbers' (2001: 9). I have personally encountered the same infatuation with statistics in postrevolutionary Iran, where sociology has moved increasingly towards including mathematics and statistics in its curriculum. In this regard, we must, however, point critically to a typical feature of the education system in Iran. In a country where there is emphasis on memorization rather than analysis and comprehension, an overwhelming use of statistics in the social sciences is the last thing we need. It is in the social and human sciences that we can finally teach our students to think and analyse, yet they are pushed into rote learning and simplistic statistical analysis.

A further means of disrupting anthropological growth at Iranian universities has been the teaching of anthropology by sociologists. Some sociologists use any means to criticize anthropology, even going to the extreme of deriding it in puns: the term for 'qualitative research methodology' is *keifi*, and it is made to 'play on' *keif* (having a good relaxed time), as opposed to quantitative research, that is, hard and factual statistical data gathering via questionnaires. Another form of opposition I have faced myself from some sociologists has been the attempt to reduce my anthropology courses by changing their titles, so that they would become sociology courses and I would ultimately find myself assigned to teach sociology! Judged from a distance, it could be considered a gain to ask an anthropologist to teach sociology courses. But why is there such an opposition towards anthropology?

Often there is the idea that any unimportant matter related to non-literate people can be taught as anthropology. An amazing example is the Azad University of Garmsar, where the department of anthropology annually admits some eighty students. Two instructors with MAs in sociology and anthropology from the University of Tehran run the department, which boasts a few more faculty members with lower credentials. The Azad University feels proud of admitting mostly female students who come from all over Iran with very low records of performance. It could not ignore such an income. Given that that the students with highest scientifically oriented aptitude go into medical and hard sciences, mathematics and engineering, and the better students in humanities go to law, economics, business administration, political science, philosophy, literature, languages and sociology, anthropology gets the lowest crust! So those who could not have gone to any other field are pleased to find themselves at a university. The Azad University, known for its success as a business centre, is quite proud to offer these young people student status for four years. This sort of incentive for studying anthropology is definitely opposed by the anthropologists I interviewed, none of whom resorted to anthropology because no other field was open to them. They all chose it because of their interest and curiosity, as well as for the viability of its methodology with respect to their scientific search.

Here I would like to alert readers to the activities of a centre that started up in 2004. On various billboards in Tehran advertisements can be seen for the Centre of Iranian Ethnology (Kanun-e Mardomsenasi-ye Iranian). A leaflet of the centre states that the municipality of Tehran, second arrondisement, offers 'courses in handicraft, psychology, Qu'ran, guitar, violin, computer, English language, law, social problems to all interested, particularly children during their summer vacation'. This centre has a library, a room for conferences and a restaurant with traditional Iranian food. Apparently, a graduate of Azad University from Arak is heading this project. It has been ten years since we have had a mushrooming of such centres, generally called cultural centres. Why does such an institution have a claim to ethnology (*mardomshenasi*)? I am reminded of Sadeq Hedayat's words on the museum of ethnology in Tehran, which looked more like a masquerade than a museum: 'In Iran where one ordinarily cannot hold a permanent academic research position, one is obliged to teach at a university where the enhancement of the field is next to impossible. In a few interviews that I conducted with Iranian anthropologists, they mentioned that the lack of possibility of holding a research position in Iran, and the necessity of teaching in order to hold a permanent job, made them leave the country.'[2]

Thus, for example, Dr Soraya Tremayne-Sheybani, who was the first to translate an anthropology book (Jean Cazeneuve 1970) into Persian, did not stay long enough in the country to translate the second volume of this book. Dr Shahnaz Nadjmabadi left Iran even though she wanted to stay after her Ph.D. research in Lorestan: 'The time is not yet ripe in Iran to engage in research within an institution. I also had the impression that nobody was really interested in what I was doing. Already, the fact that I had gone several years ago to live on my own with the nomads in Lorestan was quite a strange thing. There were many people who advised me to go back to Europe and stay there still for a couple of years and then come back to Iran.' Dr Homa Hoodfar reports how she was blatantly told by the 'Iranian Ministry of Higher Education ... that there were no vacancies nor did they foresee a need for my expertise in the near future [this was in 1988]. I had received an offer to teach at McGill University in Canada, therefore I went to McGill and later moved down the road to Concordia University and settled in Canada.' I personally decided to teach in order to be able to stay in Iran because my choice was to engage in research in Iran.

All of these anthropologists and a few others live and work abroad and come to Iran for short periods of time for research. Indeed, the overwhelming majority of Iranian anthropologists are dispersed in Euro-American universities and research centres. For research they come to Iran and now, increasingly more, to neighbouring or Middle Eastern countries. What would the state of anthropology in Iran be, had these trained anthropologists remained in the country and been integrated within research and academic life of Iran?

Anthropology as a Cultural Field: An Institutional Position or Power of an Academic Endeavour?

Now let us consider the situation of anthropologists within the country from another perspective. Again I shall refer to neighbouring fields to broaden our perspectives by placing anthropology within the context of all cultural professions in Iran. After I had completed the research for my dissertation, I started my own inquiries into Iranian culture, and I decided to approach this very complicated topic through one of its best manifestations, which at that time I perceived to be the world of traditional music. I followed a course for a few years, and I closely watched the activities of some experts. Here I would like to quote one of the most famous Iranian traditional musicians:

Competition in artistic society is great. Compassion and friendship have disappeared and musicians have become very inconsiderate of each other ... During the past twenty years we have not realized what has happened to us because we have been living within it. People have become pitiless and suspicious of each other. In such conditions, one becomes very tired. I find myself like someone who wants to go to the front to fight. Before, we went with a group and we were armed to fight a common enemy. Now we are the same people but we are pointing our guns towards each other. These are the conditions of our society ... There was a time when I loved to perform with the musicians I liked; now I do not relish to work with them. We don't have anything to say to each other. All has become a mirage. But what can I do all alone? (Shajariyan 1382: 32–3)

Iranian individualism and group work is not a new topic for students of Iranian society and culture. Anthropologists who should actually be experts in such issues have not gone beyond the usual trend of isolation and apparent good manners masking disregard and even deep enmity towards colleagues Having academic research centres with specific long-term programmes, which would oblige scientists to work together, could have been a first step. However, the personal approach of individuals who were made responsible for important institutions such as the Centre of Ethnological Research of the Ministry of Islamic Guidance (Bakhsh-e Tahghighat-e Mardomshenassi, part of Sazeman-e Miras-e Farhangi-ye Keshwar), the Ministry of Higher Education or the Faculty of Social Sciences at the University of Tehran (Daneshgah-e Tehran, Daneshkad- ye Ulum-e Ejtemai) has been detrimental to the progress of anthropology in Iran.

Another example is the office at the Iranian National Broadcasting Cmpany where manuscripts on Iranian folklore were gathered originally by Enjavi Shirazi. I was approached by this office many years ago, and I understood clearly that the person who was put in charge of this office definitely did not have the necessary expertise. However, looking at his position from a bureaucratic perspective he did not want to share his power with an expert. He considered his job to be just like any other job and did not ascribe any cultural or scientific meaning to it. He preferred to hold the position, and so far we have not seen any scientific work based on this rich collection of material. A great amount of raw data languishes similarly on the shelves of many ministries, academic centres and museums.

It should be noted that an important cultural centre called the Institute for Cultural Studies and Research (Pajuheshkade-ye Tahghighat-e Farhangi), which was created before the Revolution, does not have an anthropology section and has been headed by a physicist for more than ten years. Recently Iran University Press, which was famous for its publications in humanities, lost its philosopher dean, who was replaced by a geologist naturally keen on publishing journals and books in hard sciences. Research funds have been allocated for specific research projects, but what is necessary is their publication or accessibility through libraries where they could be consulted by other researchers. Although such research possibilities have been welcomed by university professors, whose income falls below the poverty line, a synthetic analysis of such data is still in demand. Certain topics might have been studied many times, others might have been ignored. Moreover, the quality of research has to be taken into consideration.

As far as collaboration with Iranian anthropologists living abroad is concerned, they are approached individually and certain specific research is done by them. However, there is no cohesion among the anthropologists themselves. Often they are alienated from research and academic centres where they could form a section with scientific aims. Instead they are employed on specific projects so that their expertise is *used* (a term very much in vogue ever since the Revolution). What is the import of such disjointed research, most of which we local anthropologists are not aware of, for the field of anthropology in Iran?

Gendered Space

Regarding the topic of this article, we have to consider the following: Anthropology, like any other public space in Iran, is a gendered space. To start with, I would like to mention a few methods of exclusion.

(1) For a long time we constantly heard male anthropologists say that there was no difference between men and women and that to talk about such a difference was to create a problem that did not exist. However since funding has become available specifically to do research on topics related to women, it has ironically been overwhelmingly men who have been doing this women-focussed research.

(2) At the university level, in group meetings, men dominate the sessions. Men who have relationships outside academia are totally at ease in this space. Women, few in number and ill at ease, remain silent. Unless they are asked to add details or respond to specific questions, they keep a low profile. I insist that keeping a low profile has been their strategy of survival.

(3) Women's books go unnoticed and forgotten because they are systematically ignored. Their articles and books are not even mentioned in bibliographic references.

(4) Non-anthropologist women are invited to participate in lectures, sessions and book editions so that female names appear, irrespective of their specialization. For example, on the list of lecturers at the University of Tehran in 2003–04 a translator was asked to speak on the anthropology of women, and at the Society for Anthropology of Iran (Anjoman-e Ensanshenasi-ye Iran) it is specialists in ancient languages, religion and mythology who are called on to do anthropological research.

(5) Scientific participation of women is channelled so as to be at the service of male colleagues. She is doing the work, he is getting the credit.

(6) Teaching by female colleagues is regulated in various ways: at times they are barred from teaching; at other times they are overloaded with teaching. In each case some kind of control is in play.

I have personally encountered great difficulties in getting my tenure, and then in publishing my works. It took fourteen years to publish my article 'Women of Iran is a Political Topic'. I have written an ethnography that has been waiting for eight years now and edited three volumes that are in press after delays of one to three years. Having edited two issues and one supplement of the journal *Anthropology* (*Ensanshenassi*), I received a letter stating that specific anthropologists were trying to stop its publication – and indeed, they succeeded. I organized a conference held at Shahid Beheshti University under the title 'Examples of Cultural Exchange between Iran and Other Civilizations: Anthropology Articles', which lost the subtitle 'Anthropology Articles' in the reportage of the journal of the International Centre of Dialogue of Civilizations (ICDC), where the sociologist who was formally invited to give a speech representing the ICDC became the focus of the article.

Language and Meaning

In general, ever since the 1970s there has been a change of the meaning of 'anthropology' in the minds of Iranian people. In the 1970s, when I said I was a *mardomshenas* (*mardom* and *shenas*), I was asked 'Do you know me?' or I was told that anthropologists were just curious or nosy (*fuzul*) (Shahbazi 2003). Today, in the wake of the cultural upheavals that we have faced, there is more of a demand on the part of Iranians for explanations from an anthropological perspective. The word 'culture' is used in popular newspapers much more than in the past. In addition, the Cultural Revolution that followed the Islamic Revolution, along with the government's cultural programmes, has brought the term into the foreground. The polemics about a 'clash of civilizations' and a 'dialogue of civilizations' have provided ample occasions for anthropology to make important contributions.

'Culture' has definitely become a political term and is on the political agenda of the country. Anthropologists could take the opportunity and express themselves more strongly in this arena. But are we prepared for such an enormous task and fantastic opportunity? Or have we been so dispersed and weakened by many years of alienation and distrust that we prefer to continue our individual work and remain suspicious and silent?

Another problem is the accessibility of anthropological literature in Iran. Students still have access only to a few introductory anthropology texts, in particular in the anthropology of politics and economics, but nothing on kinship. *The Golden Bough* was recently translated in 1384 (2005). A few years ago, when an excerpt of Malinowski's *Argonauts of the Western Pacific* was published, the publisher Zamineh, which used to review new books in the form of leaflets sent to its clients, asked why, at a time when paper was scarce, such a book should be published. Here we definitely have a serious problem: even anthropological classics are not translated. We should note that the material perhaps is too strange to the Iranian mind. When the social sciences are approached, there is curiosity towards knowledge of the developed world and of Iran. There is an implicit quest, presently becoming more and more explicit at an academic level, to find the historical reasons for not having developed in the same vein as the European world. Furthermore, there is a quest to know why Iran's level of development has continuously edged lower during the past 100 years. Reading classic anthropological literature on the non-developed world would therefore be a waste of time. Why the potential readership might ask should we read material on people who are strange to us and worse off than we are?

However, recent theoretical material is never seen on the shelves either. Students in the social sciences are usually poor in languages and cannot be expected to know enough English, French or Spanish to handle such immense literature. We should not forget that the language level necessary for the social sciences and humanities is far more complex than what is needed for the physical sciences, not to speak of mathematics. In this regard, sociology is more accessible and more attractive to students because traditionally it has been concerned with the Western world, and the positivistic trend is linguistically more accessible.

Having mentioned the problem of language, we should consider another fine point regarding the local meaning of anthropology. 'Cultural grid' is a well-known concept and we all know the example of *makarounie dam keshideh,* which means 'spaghetti Iranian-style'. Can a universal field acquire a local meaning? I once gave a lecture on Huntington's book and analysed his concept of culture and civilization. Afterwards, an elderly man came up to me and asked me how I would define culture. I understood very well that a field like anthropology defines culture in a particular way that is oftentimes very different from the terms in which it is understood in everyday common usage. It is particularly difficult for the language of an old culture like the Iranian culture to accept new meaning given to its old and well-defined terms. But as anthropologists we should be straightforward on this topic, and if we consider and practice anthropology as a universal discipline, we should keep our definitions and boundaries unambiguous and well-defined. We have to make clear that although we are using the Persian language, we are defining specific words in a scientific way different from ordinary usage. Every science develops its own terminology, which is acquired during one's education. An anthropologist uses ordinary language, but should make clear how her/his usage is defined. The language of the hard sciences is more difficult at the beginning and creates a distance; step by step it becomes easier. In anthropology we continue to use the same language, but it hides a deeper meaning that becomes clear with training. Meanwhile, the fact that one may find traces of anthropological interests in historical and geographical books does not make the writers anthropologists. Had it not been for the perspective of anthropology, such points would have remained undiscovered. There are many reasons to reread historical books and all texts with an anthropological regard, but if one has not been trained as an anthropologist to sift through this colossal body of material, how would one present and point to the problem raised?

Therefore the centrality and unity of anthropology must be retained. Otherwise we would be engaging in a copy-and-paste of Iran's well-documented history and literature. How could this be different from rereading a student's exercise in history or literature? The anthropological perspective, quest and aim should clearly be at the centre of such rereading of text and manuscripts, a perspective gained through fieldwork and theoretical work.

Where Are the Women?

What happened to the topic of this article? Where are the women anthropologists? Reading between the lines of what was said before, we can find them, but let us be more explicit. Iranian anthropologists whose books are internationally known (and here a search on the internet is recommended) are women. Let me give some examples.

Soraya Tremayne-Sheybani is the founding director (since 1998) of the Fertility and Reproduction Studies Group and a senior research associate at the Institute of Social and Cultural Anthropology at the University of

Oxford. Since 1985 she has been a member of the Centre for Cross-Cultural Research on Women at the Queen Elizabeth House, at the Department for International Development Studies of Oxford University, and in 1995 she became the director for eighteen months. In 1983 she founded and acted as the managing director of a consultancy firm called Social Analysis and Anthropology Associates that specializes in the application of anthropology in development projects. She has carried out research in Nigeria, Romania, Malaysia, Hong Kong, Iran and the U.K. She is a council member of the Royal Anthropological Institute of Great Britain and was its vice-president from 1998 to 2001. She is one of the Senior Common Room members of St. Antony's College and the International Development Studies of Queen Elizabeth House, at the University of Oxford.

Shahla Haeri is the head of the Women's Studies Program of Boston University, and her research has been on Pakistan and Iran. Homa Hood- far has worked in Egypt and Iran, and her work on the latter has included research on Afghan migrant populations. Fatemeh Givechian is the first Ira- nian anthropologist who conducted fieldwork on North American society and is now based in Canada. I need not introduce Ziba Mir-Hosseini, who is already well known for her award-winning film *Divorce Iranian Style* and her teaching career at both the New York University Law School and SOAS in London. Shahnaz Nadjmabadi, after working for six years at UNESCO Headquarters in Paris, has moved to Germany, University of Frankfurt, Uni- versity of Bamberg, Heidelberg and has done fieldwork in Lorestan, Tay- bad in Khorassan and the Persian Gulf coast near Bandar Lengeh. Fariba Adelkhah's *Being Modern in Iran* (2004) is on the bookshelves of many bookstores, in French or English.

It is striking that all of these women decided before or after the Revo- lution to live outside Iran. Almost all of them during some period of their career worked on women and lived abroad. What is the relationship, if any, between having become anthropologists and working on women? Is it be- cause of the theoretical attention devoted to the topic in anthropology in the 1970s and 1980s? Did this topic make them critical and perhaps uncomfort- able pursuing an academic career in Iran? Perhaps they were doubly alien- ated from being in Iran by the conditions of academia and of being a woman within the present context. Whatever the reason, their loss to the academic world of Iran has been consequential for the present state of anthropology in the country. In my view it is time that their expertise becomes known so that it can be integrated, not just to carry out specific research projects in connection with a national or international institution or ministry, but for the establishment of the academic field of anthropology.

In this regard a few words should be directed at our foreign colleagues who are sending anthropologists back to our academic and non-academic institutional centres. At a conference held in Paris in 1998, after I had heard a very poor presentation by a Middle Eastern anthropologist, I asked Dr Jennifer Scarce from Edinburgh: 'Why do you give doctorates to such students?' Her blatant response was: 'We need the money.' Perhaps certain universities need the money, but others do not. My question is, how is the work of local versus foreign students evaluated? Would the same rigour be demanded of a local student as of a foreign student competing in the Western academic world? And how is this affecting the development of fields in the developing world? Certainly some ink has been spilled on this topic, but the result is hurting our academic life greatly.

Conclusion

In a defiant tone, I would like to begin my conclusion with a fundamental question. Is there an Iranian anthropology? When we talk of French, British, Russian or American anthropology we assume that there is an accumulated wealth of data (material culture and books) and there is an academic centre. Do we Iranians have such a centre? Can there be an Iranian anthropology without such a centre? Who have been our theoreticians? Where are our accumulated data, and from which countries except Iran do we have odd pieces? Where and what is the centrality of our theory building? In the preface of a special edition of the journal *Nomadic Peoples* on Iran, Jean-Pierre Digard (2003) politely laments this situation. As students of our own culture, we know that we are either specialists of shortcuts with great imagination or we have partridge existence: we either take a very flowery and general tone to say that we belong to the universal world of knowledge production, or we ignore criticisms and continue our day-to-day existence. Both of these exercises in non-dialogue are detrimental to the existence of anthropology in Iran. I personally think that the centrality of anthropology has not yet been born. The perspectives of our good scholars are not Iran-centred. Iran is 'there'. It is a field, just as any other area of specialization would be, but one is just a little more emotional about it, and when going to the field one visits a few relatives and speaks the local language. Thus we exploit our advantages in the field, but is there an Iranian perspective being born and voiced here? Is it a perspective that shows the centrality of an effort to come from somewhere different from the Euro-American perspective? Is it voiced in relation to the needs of Iranian anthropology or in response to the Euro-American need to hear the voice of 'Other'? If an Iranian theorizes material from Iran, would this be Iranian anthropology? What do we mean by Iranian? Would he/she consider himself/herself Iranian? Is this a matter of passport or a matter of scientific perspective?

Scholars within the country have not had enough theoretical preparation to form such a centrality of ideas, and they have been so busy with
survival that such questions have not been their primary preoccupation.
An anthropological centrality, the centrality of anthropological theory, can
only be born if we develop our perspective in relation to our culture (if
our topic of research is indeed Iran) and from this centrality to the world
outside. With which areas are the names of our local anthropologists associated? Where is their field about which we are so ignorant? Indeed, in which
laboratory have we gathered any information on any other culture? Where
have we established the necessary grounds to create distance from ourselves
so as to engage in theorizing about our own culture? As anthropologists we
know that these are the alphabets of our field. The recent attention paid to
Iranology shows how we are just beginning to look from outside towards
ourselves. Fields such as ecology, geography, history, literature, archaeology, arts and so on have been concentrating on Iran. Why is there such
an interest in Iranology, when even the orientalists have been showing its
obsolescence? I think that by hiding under heaps of data from Iran, we have
lost dialogue with the world, and may I say with the necessities of Iran also.
Such superficial interests as are expressed in the curricula at certain universities and fashionable research centres are obsolete, while specializations are
gaining ground in all fields.

If we have not yet formed the centrality of our problems, then what
becomes of the centrality of our theoretical formations? Do we hold on
to an evolutionary perspective in relation to Iranian cultural history? Who
has worked on this elementary topic? What is the relationship between our
language and other cultural manifestations, such as music? How is space
formation related to kinship? What are the varieties of kinship terminology
found in Iran? What is the relationship between kinship and law in legal
and civic environments? We have not yet even formulated our problems, let
alone any theoretical formations thereof, and then perspectives on this.

Good theoretical work grows in academia when there is professional
security. Only geniuses for whom devotion to their work is more important than their personal lives can exert creativity in situations of upheaval.
In a country where academia is part of the government and an insecure
place, and where the needs of survival are not met by the minimum income,
people try to secure whatever power they can through other institutional
means. One becomes so involved in staying alive, and uses academia so
much like any other institutional power, that one forgets the necessity of
research, its prerogatives, its instruments and necessities. There is a definite
atmosphere of distrust, intrigue and denigration below the usual manner-
isms. Some years ago a poem that circulated at the university level pitilessly
ridiculed various members of academia. One person lost his job as a result,

but apparently he was not responsible for the poem. In such an atmosphere of low-grade opposition, how can academic work grow? I definitely think an anthropology of so-called anthropological work, and more importantly of anthropological academic space in Iran, is absolutely necessary. Only such a critical perspective could cut through the vicious circles that prevent this field from standing on its own feet, posing its essential questions and bringing about the positive spirit of scientific cooperation necessary for the present state of theory formation. This could become the nexus of an anthropology that belongs to a culture area, if not to a country. Unless we recognize, with anthropological clarity of perception, the crucible in which we are thrown, we cannot find our way out.

We are all suffocating in an entangled web that we ourselves, among others, have been creating. Untangling it is not an easy task, as some might be harmed and some might be deprived of their responsibility. We definitely need dedication, critical judgment and good common sense to put this derailed train back on track. Turning the page and starting with a more appropriate spirit would augur well for success in this project.

Turning the Page

I would like to conclude with a few important points.

(1) We have to confirm that anthropology is a field that is about the cultural life of peoples. It needs to do research and bring the results back to a centre. Its viability and uniqueness lie in this work in the field, with the compilation in a centre and theoretical work arising therefrom. There is no escape from this minimum requirement.

(2) We have to define our academic domain in relation to the general political life of the country and enter directly into negotiations about our limits and framework, and not allow sociologists to act as go-betweens.

(3) The enormous task lies ahead of us, not behind. If we realize what a colossal task we face, then we comprehend that we need all the human resources we have and even more. Instead of alienating expert colleagues and trying to dominate the field from an institutional standpoint, we have to define our expertise and work within it. Our work is in academia and not in journalism alone.

(4) We absolutely need contact with anthropologists in other countries to understand how they have developed, how they are working, what theories have been important to them in similar circumstances. Comparative work is essential in order to broaden our perspective,

so as not to fall back on regurgitation of manuscripts in history and literature but rather to plunge into active recapture of their sense, or of layers of culture that are fast disappearing.

(5) This requires a positive but critical perspective that will keep us from falling into the usual administrative methods of managing our professional lives. As anthropologists we should be subjects of our own studies also, and refrain from resorting to the usual patriarchal administrative behaviour, attempting to control others through spying, backbiting and intrigue. Through these practices we are digging our own mass grave. To continue in this vein will be detrimental to all the service we think anthropology can offer to our country – including our narcissistic tendencies towards it – instead of leaving it to the wolves. Such a chaotic situation must be prevented. If we claim to be scientists believing in the spirit of scientific endeavour, we have to realize that this demands cooperation.

Anthropology, as a field that concerns itself with culture, is quintessential in both our actual work and our perspective on what we do. If we want to this train to run on the proper rails, we have to define our share of responsibility towards engaging in the study of culture. I finish with a sentence from Adrian Johnson that was the motto of the 14th International Congress of Anthropological and Ethnological Sciences, and which I proposed to embellish the first page of the journal *Anthropology:* 'The twenty-first century is the century of anthropology: During this century no field other than anthropology could teach people about themselves and how to live with others.' Are we ready to exercise this ourselves?

NOTES

1. See the invitation leaflet for the conference 'Anthropological Perspectives on Iran: The New Millennium and Beyond', held in Frankfurt in October 2004.
2. I carried out a number of short interviews with the following colleagues: Homa Hoodfar, Shahla Haeri, Ziba Mir-Hosseini, Soraya Tremayne-Sheybani (Tremeyne 2001), Shahnaz Nadjmabadi. A few years ago I had conducted longer interviews with Dr Varjavand (1998), Mr Mirshokraei (1998), and again Shahnaz Nadjmabadi (1993) and Soraya Tremayne-Sheybani (2003).

REFERENCES

Adelkhah, F. 2004. *Being Modern in Iran*. New York.

Bartu, A.1996. 'Anthropology in Turkey', *Anthropology News* (December). Retrieved in from http://www.aaanet.org/mes/decbar.htm, 2004.

Beeman, W.O. 1999. 'Anthropological Research in Tajikistan', *Anthropology News* (December). Retrieved from http://www.aaanet.org /mes/decbee.htm, 2004.

Digard, J.-P. 2003. 'Preface', *Nomadic Peoples* 7(2): 17–20.

Givechian, F. 1991. *Work in Retirement: The Persistence of an American.* Cambridge.

Haeri, S. 1989. *The Law of Desire, Temporary Marriage, Mut'a, in Iran.* London.

———. 2002. *No Shame for the Sun: Lives of Professional Pakistani Women.* Oxford.

———. 2002 (ed.). *Iran Nameh* 15(3).

Hedayat, S. 1310. *Owsaneh.* Tehran.

———. 1312. *Neyrangestan.* Tehran.

———. 1323–24. 'Folklor ya farhang-e tudeh', *Sokhan* 2–6, Tehran (republication in *Neveshtehaye parakandeye Sadeqe Hedayat*, Amirkabir, 1944/1334: 448–483).

Hoodfar, H. 1997. *Between Marriage and the Market: Intimate Politics And Survival in Cairo.* Berkeley.

Hopkins, N.S. 1998. 'Anthropology in Egypt', *Anthropology News* (February). Retrieved from http://www.aaanet.org/mes/febhop.htm, 2004.

Huxley, J. 1998. *Anthropology News* (May). Retrieved from www.aaanet.org/mes/mayhux.htm (2004).

Mir-Hosseini, Z. 1993. *Marriage on Trial: A Study of Islamic Family Law: Iran and Morocco Compared.* London.

———. 1999. *Islam and Gender: The Religious Debate in Contemporary Iran.* Princeton, NJ.

Shafaq, Dr. 1335. 'Mardomshenasi chist?' *Majaleye mardomshenasi* 1: 1–7.

Shahbazi, M. 2003. 'Anthropological Fieldwork Endeavour and Indigenous Researchers', *Nomadic Peoples* 7(2): 98–107.

Shahshahani, S. 1986. 'History of Anthropology in Iran', *Iranian Studies* 19(1): 65–86.

———. 1987. *Four Seasons of the Sun* (in Persian). Tehran.

———. 1995. *A Pictorial History of Headdresses in Iran* (in Persian). Tehran.

———. 2005. *Meymand: We Were One People, One Territory. An Ethnographic Study of a Grotto-village* (in Persian). Kerman.

———. 1360. 'Xatare ensanshenasi va ensanshenasi dar xatar', *Arash* 5(7): 96–101.

——— (ed.). 2003. *Nomadic Peoples, Special Issue on Iran* 7(2).

——— (ed.). 2004a. *Anthropology Articles.* Tehran.

——— (ed.). 2004b. *Body as Medium of Meaning.* Muenster.

——— (ed.). 2004c. *Examples of Cultural Exchange between Iran and Other Civilizations.* Tehran.

Shajariyan. 1382. *Surush e mardom. Zendegi wa andishe haye ostad mohammad reza shajariyan. Be kushesh e orfan e ghane I rad.* Tehran.

Shamy, S. 1989. 'Socio-cultural Anthropology in Arab Universities', *Current Anthropology* 30(5): 649–54.

Sholkamy, H. 2001. 'Why Is Anthropology So Hard in Egypt?', *ISIM Newsletter* 7.

Tremayne, S. (ed.). 2001. *Managing Reproductive Life.* Oxford.

Tremayne, S. and A. Low (eds.). 2001. *Women as Sacred Custodians of the Earth?* Oxford.

Varisco, D.M. 1998. 'Deadening a Beaten Camel: Is Middle East Anthropology Relevant?' www.aaanet.org/mes/octvar.htm, 2004.

PART III

Anthropological Practice
Constraints and Possibilities

CHAPTER 7

Applied Anthropology in Iran?

Jean-Pierre Digard

Introduction

All Western anthropologists who have worked in Iran have at one time or another encountered a paradoxical attitude among Iranian academics and officials. Because they are Westerners, their capacity to understand 'Iran's soul' is challenged, but at the same time, they are being summoned to put their credentials as anthropologists to use for Iran. In other words, they supposedly cannot understand situations in the country well enough, but they are good enough to put their services at the country's disposal. This is particularly noticeable in relation to nomadic life, where the only envisaged solution to perceived problems – sedentarization through various direct and indirect forms of imposition and incentive – continuously failed and created further unresolved problems.

It is useless to devote much time to refuting the first accusation. As Claude Lévi-Strauss often emphasized, anthropology is less a 'source of particular knowledge' than an 'original mode of knowledge' grounded in an observer's perception at a distance from a culture different from his or her own. It is, therefore, meaningless to criticize anthropology for what constitutes, in fact, its strength and originality. To quote Lévi-Strauss once again:

> Those who claim that the experience – individual or collective – of others is essentially incommunicable and that it is forever impossible, or even reprehensible, to want to work out a language wherein the human experiences most removed from each other in time and space would become, at least in part, mutually comprehensible, they are doing nothing other than taking refuge in a new obscurantism. (1977: 10)

Let us then turn to the second accusation, which deserves more thought. Like Maxime Rodinson, I do not have what he called 'Third World mysticism', and 'I do not beat my breast every day out of desperation about not having been born in some sort of Congo' (Rodinson 1966: 7). Yet this call to serve, since it comes from a country to which I have devoted much of my life, does not fall on deaf ears. How could it, given that the country faces problems, such as desertification and impoverishment, that jeopardize human life and dignity? The moral and institutional pressure brought to bear on Iranian anthropologists is even heavier, for reasons that are easy to understand. Thus, in a recent sample of Iranian studies on the country's nomads in a special issue of *Nomadic Peoples,* edited by Soheila Shahshahni (2003), a clear majority of the subjects were directly or indirectly related to social or economic development.

The Feasibility of Applied Anthropology

The legitimacy or acceptability of a 'social demand' for anthropology is one point, but the feasibility of applied anthropology is an issue calling for special attention. The obstructions to actually applying anthropology loom large.

Many problems, such as those related to public health or the environment, are becoming much more serious. In this context, anthropology, just like other sciences, is more than ever under pressure to be 'useful' and serve a purpose. 'Finalized' research is receiving funds; budgetary incentives are granted to studies resolutely oriented towards economic or industrial applications, or towards social development. This targeting of funds and programmes is evidently taking place to the detriment of basic research with its single purpose of developing knowledge – all kinds of knowledge – independent of any concern for applications. The dispute between the supporters of 'practical' and 'basic' research revolves around the degree of autonomy or integration of these two approaches.

For the advocates of the first approach, science can be applied without doing basic research, since engineering and basic research are independent. In their opinion, this is precisely what should be done, given that basic research has high costs but no returns. Supporters of 'basic' research' argue instead that the two approaches cannot be separated and applications must be grounded in basic research. For them, as for Louis Pasteur, there actually is no 'applied science', but only applications of science. Since advances in basic research are unforeseeable – or as Marcel Granet put it, '[t]he method is the road once you've taken it' – it would be vain, even useless, to try to channel science towards possible applications.

Contrary to the view of the proponents of applied sciences, anthropology cannot be likened, let alone be reduced, to 'social and cultural engineering'. At best, it might contribute to the latter in certain fields and in certain ways. These contributions must be examined case by case, by taking into account the specific obstacles that crop up in each field of research. I therefore would like to devote the remaining part of this article to delimiting the fields and ways that anthropology might contribute to social development. I shall do this by using examples from Iran.

Anthropology's Potential Contributions to Social Development

Anthropology can serve in operations that have to do with preserving a cultural heritage. For several years, Christian Bromberger has devoted much of his time and energy (not in vain, we hope) to creating an ecomuseum in Gilan. However, any museum-related activity risks focusing exclusively on what is 'dead' and might even help a heritage die by prematurely fossilizing it. Much the same might be said about 'salvage anthropology', as it tries to save what can be, which, alas, very often amounts to nothing more than souvenirs.

For these reasons, I think it worthwhile to ask how the past can be used to build the future. This might lead to making something new out of something old, to innovations that 'revive traditions' (Bromberger and Chevallier 1999). Examples of this range widely, from adapting a Persian barber's stool to medical computer technology (Gazagnadou 1999) to reviving certain tribal institutions as a means for regulating pasture rights. And let us not forget the rehabilitation of traditional buildings in contemporary architectural projects (Roaf 2003) – a procedure already used by Hassan Fathi (1970) and by what then was called 'implicated anthropology'. Although something new is created from something old or in a style borrowed from the past (as in certain operations for replacing nomadism with transhumance), the goal is to discover a coherent, harmonious transition towards better forms thanks to a positive critique of past forms.

Why moor innovations in the past? Because societies, just like people, need to know where they come from in order to learn where they are going. To quote André Leroi-Gourhan:

> Tradition is as biologically indispensable to the human species as genetic conditioning is to societies of insects. Ethnic survival depends on routines, the dialogue that arises [between the individual and social group] leads to an equilibrium between routine and progress, with routine symbolizing the capital necessary for the group's survival and progress representing the intervention of individual innovations for improving on survival. (1965: 25)

Both Gustav von Grünebaum and Jacques Berque (1970) claimed that we should 'remain ourselves in modernity'. The former did not believe this would actually happen, but Berque took this to mean that 'other hypotheses about humanity' were possible – indeed, were the only way of offering Muslim peoples a future.

Dispelling Ambiguities

This is a beautiful project to which anthropologists might contribute – under the condition, however, that a few ambiguities are dispelled. The first ambiguity is best expressed in question form. Whom are anthropologists working for? To borrow two figures of speech from Raymond Aron, are we the 'prince's counsel' or the 'people's doctor'? In the past it was admitted, even by anthropologists themselves, that they should work openly with authorities, even colonial officials. In his 1954 book about the Nupe in Nigeria, Siegfried Nadel definitely set his research in the framework of cooperation between anthropologists and colonial administrators with the aim of building within the British Empire a native administration based on indirect rule.[1]

Things have changed in the new context of independent nation-states. Anthropological research can no longer be conducted without the agreement of host country authorities or, in the case of applied anthropology, without a request from them or their consent. The lack of political determination in the early 1970s probably hampered 'integrated development' programmes such as the wildlife sanctuary in Turan in northern Khorasan,[2] or the Alishtar project in Lorestan (Black-Michaud 1974). These two projects and others like them could have produced much better results if the central government had had a genuine interest in their success and had supported them until the end.

In the meantime, anthropologists' opinions about professional standards have evolved, and nowadays many of them deem this subordination unacceptable. Although this mistrust is easy to understand, it is not easy to imagine how such interventions could take place without agreements with officials. Yet we must avoid dogmatic posturing on this topic. With regard to nomadism, for instance, authorities of the Islamic Republic express serious concern for the problems encountered by nomads – unlike under the Shah, when the focus was on the problems that nomads raised for the central government (Shahshahani 2003a). Unfortunately, this new concern does not suffice to prevent blunders in carrying out programmes or mistakes in drawing up assessments, even though such errors were supposed to be painlessly remedied by policy changes. In the case of the Bakhtiari, official policy supported nomadism for a decade and then, as of 1989, shifted towards giving nomads the choice between incentives for transhumance or for settlement around approximately forty centres that were equipped to host between fifty and two hundred families. Using census data about nomads collected between 1987 and 1998, Seyed Saydaie (2003) has shown that the plight of this population has worsened in nearly all respects. Since then, a third policy has been drafted as part of a twenty-year plan that, based on sustainable development, implies protecting the environment and the natural resources necessary for transhumance and for an agriculture attuned to the needs of animal husbandry.

This ambiguity about whom anthropologists are working for is not just a matter of professional standards. Difficulties related to this question crop up in places other than the Islamic Republic, and they have a technical dimension too. Both in contemporary Iran and elsewhere, several factors breed misunderstanding and hamper the relations that must be woven between social scientists and decision makers. For one, authorities demand prescriptions, whereas social scientists provide knowledge. Moreover, decision makers accept as certitudes, either positive or negative depending on their options, statements that scientists never consider to be anything more than hypotheses or possibilities. Some of these technical misunderstandings might be, at least in part, smoothed out by broader cooperation between foreign researchers (whose vantage point is shaped by their distance) and Iranian academics (who have the advantage of a fuller understanding of facts in the field). This cooperation should start with fieldwork and continue up through the phase of interpreting the results. Difficulties of this sort might also be ironed out thanks to mediators between the rural and urban worlds, specifically tribe members who play an updated role of '*middleman*' as described by Fredrik Barth in the early 1960s (1964: chapter 7). This 'mediation' will probably be more effective in the absence of a rift running between these two worlds. As Soheila Shahshahani (2003b) has shown, some of the Mamassani in Fars have become lawyers, doctors or professors who are trying to improve living conditions for their still nomadic tribesmen. Their efforts will be all the more effective insofar as these middlemen have acquired social positions outside the tribal sphere and territory.

Nomads who have become specialists on nomads provide a particular case in point of this mediating position. One such example is the stance taken by leaders of the Organization of Tribal Affairs of Iran (*Sāzmān-i Umur-i ʿAshāyirī*, part of the development organization *Jahād-i Sāzandigī*). Another example is our colleague Mohammad Shahbazi, who in a recent article humorously described his intellectual itinerary as a 'native' of the Qashqa'i tribe and an anthropologist in the United States (2003). In doing so he drew attention to the discomfort and ambivalence of such a position in a country like Iran (see also Shahbazi's contribution in this volume). He criticizes both the dominant culture in Iran, which has politicized and discredited the social sciences, and Iranian anthropologists who labour to maintain the right distance from the people they are studying and from Iranian society.

Although anthropologists are usually unable to avoid playing a leading or, more likely, minor role as the 'prince's counsel', we continuously must make an effort to play a part as the 'people's doctor'. We must always have a stethoscope hanging from our ears and never let anyone dictate the diagnosis – not even when we have no illusions about the treatment. For example, we must refuse to answer questions such as 'How to settle the nomads?' and instead ask questions along the lines of 'Should nomads be made to settle?' Change is, of course, inevitable – but it is not an end in and of itself. Nor is it necessarily desirable. To form an opinion about possible changes, it is important for us to listen to what people want. I would be demagogical, were I to claim that 'social actors' are always the best placed to know what is good for them. But it is useless to go against what they want or expect, or to be in contradiction with their values. In general, it is easier to set off a fundamental change from within a social system, from within its set of values, than from without it, in opposition to those values. (Moore 1950: 416).

We can cite many cases where opposition to an innovation has been blamed on Islam, even though the innovation simply did not correspond to the people's material needs (Rodinson 1972: 218). And let us not forget that the rising expectations of the people are often, and sometimes too hastily, pushing towards modernity. Christian Bromberger has reminded us of this: 'Living in a modern house in Gilân, as in many areas in the world, is not just a quest for more comfortable conditions. It is also a rejection of a past of toil and hard labour, an appropriation of the signs – often illusory – of emancipation. These are feelings that the well-to-do have trouble understanding since they perceive a "past" that they have not experienced as a golden age and with nostalgia' (1986: 118)

In anthropology as in medicine, emergency situations always introduce aggravating factors. The worst situation is the following. After anthropologists have been shunned or their advice ignored for twenty years, they are suddenly summoned to the scene. Usually there is nothing left to do save issue a death certificate or, at best, perform an autopsy – the previous situation is a thing of the past and anthropology is incapable of resurrecting it. When this happens, we must refuse the summons lest we be blamed, sooner or later, for the failure.

Closing Remarks

Here I would like to close, unfortunately without mentioning critical anthropology with its almost Weberian tonality and its critical description of social experience, as practised, for instance, by Ziba Mir-Hosseini. (1999)

As seen above, my assessment is mixed. We cannot avoid noticing that Iran is facing many urgent problems. For this reason, we deem legitimate the interest usually shown for problems related to change and development. It would be misguided to refuse to apply anthropology when possible and under the right conditions. Nonetheless, it would be suicidal for anthropology (and for those to whom it could be of use) if our discipline were to be reduced to an applied anthropology, or if applied anthropology were to become a separate discipline with its own specialists, as called for by some pundits.[3] It would be fatal if applied anthropology were to swell up because of its supposed 'usefulness' and smother basic anthropology. We must always bear in mind that the validity of results never depends on how serious or urgent a problem is, and that the dictate 'What is it good for?' or 'Whom is it good for?' has never been a driving force in scientific innovation. True science works with its eyes focused on the long term. It constantly risks not knowing in advance what it is going to discover. Beware, lest we put ourselves in the ridiculous situation of becoming 'experts' with fake learning who will know tomorrow why what they predicted yesterday is not happening today!

NOTES

Translated from French by Noal Mellott, CNRS, Paris.
1. By contrast, in the French Empire 'direct government' was the rule, and officials did not want to bother with intermediate levels except when absolutely necessary.
2. See the special issue of *Exploration* (1980): 22(4).
3. For example, Mars (2004).

REFERENCES

Barth, F. 1964. *Nomads of South Persia: The Basseri Tribe of the Khamseh Confederacy.* Oslo.

Berque, J. 1970. *L'Orient second.* Paris.

Black-Michaud, J. 1974. 'An Ethnographic and Ecological Survey of Luristan, Western Persia: Modernization in a Nomadic Pastoral Society', *Middle Eastern Studies* 10(2): 210–28.

Bromberger, C. 1986. *Habitat, architecure et société rurale dans la plaîne du Gilân (Iran septentrional).* Paris.

Bromberger, C. and D. Chevallier (eds). 1999. *Carrières d'objets: Innovations et relances.* Paris.

Exploration. 1980. Special issue, 22(4).

Fathi, H. 1970. *Construire avec le peuple.* Paris.

Gazagnadou, D. 1999. 'L'ordinateur américain et la chaise de coiffeur persane', in C. Bromberger and D. Chevallier (eds), *Carrières d'objets: Innovations et relances.* Paris: 123–31.

Leroi-Gourhan, A. 1965. *Le geste et la parole: II. La mémoire et les rythmes*. Paris.

Lévi-Strauss, C. 1977. *L'identité*. Paris.

Mars, G. 2004. 'Refocusing with Applied Anthropology', *Anthropology Today* 20(1): 1–2.

Mir-Hosseini, Z. 1999. *Islam and Gender: The Religious Debate in Contemporary Iran*. Princeton, NJ.

Moore, B. Jr. 1950. *Soviet Politics: The Dilemma of Power, the Role of Ideas in Social Change*. Cambridge, MA.

Nadel, S. 1954. *Nupe Religion*. London.

Roaf, S. 2003. 'Sustainable Buildings: Middle Eastern Traditional Systems for the Future', in R. Tapper and K. McLachlan (eds.), *Technology, Tradition and Survival: Aspects of Material Culture in the Middle East and Central Asia*. London: 132–47.

Rodinson, M. 1966. *Islam et capitalisme*. Paris.

———. 1972. *Marxisme et monde musulman*. Paris.

Saydaie, S. 2003. 'Sustainable Development among the Bakhtiari Tribe', *Nomadic Peoples* 7(2): 70–77.

Shahbazi, M. 2003. 'Anthropological Fieldwork Endeavour and Indigenous Researchers', *Nomadic Peoples* 7(2): 98–107.

Shahshahani, S. (ed.). 2003a. *Nomadic Peoples: Special Issue on Nomads and Nomadism in Post-revolutionary Iran* 7(2).

———. 2003b. 'Interview with Jafar Alipour', *Nomadic Peoples: Special Issue on Nomads and Nomadism in Post-revolutionary Iran* 7(2): 62–69.

———. 2003c. 'The Mamassani of Iran: At the Juncture of Two Modes of Subsistence', *Nomadic Peoples: Special Issue on Nomads and Nomadism in Post-revolutionary Iran* 7(2): 87–97.

Von Grunebaum, G. 1962. *Modern Islam - the search for cultural identity*. Berkeley.

CHAPTER 8

Past Experiences and Future Perspectives of an Indigenous Anthropologist on Anthropological Work in Iran

Mohammad Shahbazi 𝕩

> Anthropology is about all of us who participated in Frankfurt's
> 2004 Conference on 'Anthropological Perspective in Iran: The
> New Millennium and Beyond' and its results ought to apply to all
> of us equally – indigenous or otherwise.

Introduction

During my anthropological fieldwork in Iran, I faced three key challenges in
using ethnographic research methodologies: (1) identifying and dealing with
the realities in the field, (2) gaining access to the subjects and the archived
data about them, and (3) adjusting theories and methodologies to the 'reality' of actual conditions and findings in the field and later during data analysis and writing. In this chapter I briefly discuss a few well-known works on
issues related to the 'native anthropologists' and indigenous anthropology
and reflect on where I fit in this picture, addressing the first two challenges,
succinctly comparing my 1990s fieldwork and health-related research conducted beginning in 2000 and, finally, offering several recommendations for
the future of anthropology and anthropological work in Iran. I do this with
optimally optimistic thinking, in the belief that positive thinking can yield
good results.

One might think that indigenous researchers have a great advantage in
the field, yet their difficulties are not much different from those of foreigners who became acquainted with their research groups only as adults – that
is, when conducting typical anthropological research. However, as I will
discuss later in the chapter, a shift in the nature of fieldwork from anthro-

pology to applied anthropology may also create a positive working environment, which I have experienced in recent years. As a native Iranian – first as a student of anthropology and since 2000 as a medical anthropologist, educated and based in the United States with ongoing research in Iran – I can speak about this topic based on my own experiences. In the following I discuss some of the insights I gained while conducting research among Qashqa'i nomadic pastoral tribespeople[1] among whom I had grown up. But before I discuss my insights, I want to include a few words on what has been said about native/indigenous anthropologists and anthropological work.

Having Feet in Two Worlds

The debate on 'indigenous anthropology' (Fahim 1982; Motzafi-Haller 1997; Narayan 1993) was formally documented when dozens of participants from over twenty countries met at Burg Wartenstein, Austria, to present/discuss issues related to indigenous anthropology in the late 1970s. A close reading of the contents of the debate on indigenous anthropology seems to indicate that there were relatively supportive/favourable environment for the Western anthropologists to conduct fieldworks in some developing countries up to 1970s. However, as such countries have become politically sensitive (sensitive in terms of questioning the hidden agenda for research and other sociopolitical/economic activities by the Westerners), they have set restrictions on foreign anthropological research – vigorously encouraging indigenous anthropologists to do 'untainted' fieldwork (Fahim and Helmer 1980). Prior to this event Jones (1970) discusses the concept of native anthropology, identifying it as a facet of indigenous anthropology where the latter accommodates the various relationships that may exist between the local researcher and the people studied, focusing on both the epistemological and the operational consequences of such relationships.

As for the role of the indigenous anthropologists in agency-sponsored development research, it has been emphasized that the indigenous anthropologist's commitment, cultural understandings and potential for activism concerning development projects in line with needs of the local people makes them favoured over foreign anthropologists. It is often the capacity for activism that makes governments distrustful and suspicious of their competent social scientists (Fahim 1982).

Indigenous anthropologists can be engaged by the government development projects or be engaged in research that generates 'scientific' products, legitimizing the projects with political agendas. For example, Mexico in the 1940s actively engaged anthropologists with such agendas. However, seeing the consequences of the projects, Mexican anthropologists disassociated themselves from such activities and used university classrooms to criticize the development model in their country (Fahim and Helmer 1980). Other indigenous anthropologists have been able to resolve such dilemmas by presenting facts and alternatives and by establishing rapport with the planners, hence influencing the design of plans and maximizing benefits for the local people. (See the comments of Nader Afshar Naderi, who worked with the Iranian Institute for Peasant and Rural Studies, in Fahim 1982.)

Some participants in the work that Fahim documented present a debate on how social scientists in general and native anthropologists in particular can work with elites of ethnic or minority groups and either benefit them through or deprive them of their fair share of national resources. But as an indigenous anthropologist with feet in two worlds, I think such a dichotomy is both unhealthy and useful. In the same way that placement of academics in the process of development – in its broadest sense – increases chances of collaboration between decision makers and researchers, so collaboration of indigenous and non-indigenous anthropologists, as a world scholarly community, may promote synergies for future capacity building for the stakeholders.

The discussion of my experience as an indigenous anthropologist here, similar to what the literature has to offer on this subject, barely scratches the surface of the subject at hand. I will now return to my field experience, following it with commentary on how a single indigenous researcher may undergo contrasting experiences as an indigenous anthropologist that I believe need to be explored in a depth that is outside of the scope of this paper.

Backgrounds

Being myself a result of the literacy programme and a member of this very generation, I developed a research interest in examining the impacts of this state-supported formal education on Qashqa'i culture. I soon learned that a key question in research on the Middle East since the 1950s has been the connection between the state and its resident tribes and nomads. The use of force and coercion by state officials to control tribal and nomadic groups is well documented (Amanolahi-Baharvand 1991; Barth 1961; Beck 1986, 1991; Tapper 1979 and 1993). However, less well known are the ideological controls instituted through systematic state-supported apparatuses and the ways in which tribal and nomadic people have responded to them. One such apparatus was education, which I researched.

Thirteen years after I had left for my education abroad, I returned to Iran and began a twenty-four month research project to study a state-supported formal education programme specifically designed for the needs of nomadic and transhumant tribal groups. My study focused on Qashqa'i schoolteach-ers, in particular the roles they played in the processes of formally educat-ing Qashqa'i tribespeople, how they prepared their students for new roles within a changing Iran and the extent to which they enculturated them with values held by earlier generations. I conducted this study in Fars Province (southern Iran), and I also travelled to neighbouring and other provinces to interview formally educated Qashqa'i and others who were involved with the literacy programme. Recognizing that this state-supported literacy pro-gramme was not solely for the Qashqa'i tribespeople, I intentionally focused on its impacts on Qashqa'i culture as an indigenous anthropologist.

The brief presentation of one cycle of a Qashqa'i year projects a picture of integrated activities in a unique setting.[2] These activities accompanied other expressive cultural activities, such as dance, song, music, poetry, story-telling, sport, dress, cuisine, technology etc.[3] The change of seasons divided events and presented them in meaningful rotation. These activities became meaningful through migration – an organized, systematic and highly man-aged act. Repetition of this communal act, combined with the use of the Turkish language over time with minimal influence from outside, produced explicit and distinct Qashqa'i cultural patterns. In fact, the repetition of similar communal acts over time, with the consequent production of distinc-tive cultural patterns, is not unique to the Qashqa'i but is a universal human sociocultural experience. In this connection I view indigenous anthropolo-gists as social actors who were reared in accordance with explicit and dis-tinct cultural patterns. They then drifted away from a culturally embedded status, but return as formally trained anthropologists to critically examine certain aspects of their own cultures and societies.

Identifying and Dealing with Realities in the Field

I was not old enough to be aware of popular views of social scientists and their practices in the 1970s, when I was a high school student of Qashqa'i descent in a relatively big city in Fars Province. The idea that anybody would want to study people, especially strangers, was alien to me, my friends and my kin. I observed privileged foreigners (*ajnabi*), predominantly Americans, who enjoyed a lavish lifestyle but did not seem to have any interest in the place where they lived. I could not imagine that some of those foreigners actually lived with rural and pastoral nomadic populations to study them. Indeed, I think few people from among the public actually knew about or understood the nature of the work of these researchers. For example, I learned from some members of a Qashqa'i group who had been studied in the 1970s (Beck 1986) that most of them did not know the aim of the for-

eigner among them, nor did they know they had been studied anthropologically. 'Why should anyone study other people?' a Qashqa'i man commented
in 1992. In 1996, a friend's six-year-old daughter asked me what I did for a
living. When I replied that I was conducting anthropological research, she
promptly asked, 'Does that mean you're nosy about other people's business?' These examples express a general sentiment, a somewhat dismissive
attitude towards this kind of work, or even a mistrust of anybody studying
other people closely. Many problems I had to solve in the field were based
on this pervasive attitude.

I would argue that this scepticism is linked to certain sociohistorical developments, in particular the development of modern state-supported formal
education, especially modern secular education. This led to the creation of a
popular culture that arguably politicized and devalued the social sciences. In
the nineteenth century, the desire on the part of rulers in Iran for a modern
military and state bureaucracy encouraged them to establish schools, bring
foreign teachers to Iran and dispatch young Iranians to Europe to study. The
first modern school in Iran, founded to educate officers and civil servants,
served as a cultural centre and employed foreign teachers trained in military
sciences, engineering, medicine and mineralogy. There were no social scientists among them. In the 1930s, the Ministry of Education was established.
Formally educated people were seen as able and skilful citizens who could
serve their country and their fellow citizens in any capacity.

If one looks at the Iranians who were sent to Europe to study, they were
at first all male children of well-off/wealthy elite families. In general they
studied medicine and engineering-technical fields; only at a later stage did
some study law and other subjects too. This contributed to a conception
that associated the earning of degrees with technical fields that would mod-
ernize the country. Most of these Western-educated individuals ended up in
decision-making positions and in turn perhaps contributed to the emerging
perception that 'hard science' was good. The social sciences, by contrast,
were seen as fields that created political consciousness among students and
stimulated them to ask political questions in the late 1940s and early 1950s
– particularly during the later part of the Mossadeq era when pro-Shah and
pro-American media labelled Mossadeq's supporters communists.

After 1953, the Shah, wishing to reconstruct the country's glorious
past with the help of modern science and technology, prized these fields
(medicine and engineering-technical fields) over all others. At the same time,
many educated people were critical of the Shah. Academics, intellectuals
and political activists (including religious ones) were perceived as opposing many of the Shah's policies and were labelled Marxists, socialists and
communists by the ruling establishment. This prepared the ground for the
general notion among the public that educated people, especially social sci-

entists, opposed the government and were subversive and untrustworthy. Moreover, the Shah's regime promoted and strengthened a mass culture in which technical fields, the natural sciences and medicine were viewed as more important than the social sciences. Indeed, at that time the first two career choices of most ambitious Iranians were engineering and medicine. This pattern prevails even today, including among expatriate Iranians.

The social sciences thus remained comparatively unexplored fields. They were associated with the potentially dangerous raising of political consciousness and with poorly paid jobs. Anthropologists were seen as living and working in unattractive places and studying the ways of life of 'backward' people to no obvious reasonable end – except to benefit their respective governments in the long term. Nevertheless, universities, operated by pro-Western government establishments, created social science departments. Meanwhile, increasing interest in Iran in the early 1970s attracted foreign anthropologists to the country. Simultaneously, some young Iranian university students became interested in the field of anthropology, despite the field's unpopularity. Most of them started studying anthropology abroad, but by the time they returned, prepared to contribute to the consistent formation and growth of anthropology, Iran's Revolution of 1978–79 disturbed this development.

Following the Revolution, higher education institutions remained inactive. Many Western-educated social scientists, including anthropologists, left the country. A few anthropologists trained in the West who were staying in Iran struggled to keep their courses/positions. Meanwhile, Western anthropologists who had conducted research projects in Iran in the 1960s and 1970s did not return or could not enter the country easily. Even if they managed to get in, the visas were granted only for a short visit (not exceeding one or two months). For years Iranians, including anthropologists, could not easily obtain visas for European and North American countries. In addition, the higher learning institutions, including the Ministry of Education, did not support students' efforts to leave the country to pursue higher education in fields other than medicine and/or technological subjects. The social movements of 1978–79 and the Revolution thus reinforced earlier misconceptions about the social sciences in Iran. When revolutionary ideologues examined the activities of foreigners in Iran, including anthropologists, the social sciences by and large did not fare well. As one Iranian told me: 'The American military advisors trained some officers, and the training of personnel in the petroleum industry was of some value to our nation, but in what ways have those so-called researchers benefited us? The information they collected was used for political purposes.'

In sum, the social sciences in general and anthropology in particular have had an unsteady history in modern Iran. Events following the Revolution of 1978–79 contributed negatively to the unstable status of this field. Anthropology, an important discipline within the social sciences, was born in a political storm half a century previously in Iran – and it has yet to mature, yet to claim its unique identity, yet to survey the storm, yet to hatch and earn appreciation in popular culture.[4]

Suspicious Anthropologist in the Field

In such a negatively charged climate, I had to justify even to my own kin in Iran what I was doing and why I was doing it. I learned to avoid asking direct questions in interviews and to use questionnaires where I was not well known. Through trial and error I found that I aroused the least suspicion and got the best results when I started a conversation casually and only gradually led the discussion to the topic about which I needed information. Although I informed the people I interviewed of my intent and purpose and talked only to those who agreed to an interview, I felt I had to approach my questions obliquely and casually, discussing my topics in open-ended interviews. I felt the need to be circumspect and to avoid raising suspicions in the minds of overly politicized individuals, especially since tribal people in southern Iran have a long history of insubordination and thus are viewed by many officials and non-Qashqa'i as potentially dangerous.

Another set of problems arose from the way the bureaucracy works in Iran and from the need to deal with officials in various circumstances. As an Iranian with a passport from the Islamic Republic, I generally had no problems with research permits. However, rules and regulations that affect research on the local level, and particularly decisions made by local officials in the absence of established administrative procedures for research, did cause difficulties. One issue for the officials, in regions with a sizeable population of settled Qashqa'i, was the nature of my research and why I had included those regions in my study. Some officials had a pervasively negative attitude towards any research in areas containing groups considered to be politically charged, such as the Qashqa'i. I felt considerable pressure to stop my research on numerous occasions and frequently had to engage in long debates on this topic. On one occasion the secret police questioned my host, a former Qashqa'i schoolteacher, on my activities, the devices I used to record the interviews and the kinds of information I was interested in. When I applied to government officials for permission to take my audiotapes out of the country, the tapes were confiscated. It took me over three months and much strategic networking to get them back. With each of the standard methodologies mentioned in the introduction I encountered obstacles. As my fieldwork progressed, I developed other, locally more appropriate means of collecting data while dealing with these obstacles. This was one way my fieldwork methodology evolved as I adjusted to local conditions.

The politically sensitive setting I found in Iran had another consequence for my research methodology. I realized early on that in order to be successful, I had to painstakingly adjust my research methodologies to requirements of conduct and procedures informed by local values and sensitivities. For example, it soon became obvious that interviews I conducted in the presence of other people were less fruitful than private conversations. My interviews primarily focused on the state-supported literacy programme that was provided to Qashqa'i and other tribespeople in the south and southwest of Iran. The educated Qashqa'i I talked to interacted with me much more freely in private interviews than when others were present. The interviewees often repeated in private that they could not speak their minds when others – particularly members of other tribes and subtribes – were present. When I asked what made them feel that way, I was told that there were individuals who believed that the literacy programme directed by Mohammad Bahman-begi benefited the Qashqa'i. Therefore, they preferred to speak privately so as not to offend others or hurt their feelings. In addition, private conversations resulted in more spontaneous and frank responses to my questions than what I received in public dialogues, even if the conversations were totally apolitical. Most of the schoolteachers I interviewed were males. The few interviews I did with women had to be done in the presence of other members of the household to make them culturally appropriate.

Regarding methodology, the point here is that even though I was a 'native' with the intent to be as supportive and culturally sensitive as possible, and even though I was a bona fide researcher with written support from the government, I needed to reenter my own ethnic group with caution. Although I was a Qashqa'i, had grown up among Qashqa'i in Iran and spoke the relevant languages, I was not personally known to many of my subjects. I had been living abroad for years, which had interrupted the growth of my social circles in Iran. I thus needed to approach members of my ethnic group who did not know me or my family, through individuals who were trusted by them, much as any outsider would. Barth's celebrated claim of 1969 that the key criterion for ethnic membership is an acknowledged and self-conscious distinctiveness within whatever larger social whole exists could not be fully applied in my case. Anthropologists usually enter the community they want to study through somebody known to the community. In my case, however, there was a twist: I was an indigenous anthropologist working among people with whom I shared a common culture (was born to a sub-tribe of the Qashqa'i tribespeople) had been reared. This made me an insider with the difficulties of an outsider.

When I shifted my focus of research from typical anthropological work in the 1990s to more applied anthropology beginning in 2000, my experience was altered considerably. Whereas in the 1990s I had wandered around wearing my anthropologist hat as a Qashqa'i, during my latter medical anthropological research I instead kept my spruce-root hat loose or off, metaphorically, and displayed an engraved image of a researcher on my forehead. Is this experience unique? Below are further observations/experiences worth discussing.

Indigenous Anthropologists Facing the Reality

I saw myself as intellectually isolated, there being only a few local colleagues – students during my initial research – who knew about my work. Often I felt restricted in my research, trying to avoid any political sensitivity on the part of government agencies. When I was asked to serve on a national committee to review the literacy programme with intention to further integrate tribespeople into larger Iranian society, I was reluctant to support the effort for fear that it would cut tribespeoples – my own people – free from their past. I knew of no suitable role for myself, which left me minimally participatory in activities other than focusing on my own research in progress. My mind was constantly preoccupied with the doctrines of assimilation and cultural homogenization, and with theories of modernization vs. traditionalism. At the time, though I received logistical support, there were no professional opportunities that would generate income locally, nor was I eligible to draw on grants available to my fellow graduate students (Americans and Europeans). Of course, there were also questions about the methodology I applied and my own concern about synthesizing and or analysing the data I was collecting.

Conducting research as a medical anthropologist beginning in 2000, I have neither been concerned nor been subjected to any of the above conditions. However, while I was not much concerned about the number of anthropologists who would critique my work locally and internationally in the 1990s, now I am quite concerned about criticisms coming from all directions with every step I take, for I have been working in health-related areas that boast many experts with defined scientific parameters, measurements, and measuring 'tools'. In a parallel way, I think that with the increasing number of indigenous anthropologists and the existing technologies for virtual communication, any anthropological fieldwork (indigenous or otherwise) will pose a daunting yet exciting prospect for the fresh generation of anthropologists.

Another contributing factor to my relatively easy task in conducting health-related research in Iran could be that ever since the latter nineteenth century, Western, modern educational institutions – from elementary grades through to post-secondary and graduate training – all have increasingly pitched themselves to vocational and practical objectives. The aim has been to benefit individuals by preparing them for well-paid jobs and providing the respective societies/nations with more productive workforces and stronger economic output. Thus it is market forces that have, at least in the past several decades, driven education in this direction. Since Iran's perceived needs were determined by Westerners or Iranians operating under Westerners' sociocultural/sociopolitical influence, Iran promoted 'vocationalism'. In fact the educational systems of those influencing Iran's political scene have entered an era where it is not ideas but money that matters. Whereas the social sciences might be seen as promoting ideas, vocational courses are associated with money. In my view such perceptions and associations have played significant roles, all contributing to the failure of the social and behavioural sciences to blossom in Iran.

The international community of scholars in the social sciences interested in Iran is rather small, too. Several factors contributed to the lack of growth in the number of North American trained social and behavioural scientists with research interests in Iran in the 1980s and 1990s, most notably: the small number of Iranian students in U.S. universities in this period, Iranian students' lack of interest in the social and behavioural sciences, the difficulties involved in carrying out fieldwork in Iran, and a lack of interest, perhaps even a calculated disinterest, in recruiting and retaining students interested in Iran on the part of some faculties and administrators in the United States.

In the absence of a strong cohort of younger social scientists working in Iran, locally successful preceptors and mentors for guiding fieldwork could not be developed. Thus it is necessary for everybody to start from zero in the field in Iran. This includes not only overcoming the lack of a cohort and a professional tradition but, as mentioned earlier, also includes dealing with reluctant bureaucrats and lacking administrative procedures for permits and support, as well as addressing a mass culture that reflects negative attitudes towards social scientists. In my view these gaps must be bridged. It seems that the insiders are not going to trust the outsiders; and the outsiders may not view the insiders as competent or politically interested in building a trusting professional working relationship. Iranians who have gained the trust and respect of the insiders as well as the support of the outsiders can play a major role in this process. I believe that the conference in Frankfurt in 2004 was a good start. Regular regional and/or intercontinental gatherings could gradually iron out many of the politically created differences. I suggest that anthropologists living and working within Iran also arrange a conference in Iran (I was pleased to learn that one such conference has been arranged in Iran since I wrote the first draft of this essay), and perhaps a series of lectures on the importance of social and behavioural sciences to be delivered on various campuses in Iran. Finally, I am hoping that within the next few years I may be able to start such activities with a focus on health and can find ways to connect it to the social sciences in general and anthropology in particular.

Perspectives on the Future of Anthropology and Anthropological Studies in Iran

In conclusion, I wish to make a number of recommendations on where to go from here. In light of the difficulties I experienced in the field, I consider it necessary for anthropologists conducting research in Iran to work towards changing the ambivalent public view about social scientists. On the personal level, we ought to be prepared to engage officials as well as ordinary people in discussions about our work. In the interim there is a pressing need for large-scale production of brochures and flyers to publicize facts on anthropology and anthropologists. Such materials designed to create awareness among the public and officials can be disseminated at universities and other related institutions through the proper channels. Moreover, such media could be utilized to expose officials as well as the public to our published work.

On the academic level, attempts should have been made long ago to reach out to Iranian social scientists working in Iranian universities through collaborative work (for example, by conducting research on certain aspects of a social or economic issue in which two or more scholars from within and outside of Iran could participate). Such collaboration would provide an opportunity for the growing number of educated Iranians who show interest in our work to inform themselves of the value of what we do. Obviously, collaborative work may mean one thing in the Western academic environment and other things in Iran, ranging from a political agenda to access to funds to securing a visa to the United States. However, these differences can be worked out.

To bridge the existing gulf in understanding, social scientists in general and anthropologists in particular need to walk a fine line of diplomacy. Although most contacts between foreign and native scientists that I know of in the last few years have been positive, I am aware of cases in which the conduct of a foreign anthropologist led to conflicts that angered and isolated native anthropologists – the very scholars who could serve as cultural brokers and facilitators of collaborative partnerships and professional networks. Overall, though, in the complex, dynamic cultural situation in Iran today, anthropologists and other social scientists need to avoid working in isolation. Researching the new social realities of Iran requires new tools and techniques, new methodologies. In addition we should apply currently available technological tools to accomplish this goal.

Some twenty years ago anthropologists working in Iran collected data in isolation, often disconnected from the rest of world for months and years. They went to the field equipped with the latest theoretical frameworks and methodologies, but by the time they returned to their office much might have changed. They often struggled between what they knew when they departed for the field and what they learned upon return to be able to make sense of their data. It frequently took months and years for the anthropologists to analyse their data and publish their findings. This often meant that they had to return to their respective institutions and use the resources (library, etc.) available to them to analyse and write up their findings.

Today, different technological facilities are available in Iran. Through wireless phone services one can easily connect with any colleague in any part of the world. In most cases one can also connect, via the internet, from almost any village in any part of the country. Thus it is possible to put a burning question or a pressing idea to a colleague in a matter of minutes and benefit from feedback and inputs immediately. Hence, new communication technologies can save anthropologists from living and working in isolation. I urge anthropologists working on projects in Iran to make use of the currently emerging and already available technologies. To that end, I suggest establishing virtual centres using the latest available technologies, such as web-based tools with chat rooms and virtual discussion board capabilities, through which ideas can be exchanged and dialogued instantly. Researchers and students with similar interests thus can get acquainted with one another and perhaps even start working together collaboratively. Such tools can also house an electronic index of projects or perhaps maintain electronic copies of major anthropological work on Iran. Regarding methodology, theoretical frameworks and new research proposals, the application of such a virtual centre can benefit anthropologists in many ways, providing an opportunity for collaborative projects, stimulating and generating new ideas for old concepts and sparking university students' interest in the field of anthropology – particularly if the applied aspects of this field are presented. In general this should reflect a team-oriented approach and collaborative spirit.

In recent years the atmosphere in Iran's universities has been changing. In 2003 several university officials told me that they were directed to promote collaborative research with foreign scholars. Consequently, there is less fear among Iranian scientists of contact with anthropologists outside the country. Now it may become possible to exchange individual and private research practices for collaborative enterprises with Iranian social scientists to benefit our scholarly community as a whole, rather than just individual researchers. While advocating collaborative work, I am also cognizant of our individualistic field-related culture – after all, we are talking about anthropologists, not laboratory scientists – where people work in continuous shifts to get the work done. Nonetheless, despite the advantages and disadvantages of being an indigenous/native or non-native anthropologist, I believe one's weaknesses could be another anthropologist's strength. We therefore should work together to shift the focus from the current individualistic approach to a team-based collaborative endeavour. I sincerely believe that Dr Shahnaz Nadjmabadi's efforts in bringing us together in Frankfurt paved the way for such an endeavour. We must now follow it through to the next conference and beyond.

NOTES

1. The Qashqa'i comprise about half a million Turkish-speaking ethnic tribespeople in southwestern Iran. They were once predominantly nomadic pastoralists, but their lifestyle started changing in the 1950s. Some families still migrate and are recognized as 'ashayir-e sayyar' (migrating nomads). The nomadic lifestyle provided cultural symbols, sentiments and memories, passed on from one generation to the next. Previously, Qashqa'i youths did not have many non-Qashqa'i cultural experiences. Then, in the 1950s, a state-supported literacy programme, adapted to the nomadic way of life, was introduced. By the late 1970s it had provided literacy skills to more than a hundred thousand Qashqa'i. The Iranian Revolution in 1979 interrupted the literacy programme (Kazimi 1990; Sohrabi 1995) but created fertile ideological ground for self-reflection and an opportunity for formally educated Qashqa'i tribespeople to reflect upon their cultural assumptions – their 'Qashqa'iness' – as well as their current and future roles and activities in their own and wider Iranian society.

2. Qashqa'i tribespeople migrated seasonally in groups of households. The activities involved in migrating provided meanings for cultural symbols, sentiments and memories. The people reproduced their culture and taught their offspring. For a detailed description of one such cycle, see Shahbazi 1989.

3. For work on Qashqa'i culture, see for example Beck (1991), Kayani (1992) and Ruhani (1992).

4. While it is difficult to define popular culture, my understanding is that popular culture prevails in any given society. It results from the daily interactions, needs and desires that make up the daily lives of the mainstream. It typically includes any number of practices, including those pertaining to cooking, clothing, mass media and the many facets of entertainment, including sports, arts, literature and so on.

REFERENCES

Amanolahi-Baharvand, S. 1991. *Qum-i Lor: Pizhuhishi dar barih-yi payvastagi-yi qumi va parakandagi-yi joghrafiyayeiyi Lorha dar Iran*. Shiraz.

Barth, F. 1961. *Nomads of South Persia: The Basseri Tribe of the Khamseh Confederacy*. London.

——. 1969. 'Introduction', in F. Barth (ed.), *Ethnic Groups and Boundaries: The Social Organization of Culture Difference*. Long Grove, IL: 9–38.

Beck, L. 1986. *The Qashqa'i of Iran*. New Haven, CT.

——. 1991. *Nomad: A Year in the Life of a Qashqa'i Tribesman in Iran*. Berkeley, CA.

Fahim, H. (ed.). 1982. *Indigenous Anthropology in Non-Western Countries*. Durham, NC.

Fahim, H. and K. Helmer. 1980. 'Indigenous Anthropology in Non-Western Countries: A Further Elaboration', *Current Anthropology* 21(5): 644-63.

Jones, D.J. 1970. 'Towards a native anthropology', *Human Organization* 29: 251–59.

Kayani, M. 1992. *Siyah chadorha: Tahqeqi dar zindagi-yi mardom-i il-i Qashqa'i*. Shiraz.

Kazimi, S. A. 1990. 'Tavanaeiha va natavanaeihay-i amuzish va parvarish 'ashayir az aghaz ta inqilab-i Islami', MA thesis. Shiraz: Shiraz University.

Motzafi-Haller, P. 1997. 'Native Anthropologists and the Politics of Representation', in Deborah Reed-Danahay (ed.), *Auto/ethnography: Rewriting the Self and the Social*. Oxford: 169–95.

Naryan, K. 1993. 'How Native is a "Native" Anthropologist?' *American Anthropologist* 95: 671–86.

Tapper, R. 1979. *Pasture and Politics: Economics, Conflict and Ritual among Shahsevan Nomads of Northwestern Iran*. London.

——. (ed.). 1993. *The Conflict of Tribe and State in Iran and Afghanistan*. London.

Ruhani, F. 1992. *Chadorha-yi siyah: Pizuhishi piramun-i jami'ah va iqtisad-i 'ashayiri-i il-i Qashqa'i*. Stockholm.

Shahbazi, M. 1989. 'Formal Education, Schoolteachers, and Ethnic Identity among the Qashqa'i of Iran', Ph.D. dissertation. St. Louis, MO: Washington University.

Sohrabi, A. 1995. *Amuzish va parvarish dar 'ashayir-i Iran*. Shiraz, Shiraz University Press.

CHAPTER 9

Anthropological Research in Iran

Lois Beck

Introduction

I base this chapter on my experience as a cultural anthropologist in Iran, and among Iranians, over a span of forty-six years. I began research in Iran from 1963 to 1964, when I was an undergraduate student at Shiraz University. Then I conducted research in Iran for a doctoral dissertation from 1969 to 1971 and returned to the country on two occasions in 1977 to begin new projects. I continued research in Iran during twelve visits after the Revolution of 1978–79, first in 1979 and most recently in 2004. Since 1977, as part of an oral-history project, I have interviewed Iranians in Iran and abroad, many of whom are in involuntary exile in Europe and the United States. Although my discussion here pertains only to research *in* Iran, my time spent with Iranians outside the country has enriched my understanding of Iranian societies and cultures. I have cooperated on long-term projects with Iranian anthropologists in Iran and elsewhere and have worked with Iranian and foreign scholars on topics relating to the country.

Here I outline some interlinking issues in past and current anthropological research in Iran and suggest to future researchers there some ways to enhance the discipline. (The term 'anthropology' throughout this discussion refers to cultural and social anthropology.) Attendees of the conference on anthropology in Iran, held in Frankfurt (Germany) in 2004, have continued since then to consider solutions to the problems we all face.[1] I discuss theoretical, methodological and ethical issues but do not aim to review or critique the existing literature and do not always provide references. If I mention, for example, that some anthropologists use the present tense in their writings to describe societies in the past, I do not necessarily cite published examples. In addition, people at the conference offered varying views that published work does not always depict, and I comment on these perspectives as well.

I do not address here many of the practical matters related to research and writing, such as visas for foreigners, institutional support in Iran and abroad, research stipends and family circumstances. Some contributors to this volume address these points, as do some authors in the special issue of *Iranian Studies* (2004) on ethnographic research in Iran. However important these topics are for individual researchers, focus on them can detract from fundamental intellectual, theoretical, analytical, methodological and ethical issues.[2]

Misconceptions about Anthropological Research

Some scholars (including some young anthropologists) and others may not fully understand the anthropological research that foreigners and Iranians have conducted in Iran. In their writings and discussions, they often imply that if an anthropologist engages in research within a community, the written results describe only that community and are irrelevant for other purposes. Even if an anthropologist studies in a specific place, or among a specific population, the resulting work can be as problem-oriented, analytical and comparative as other kinds of studies. The research that a few scholars in the early 2000s denounce as 'village and community studies' or 'studies of villages, tribes and nomads' does not necessarily aim to describe small communities. Instead, researchers usually focus on certain topics, such as occupational changes or new forms of spatial mobility. Anthropologists often undertake such studies in local communities, for reasons related to the perspectives and methodologies of the discipline, but may not intend to describe such places or peoples. William Beeman (1986), for example, conducted research in a village north of Shiraz, but his book concerns the sociolinguistics of the Persian language in Iran and tells us little about the place he visited.

Many of the major anthropological studies on Iran, based on research conducted mostly in the 1960s and 1970s by foreigners and Iranians, demonstrate an interest in certain topics and are not necessarily or strictly descriptive works. Anthropologists who studied kinship patterns in Iran, for example, could have lived in rural Azerbaijan or in an upper-class urban neighbourhood; their point of focus is kinship and not the specific setting. (Of course, the setting and its history and social organization affect the *kinds* of kinship practises found in each place.) Christian Bromberger's distinction between 'local studies' (studies of a community) and 'localised studies' (studies of a topic conducted in a place) is apt here.[3]

Despite these misconceptions, the anthropology of Iran has not been as problem-oriented as it could be. Yet, many scholars are already adjusting their focus to encompass a wide range of topics and perspectives (as witnessed by this volume's chapters and the new literature on which their authors draw).

Anthropologists and Other Scholars

Anthropologists and other scholars on Iran (particularly historians and political scientists) do not always rely on one another's work. Their frames of reference and methodologies do differ, but other factors are also pertinent. These two groups of scholars could benefit from one another's work if they each paid more attention to the sectors of society that they otherwise often neglect.

Many anthropologists do not adequately examine broad, nationwide issues in their usually local-level studies. Hence, other scholars often disregard their work or consider it to be inapplicable to their own; they tend to focus on national events and issues and may assume that circumstances at the local level and outside the capital of Tehran are unimportant to their scholarly pursuits. For example, those who study the ruling elite in Tehran do not usually address the broader social spectrum of the country. They rarely invoke the rich complexity of Iranian society, even though this complexity has national implications. Most historians and political scientists who write about the Revolution of 1978–79, for instance, ignore the small but still readily available anthropological literature on the activities of Iranians in different parts of the country during that period and afterwards.

Many scholars who are not anthropologists tend to regard (explicitly and implicitly) the citizens of Iran as 'Persians' who are integrated (to a greater or a lesser extent) in the nation-state. They often use the terms 'Iranians' and 'Persians' interchangeably, as if they are synonymous. If they acknowledge other categories of Iranians (such as Turks and Kurds), they often consider them to be Persianised and assimilated, and they equate Iran with Shi'a Islam and the 'Persian' culture despite the importance of other religions and other cultures in the country.[4] By contrast, anthropologists often describe and discuss the diversity and complexity of Iran's societies and cultures, which manifest varying socioeconomic, political, social organizational, regional, ethnic, linguistic, religious, tribal, educational, occupational and gender traits. They explain the ways people actually lived at the local level, a focus that other scholars tend not to have.

A political scientist, for example, may note that a certain percentage of Iranian citizens voted in a presidential election and may speculate on the reasons for the high or the low turnout. An anthropologist may know the voting patterns of a specific region and the reasons that people gave for their participation or absence at the polls. By situating this information in a wider context, aided by the political scientist's writings, the anthropologist can then explain how and why this region differs from or is similar to other parts of the country and can augment the political scientist's formulations. As another example, Bahman Baktiari (a political scientist) examines Iran's postrevolutionary parliaments (1996) and follows trends in sequential parliamentary sessions by connecting them with national politics. In conducting research on specific parliamentary deputies and their electoral campaigns, I saw that Baktiari's and my separate pursuits could be mutually beneficial. He understands the parliament as a whole; I study specific regions and the interests of their residents in parliamentary representation. In a further instance, I saw the utility of a discussion of anthropological methods and materials for linguists who studied endangered Iranian languages, and I too have benefited from the wealth of information they are collecting and analysing.[5] Some young scholars – such as Arang Keshavarzian (a political scientist) who used anthropological (and other) techniques to study the contemporary Tehran bazaar (2007) – demonstrate the productivity of interdisciplinary efforts.

Comparative and Problem-oriented Studies

The anthropologists of Iran tend to focus on only a single localised community (whatever their topic of study) and do not engage in or draw on comparative studies, done elsewhere in Iran and in other countries, as much as they could. They do not usually rely on the frameworks and analyses of anthropologists who conduct research elsewhere in the world. As anthropologists become more problem-oriented and less interested in describing specific communities, such comparative approaches become essential. By applying a wider literature to their research in Iran, they would appeal to a broader audience than they have found in the past. Some scholars comment that the anthropologists of Iran have not contributed much to anthropology in general. A certain truth lies in this statement, in part because these anthropologists do not often enough tie their findings to a wider literature.

Few anthropologists analyse specific topics as they pertain to two or more sectors of Iranian society. One exception is Philip Salzman, who compares his observations of nomadic pastoralists in Baluchistan with the reports of scholars on similar peoples in other parts of Iran (and in the wider Middle East and beyond). In focusing on ecology, economics and sociopolitical organizations, Salzman (2000, 2004) offers insights about how and why pastoralists differ from or are similar to one another. Janet Bauer (1983) conducted research in Tehran and four rural areas on the topic of rural-urban migration. Soheila Shahshahani (2003) mentions the spatial dispersion of some Mamassani Lurs (a community she originally studied decades earlier) and suggests how anthropologists could expand their focus beyond a certain locale. Comparative studies based on research in multiple locales, in Iran and elsewhere, are productive. Ziba Mir-Hosseini's work on marriage and family law in Iran and Morocco (1993) illustrates the benefits of multiple sites for research.

Examples of potential, problem-oriented studies in Iran, possibly conducted in more than one location, could include many kinds of topics, such as: state-directed Islamization and local religious practices, forms of resistance and protest, sources of societal conflict and integration, crises in local political leadership, emerging forms of gender politics, expanding emphases on ethnic identity and affiliation, divergent notions of Iranian nationalism, local economic transformations related to national and global markets, environmental conservation and sustainable livelihoods, new educational institutions (such as independent, *azad,* universities), new governmental ministries (such as Jihad Sazandegi) and parastatal agencies (such as charitable foundations), changing forms of communication (such as use of the internet), emerging nongovernmental organizations (NGOs) and new publications serving special interests (such as those published in languages other than Persian).[6] Even a limited study, such as Niloofar Haeri's on the clothing of Muslim clerics in Iran (2005), offers intriguing issues for comparison and analysis. Some studies may be difficult to pursue, such as the pilgrimages of Iranians to Shi'a shrines in Iraq.

Fariba Adelkhah's book, *Being Modern in Iran* (2000), offers an example of the changing face of anthropology in Iran. She discusses trends related to evolving political cultures and describes a society undergoing revolutionary changes and modernization. She does not base the study in one community but, rather, draws information from diverse sources, mostly published (such as newspapers). The book focuses on political events centred in Tehran but could also have included some perspectives outside the capital. Shahram Khosravi's work (2008) on emerging forms of politicised culture among Tehran's alienated youth is another example of new approaches.[7]

Local-level Studies and the Wider Context

Anthropologists need to examine the wider context of their usually local-level or localised studies. They could show how local communities relate to regions, provinces, the nation-state and, where relevant, the Middle East, the Muslim world and the international arena. Yet, descriptions of life at the local level, however related to this wider scope, will probably remain the strength of anthropology in Iran for the near future.

The works of historians, political scientists, journalists and autobiographers often present Iran as a relatively homogeneous country, society and culture. If only to broaden the scope and encourage a more realistic depiction, anthropologists could influence other writers more than they currently do. They could contribute to the wider literature by connecting the local setting to the regional and national context and by drawing on the works of other kinds of scholars to understand better this broader dimension. Over time, scholars and writers who are not anthropologists may come to appreciate Iran's rich diversity and may learn about peoples and regions with which they had been unfamiliar.

While writing a book on postrevolutionary Iran (Beck n. d.), I saw that authors who examine this period (and who are not anthropologists) rarely consider the ways that national events affect local communities, especially beyond central and northern Tehran. I also found little relevant material in the small anthropological literature on this period and thus needed to rely on the works of historians, political scientists and journalists, despite their Tehran-focused approaches. A political scientist's report (2000) on the nationwide elections in 1999 for local councils (*shuras*), for example, notes that 'technocrats' won the majority of the seats in hundreds of municipalities.[8] The author did not define 'technocrat', a word whose application in different parts of Iran would likely vary. This general study is informative, but I also wanted to read about a few specific councils to understand better why, in any given place, certain people ran for election and why they won or lost. The identities of the candidates (birthplace, gender, ethnicity, socioeconomic background, formal education, occupation and political affiliation) and their platforms are also important. I needed to compare my findings on specific councils (where no 'technocrats', however defined, were elected) with information from other parts of Iran, but comparable publications did not exist.

The kinds of information and insights that anthropologists gain for the communities they study are important for other scholars who, at least until now, focus primarily on national events and issues without discussing similarities across or variations within Iran. In writing about postrevolutionary Iran, I saw that the circumstances I could confirm for one part of the country did not always accord with published material about Iran as a whole. Was the situation I had observed over a long period relatively unique? Or did the authors of purportedly nationwide studies ignore circumstances outside certain sectors of Tehran?

The Purpose of Anthropological Research and Writing

The issue of the purpose of anthropology was like a camel browsing in the conference room in Frankfurt in 2004. We all saw it, but no one acknowledged its presence. What is the aim of anthropological research and writing as they pertain to Iran? Why do anthropologists pursue these activities? Who gains from these endeavours? Does anthropological research address the needs of the studied communities? How does applied anthropology relate to and differ from other forms? Who are the audiences for anthropological writings? What publications and reports are appropriate, and for what purposes? How could anthropologists expand their writings in new directions? I address some of these questions here; contributors to this volume discuss others.

Anthropological research without the next step – dissemination of the findings – is on some level meaningless. A researcher may enjoy the work, but without others benefiting from the effort, it remains a solitary, personal venture, similar perhaps to tourism. Some anthropologists engage in one research project after another without distributing the results. Possibly despite their intentions, all anthropologists have material they have never compiled, analysed, written, published or displayed (such as in films and museum exhibits). Anthropologists who are also teachers and lecturers do have another forum for their work. Even if they only teach and lecture, they may positively influence their audiences.

Anthropologists conduct research in Iran for a variety of reasons. Some want to draw attention to societal problems (such as the negative impact of gender-biased laws) and may regard their work as a step towards lessening them. Others frame their studies more broadly to address critical global issues, such as public health crises and people's responses to desertification, and their work may have policy implications. Some anthropologists want to chronicle diverse societies and cultures in Iran and may seek an audience only within Iranian studies and the discipline, while others may also address a wider range of scholars in Middle Eastern and Islamic studies. Some projects (such as the study of a local craft) may have few ramifications unless researchers also consider broader frameworks (such as the transformation of economic practices). Some cultural anthropologists say that any gathered information has intrinsic value, perhaps in the future if not currently. They liken their data to those excavated and analysed by archaeologists, each coin and seed and fabric-imprinted shard being potentially valuable to them.

Many kinds of approaches, methods and writing styles exist in anthropology, which anthropologists and others identify (accurately or not) by a vast array of sometimes overlapping terms: scientific, empirical, ecological, demographic, descriptive, comparative, analytical, dialogic, interpretive, autobiographical, self-reflexive, critical and postmodernist (including culture studies). How do these and other perspectives in anthropology relate to the ways anthropologists, other scholars and general readers regard the disseminated results? Reflexive and postmodernist anthropology seems, on the surface, to offer less to other kinds of scholars than do other approaches, particularly descriptive, comparative and analytical ones. Yet, such innovative forms may appeal to a broad, nonscholarly audience, including people who might not otherwise be interested in Iran.

In *Reading Lolita in Tehran* (2003), Azar Nafisi (who is not an anthropologist) demonstrates how an accessible approach to controversial issues can draw intense interest around the world. Autobiographies such as hers explain specific situations and times in comprehensible fashion.[9] Shirin Ebadi's memoir (2007) offers a vivid account of her life in Iran leading up to her receiving the Nobel Peace Prize in 2003. In *Blood and Oil* (2005), Manucher Farmanfarmaian and Roxane Farmanfarmaian provide rich descriptions of the historical circumstances under which their large extended family lived.

In anthropology, some autobiographical approaches include personal details for no scholarly purpose, especially when the works contain little sociocultural information or analysis.[10] When personal information seems warranted, as when Ziba Mir-Hosseini (2002) discusses her research on divorce and women's rights, it adds substance to the account. Similarly, Shahla Haeri (1989: 12) explains how her identities as an Iranian, a woman and an ayatollah's granddaughter facilitated her research on temporary marriage (*sigheh*) among Shi'a Muslims in Iran.[11] As a third illustration, Asef Bayat states that his origins in an impoverished community in Iran contributed to his study of poor people's movements there: 'I consider my own life experience to be the single most important source of my insights and data' (1997: xiii). For some other Iranian anthropologists, and for most non-Iranian anthropologists who conduct research in Iran, personal and biographical details may serve no purpose in their writings and could be avoided if they contribute little substance or value to the works.

So far, only a few anthropologists of Iran have made their work accessible to wide audiences, and not all anthropologists want to focus their efforts in this direction. Ziba Mir-Hosseini's popular documentary films on Iran (made in collaboration with K. Longinotto), *Divorce Iranian Style* (1998) and *Runaway* (2001), show the impact of societal problems on individuals and enable general as well as specialist audiences to understand the circumstances. Erika Friedl's *Women of Deh Koh* (1991) attracts a larger audience than perhaps any other anthropological publication on Iran. The author's engaging writing style, and the book's brevity and content (stories of twelve village women), make the volume intriguing to many. Christian Bromberger's discussion of Iranian soccer (1998) could potentially reach many readers if he expanded it as a short volume. A few anthropologists of the Middle East (but not Iran) write fiction that reaches a wider audience than their analytical work does.[12] For these kinds of works, English is the most accessible language and thus draws international attention.

I do not suggest that anthropologists concentrate on writing for general audiences. Yet, many of them could occasionally write less specialised pieces, if only to reach people who might not otherwise read about Iran or who are exposed only to negative stereotypes about the country and its people. My article 'With My Daughter' (1993) offers a positive portrayal of one sector of Iran, draws the interest of Westerners, and appeals to Iranians, especially those who resent the negative images in the book *Not Without My Daughter* (Mahmoody 1987) and the film based on it.[13]

Some anthropologists of Iran state that their main audiences should be scholars and academics within the discipline. Yet, if the attendees at the 2004 conference had taken a poll on the anthropological works they each admire, the gathering would not have agreed on any single publication. Some anthropologists criticize studies of 'folklore', others dislike descriptions of material culture, some decry applied research projects, others disparage postmodernist writings, some object to research on Iranians abroad, others complain about studies of Tehran's youth, some dismiss fictionalised stories with narrative plots and others reject studies of 'nomads, tribes and villagers' ('the dead past', they say).[14] Even the issue of defining anthropology raises spirited debate. Some who say that anthropologists should direct their writings towards other anthropologists do not agree on the purpose and content of this work or the forms it should take.

One way (among others) to understand the many different perspectives in the research and writing of anthropologists on Iran is to account for their locations and circumstances. For the analytical purpose of the discussion here, these anthropologists fall into three broad categories (each of which is heterogeneous): Iranians living in Iran, Iranians living abroad and foreigners. Some attendees at the conference raised distinctions (subtly or explicitly and sometimes contentiously) between and among anthropologists based on these categories. I focus here on written work, because research by itself means little unless it results in some accessible medium. Also, we can compare the publications of anthropologists; we may never know about the specifics of the actual research.

The first group of anthropologists – Iranians living in Iran – has more intimate, day-to-day knowledge of the country than the two other groups. Many of them have written prolifically, almost always in Persian, about different sectors of Iran (see Fazeli 2006). Yet, Iranian anthropologists, as well as foreign scholars who know Persian, rarely cite this vast literature in their own writings, perhaps because the works are not widely known or available. Scholars in this first group may have difficulty orienting their writings to other anthropologists and other kinds of scholars, in part because they do not often take a comparative or problem-oriented approach, and they may sometimes lack the distance often necessary to view society and culture analytically and dispassionately. They tend to take for granted the facts and circumstances familiar to them and offer insufficient explanations for non-Iranian readers. They experience firsthand the difficulties of living through troubling times, which influence the direction and content of their research and writing. Concerned about political and other repercussions from employers and governmental officials, they are cautious in choosing topics and sites of research and in publishing certain information. They face problems in writing in languages other than Persian and in reaching publishers and audiences outside of Iran. Some lack the international networks of scholars on which the second two groups rely. The internet has been changing this situation for them.

The second group – Iranians living abroad – sometimes faces similar problems in taking the familiar circumstances of Iran for granted, but these anthropologists understand more clearly the kinds of information that non-Iranian readers require. They too cope with difficult situations, which for some of them include leaving their homeland, adjusting to life abroad and facing possible discrimination there. Those who were born or raised abroad (a rapidly growing group) may also undergo problems there because of their country of origin and their political, ethnic and religious identities. These difficulties may influence their choices of topics and research locations, but these scholars are better positioned than those in the previous group to write openly about actual conditions in Iran. They may be more amenable to innovative forms of writing than those in the previous group, if only because the trends in the countries where they reside influence their work. They benefit from having access to international networks of scholars and research institutions. They may not have ready access to publications appearing only in Iran and only in Persian, and increasing numbers of those born or raised abroad do not read Persian.

Some of the distinctions between these two categories reflect ideological, political and personal issues that are found among Iranians in general. Those who stayed in Iran experience the consequences of the change in regimes, and some of them express strong sentiments about those who left and created new lives for themselves abroad.

The third group – foreign anthropologists – does not have the understanding of and intimacy with Iran that most Iranian anthropologists have, including those who live abroad but visit periodically. Its members lack the networks of family, kinship, neighbourhood, community, and socioeconomic class that often assist Iranians in their scholarly pursuits. (Some foreign anthropologists married to Iranians are able to tap into such networks.) Yet, foreign scholars have the advantage of distance, of potentially being able to analyse their findings more objectively (however the term is defined) than those in the two previous groups. They are perhaps better prepared to write for non-Iranian readers than those in the other groups; they understand the extent to which most non-Iranians lack even basic knowledge about Iran. They have access to publishers, especially those who produce works in languages other than Persian. Some in this group are privileged in their opportunities for employment, teaching, subsidised research and publishing. Some anthropologists in the two previous groups express ambivalent attitudes about the work of foreign anthropologists on Iran.

Each of these three groups faces its own challenges in writing for diverse audiences. They disagree with one another about how to write for fellow anthropologists. The dilemma they all face is to move from the intense experience of research to a written (or film) version of the work. Their professional (and personal) interests, the interests of the studied communities and those of the intended audiences may possibly conflict. Research and writing, however densely interrelated, are also two quite separate processes, which hardly any anthropologists of Iran have examined as such in print.

A final point in this section on the purpose of anthropology concerns the possibly negative and/or unintended results of some anthropological writings. State and foreign agencies as well as individual Iranians and foreigners might use the findings for their own nonscholarly, perhaps harmful, purposes. For example, a U.S. army lieutenant colonel (Eisenstadt 2007) draws on the scholarly publications of anthropologists and others to suggest ways to exploit the tribes of Iraq for the purpose of supporting the U.S. occupation there. Should anthropologists, then, avoid certain locations, populations and topics because such kinds of results are possible?

Journalists, photographers, filmmakers and authors of memoirs, travelogues and novels probably play a larger role than do anthropologists in disseminating information about Iran's diverse peoples that might prove damaging or detrimental to such peoples. Filmmakers in particular may depict sectors of Iranian society with which many Iranians and others are often unfamiliar. For example, the film *Gabbeh* (Makhmalbaf 1996), popular in Iran and abroad, presents romanticised images of Qashqa'i society and culture to previously uninformed audiences. As a consequence, eager tourists, both Iranian and foreign, want to experience the life they saw depicted on film. Yet, they seek out only those Qashqa'i who still live in goat-hair tents, migrate, weave textiles and otherwise manifest 'traditional' society – and who cannot afford to care for multitudes of unwelcome visitors.[15]

Applicability of Western Theories and Methods

Some social-scientific theories and methods developed in the West may apply to Iran, while others may not. Iranian anthropologists are positioned to assess these perspectives and judge their relative merits. At the turn of the twenty-first century, foreign as well as Iranian anthropologists face a world that differs substantially from the one that even their immediate predecessors had experienced. Some anthropologists and other scholars in the early 2000s criticise anthropological studies published only several decades previously. Yet, the political and social conditions that anthropologists underwent then were different, and the work of these scholars was similar to that conducted at the same time in other parts of the world.

Facing the new century, anthropologists have new and revised interpretative and analytical frameworks. Scholars often use certain terms to help them understand, describe and analyse the complex set of often changing (or emerging) processes they see in Iran. Such terms include tradition, modernity, ethnic and tribal resurgence, civil society, political reform, democratization, westernization, globalization, secularization, Islamization, conservatism, fundamentalism, nationalism, colonialism, neocolonialism and imperialism. What do these terms mean in a particularly Iranian context and in different sectors of Iranian society, and how do these meanings vary from their use by scholars elsewhere in the world? What are the current anthropological understandings about how and why societies and cultures change, in Iran and elsewhere, and what are the short-term and long-term consequences? Given the discipline's particular orientation, how are people at the local level affected by changes occurring in Iran as a whole? What impact did the Revolution and the war with Iraq (1980–88) have on the many dimensions of people's lives?

The scholarly (and general) controversy about certain processes seen (or imagined) at the national level occurs in the ongoing debates among Iranian intellectuals in Iran and abroad about the 'dialogue' between 'tradition' and 'modernity' and its consequences. What aspects of these processes do anthropologists pursue with regard to the local communities where they often conduct research? What alternative formulations do they suggest for the phrase 'the transition from tradition to modernity'? How do anthropologists explain the persistence of 'tradition' in modern contexts? How does 'tradition' serve the interests of people who are also adapting to modern elements of life?[16] A second set of issues concerns Iranian national and regional cultural identities and their various manifestations. How do the debates among Iranian scholars, writers and journalists in Iran and abroad on these two topics affect the work of Iranian and foreign anthropologists in Iran? Could the efforts of these two groups be mutually beneficial? Anthropologists have barely begun to raise these issues (but see Tapper's discussion in this volume, especially on Iranian film). Yet, they expect that the new generation of scholars will confront these tasks with some success.

Cooperation with People in the Studied Communities

If anthropologists could more effectively encourage and engage the coop-eration of people in their studied communities, the results would probably demonstrate a deeper understanding than is often apparent in most pub-lished studies. Ziba Mir-Hosseini (2002) explains the process as it relates to filming, but it also applies to ethnographic research and writing, as demon-strated in her study of the Muslim clergy (1999; see also Mir-Hosseini and Tapper 2006). Julia Huang formed close ties with Qashqa'i schoolchildren over a span of fourteen years as they grew up together and passed through the same stages in their formal education. Their joint projects, which dem-onstrate perspectives not found in the publications of formally trained adult anthropologists, contain insights that would interest scholars who study so-cialization and education in Iran.[17] Some anthropologists interact with local experts (such as historians, poets, linguists, musicians and weavers) in the societies where they conduct research. They could assist these individuals in the dissemination of their works, and future anthropologists might want to participate in joint projects with such experts.

Ethics

Ethical issues of all sorts, especially as they pertain to the people among whom anthropologists conduct research, relate to other points included in this chapter. During the 2004 conference, only several people explicitly raised the issue of ethics in research and writing, and so I address the topic here.[18]

One ethical issue concerns the relationship of Iranian and foreign an-thropologists to state institutions and international organizations in Iran. Anthropologists talk among themselves about the political implications of such contact and the way it may restrict research and writing, but they may not want to publicise their views more widely. International agencies in Iran and scholars who engage in applied research projects cannot avoid an as-sociation with the government. If the World Health Organization, for exam-ple, wants to settle nomads in newly constructed villages, what role (if any) should anthropologists play in assisting the effort? If the WHO offers fund-ing to anthropologists to conduct research preliminary to the settlement, how should these individuals respond, and what are the implications?

Another kind of ethical issue concerns confidentiality and anonymity and the ways that anthropologists treat personal, group and place names in their writings. They may use the actual names or decide to change, conceal or omit them. They need to explain their policies on these matters in every relevant publication.

After the Revolution of 1978–79, some anthropologists avoided using actual names in their publications on Iran, for political reasons, but they had often included the true names of the same people and places in their earlier writings. If the point of applying anonymity is to protect the people who interact with anthropologists, then this effort has failed. Any person or agency that wants to interfere with or harm these people could simply consult the earlier publications to discover who they are and where they are located. Also, many state agencies have *always* known the precise locations, schedules and activities of anthropologists and can easily connect almost any publication with the place where the research occurred, regardless of pseudonyms. These agencies (and their successors) are the ones most likely to act on this knowledge, perhaps in ways detrimental to the studied people. Regional and community elites also hold information about the activities of anthropologists; researchers often depend on their assistance and goodwill. Anthropologists worry about governmental officials acquiring information about their research and the people they study and acting on this information in harmful ways. Yet, state agencies already know the details. Does anonymity actually protect anyone, then, and what is the purpose of continuing the practice if it usually fails in its objective?

Academic institutions, professional organizations and funding agencies in the United States often oblige certain social scientists (and others) to abide by the rules of 'informed consent'. These scholars must inform (in writing) the people among whom they conduct research about the true purpose of their study, and they must guarantee them confidentiality. Having this information, people can presumably choose to consent to the study or not. Research in other countries, particularly non-Western ones, poses difficulties for this process, and the nature of anthropology makes the practicalities of research different from those in other disciplines. Specifically, anthropologists usually live within communities for extended periods, observe activities around them (regardless of the research topic), and talk with many people about multiple issues (again, regardless of the topic). Even if the studied people supposedly give their consent, they may not understand the implications (such as the government discovering damaging information and punishing them). Anthropologists who study within communities may consult leaders and other key figures, but they cannot seek consent from everyone with whom they interact. Most likely, individuals in any community will react differently to an anthropologist's presence and may or may not consent to participate if the anthropologist gives them an opportunity to do so.[19]

The photographs that anthropologists include in their publications (and films) raise similar ethical issues. Whose photographs do they use, have these individuals consented to the inclusion, and do people understand the role their images play in the work's impact?[20] During research, anthropologists do not know which of their photographs may be published and in what forums. If anthropologists invent pseudonyms, should their publications include photographs of the people so identified?[21] Would not such a practice negate the purpose of anonymity? Anthropologists should provide their publications to the people among whom they conduct research, especially so these people can be better informed in the future about their decisions concerning consent and anonymity.

One person attending the 2004 conference intentionally publicised the true names of places where other anthropologists conduct research in Iran. Without consulting these scholars first, the person divulged the actual names, despite the anthropologists over the years having told the people among whom they conducted research that they would never reveal their names or locations. This person asserted that Iranians, in particular, had a right to know precisely where anthropologists, especially foreigners, conduct research. Should the anthropologists in question continue to use pseudonyms if others disclose the actual names? Do colleagues in the same enterprise share certain expectations about their individual and collective responsibilities?

Another anthropological technique has related ethical implications. Without indicating explicitly that they have done so, a few anthropologists combine information about multiple people when they write about single individuals. By constructing composite characters, they may aim to protect the people with whom they interact, but by doing so they create fiction (and not factual social science) for readers.[22] If the people about whom some anthropologists write are fictional, do we presume that the circumstances of these characters are also falsely depicted?

Some anthropologists explain their techniques in their publications (in a footnote or a separate section on methodology), but others do not. Approaching a work, readers need to know if, and why, the anthropologist offered confidentiality to people, uses pseudonyms or not, creates composite characters, depicts accurately the surrounding circumstances and renders quoted remarks correctly (such as through use of audio-recorders). Readers must also know specifically when the anthropologist resided in or visited the community (see the discussion of this topic below).

On these issues, as well as others, anthropologists confront many dilemmas in research and writing. If, by their methods, they harm or otherwise disrupt the lives of the people with whom they interact, should they conduct research there at all? Who is served, or harmed, by their work? Do the benefits outweigh the detriments? What has their work contributed, and to whom, and at what cost?

Some anthropologists in Iran, including Iranians writing in Persian, conducted research in the 1960s and 1970s as if no one in the studied com-

munities would ever read the resulting publications and reports. More recently, most anthropologists understand that their work will eventually be
disseminated, even translated into Persian (usually without their knowledge
or permission), and could be read by those with whom they have talked.[23]
Such a perception will likely change the content of anthropological writing,
but will it also change the way research is done?

In 1963 I visited the Basseri tribal khans about whom Fredrik Barth
writes in *Nomads of South Persia* (1961). They possessed a copy of the book
and showed it to visitors. If my memory is correct, the khans noted that
Barth himself had sent them the volume. When I saw Barth's book in the
hands of his hosts, about whom he had so recently written, I learned a lesson early in my interest in Iran. I understood that anthropologists should
write responsibly about the people with whom they live and interact, and I
knew that some people about whom anthropologists write might read these
publications. Anthropologists conducting research in Iran do not share the
same views on this issue. Some agree; others do not. Some say that the integ-
rity of the 'science' supersedes the interests of the studied people.

Unlike Barth, not all anthropologists provide the results of their research to the people about whom they have written. If, from the start, anthropologists know that they will give their publications to their hosts, they
might consider differently the kind of research they conduct and the way
they depict the people among whom they live.

Yet, anthropologists also have other audiences and other purposes and
mandates, and the issue for them is the way they reconcile these often conflicting demands. A student writing a doctoral dissertation and hoping for
employment in academia afterwards occupies a different position from that
of an established scholar who does not need to publish to retain his or her
job. The scholar could easily omit sensitive material from a manuscript,
whereas the student might feel compelled to include it, to buttress his or her
argument.

Anthropologists will never solve all of the ethical problems they encounter, but they should try to promote and safeguard the interests of the
people with whom they talk. Through people's responses to their initial
publications, they can judge the community's sentiments and possibly adjust
their methods and writings.

Anthropologists as Historians

Anthropologists could be more historical in their research and writing than
many of them have been.[24] They could increase their efforts to understand
past events and circumstances, even when they focus on the most recent

period. Anthropologists who conduct longitudinal studies in Iran, based on multiple visits over a long span of time, tend to be more specific historically than some other anthropologists. Yet, some of them still present their anthropological writings ahistorically and do not place the research, the issues and the people in a historical context.

Writers using the 'ethnographic present tense' do not adequately address the issue of situating information within history. This problematic phrase describes the use of the present tense to convey information about the past, often the time when the anthropologist conducted the research. Some writers, but not all, explain that the ethnographic present tense refers to a certain period in the past, but this inclusion alone is not sufficient. The 'ethnographic *perfect* tense' (as it could be phrased) conveys the notion that anthropologists may be depicting an idealised, even romanticised, past through the use of the present tense. Readers imagine the events they see described in the present tense as if they are occurring 'now'. They may be more intrigued by the writing if they follow along with the anthropologist, who may attempt to show, through the present tense, how the events unfolded for her or him. Some anthropologists deploy the present tense as a way to ignore or conceal changes in society and culture that occurred before, during or after the period of research. Some, perhaps wanting to simplify the task of research and writing, avoid the effort of identifying events and circumstances by dates.

Even in writing about the most recent period, anthropologists must specify the time when they conducted research and must identify the events they describe by the years and by the wider circumstances. Sometimes, for accuracy in reporting, they need to be more specific by including the months and even days when they engaged in research.[25] When I sought information about changes in women's economic activities in different parts of Iran (especially outside of middle- and upper-class Tehran) after the Revolution – to augment chapters in a book on women (Beck and Nashat 2004) – I saw that some authors in the small existing literature do not specify when they visited the studied communities or when the events they describe occurred. The authors of two separate studies published in the mid-1980s, for example, do not state if they refer to the pre- or postrevolutionary period (and they do not indicate when they were present in the communities). Changes had certainly occurred in the two places after the Revolution, and thus specifying the period is important. A third work blends together information on the pre- and postrevolutionary periods without indicating which events occurred when. A fourth work does not specify the date when a certain institution (the researcher's focus) was founded and does not provide an account of its chronological development. If the author had been specific, other scholars would be able to place these circumstances in the context of other changes occurring in Iran at the time.[26] If anthropologists would include, at the very least, the dates of their visits, then readers can presume that the written results refer to that period.[27] Still, it is better to be explicit about both issues, the timing of the research and the period discussed and analysed.

One reason anthropologists conduct research is to explain life in Iran in certain places and at certain times. If they omit even basic information about the historical period, they limit their contribution to the understanding of the country. If a person diligently conducts research, consults documents, asks questions and takes notes, she or he can easily attach dates to the crucial events and circumstances, thus situating them in a wider historical context. If anthropologists took greater care in this matter, they would find that other kinds of scholars would appreciate their writings more and would utilize this work in their own. As it stands now, few historians, political scientists and other scholars on Iran draw on the work of anthropologists there. Thus, anthropologists have a reason, as well as an obligation, to improve this state of affairs.

Conclusion

Anthropology as a discipline has much to offer the study of Iran and its rich, complex societies and cultures. Especially given the fast pace of change, anthropologists are well positioned to examine the impact of national and global circumstances on different sectors of Iranian society, especially if they pay heed to broad issues and the work of other kinds of scholars. Many young scholars in Iran and abroad will carry forward the tasks in which their predecessors had engaged. They may find some earlier studies to be useful in their work, and they will devise new methodological and analytical approaches and new forms of writing.

Still, even after presenting these arguments, it could be said that the basis of anthropological research in Iran remains that of two people talking to one another about issues that concern them both. It is hard to improve upon this human exchange.

NOTES

1. I appreciate the efforts of Shahnaz Nadjmabadi and others at the Johann Wolfgang Goethe-Universität in Frankfurt (Germany) who organised the innovative conference 'Anthropological Perspectives on Iran' in 2004. Shahnaz Nadjmabadi, Christian Bromberger, Shahla Haeri, Mary Hegland, Julia Huang, Mary Martin and Richard Tapper offered helpful comments on drafts of this chapter.

2. Brian Spooner provides two comprehensive reviews of anthropology (1987) and ethnography (1999) as they pertain to Iran. Soheila Shahshahani (1986) and Nematollah Fazeli (2006) describe the development of the discipline by Iranians within Iran.

3. Christian Bromberger (personal communication, 8 April 2005).

4. Some historians consider Iran's cultural (and economic and political) diversity and complexity; see, for example, the works of Kaveh Bayat (2003, 2008), Houchang Chehabi (1997), Stephanie Cronin (2007) and Vanessa Martin (2005).

5. Seminar, 'Documenting Endangered Iranian Languages', Christian Albrechts-Universität, Kiel, Germany, 20–31 August 2007. I thank Geoffrey Haig for inviting me to participate.

6. When I suggested these topics at the 2004 conference, an Iranian anthropologist who resides in Iran responded: 'Foreign anthropologists can't study any of those issues in Iran, and Iranian anthropologists have other priorities'. He did not suggest alternatives for either group.

7. Roxanne Varzi's work (2006) is comparable; see also Nasrin Alavi's analysis (2005) of blogging by Iranians.

8. The author of this unpublished report requested that I not cite it. The report was still unpublished in 2009 (to my knowledge).

9. In *Jasmine and Stars* (2007), Fatemeh Keshavarz critiques Nafisi's approach.

10. One author (unnamed here) treats his readers to vivid descriptions of his digestive difficulties. To what purpose, a reader might wonder.

11. Multiple identities also assisted Shahla Haeri when she interviewed formally educated, professional Muslim women in Pakistan (2002).

12. See Nancy Lindisfarne (2000), Jenny White (2006, 2008) and Camilla Gibb (2007). Lindisfarne's book is about Syria, not Iran, where she has also done research. No anthropologists have yet published works on Iran that are 'fictional', comparable to the four books listed above. The fictionalization of anthropological material and the distinction between nonfictional and fictional writing are issues for another forum.

13. Many Iranians translated 'With My Daughter' into Persian and published it in a variety of forums; for example, see *Zan-e Ruz* (no. 1511, June 1995) and *Kayhan Havai* (nos. 1097–1101, Sept.–Oct. 1994, five installments). *Not Without My Daughter* (Gilbert 1991) is the film. Julia Huang (2009) offers her own account of growing up among Qashqa'i nomads in Iran.

14. Lack of space prevents me from elaborating on each of these broad fields. Some anthropologists object to compilations of folktales, for example, yet they might appreciate a contextualised analysis of selected tales (see Friedl 1978).

15. Lois Beck and Julia Huang (2006) describe the visits of domestic and foreign tourists to Qashqa'i territory. Modern industry is complicit in marketing images of an exotic Iran. The Japanese manufacturer Nissan created a 'concept' car in 2004, the 'Nissan Qashqai', as a vehicle for 'urban nomads' in the West.

16. One example concerns the rituals and symbolic discourses of modern Shi'a Islam (Aghaie 2005). In another example, a few Qashqa'i nomads in 2004 used mobile telephones to contact people within their increasingly dispersed kin and

tribal groups – a 'traditional' practice, but using modern technology, to enhance the importance of kin and tribal ties.

17. Julia Huang explains the context of this cooperation and describes her visits to schools in Iran (2006, 2009).

18. One conference attendee noted that only two foreign anthropologists raised ethical issues. Another person added that Iranian anthropologists face so many other difficulties that they cannot worry about this issue. Foreigners have the 'luxury', as he phrased it, of considering ethics, while Iranians do not. Yet, all anthropologists need to face these issues and try to abide by the discipline's established ethical standards. Richard Tapper discusses ethics in his chapter in this volume.

19. Shahnaz Nadjmabadi (2004) offers some examples.

20. Some Qashqa'i women asked me not to photograph them wearing the outer dress mandated by the Islamic Republic of Iran. Others permitted me to photograph them in such attire but asked me not to publish the images. In both cases, the women objected to wearing the state's mandatory dress and did not want outsiders to think that they had chosen this attire out of their own free will. I respected these and similar requests.

21. An example demonstrates the complications. An influential text for courses in anthropology is *Nisa* (Shostak 1983), an account of a woman in Africa. The author says that 'Nisa' is a pseudonym; the photograph of another, also unidentified, woman is depicted on the book's cover. Yet, a second book on the same woman (Shostak 2000) features a photograph of the real 'Nisa' on the cover.

22. The 'facts' may reside in many individuals, yet the composite person is fictional.

23. Officially, Iran does not abide by international copyright regulations. Translators and publishers in Iran make their own decisions without restriction, including altering texts, omitting authors' names and substituting the names of others. Such incidents also occur outside of Iran. At least two of my publications were republished in Europe under the names of other people but, in these cases, without the apparent complicity of the editors and publishers.

24. One exception is Richard Tapper, who writes historical as well as ethnographic studies of the Shahsevan in northwestern Iran (1979, 1997).

25. The timing of Mary Hegland's research offers an example. She conducted research in Iran from June 1978 to December 1979 (1983: 171–72) and witnessed the stages of the Revolution of 1978–79. In her case and others, the months must be included and sometimes also the days. An anthropologist who begins research, for example, at the end of August and concludes it at the beginning of October has not conducted three months of research 'in August, September and October'. Some anthropologists indicate the seasons, but does 'spring and summer' mean six months of research or perhaps only several weeks? Along with many others, I have not always been as specific as I should have been in this matter. Tending to be precise, journalists usually date and situate their interviews because they often pursue specific events (such as elections) and visit Iran only briefly. Most anthropologists in their publications do not date their interviews, in part because they talk with certain people on multiple occasions over a span of time. Still, they should list the timing and circumstances of cru-

cial discussions, especially if the subject matter relates to specific, time-bound events.

26. The problems I address are not unique to these four works or their authors, and I omit references to them.

27. In some cases, researchers were present only briefly or went to the research site periodically. This issue is pertinent for Iranian anthropologists who reside abroad and visit Iran to see their families. Foreign anthropologists in Iran may devote most of their time there to research, which may not be the case for visiting Iranian anthropologists.

REFERENCES

Adelkhah, F. 2000. *Being Modern in Iran*. New York.

Aghaie, K. (ed.). 2005. *The Women of Karbala: Ritual Performance and Symbolic Discourses in Modern Shi'i Islam*. Austin, TX.

Alavi, N. 2005. *We are Iran: The Persian Blogs*. Brooklyn, NY.

Baktiari, B. 1996. *Parliamentary Politics in Revolutionary Iran: The Institutionalization of Factional Politics*. Gainesville, FL.

Barth, F. 1961. *Nomads of South Persia: The Basseri Tribe of the Khamseh Confederacy*. London.

Bauer, J. 1983. 'Poor Women and Social Consciousness in Revolutionary Iran', in G. Nashat (ed.), *Women and Revolution in Iran*. Boulder, CO: 141–69.

Bayat, A. 1997. *Street Politics: Poor People's Movements in Iran*. New York.

Bayat, K. 2003. 'Reza Shah and the Tribes: An Overview', in S. Cronin (ed.), *The Making of Modern Iran: State and Society Under Riza Shah, 1921–1941*. London: 213–19.

———. 2008. 'Iran and the "Kurdish Question"', *Middle East Report* 38(2): 28–35.

Beck, L. 1993. 'With My Daughter: In Mountainous Iran, An Anthropologist's Five-Year-Old Child Adapts Quickly to Pastoral Life', *Natural History* 102(3): 6–13.

———. n. d. *Nomads Move On: Qashqa'i Tribespeople in Post-Revolutionary Iran*. Unpublished book manuscript.

Beck, L. and J. Huang. 2006. 'Manipulating Private Lives and Public Spaces in Qashqa'i Society in Iran', *Comparative Studies of South Asia, Africa and the Middle East* 26(2): 303–25.

Beck, L. and G. Nashat (eds). 2004. *Women in Iran from 1800 to the Islamic Republic*. Urbana, IL.

Beeman, W. 1986. *Language, Status, and Power in Iran*. Bloomington, IN.

Bromberger, C. 1998. 'Le football en Iran', *Sociétés et représentations* 7 (Dec.): 101–15.

Chehabi, H. 1997. 'Ardabil Becomes a Province: Center-Periphery Relations in Iran', *International Journal of Middle Eastern Studies* 29(2): 235–53.

Cronin, S. 2007. *Tribal Politics in Iran: Rural Conflict and the New State, 1921–1941*. London.

Ebadi, S. 2007. *Iran Awakening: One Woman's Journey to Reclaim Her Life and Country*. New York.

Eisenstadt, M. 2007. 'Iraq: Tribal Engagement, Lessons Learned', *Military Review* (Sept.–Oct.): 16–31.

Farmanfarmaian, M. and R. Farmanfarmaian. 2005. *Blood and Oil: A Prince's Memoir of Iran from the Shah to the Ayatollah.* 2nd ed. New York.

Fazeli, N. 2006. *Politics of Culture in Iran: Anthropology, Politics and Society in the Twentieth Century.* London.

Friedl, E. 1978. 'Women in Contemporary Persian Folktales', in L. Beck and N. Keddie (eds), *Women in the Muslim World.* Cambridge, MA: 629–50.

———. 1991. *Women of Deh Koh: Lives in an Iranian Village.* New York.

Gibb, C. 2007. *Sweetness in the Belly.* New York.

Gilbert, B. 1991. *Not Without My Daughter.* 107 minutes. United States.

Haeri, N. 2005. 'Clerical Chic', *The Guardian*, 5 January 2005. Retrieved 13 January 2005 from www.guardian.co.uk/print/

Haeri, S. 1989. *Law of Desire: Temporary Marriage in Shi'i Iran.* Syracuse, NY.

———. 2002. *No Shame for the Sun: Lives of Professional Pakistani Women.* Syracuse, NY.

Hegland, M. 1983. 'Aliabad Women: Revolution as Religious Activity', in G. Nashat (ed.), *Women and Revolution in Iran.* Boulder, CO: 171–94.

Huang, J. 2006. 'Integration, Modernization, and Resistance: Qashqa'i Nomads in Iran Since the Revolution of 1978–1979', in D. Chatty (ed.), *Nomadic Societies in the Middle East and North Africa: Entering the 21st Century.* Leiden: 805–39.

———. 2009. *Tribeswomen of Iran: Weaving Memories among Qashqa'i Nomads.* London.

Iranian Studies: Special Issue on Ethnographic Fieldwork in Iran (2004). 37(4).

Keshavarz, F. 2007. *Jasmine and Stars: Reading More than Lolita in Tehran.* Chapel Hill, NC.

Keshavarzian, A. 2007. *Bazaar and State in Iran: The Politics of the Tehran Marketplace.* Cambridge.

Khosravi, S. 2008. *Young and Defiant in Tehran.* Philadelphia, PA.

Lindisfarne, N. 2000. *Dancing in Damascus: Stories.* Albany, NY.

Mahmoody, B. with W. Hoffer. 1987. *Not Without My Daughter.* New York.

Makhmalbaf, M. 1996. *Gabbeh.* 75 minutes. Iran.

Martin, V. 2005. *The Qajar Pact: Bargaining, Protest and the State in Nineteenth-Century Persia.* London.

Mir-Hosseini, Z. 1993. *Marriage on Trial: A Study of Islamic Family Law. Iran and Morocco Compared.* London.

———. 1999. *Islam and Gender: The Religious Debate in Contemporary Iran.* Princeton, NJ.

———. 2002. 'Negotiating the Politics of Gender in Iran: An Ethnography of a Documentary', in R. Tapper (ed.), *The New Iranian Cinema: Politics, Representation, and Identity.* London: 167–99.

Mir-Hosseini, Z. and K. Longinotto. 1998. *Divorce Iranian Style.* 80 minutes. London.

———. 2001. *Runaway.* 87 minutes. London.

Mir-Hosseini, Z. and R. Tapper. 2006. *Islam and Democracy in Iran: Eshkevari and the Quest for Reform.* London.

Nadjmabadi, S. 2004. 'From "Alien" to "One of Us" and Back: Field Experiences in Iran', *Iranian Studies* 37(4): 603–12.

Nafisi, A. 2003. *Reading Lolita in Tehran: A Memoir in Books.* New York.

Salzman, P. 2000. *Black Tents of Baluchistan.* Washington, DC.

——. 2004. *Pastoralists: Equality, Hierarchy, and the State.* Boulder, CO.

Shahshahani, S. 1986. 'History of Anthropology of Iran', *Iranian Studies* 19(1): 65–86.

——. 2003. 'The Mamassani of Iran: At the Juncture of Two Modes of Subsistence', *Nomadic Peoples* 7(2): 87–97.

Shostak, M. 1983. *Nisa: The Life and Words of a !Kung Woman.* New York.

——. 2000. *Return to Nisa.* Cambridge, MA.

Spooner, B. 1987. 'Anthropology', *Encyclopaedia Iranica* 2: 107–16.

——. 1999. 'Ethnography', *Encyclopaedia Iranica* 8: 9–45.

Tapper, R. 1979. *Pasture and Politics: Economics, Conflict and Ritual among Shahsevan Nomads of Northwestern Iran.* London.

——. 1997. *Frontier Nomads of Iran: A Political and Social History of the Shahsevan.* Cambridge.

Varzi, R. 2006. *Warring Souls: Youth, Media, and Martyrdom in Post-Revolution Iran.* Durham, NC.

White, J. 2006. *The Sultan's Seal.* New York.

——. 2008. *The Abyssinian Proof.* New York.

CHAPTER 10

Being From There

Dilemmas of a 'Native Anthropologist'

Ziba Mir-Hosseini

Introduction

The Revolution of 1978–79 brought a rupture in anthropological studies of Iran. After more than a decade during which, at any one time, probably more than a score of non-Iranian anthropologists were engaged in field studies in the country, suddenly this 'field' was closed to them.[1] At the same time, for native Iranians, the 'Cultural Revolution' of the early 1980s closed the universities for two years and led to a restructuring of the curriculum in social sciences and their 'purification' from 'non-Islamic' elements, mainly done by purging 'corrupt and westernized' teachers and replacing them with 'honest and committed' ones, i.e. those able to teach from an 'Islamic' perspective.[2]

Meanwhile, anthropology as a discipline was grappling with the issue of authorial responsibility in ethnographic writing and such hoary dichotomies as insider/outsider, activist/scholar and observer/participant. The production of anthropological knowledge and texts was coming under increasing scrutiny; the old certainties and the 'scientific objectivity' of the classical anthropological texts had lost their authority. Anthropologists began to situate themselves in their texts, to tell something of their interactions with the 'natives' and the processes through which they came to construct their ethnographic accounts.[3] By the early 1980s a new genre of ethnography was emerging, which Barbara Tedlock (1991) calls 'narrative ethnography', reflecting a move from 'participant observation' to the 'observation of the participation'. This methodological shift not only made the public revelation of fieldwork experiences less of a taboo but also broke down the strict dichotomy between 'Self' and 'Other' (the ethnographer and the subject) – the hallmark of the 'objectivity' of the ethnographer, a token of the 'scientific' nature of the endeavour.[4] All this has been accompanied by the recognition of two important features of dialogue. First, it is in the dialogue between the ethnographer and the subject that the latter's 'culture' is produced. Second, dialogue, conversation and debate actually change the participants' views and perceptions – their 'culture' (Dennis Tedlock 1987). A new breed of ethnographers emerged who 'cannot be tucked away or pigeonholed within any of the four historical archetypes ... the amateur observer, the armchair anthropologist, the professional ethnographer, or the "gone native" field-worker'. They are interested 'in the co-production of ethnographic knowledge, created and represented in the only way it can be, within an interactive Self/Other dialogue'; and many of them 'are themselves subaltern because of their class, gender, or ethnicity' (Barbara Tedlock 1991: 82).

In what follows I explore the ways in which these developments in anthropology and my own involvement in the politics of gender in Islam have come to shape my experience of fieldwork and to shape the ethnographies (two of them documentary films) that I have produced since completing my doctoral thesis in 1980. I narrate the stories behind the production of my ethnographies not because I consider my own trajectory particularly important or representative of Iranian anthropology but because I think it highlights some of the issues central to the theme of anthropological perspectives on Iran. The central question that I want to explore is one that has occupied my mind since the early 1990s. What kind of ethnography can I produce as a 'native feminist' anthropologist? I use the term not only to indicate my Iranian identity, but in the sense of a certain consciousness, and the way in which it interacts with the anthropological and feminist epistemologies that are rooted in Euro-American traditions.

How I Turned to Anthropology

My conversion to anthropology was gradual. My first degree at Tehran University was in sociology; soon after graduation in 1974 I went to England to continue my studies. In 1976 I registered as a doctoral student in the Social and Political Sciences (SPS) at Cambridge University to do a thesis on the changing family structure in Iran under Esther Goody, an anthropologist of Africa with an interest in the family. All I knew then about anthropology came from a two-credit course in the third year of my BA, and from reading Henry Field's *Contributions to the Anthropology of Iran* (1939). Now, since my supervisor was from the Department of Social Anthropology, and since my research entailed fieldwork, I joined the departmental pre-fieldwork seminars and read and attended classes in anthropology. In 1977–78, I did fieldwork in Kalardasht, a picturesque mountainous district in northern Iran experiencing a tourism boom that had transformed previous agricultural land into a market commodity. When I was writing up my research, Esther was abroad and I was supervised by John Barnes, another distinguished an-

thropologist of Africa. Andre Beteille, an anthropologist of India who was
visiting the department that year, also read and commented on my work.
In my thesis, I explored the impact of the changed economy on marriage
rituals and family relations in four Kalardasht villages with different ethnic
compositions and varying degrees of exposure to tourism. In short, by June
1980, when I submitted my thesis, I was fully integrated into the anthropology department and had come to see myself as an anthropologist.

In late 1980 I returned to Iran, full of hope. In my late twenties, newly
married, my doctorate in hand, I looked forward to teaching anthropology and living happily with my new husband. Neither aim was to be fulfilled. Like many other Iranian women of my background, I found myself
rejected by the Islamic Republic soon after it became established and began
to restructure Iranian society. Soon after the reopening of the universities in
1983, I taught English for two semesters to social science students in Shahid
Beheshti University; meanwhile I applied for a teaching post in anthropology, which had to be done through the Committee of Cultural Revolution. I
was called for an interview to the committee's headquarters and appeared in
front of a small board, two members of which were sociology professors at
Tehran University whose courses I had attended as an undergraduate. The
interview went well. I was asked about my research and study in Cambridge
and was given the impression that they would welcome me as a colleague.
A week later, at seven in the morning, I received a call from the man in the
committee who had arranged the first interview, asking me to come for an
interview that very morning. 'I had my interview last week', I told him.
'That was the academic interview, this is the ideological one', he said. Later
I learned that applicants were called for their 'ideological interview' at the
very last minute so that they would not have time to prepare using the
booklets and pamphlets, sold in bookstalls in front of Tehran University,
containing a range of questions and the 'correct' answers for the ideological
tests that had become part of the university entrance exams.

For my 'ideological interview' I went to a different location from the
first one, wearing what I thought was proper dress: matching trousers and
overcoat (rū-pūsh), with a large scarf (rū-sarī) tightly tied under my chin
and no make-up, of course. After a short wait, I was ushered into a large
room. There were two tables in the room; I was directed to sit at the one
near the door. At the other table – at the far end of the room – sat my in-
terviewer. A large lamp hung over his table, leaving his face in shadow so
that I could not see him but only hear his voice. The interview lasted for
over two hours, in the course of which I was asked a gamut of questions. In
retrospect it is clear that these were meant to enable him to ascertain two
facts: my religious/ideological correctness and ability to teach anthropology
from what he called 'the Qur'anic perspective'. 'Why did you go to England

to study? Did you cover your hair when studying in England? How much of the Qur'an do you know by heart? How do you propose to study a social problem, such as divorce, in the perspective of Qur'anic anthropology?' My answer to each question was evidently problematic, leading to new ones, my answers to which became more and more incriminating. For instance, I said I had gone to England to study because my sister was living there, which led to a host of questions about her British husband and the reasons for their marriage, his line of work, his trips to Iran, etc. Similarly, not knowing that he had a file in front of him containing a report based on inquiries made from our neighbours about my conduct and appearance, I claimed that I had observed *hijab* while studying in England. This then led to a chain of questions that lasted for over half an hour wherein he tried to force my hand and I tried to cover my lie.

I did even worse when we moved on to teaching anthropology. What I did not appreciate then was that his questions were based on a theological concept of anthropology, the nature of human nature. My responses came from a different notion of anthropology, the study of human societies and cultures. The interview eventually came to a close when he asked me whether I prayed, and then to recite the *fatiha*, the Qur'anic verse that is recited in daily prayers. By this stage I was in a panic and when I had finished reciting the verse, I knew that I had missed something. I finally turned on him and protested angrily: 'Is this an interview or a trial? What are these questions for? Is it a crime to study abroad and to want to teach in one's own country?' His response, in a nutshell, was: 'Blood has been given for this Revolution, we want an Islamic university, and we cannot allow people like you, trained in the West, to teach in our universities.'

I relate this experience because it tells not only something of the way in which the advocates and operatives of the 'Cultural Revolution' in the early 1980s viewed both the subject of anthropology and women from my social background, but also something of the dissonance, of the gap, between us in our cultural assumptions and language. I came to feel the shock more intensely when my marriage broke down shortly after. The dismantling of the Family Protection Act shortly after the Revolution put me at the mercy of my husband: he refused to grant me a divorce or permission to leave the country. My only option was to negotiate my divorce in the new courts presided over by religious judges. I started to educate myself in Islamic family law, and I learned it well enough to secure my release.

I had come to realize that I did not understand the cultural codes of the new regime that was shaping and changing society. It was as though the cocoon in which I had lived was shattered, the ground taken from under my feet. My response to both these experiences was to try to treat them anthropologically – in the sense that I sought an intellectual understanding of the revolutionary culture that was so different from the one in which I had grown up.

New Field, New Approach

In 1984, following my divorce, I returned to Cambridge, where my former supervisor, Esther Goody, took me under her wing again. I started a post-doctoral project as a research associate of the Department of Social Anthropology. My experiences in revolutionary Iran had given me a passionate interest in the issue of women's rights and the working of the sharia. I began a project on the theory and practice of Islamic family law, focusing on marital disputes and litigants' strategies. Between 1985 and 1988, I spent three months conducting fieldwork in family courts in Tehran – then called Special Civil Courts. In 1988, I managed to obtain two grants for field research in Morocco, where I spent a year doing research in the family courts of Rabat, Sale and Casablanca.

This was the first time I had done fieldwork outside Iran. Not being emotionally involved in Moroccan society and politics, I was able to keep some distance and to be more an observer than a participant; at the same time, living at close quarters with Muslims from a very different tradition gave me the intense 'culture shock' I had not experienced when working in Iran. In both countries, however, I was collecting the same kind of data and dealing with the same issues. My own divorce experience brought me close to the litigants, most of them women, in both countries. When meeting women outside court and asking them about their cases, I often started by relating how my own marriage had broken down and how I had obtained my divorce, which created an immediate bond between us. After a while, I noticed that each time I told my story, it sounded different – I would emphasize aspects of my experience that related to the situation of the woman I was talking to. I became increasingly sensitive to situation, to how different contexts produce different narratives, how one can control this production, how much was dependent on one's perspective, how one can resolve what might seem palpable contradictions.

I completed my first monograph, *Marriage on Trial*, in 1992, when I was still feeling my way in terms of my own academic and personal engagement with both feminist discourses and Islam. I was concerned and often dismayed by a dominant approach in the academic literature of the 1980s on women in Muslim societies, mostly produced by women from Muslim backgrounds writing in English or French. These writers, it seemed to me, shared – and thus helped to reproduce – the same essentialist and orientalist assumptions about gender in Islam that were held by many of their Islamist antagonists: that the Islamic position on gender was divinely ordained and immutable. My own experience, as both a litigant and an ethnographer, was quite different: 'Islamic' positions on gender were changing and thus open to negotiation and modification. Like the Islamists, many of these academics were selective in their arguments, had an ahistorical understanding of Islam and gender, resorted to the same kinds of sophistry, and resisted any readings of Islamic law that treated it like any other system of law; and they disguised their polemics by obfuscation and misrepresentation. Both sets of antagonists, in other words, had a strongly ideological approach, and in the final analysis they read what they wanted into Islam, though in pursuit of different agendas, the one Islamist and the other feminist.

In *Marriage on Trial,* I tried to shift the debate on the relation between Islamic law and women to a different level. Instead of condemning the sharia as responsible for all women's problems, I sought to understand how it operates and in what ways it is relevant to today's Muslim societies: how individuals, both men and women, make sense of the religious precepts that underlie every piece of legislation regulating their marriages. I also tried to shift the focus from how women are oppressed by sharia rules to how women can manipulate the contradictions embedded in these rules and use the courts as an arena for negotiation. In the court cases I witnessed and recorded in Iran and Morocco, I noticed that many women were aware of these contradictions and manipulated them in order to renegotiate, and at times to rewrite, the terms of their marriages. In so doing, they could turn the most patriarchal elements of sharia law to their advantage in order to achieve their personal and marital aims. I was sensitive to this, in part because it was exactly what I had managed to do myself some years earlier when my own marriage broke down.

When I started field research in Tehran family courts in 1985, I sought to retain the impartiality of the 'objective' academic observer, firmly instilled in me by my 1970s training in 'participant observation'. But at times I caught myself being more a 'participant' – and certainly not an impartial observer. My own gender identity and my own experience of divorce often mediated many of my 'observations'. My 1989 fieldwork in Morocco helped me to come to terms with my own Muslim identity and to reexamine my relationship with the faith into which I was born, yet I still found it difficult to reconcile my growing personal involvement in feminist discourses and Islam with my academic aim of 'objectivity'. By the time my research in Morocco ended, I had realized that this aim was impossible but still hesitated to acknowledge it, let alone to participate actively in what I was studying: I still carried a heavy baggage of conflicting identities and politics, too painful to unpack in the aftermath of the 1979 Revolution in my own country. So, while writing up my field material from Iran and Morocco, I tried as far as possible to keep my distance and not to insert my own voice into the text.

From Observation to Participant Activism

In 1992, after completing *Marriage on Trial,* and after four years' absence from Iran, I returned for six months to pursue an earlier and rather different research interest: the mystical tradition of a sect, the Ahl-i Haqq.[5] I found Iran less ideological, now boasting a wider range of journals to read, more tolerance of different ideas and a lively debate on women's rights in Islam, aired in women's magazines. Between 1993 and 1995, I returned to Iran several times a year to do both research and consultancies for the Food and Agriculture Organization, which took me to various parts of Iran, rural and urban, where I met and talked with women from different walks of life. These consultancies gave me access to women working in government, as well as the opportunity to contact those who had contributed to gender debates through either their writings or their activities in women's organizations. In time, I made close friendships with some of these women, who came from very different backgrounds and held divergent views. It was during one of these trips that I started collaboration with Hojjat ol-Eslam Sa'idzadeh, a cleric who used to write for women's magazines, under different pseudonyms, on gender equality and women's rights in Islamic law. He introduced me to the clerical debates on gender and facilitated my fieldwork in Qom in 1995.

If *Marriage on Trial* was my initiation into the politics of gender in Islam, in my second published ethnography, *Islam and Gender* (1999), I abandoned the impossible ideal of 'academic' detachment and described my own engagements with a series of clerics and their texts as a personal search for understanding. I wrote not only as an anthropologist but also as an Iranian Muslim woman who needed to make sense of her faith and culture. True, the book owes its format to a traumatic experience in Tehran airport in November 1995, and the loss of my field material, but by then my approach to fieldwork in Iran and my involvement in the politics of Islam had already changed.[6] Not only was I now deeply involved in gender debates in Islam, I was also interested in collaborative work.

During the writing of *Islam and Gender,* I started working with an independent British filmmaker, Kim Longinotto. When I met Kim through a mutual friend in March 1996, we discovered that we shared the same frustrations with media stereotypes of the Muslim world. We decided to make a documentary film in Iran, inspired by the court cases in *Marriage on Trial.* The first step was to apply to British TV commissioning editors for funding, and to Iranian officials for access and permission to film. Kim focused on the first and I on the second. This, my first experience in filmmaking, involved me in a long series of negotiations, not only with the Iranian authorities for permission and access, but also with myself: I had to deal with personal ethical and professional dilemmas as well as with theoretical and methodological issues of representation.[7] The film's subject matter inevitably entailed both exposing individuals' private lives in the public domain and tackling a major issue dividing Islamists and feminists: women's position in Islamic family law.

In the course of these negotiations I came once again to confront my own multiple identities. I found myself in an uncannily familiar situation of shifting perspectives and self-redefinition. When I started the film project, I was fresh from fieldwork in Qom. In my discussions with the clerics I had had to justify my feminist stance, whereas in making the film I wanted to honour the Muslim and Iranian aspects of my identity. I came to realize that the problem was also inside me. I could not integrate the multiple discourses and representations of women in Iran, nor could I synthesize my own identities and positions. I disagreed equally with Iranian and Western stereotypes of 'women in Islam', images that did not reflect a complex reality. As a feminist, an Iranian and a Muslim, I objected to how women were treated in Iranian law and wanted to change it. But my objections were not the same as those implied in Western media discourses or those aired by feminists after the Revolution: I did not see women in Iran as victims, but as pioneers in a legal system caught between religious tradition and modern reality.

This was not the kind of 'reality' the women's organizations and authorities in prereformist Iran wanted shown to the outside world. Both the officials in the Ministry of Culture and Islamic Guidance and women's organizations with close ties with the government refused to cooperate with us. Our chosen topic – divorce – was a 'reality' denied by their ideological discourse, a taboo theme that threatened to undermine a central tenet of the early rhetoric of the Islamic Republic. At the very core of their critique of the West was that family values had broken down, as witnessed by rising divorce rates; the Islamic Republic prided itself on the stability of the family. I understood why officials in the Ministry of Islamic Culture and Guidance rejected our proposal and why no Islamic women's organization wanted to be associated with us: it would be like washing dirty linen in public. But at the same time, I felt strongly that it was an issue that should be addressed, as divorce laws had become the most visible yardstick, after the 'Islamic' dress code, for measuring women's emancipation or repression in Islam. Both Western media and Islamist rhetoric treated the whole issue of family law ideologically and ignored the complex reality on the ground. It was used as a means of 'othering' – and there lay the importance of addressing it.

We spent eighteen months negotiating for permission to make our film and had no success until Khatami's election to the presidency brought a shift in government discourse and policies. In autumn 1997, we finally got our permit to make a film about 'reality' as seen through the eyes of women going through divorce. The women who agreed to be in our film shared our vision and seized the opportunity to have their voices heard, to express themselves – to make the film with us. In this way, the film became part of the debate on women's rights in Iran, which I had been passionately involved in since the early 1990s. I wanted to show that there are different voices in Islam and Iran. The voice most often heard is that of the law: highly authoritarian and patriarchal, and increasingly out of touch with people's aspirations and lived realities. But there is also an egalitarian voice in everyday life, seldom heard by outsiders or acknowledged by the authorities. It is this voice that women are expressing – the true voice of 'Islamic feminism'. It is by hearing this voice that we can come to see the anachronistic nature of the law, and how social change is daily chipping away at its monolithic authority. Just as my 1995 debates with the clerics in Qom and my collaboration with Sa'idzadeh made me realize that I wanted to be not just an observer but also a participant in defining the terms of gender discourse in Islam, so my involvement in making the film with Kim, and my subsequent engagement with its various audiences, enabled me to continue my transition from the detached world of academia to that of a scholar activist.

In 2000, I codirected another feature-length documentary with Kim Longinotto for Channel 4. This time we filmed in a shelter for runaway girls, exploring issues like child abuse and the unbearable family situations that force these girls to run away. And recently I completed a book with Richard Tapper about a reformist cleric – Hassan Yousefi Eshkevari – who was imprisoned for over four years (2000–05) because of his liberal views on Islamic law and his advocacy of democracy and women's rights. Our book traces the development of his thought and places in context the writings he produced between 1995 and 2000, when the reformist movement was in formation (Mir-Hosseini and Tapper 2006).

Concluding Remarks

I conclude by reflecting on certain issues implicit in my account, and try to suggest some answers to questions with which I have grappled since the early 1990s. What does it mean to be a 'native' ethnographer? In what ways, if any, do the fieldwork experiences and the ethnographic accounts of 'insider' and 'outsider' anthropologists differ?

I explored these questions in the context of the rupture brought to Iranian anthropology by the Revolution of 1978–79 and its impact on my own anthropological trajectory. As stated above, I did my first fieldwork in Kalardasht in 1977–78, but by the time I had completed my thesis two years later, the ethnography had already become history. When the Iranian universities reopened after the 'Cultural Revolution', they had been 'Islamized' and had no room for teachers trained in the West. I returned to Cambridge in 1984 to resume my academic career, but I was no longer interested in 'traditional' fieldwork in villages or tribes – the 'Other', for an urban middle-class Iranian anthropologist like me. The research I have done since then does not fit the image of anthropology and its subject matter in Iran and other non-Western countries (see Fazeli 2006). I have often been reminded of this. Moroccans told me that I should not call myself an 'anthropologist' because I was one of them: a Muslim, not an 'Other'. In Iran, I have often been told that what I am doing is 'not really anthropology' but sociology. Above all, I am writing about city people. Yet I continue to see myself as an anthropologist, not only because I have remained faithful to its time-honoured methodology but also because of what attracted me to it in the first place: the peculiar way that anthropology makes the familiar strange in one's own society and the strange familiar in another. For me, 'doing anthropology' is more than an academic discipline: it is a way of life, a means of making sense of, belonging to and yet being able to transcend both the society that I was born into and the society that I now inhabit.

It is in this sense that see myself as a 'native' anthropologist. It is not only a matter of my Iranian/Muslim identity; rather, it concerns a certain consciousness of the link between epistemology and politics. It is this consciousness that, in my view, separates the ethnography done by a 'native' anthropologist from that of others – whether 'insiders' or 'outsiders'. In Barbara Tedlock's words:

> Just as being born a female does not automatically result in 'feminist' consciousness, being born [in] an ethnic minority does not automatically result in 'native' consciousness. Native ethnographers ... have worked to bridge the gulf between Self and Other by revealing both parties as vulnerable experiencing subjects, working to coproduce knowledge. They have argued that the observer and the observed are not entirely separate categories. To them theory is not a transparent, culture-free zone, not a duty-free intellectual market hovering between cultures, lacking all connection to embodied lived experience. They believe that both knowledge and experience from outside fieldwork should be brought into our narratives and that we should

demonstrate how ideas matter to us, bridging the gap between our narrow academic world and our wider cultural experiences. These strategies should help us simultaneously deepen and invigorate our writing and our selves. (1991: 80–81)

This 'native' anthropology, for me, also comes with a promise and a commitment to engage in productive dialogue between persons inhabiting different societies and differing political realities.

NOTES

1. I am of course aware of the small number of foreign anthropologists who either continued to conduct fieldwork during the Revolution or were able to revisit Iran afterwards.
2. On the development of anthropology in pre- and postrevolutionary Iran, see Fazeli (2006).
3. See for instance, Abu Lughod (1993), Appadurai (1988), Clifford (1988), Clifford and Marcus (1986), Kondo (1986), Barbara Tedlock (1991) and Dennis Tedlock (1987).
4. The previous generation of anthropologists dealt with this problem either by publishing accounts of their field experiences under a pseudonym and in a semi-fictionalized form, or by keeping personal records and comments in the form of a diary; see Barbara Tedlock (1991: 70–76).
5. I published four articles based on this fieldwork (1994, 1995, 1996, 1997), but have not yet completed the monograph I originally planned.
6. See preface to Mir-Hosseini (1999).
7. For a detailed account see Mir-Hosseini (2002).

REFERENCES

Abu Lughod, L. 1993. *Writing Women's Worlds: Bedouin Stories*. Berkeley, CA.
Appadurai, A.1988. 'Putting Hierarchy in Its Place', *Cultural Anthropology* 3(1): 36–49.
Bradburd, D. 1998. *Being There: The Necessity of Fieldwork*. Washington, D.C.
Clifford, J. 1988. *The Predicament of Culture*. Cambridge, MA.
Clifford, J. and G. Marcus (eds). 1986. *Writing Culture: The Poetics and Politics of Ethnography*. Berkeley, CA.
Fazeli, N. 2006. *The Politics of Culture in Iran: Anthropology, Politics and Society in the Twentieth Century*. London.
Field, H. 1939. *Contributions to the Anthropology of Iran*. Chicago.
Kondo, D.K. 1986. 'Dissolution and Reconstitution of Self: Implications for Anthropological Epistemology', *Cultural Anthropology* 1(1): 74–88.
Mir-Hosseini, Z. 1980. *Changing Aspects of Economy and Family in Kalardasht, A District in Northern Iran*, unpublished Ph.D. thesis. University of Cambridge.

———. 1993. *Marriage on Trial: A Study of Islamic Family Law in Iran and Morocco*. London.

———. 1994. 'Inner Truth and Outer History: The Two Worlds of Ahl-i Haqq of Kurdistan', *International Journal of Middle East Studies* 26(2): 267–85.

———. 1995. 'Redefining the Truth: Ahl-i Haqq and the Islamic Republic of Iran', *British Journal of Middle Eastern Studies* 21(2): 211–28.

———. 1996. 'Faith, Ritual and Culture among the Ahl-i Haqq', in P. Kreyenbroek and C. Allison (eds), *Kurdish Culture and Identity*. London: 111–34.

———. 1997. 'Breaking the Seal: The New Face of the Ahl-e Haqq', in K. Kehl-Bodrogi et al. (eds), *Syncretistic Religious Communities in the Near East*. Leiden: 175–94.

———. 1999. *Islam and Gender: The Religious Debate in Contemporary Iran*. Princeton, NJ.

———. 2002. 'Negotiating the Politics of Gender in Iran: An Ethnography of a Documentary', in R. Tapper (ed.), *The New Iranian Cinema: Politics, Representation and Identity*. London: 167–99.

Mir-Hosseini, Z. and R. Tapper. 2006. *Islam and Democracy in Iran: Eshkevari and the Quest for Reform*. London.

Tedlock, B. 1991. 'From Participant Observation to Observation of Participation: The Emergence of Narrative Ethnography', *Journal of Anthropological Research* 47(1): 69–94.

Tedlock, D. 1987. 'Questions Concerning Dialogical Anthropology', *Journal of Anthropological Research* 43(4): 325–37.

PART IV

Past and Present Perspectives

Challenging the Future

 CHAPTER 11

Usual Topics
Taboo Themes and New Objects in Iranian Anthropology

Christian Bromberger

Introduction

Anthropology is the totality of human life. But which human has been and remains the object of Iranian studies? It is obviously a truncated human, an incomplete human, identified only through a few activities that seem well-founded to deserve anthropological attention. What is the reason behind the limited notion of anthropology in Iran? In what follows I would like to share a few critical thoughts on the subject.[1]

To start with, I would like to make two preliminary remarks. On the one hand, these critical thoughts concern the anthropology of Iran as studied by Iranians and so-called halfies,[2] or by foreigners, including myself. In addition, these critical thoughts apply specifically to the anthropology of Iran, but also to the anthropology of other cultural areas, even to anthropology in general. I have devoted my anthropological life to several different fields – Iran, the Mediterranean world, societies of Western Europe – and thus have had the opportunity to consider fields[3] other than Iran as well. The anthropology of Iran undoubtedly shares many of the same problems as the discipline in general, in particular the considerable difficulty in adapting its conceptual grids to the analysis of the present, although these problems are more striking here than elsewhere for a number of reasons that I shall consider.

Weaknesses of Anthropology of Iran

A symptom of this incongruous situation is the generally weak contribution of Iranian anthropology to anthropology in general. On this point, I do not share Brian Spooner's opinion when he writes: 'Iranian material is now becoming commonplace in anthropological literature because of its intrinsic cultural and historical as well as theoretical interest' (1987: 110–11). In the contemporary anthropological debate few references are made to the anthropology of Iran, and it would be quite difficult to find an emblematic text that – in the manner of Evans-Pritchard's *The Nuer* (1940), Lévi-Strauss' *Tristes Tropiques* (1955), or Dumont's *Homo Hierarchicus* (1966), or even Geertz's 'Deep Play: Notes on the Balinese Cockfight' (1973) – testifies to the originality of a recognized intellectual tradition based on the study of the Iranian world (except perhaps Barth's work on the Pathans, published in 1981, which fed his innovative theory of ethnicity). If we wonder about the place of anthropology in Iran, no longer from a general anthropological point of view but from an Iranological one, we reach the same conclusions: in the pantheon of great leaders, there are archaeologists, specialists in Islamic philosophy and historians, but few, indeed almost no anthropologists at all.

This weakness and the late start of anthropology in this part of the world are due to three interrelated factors. First, Iran was never colonized, and we know how close the tie is between colonialism and the rise of anthropology and its development in certain specific regions. Second, Iranian societies are not primitive enough to raise broad anthropological interest. Third, prevailing studies of the monumental heritage and learned written traditions have left little space for studies of daily life. Nevertheless, the anthropology of Iran can be credited with considerable merits in certain fields[4] on which outsiders and insiders alike have focused their research: (1) nomadic pastoralism, in particular F. Barth's study of the Basseris (1961), which was crucial in the emergence of this field of study; (2) techniques, a field long underrepresented in English and American anthropology in which museographers, 'true' technologists such as H. E. Wulff (1966) and the great French masters A. Leroi-Gourhan and A.-G. Haudricourt have contributed directly or indirectly to the development of research;[5] (3) cooperative forms of agricultural work, for example, Safi Nezhâd's book on the [Bone] (1353/1974); (4) folklore, interest in which has produced countless books of tales and lists of traditions that consist mostly of compilations and ignore performance and contextualization.[6] More recently, some topics have drawn much more attention since the Revolution than they did before it, particularly research on women, Islam and politics, which have become privileged topics.[7]

However, whole sectors of the social and cultural experience have been neglected and research on present-day anthropology in Iran has barely begun. Urban anthropology has hardly developed, an anthropology of industrial companies and factories is practically non-existent and the study of today's family consumption practices, leisure, new means of expression and communication remain a nearly unexplored field. In addition, political anthropology (which must not be confused with political science) is desperately lacking in today's Iranian society, although it was a major issue in the study of nomadic pastoral societies. How can we explain these gaps, which do not apply to anthropology in other areas of the world in the same way?

Obstacles for the Anthropology of Iran

The development of the anthropology of Iran has been and continues to be confronted with political and ideological obstacles that I would like to briefly review.

Political obstacles are obvious. Revolutionary and postrevolutionary events brought ongoing research to a halt and led to the departure of a great number of anthropologists for other fields. Obtaining a visa today has become impossible for many anthropologists. For others it is a hit-or-miss endeavour, while still others can gain permission for short visits only and must limit their research to 'zip in and zip out fieldwork' and a 'quick ethnography' (Hegland 2004). Nevertheless, some 'tenacious, doggedly determined scholars' (Friedl and Hegland 2004: 569) kept doing fieldwork, even under difficult circumstances. Meanwhile, Iran's negative image in the West has dissuaded the younger generation from pursuing research interests in a country so difficult to access. It should be noted, however, that from the mid 1990s to the mid 2000s a limited open-door policy, a less unilateral and negative image of the country as well as less restrictive travel conditions for movement within the country have encouraged a slight increase in the number of researchers.[8]

The ideological climate has also been an obstacle to the development of anthropology. Even though, like other social and publishing activities, it had to submit to restrictive police supervision, the discipline was relatively well-perceived under the Pahlavi regime and was supposed to testify to Iran's own cultural traditions, anchored in an impressive pre-Islamic past. Within the overall national project, however, anthropology played a less significant role than archaeology. The Islamic Revolution broke away from this form of cultural nationalism, and anthropology became a suspicious discipline, responsible for perpetuating archaisms, for disconnecting Iranian culture from its Islamic foundations and for using Western concepts to reduce irreducible phenomena (such as religion) to sociological or anthropological interpretation.

Although anthropology is more tolerated today, the political situation excludes analyses of a certain number of topics that have been the subject of very interesting research elsewhere. Can we imagine an anthropology of prisons, such as those completed by Cunha in Portugal (1995), Khosrokhavar in France (2004) or Wacquant (1999)? Can we imagine an anthropology of stigmatized minorities (Bahai, Jews, Afghans, homosexuals, etc.), or of racism in Iran? Is it possible to develop a political anthropology of Iran – not one that would deal with old conflicts between state and tribes, or with current arguments between 'conservatives' and 'reformists', or with the vote of young people and women, but an anthropology that would analyse Parliament, its daily operations, the access to power on a local or national scale, clientelism, etc? Is an anthropology of life at the office, dealing with promotions, sanctions and other daily schemes, a prospect for research? Is an anthropology of anti-religiosity or anti-clericalism thinkable? On some of these subjects, discreet investigations are undoubtedly feasible, but they are high-risk exercises that pose frightening ethical problems, not so much for the anthropologist as for those who involuntarily or voluntarily lend themselves to such studies.

Anthropologists definitely have also remained prudently silent on less sensitive, yet decisive issues for the future of Iran, among them questions of regionalism – a subject that has developed at an accelerating pace over the past ten years. Following the rapid breakdown of traditions (such as vernacular architecture, folktales, local games) and a spreading Persianization, 'regionalist' movements have arisen. For example, in Gilan regionalism is promoted by numerous formal and informal associations and publications (including the publication of six important journals dealing more or less with regional culture, three of which are specifically devoted to Talesh and some of which emphasize the province's lack of autonomy). This process of growing regional awareness is undoubtedly also apparent elsewhere, and not only in Azerbaijan and Kurdistan, where it has been deep-rooted for a long time.

Political considerations weigh heavily on each phase of research (from fieldwork to publishing), raising practical, intellectual and de-ontologically sensitive issues, such as the question of which institutions we should cooperate with. The Iranian state is neither monolithic nor lacking in contradictions. What are the appropriate limits of enquiry with respect to informants' safety? Should researchers report observed injustices and violence? Where and how should the line be drawn between scientific cooperation and political accommodation?

Ungrounded Prejudices against Anthropology

The development of anthropology in Iran has also been hampered by local opinions regarding the discipline that subject it to constraints, confining it to local traditions, tribes, villages, craftsmanship and folklore.

Doubts relating to the benefits of social sciences are legitimate, *a fortiori* in societies where disinterested knowledge appears far removed from daily problems. It is striking, however, that anthropology is frequently confronted with the issue of uselessness,[9] whereas other disciplines, such as archaeology, art history, even literary studies, are not. It should be specifically noted that anthropology is rather more 'mediately' than 'immediately' useful. However, the discipline can be of immediate use in the preservation of heritage and diversity, which is particularly urgent in the current context of disappearing techniques, customs and 'traditional' modes of expression in a country such as Iran that is not yet burning with the 'preservation' fever.

Actually, it was in this dramatic context, as I realized the almost complete disappearance of local vernacular architecture, that I had the idea of an open-air museum in Gilan. This project is now carried on by the Organization of Cultural Heritage (Sâzemân-e Mirâs-e Farhangi) in cooperation with French specialists, under the aegis of the United Nations Educational, Scientific and Cultural Organization. However, crucial issues relating to folklorization, reification and authenticity rebuilding are raised by exhibiting traditional houses in an open-air museum. In doing so, we have to recontextualize buildings that have been taken out of their original contexts and avoid aestheticizing them – an undesirable tendency, from the anthropological viewpoint, widespread specifically among photographers. For instance, many lovely pictures by M. Kuchekpur are nowadays very popular in Gilan, some of them included in the excellent *Book of Gilan* (*Ketâb-e G ilân*), edited by Eslah 'Arbâni (1995–96). However, these photos depict recreated sequences and scenes, such as of women working in rice fields wearing their best clothes, or weaving fabric on a loom with treadles located in a garden!

In the process of change, anthropology can also suggest ways to adapt, for example techniques, trades, inhabited or cultivated land usage, transitions from nomadism to transhumance. The 'mediate' benefits of the discipline seem somewhat more important than its 'immediate' benefits. The anthropologist's principal role is to uncover false obviousness and eradicate stereotypes, to identify hidden categories and unspoken reasoning that escape ordinary observation. In short, the role of the anthropologist is to encourage thinking wherever possible. For this reason, it is as much a point of view on culture as it is a part of culture. This statement concerns both the society under study – most of our texts are today translated into Persian and can thus stir discussion – and the anthropologist's society, overburdened with stereotypes. From myths about local history and identity to generalizations about women's status, from interpreting local and contemporary crazes such as pigeon fancying (see Goushegir 1997), bullfighting in the Caspian provinces (see Bromberger 1997b) or football all over Iran (see Bromberger 1998) to documenting and analysing new forms of consumption, anthropology provides many opportunities to rethink society.

Distance, looking from the outside, and comparativism enable anthropologists to raise major as well as trivial issues that otherwise escape the awareness of local people imprisoned within their daily routines and even of native anthropologists too much accustomed to local habits. Why do men and not women, as is usual elsewhere, feed silkworms in Gilan? Why do men and not women, as elsewhere, milk sheep in Tâlesh? Only an outsider can be aware of the 'strangeness' of these practices and raise questions about them.

Regarding the traditional fields to which anthropology in Iran tends to be confined, they remain unquestionably legitimate and definitely demand ethnohistorical research.[10] But the majority of Iranians live in other frames of mind. The organization of work in industrial companies, the equipment of modern houses, the use of freezers, the consumption of pizza,[11] private and collective means of transportation, cosmetic care, reconstructive surgery, modern sports, everyday rumours and jokes, and children's birthdays deserve as much anthropological attention as craftsmen's skills, rural architecture, traditional techniques of food storage, provincial culinary recipes, horseback travel, past ornamental fashions, local games, fairy tales or weddings of the old days. The former topics well illustrate the dramatic changes of recent years. For instance, the marked increase in children's birthday celebrations clearly exemplifies a reversal in trend among Iranian families, who are becoming more 'child-focused' in a context of demographic transition.

Therefore, in Iran, as is often the case elsewhere, a rebalancing of the objects studied is undoubtedly needed. This rebalancing, however, poses two main problems: the legitimacy of these 'new objects' in Iran even more than elsewhere, and the need for a readjustment of our methods to grasp them.

Controversial but Necessary Shifts in Emphasis

Freezers, washing machines, jokes, swear words, football or pets are not 'noble' topics and are generally not regarded as subjects of anthropological studies, even less so of publications – instead, writings are largely reserved for famous 'serious' or 'exotic' topics. Daily life apparently does not deserve this attention. Orientalists have always looked down upon our usual objects of study (villages, ploughs, tents, rural houses, etc.). Being interested in the commonplace aspects of everyday life – now, that seems perfectly inappropriate!

I personally experienced the limits of the cultural legitimacy of the objects studied when I devoted an article (1986) to 'ethnic jokes in Northern

Iran' (*jok-e rashti*). This text caused passionate reactions among Iranian scholars who did not consider it legitimate to put *in writing* corrosive vulgarities usually narrated orally by natives. Moreover, this type of analysis revealed aspects of the phenomenon that it is thought to be wiser to conceal from public view (such as sexuality, illicit male-female relations, etc.). Nevertheless, the question why Rashti jokes are so popular deserves to be asked. (Even today, a 'jokestan' exists on the internet where Rashti jokes occupy the first place![12]) What exactly is the actual meaning of this reputation for phlegmatism and laziness on the part of men and frivolousness on the part of women of that province?

Analysis shows that this popular anthropology echoes the scientific traditions of Arab-Persian geography, ascribing to the climate a determining influence on popular virtue, and principles inherited from Hippocrates and Galen, classifying body humours and foods in two major categories, cold (*sard*) and hot (*garm*), and two minor categories, dry (*khoshk*) and humid (*martub*). According to these food classifications, the Gilanis are perceived by the so-called 'Araqis (inhabitants of the plateau) eaters of cold food, consuming rice, eggs, fish, vegetables and fresh fruit in abundance. They are therefore reputed to lack manliness. Moreover, to the 'Araqi people, the neighbouring Caspian region is like the world turned upside down, the negative pole of their own identity: it is wet, not dry; it is green, not ochre; its people grow rice, not corn; they eat fish, not meat; they have cows, not sheep, donkeys or dromedaries; their traditional houses are wide open, not enclosed by exterior walls. It is a society where the sense of honour (*nâmus*) and violence between individuals and groups is less obvious than in the Iranian interior. It is in a way a feminine as opposed to masculine society, with a greater participation of women, who are seldom veiled, in production activities, and a greater flexibility in male-female relations – though not, of course, to the extent suggested by the jokes. Thus Gilan appears in 'Araqi representations as a paragon of otherness, a situation that often invites a smile. Ultimately, these jokes and anecdotes about the Rashti-s teach us as much about the specificities (grossly exaggerated in these texts) of the Caspian populations as they do about the dominant values of those in the Iranian interior, who make up the jokes and laugh at them. For all these reasons, these trivial texts deserve analysis.

In addition, the 'new objects' seem to belong to the domain of sociology or cultural studies rather than anthropology. But anthropological studies in these new fields – for example, on the way meat is consumed today, on reconstituting families, on the ways of life of the urban middle class, on pets (see Digard 2003b), on football – have proven to be of great heuristic value, for they are based on long, meticulous field investigations and measured comparativism. It would be absurd for anthropology to show such overcautious fundamentalism as to refuse the study of these objects and confine itself to some sort of archaeology.

In order to analyse modern life, it is undoubtedly necessary to adjust our paradigms. It no longer seems possible to write monographs on villages while being confined there, as was done in the past. Life today, although anchored in a specific place, is organized in translocal networks. Not one member of the family that I am currently studying (Bromberger 2005) resides today in the village where I met them all twenty years ago. They keep their land, their memory and a feeling of belonging (for instance, the men continue to be a part of the village *daste,* or group of penitents), but our study must expand from rural areas to the city, even abroad, in order to keep up with contemporary reality. Hence we need a multi-scale analysis, considering individuals in the different social spaces and networks that they are related to, and a 'multi-sited' approach.[13]

As mentioned earlier, the anthropology of Iran – though the situation is not unique and could well apply to other countries or regions – has been one way to reinforce the feeling of national identity. The early advocates of this area of study and the writers interested in folklore (such as the great Sadeq Hedayat[14]), along with most of their successors, were all driven by a strong feeling of the singularity of the country's culture and tended to over-Iranize the facts. For that reason, many modern-day customs are considered to be the legacy of Zoroastrian Iran. The same tendency is found in Greek anthropology (laography, the study of the people) due to a constant effort to find the remnants of a brilliant past in recent contemporary rituals. The intentional over-Iranization and over-antiquation of folklore and traditions have been pitfalls on the path to the knowledge about the history and cultural specifics of Iran.[15] Thus, for example, recent studies have dismantled the myth of the ancient origin of *zurkhâne* (see Rochard 2002). When authors evoke the *chahârshanbe suri,* they always recall its Zoroastrian origins, but they rarely mention the existence of similar pre-springtime fires in many areas of the ancient world.[16]

This tendency to over-Iranize the facts could have been and could still be moderated by comparativism. However, one of the problems of the anthropology of Iran is the weakness of its comparative dimension on several levels: comparisons with other societies and cultures that would be conducive to interpretation are exceptions rather than the rule;[17] systematic comparisons within the Iranian world are rare, too.[18] However, it would be of greater interest to compare, for instance, the systems of descent and alliance in the Iranian world, although monographic studies on this topic conducted in various areas are not lacking. A third type of comparison could also be useful – that of diachronic comparison focused on the transformation of customs and practices, whether technical (for example, methods of ploughing and their organization), recreational (*zurkhâne,* Greco-Roman wrestling, combat sports from the Far East, etc.) or social (such as marriage rituals or children's birthdays), etc. In particular this third type of comparison is an invitation to pay more attention to the phenomena of innovation, transmission, resistance and barriers to change.

In order to undertake such comparative work, there must exist a 'community' of anthropologists working on Iran. However, no such 'community' or institution has yet been established. The political context, competition between individuals and organizations (which itself merits ethnographic investigation), and difficulties gaining access to the field, as well as the diversity of interests, by and large explain this fragmentation. At an international level, the anthropology of Iran now belongs either to the field of Iranology, where it holds a negligible and often misunderstood position, or to the vast field of Middle Eastern Studies, which may promote the first type of comparisons but not the second type.

Such cooperation is needed and should take the form of an international association where members meet periodically on a specific topic. It should also contribute to making local people understand what ethnographic work really is: not a team project, with assigned drivers and complicated bureaucracy – a method really only acceptable in the context of systematic collection campaigns – but rather solitary, discreet, autonomous, long-term work where listening and looking without asking too many questions becomes possible.

NOTES

1. Many thanks to Lois Beck and Shahnaz Nadjmabadi, who offered helpful comments on an earlier draft of this text.
2. 'Halfies' refer to those anthropologists with local origins who were raised or are living elsewhere and doing research in the place of their origins.
3. See, among others, Bromberger (1997a: 294–313) as well as Albera, Blok and Bromberger (2001: 756).
4. For comprehensive reviews, see Spooner (1987: 107–16, 1999: 9–45).
5. 'Material culture would have been an obvious avenue to explore, but it was often missed because it did not fit the theoretical interests of the time', observes Spooner (1999: 12). It should be pointed out that although it did not fit the theoretical interests of English and American anthropology, it did by contrast comply with the theoretical interests of an important trend in French anthropology and incidentally in German, Austrian and Scandinavian anthropology as well.
6. There are, however, also outstanding contributions to Iranian folklore, such as Enjavi-Shirazi (2001) and Marzolph's works (see his article in this volume).
7. Let us mention, among others, Beck and Keddie (eds), *Women in the Muslim World* (1978); M.M.J. Fischer, *Iran: From Religious Dispute to Revolution*

(1980); G. Nashat (ed.), *Women and Revolution in Iran* (1983); F. Adelkhah, *Être moderne en Iran* (1998).

8. Among the young French scholars who have recently carried out outstanding fieldwork research are Philippe Rochard, *Le 'sport antique' des zurkhâne de Téhéran: Formes et significations d'une pratique contemporaine* (thesis), Aix-en-Provence, Université de Provence (2000) and Anne-Sophie Vivier, *Comment peut-on être Afzadi? Individu et société dans un village persan* (thesis), Ecole des hautes études en sciences sociales, Paris (2004).

9. On the question of the benefits of anthropology, see Digard (2003a) and Hourcade (2003).

10. On this point, I should be quite clear again: folklore and traditional techniques are not peripheral matters, as in Anglo-American anthropology, but belong to the core of our discipline, if they are related to social context.

11. On this process of Westernization of cuisine, see Chehabi (2003).

12. www.jokestan.com. Retrieved December 2006.

13. On this kind of approach, see especially Marcus (1995).

14. See, in particular, *Neyrangestân* (1955).

15. On this tendency towards over-Iranization, see the provocative work by Vaziri (1993).

16. However, some comparative articles were presented at the *First Symposium on Nowruz*, Tehran, Anthropology Research Centre, in 2001.

17. Among these exceptions are, for instance, the comparative studies on nomadism by Digard (1977), Mir-Hosseini's work on Islamic family law (1993) and Salzman (2004).

18. Exceptions are, for example, Digard (1988) and Tapper (1983).

REFERENCES

Adelkhah, F. 1998. *Être moderne en Iran*. Paris.

Albera, D., A. Blok and C. Bromberger (eds). 2001. *L'anthropologie de la Méditerranée/Anthropology of the Mediterranean*. Paris.

Barth, F. 1961. *Nomads of South Persia: The Basseri Tribe of the Khamseh Confederacy*. Oslo.

———. 1981. *Features of Persons and Society in Swat: Collected Essays on Pathans*. London.

Beck, L. and N. Keddie (eds). 1978. *Women in the Muslim World*. Cambridge, MA.

Bromberger, C. 1986. 'Les blagues ethniques dans le nord de l'Iran. Sens et fonction d'un corpus de récits facétieux', *Cahiers de littérature orale* 20 : 73–101.

———. 1997a. 'L'ethnologie de la France et ses nouveaux objets. Crise, tâtonnements et jouvence d'une discipline dérangeante', *Ethnologie Française* 3: 294–313.

———. 1997b. 'La guerre des taureaux n'aura pas lieu. Note sur les infortunes d'un divertissement populaire dans le nord de l'Iran', in J. Hainard and R. Kaehr (eds), *Dire les autres. Réflexions et pratiques ethnologiques. Textes offerts à Pierre Centlivres*. Lausanne: 121–37.

———. 1998. 'Le football en Iran', *Sociétés et representations* 7: 101–15.

————. 2005. 'Famille et parenté dans la plaine du Gilân (Iran)', in A. Kian et M. Ladier-Fouladi (eds), *Familles et mutations socio-politiques*. Paris: 125–42.

Chehabi, H. 2003. 'The Westernization of Iranian Culinary Culture', *Iranian Studies* 36(1): 43–61.

Cunha, M. 1995. 'Sociabilité, « société », « culture », carcérales. La prison féminine de Tires (Portugal)', *Terrain* 24: 119–32.

Digard, J.-P. 1977. 'Caractères et problèmes spécifiques du nomadisme en Iran: l'exemple Baxtyâri', in Commission Nationale Suisse pour l'UNESCO (ed.), *Séminaire sur le nomadisme en Asie centrale (Afghanistan, Iran, URSS)*. Bern: 51–75.

————. 2003a. 'Pour une ethnologie du "superflu" en Iran', in B. Hourcade (ed.), *Iran. Questions et Connaissances : Actes de la IVe Conférence européenne des études iraniennes*, Paris 1999: vol. III. *Cultures et sociétés contemporaines*. (Cahiers de Studia Iranica no 27). Louvain and Paris : 153–160.

————. 2003b. 'Les animaux révélateurs des tensions politiques en République islamique d'Iran', *Études Rurales* 165–66: 123–32.

———— (ed.). 1988. *Le fait ethnique en Iran et en Afghanistan*. Paris.

Dumont, L. 1966. *Homo Hierarchicus: Essai sur le Système des Castes*. Paris.

Enjavi-Shirazi, A. 2001. *Jashnhâ va âdâb va mo'taqedât-e zamestân*. 2 vols. Tehran.

Eslah 'Arbâni, E. (ed.). 1995–96. *Ketâb-e Gilân*. 3 vols. Tehran.

Evans-Pritchard, E.E. 1940. *The Nuer: A Description of the Modes of Livelihood and Political Institutions of a Nilotic People*. Oxford.

Fischer, M.M.J. 1980. *Iran: From Religious Dispute to Revolution*. Cambridge, MA.

Friedl, E. and M.E. Hegland. 2004. 'Guest Editors' Introduction', *Iranian Studies* 37(4): 569–73.

Geertz, C. 1973. 'Deep Play: Notes on the Balinese Cockfight', in C. Geertz, *The Interpretation of Cultures: Selected Essays by Clifford Geertz*. New York: 412–53.

Goushegir, A. 1997. *Le combat du colombophile (jeu aux pigeons et stigmatisation sociale)*. Tehran.

Hedayat, S. 1955. *Neyrangestân*. Tehran.

Hegland M.E. 2004. 'Zip in and Zip out Fieldwork', *Iranian Studies* 37(4): 575–83.

Hourcade, B. (ed.) 2003. *Iran.Questions et Connaissances : Cultures et sociétés contemporaines*. (Cahiers de Studia Iranica). Louvain and Paris.

Khosrokhavar, F. 2004. *L'islam dans les prisons*. Paris.

Levi-Strauss, C. 1955. *Tristes tropiques*. Paris.

Marcus, G.E. 1995. 'Ethnography In/Of the World System: The Emergence of Multi-Sited Ethnography', *Annual Review of Anthropology* 24: 95–117.

Mir-Hosseini, Z. 1993. *Marriage on Trial: A Study of Islamic Family Law. Iran and Morocco Compared*. London.

Nashat, G. (ed.). 1983. *Women and Revolution in Iran*. Boulder, CO.

Rochard, P. 2000. *Le 'sport antique' des zurkhâne de Téhéran. Formes et significations d'une pratique contemporaine*, Ph.D. thesis. Université de Provence. Aix-Marseille.

————. 2002. 'Les identités du *zurkhâne* iranien', *Techniques et culture* 39: 29–57.

Safi Nezhâd, J. 1974. *Bone.* Tehran.

Salzman, P. C. 2004. *Pastoralists: Equality, Hierarchy, and the State.* Boulder, CO.

Spooner, B. 1987. 'Anthropology', *Encyclopaedia Iranica* 2: 107–16.

————. 1999. 'Ethnography', *Encyclopaedia Iranica* 9: 9–45.

Tapper, R. (ed.). 1983. *The Conflict of Tribe and State in Iran and Afghanistan.* London.

Vaziri, M. 1993. *Iran as Imagined Nation: The Construction of National Identity.* New York.

Vivier, A.-S. 2004. *Comment peut-on être Afzadi?Individu et société dans un village persan,* Ph.D. thesis. École des Hautes Études en Sciences Sociales. Paris.

Wacquant, L. 1999. *Les prisons de la misère.* Paris.

Wulff, H.E. 1966. *The Traditional Crafts of Persia.* Cambridge, MA, and London.

CHAPTER 12

Islamophobia and Malaise in Anthropology

Fariba Adelkhah 〽

How would you react if someone told you that many Iranian women have never been as free, as independent, and as active as they have been since the 1979 Revolution; that they are actually able to make money, travel, and be 'breadwinners'? Most likely by suspecting your interlocutor of being an Islamist or defender of the regime. And so, after reading my *Revolution under the Veil* (1991), an eminent professor of political science in Paris asked me, with a tone of gravity, whether I was the Han Suyin of the Islamic Republic. It goes without saying that this scenario could have played itself out in any Western capital, as well as in Iran itself.

The fact is that we continue to react to the mere mention of the postrevolutionary situation in Iran in a Pavlovian manner. The morsel of food that makes the dog quiver in the absence of all electric shocks is, of course, Islam – the Islam that is now automatically associated with terrorism and hostage-taking; the Islam that is symbolic of anti-secular sentiment, at least in France but increasingly in other European countries as well; the Islam that is bound up with problems of immigration, negations of gender equality and, most recently, the development of the atomic bomb. Islam, or more precisely the veil or *hijab* – the 'abbreviated translation'[1] of the former – is today's controversial subject par excellence.

When giving a conference paper on the practice of *hijab*, for example, there is inevitably to expect a clash between the apostles of secularism and the zealots of faith. By merely mentioning such basic facts as the increased mobility of women or the spectacular drop in fertility rates in contemporary Iran, one runs the risk of being labeled a supporter of the Islamic Republic. This is due, in part, to a widespread misunderstanding whereby an acknowledgement of the 'merit' of such social practices is perceived as an approbation of institutions or leaders. Similar reactions are also common among Iranians, who have been traumatized by the experience of revolution, near-civil war, waves of epuration and repression, the conflict with Iraq and the pain of exile. Shirin Ebadi, the 2004 Nobel Peace Prize Laureate, hit the core of this contradiction by arriving in Stockholm unveiled, thereby making herself a target for Islamists who attacked her for allegedly renouncing her society and religion. But at the same time she was condemned by the secular community as well, which accused her of wearing the *hijab* in Iran and practising a regime of shame.

This misunderstanding polarizes certain areas of research in the social sciences to such an extent that it becomes impossible to escape fixed ideological categories, even if it is evident that social practices can never be divided up quite so neatly along political or ideological lines. As Farhad Khosrokhavar wrote:

> The veil can be repressive in two distinct ways, even in a Muslim country. On the one hand, once a young girl starts wearing the veil, she cannot stop even if she wants to; the constraints of the community, as well as outright State repression, forbid her from doing so. In other words, she is free to wear the veil as long as she wants, but if she wants to take it off later, she is denied this freedom. On the other hand, the veil as an expression of personal autonomy can be transformed, in the hands of social powers not controlled by the women themselves, into a means of pressuring women and girls who do not wear the veil. (Khosrokhawar and Chafiq 1995: 162)

Thus the political and normative approach proscribes any direct discussion of the *person* wearing the veil, concentrating uniquely on the environment (family, regime) or the history that exerts power over her. When it considers Islam, man is no longer is the master of history – he is subjugated to it, and there is no necessity to deconstruct the consensus between the dominated and the dominant according to class, context or even generation. In short, this approach holds processes, agents and contexts in contempt. It is possible, of course, to cite many examples, but the crucial issue here – without going back into the history of the social sciences – is to understand the contemporary context, particularly in Iran, that gave rise to this confusion and continues to fuel it today. Founded upon a reification of the conflict between state and society, this confusion emerged from a deterministic tendency in contemporary social research, a tendency that is at once religious and political.

'State versus Society': Impossible Reconciliation or Domestic Reification?

For better or for worse, one of the salient traits of social science research in Iran from the Revolution roughly through the year 2000 is that it was largely cut off from two major intellectual trends: on the one hand, the Marxist and neo-Marxist tradition, which accorded special importance to conflicts between social groups, relationships between town and country-side (or tribes), and effects of domination and inequality; and, on the other hand, development studies, which accompanied the White Revolution (1963–1967). This authoritarian modernizing program with developmentalist in-spiration was started by the Shah in order to respond, in part, to the attacks of the Kennedy administration, and contributed to a better understanding of (or at least greater familiarity with) processes of urbanization and issues of social change in rural areas. The decline of these paradigms went alongside the rupture produced by the Revolution – well before the crumbling of the Soviet Union. Research concerning changes in Iranian society since the Rev-olution tends to be dominated by political concerns. Thus, schematically, there would be no state without its oppression of society, and no society without its resistance to the state. What results, then, is a highly dichoto-mous vision of the Revolution and the Islamic Republic, one that oscillates continually between two opposing poles:

- insistence on the active role of the clergy, or a portion of the clergy, in controlling the revolutionary process, functions of state and soci-ety itself by means of repression, cooptation and the imposition of a totalitarian ideology.
- insistence on the role of autonomous social movements that exist out-side of the realms of power and state, movements that are bound either to suffer repression or to resist and triumph in a form of 'Tehran Spring' (before, of course, being snuffed out by the totalitarian regime).

According to the terms of this often militant and state-centric alterna-tive, the researcher faces a supposedly absolute rift between despotism and freedom. The aim of social science research, according to this biased view, is to detect the origins of despotism and freedom in their natural state without considering either the forces that produce them or the processes of their fulfillment and functionality, nor even the various and contradictory invest-ments in social and political institutions. Of even less concern to this mode of thinking is the possibility of protecting (where freedom is concerned) or softening (where oppression is concerned). The researcher is expected to walk this line without questioning how the state – which concomitantly generates one thing and its opposite, i.e. civil society and its repression – can weigh on the balance of power or shape social organization. The politi-cal arena is considered a domain of irreconcilable oppositions. One is not meant to question the interpenetrations of power and society, for their dis-tinction constitutes a line that nobody is supposed to cross.

I do not seek to question the results of these studies: I myself have contributed to such formulations. What one can dispute in such a vision today, however, is the 'no exit' situation in which it frequently situates social actors, and the concomitant refusal to question the ways in which these actors are linked to power structures to which they are systematically opposed. The result seems to be the marginalization of research that would allow one to understand, for example, the sociopolitical changes of the country, rendered visible in each election cycle since the reelection of Hachemi Rafsandjani as president in 1993. It is not a matter of opposing an alternative angle. Rather, we seek simply to clear a path for a serious reflection on this dichotomous approach and the confusion that results.

We might begin by underscoring the weaknesses of this vision that I hold today as responsible for the impasse – at once political and analytical – in which we find ourselves. First of all, the aforementioned approach is problematically anachronistic: it reformulates traditional Iranian wisdom and repackages it as new, dressing it up in analytical language. This wisdom is characterized by an irreconcilable antagonism between good and evil, a framework that is utterly foreign to a more accurate representation of shifts in modern society that a more dynamic approach towards social change might afford. Furthermore, according to this dual interpretation, society depends on the state and its manifestations, and vice-versa. From the outset, this viewpoint should raise the question of how to understand the autonomy of social movements, about which it is common for researchers in the social sciences to hypothesize. In other words, this autonomy should be considered in its context, namely, that of thirty years of an Islamic Republic, and not normatively or in the abstract. Lastly, behind this highly critical vision of the revolutionary state remains the ideal of another, no less authoritarian state. Although seeking to be alternative, this approach holds differences, stratifications and social contradictions in contempt. For it, the only way to salvation is a unanimous front against segregation, the veil and Islamization itself.

A concern for the management of everyday life by social movements – in particular at the hands of women, students and other intellectuals – has been largely neglected, at least until 1997, in favour of the study of religious legal codes, writings by Islamic saints or scholars and political discourses. The latter were shown to be irreconcilable with modern times, calling for their subversion by women. What is surprising here is precisely the great divide that separates the periods before and after the Revolution, insofar as our interest in 'Islam' is concerned. This absolutely does not mean that religiosity after 1979 is of the same nature as it had been in the 1960s or 1970s. Rather, there still remains this gap, which we must one day interrogate concerning the change in our perception.

On the one hand, before the 1979 Revolution the future of religion, relegated often to folkloric practices, was thought of as being inversely proportional to the literacy rate and the speed of civilizing progress – in spite of the increase of modern centres of religiosity, including Tehran, or the arrival of a growing number of veiled women at the university. On the other hand, after the Revolution, which seemed to suddenly consecrate the failure of secularism, Islam became the alpha and the omega of our societies and their future, even secular ones such as France.[2] Never have Iranian men or women – especially Iranian women – been so interested in Islamic practices, codes, writings, principles, and authors as since the Revolution. In the social sciences, North American and European professors were frequently interested in the history of religious practices.[3] Iranians, on the other hand, considered such practices as surviving elements from the past, muffled in the background of the private sphere, elements that modernity, through force of persuasion and not violence, was seeking to dissipate. Such opinions were not, of course, without effect on the results of social science research published before or during the Revolution.[4] And this Islamic remainder was even more unappealing, according to Nikki Keddie, since it was made up largely of 'disadvantaged' or 'lower middle-class' urban strata (Keddie 1972).

Might we not say that the modernizing aspirations of the 1960s and 1970s – with their certainties based on the occlusion of whole sections of social reality – led us to consider Islam's hegemony as the result of the Republic's public policy, as if to reassure us of the solid foundations of our former modes of reasoning? By considering religiosity as the monopoly of postrevolutionary power, or even as its invention, did Islam not become the popular name for the state?[5] Is criticism of the Iranian government not a euphemized form of critiquing Islam or theocracy? Has the political analysis of the state not been substituted by the political analysis of Islam, and has the resistance to clerical power not become the form through which one has sought to consider political change in the aftermath of the Revolution?

In sum, the vision that emerges from the majority of analyses dealing with Iranian society is of an excessively political or militant nature. Society is often depicted as either wretched or exotic: everything boils down to domination or contestation. There is the illegitimate clerical power – a phoenix continually reborn from its ashes as it recovers and renews itself through crises – even as there is a society that is preferentially called 'civil', but which should actually be called 'civilized', even 'libertarian', since it is entirely mobilized towards the aims of the Constitutional Revolution (1906–1909).[6] The latter was the founding moment of progressive Iranian ideology, the realization of liberty and equality. Having arrived at this point in our critical discussion, a doubt arises: has anthropology in Iran not remained an organic science of the people (*mellat*) held hostage to the master narrative (*grand récit*) (Duara 1995) of the nation? This narrative seems to exercise a form of 'tyranny', in the words of Naghmeh Sohrabi, not only over the period that followed the Constitutional Revolution but also, retrospectively, over that which preceded it (Sohrabi 2005): the history of the Qajar period is reread anachronistically, once and for all, through the prism of the Revolution's inevitable arrival.

The weight of this nationalism, a stumbling block to any serious analysis of Iranian society's recent evolution, has given rise to a number of consequences that limit social science research. For one, it has helped make anthropology a Farsi-centred discipline, despite the spectacular increase in bilingual Persian-Baloutch, Arabic, Kurdish and Turkish publications over the last few years. Secondly, it has provoked a general indifference to attempts at situating Iranian society in its regional environment by means of investigations into migration, cross-border trade, tourism and pilgrimages. Furthermore, the social sciences in Iran continue to take for granted the 'naturalness' of the nation-state, even if they play on ethnic, regional or local variations, which is all the more surprising at a time when globalization should tend to minimize such state-centred dimensions.

On the basis of the preceding discussion, which some may find too harsh, our goal is neither to ask how this 'national' or nationalistic tradition persists in the discipline of anthropology nor to proffer a possible or more desirable alternative to such enclosure. Rather, our aim is to interrogate the limits of the paradigm of 'civil society' that has, over the last few years, substituted itself for the nationalist narrative. Is this Manichean alternative between a virtuous 'civil society' and an oppressive 'power' – or between the Islamic Republic's stigmatization on the one hand and civil society's sublimation on the other – not essentially a cheap remake of the old dolorist schema that opposes *dolat* to *mellat,* as discussed by Katouzian in his famous book (2003)?[7] The problem is that this old schema, by becoming reified, is reinforced and nourished today by another generalized confusion in the face of Muslim societies: that having to do with 'an understood question', as historian Jocelyn Dakhlia's expresses it (1998) – in other words the stereotyped postulate of nondistinction between religion and politics or, moreover, the theocratic functioning of politics in Islamic countries.[8] Thus, notwithstanding an essentialist argument, if Islam is at once *din* and *dowlat* (religion and politics), it is not surprising to find that the opposition *dollat/ mellat* (state/society) finds a new extension, transforming itself, according to some, into an opposition between Islam and *mellat.*

If the veil – including that of Shirine Ebadi – seems to have crystallized better than anything else the dualism or irreconcilability of power and society, it deserves reexamination. We may need to show that it is not possible to reduce the veil to a question of power or Islam, and demonstrate that it has become a terrain of negotiation between state and society. To do so, however, we must accept the idea that the veil, as a social contract rather than a religious practice (and, more generally, Islam, as a debate rather than a series of categorical prescriptions) is not Iran's past, but its present. Indeed, neither the specific practice of *hijab* nor Islam in general is able to refer to any such tradition. Both catalyse crucial and autonomous movements in the fields of social and political change. One need only think of the considerable number of Islamic publishing houses, discussion groups or encyclopedias; the highly colourful and controversial ritual mourning ceremonies for Ashoura, which year after year stir debate and conflict; or the regular mobilization of Islamic tribunals that condemn, and sometimes liberate, those accused of blasphemy. The result of a religious debate is not merely in the hands of clerics, and it is not simply a question of the famous divide between reformers and conservatives. Today the competition is fierce, and various social groups play important parts: *mojtahed* women (i.e. female clerics, whose numbers are growing), secular Islamic thinkers (i.e. those who do not wear the turban), Sufis, religious singers, university professors, journalists and feminists are all able to galvanize the public.

The Veil of Discord, or the Limits of Civil Society

By taking up, as planned, that most controversial of subjects – i.e. the veil – we do not intend to claim its centrality in Iranian society. It was not the subject of political demands until 2000, when, rather timidly, the question of a referendum on its practice surged forth in a few speeches. 'We have other battles to fight', said Iranian women who had turned their backs on Faezeh Hachemi, the athletic daughter of the president, member of Parliament in Tehran elected in 1996 and founder of the female Olympics in Islamic countries, who fought for such a referendum and lauded horseback riding, cycling and pants-wearing for women at the legislative elections of 1999. Rather, we should remember that if there was instrumentalization of the veil, it was a general phenomenon. As an instrument of the exercise of power, the veil allowed the Islamic Republic to recentre the question of discrimination against women to the sole domain of religion, demanding that women obey Islamic norms before exercising the right to exist in public space.

But the veil was likewise instrumentalized by critics of the government and even by social scientists. It became a self-sufficient analytical category used to typify the state and evoke its repressive policies towards women. Considered as a symbol of political obscurantism, the veil fed claims of antagonism between state and society, meanwhile making it easy to forget the multiple ways in which it actually permitted communication between the

two. It was similarly surprising to see these women, who were not particularly active politically until 1997, mobilized in a great reform movement behind Mohammad Khatami, a political leader who, although an enlightened
cleric, never publicly questioned the obligation to wear the veil. In other
words, did we not keep ourselves from properly understanding Iranian society in all its complexity by condemning the political seraglio, and by stig-
matizing its religious discourse and its desire to maintain the obligation to
wear the veil?

I would like to recall several arguments that undermine the thesis of absolute antagonism by looking briefly at the results of a study conducted on a
group of Muslim women between 1985 and 1987.[9] These arguments, while
emphasizing the relative autonomy of society, nevertheless permit one to ap-
prehend the possible linkages between power and its subjects – connections
whose changes are not irrelevant to current sociopolitical developments.

Preference should be given to the points of juncture or overlap between
phenomena, not the lines that separate or delimit them. For anthropologists,
then, social life cannot be seen as organized or divided into compartments
such as religious and nonreligious, national and international, state and civil
society. All of these dimensions tend to intermix in history. The fact that one
must create categories like the clergy, the bazaar and the state in order to
analyse them is one thing. But this does not mean that they should be reified or necessarily opposed to each other. Indeed, nothing prevents us from
forging new notions that transcend our usual categories, allowing relationships and mutual interactions to become visible. For example, distinctions
are often drawn between bazaar, clergy and state in the anthropological
literature. Yet one knows that clerics and politicians often maintain tight
relations with the bazaar, either because they themselves are economic op-
erators or because members of their families are *bazaari*. Thus one of the
most widespread interpretative schemas of political change in Iran, which
presupposes a pattern of regular conflict between the bazaar and the state,
finds itself vitiated at its very base.

In the same way, so-called religious practices are in reality much more
than that, even though their actors do not find the least contradiction.
Wherever anthropologists or sociologists of religion seek to find pure manifestations of faith, they will encounter matrimonial, economical and political practices, effects of distinction and power, and the social affirmation of
women or youth.[10] The study of *jaleseh* (Adelkhah 1991) is revealing in
this regard: these female religious meetings are privileged instances of the
self-organization of the 'second sex'. They have proven to be successful in
the practice of commerce and in the informal savings of their participants,
in their progressive religious autonomy in relation to the clergy and in their
politicization and electoral participation. They function as the substructure
of a real charitable organization.

As for *hijab,* it is not limited by the refusal to wear *hijab,* as is suggested by the impassioned debate concerning the practice of the veil. Indeed, most of the time women do not experience any related pathos, whether wearing it or not. The most significant divisions often occur among the practitioners of veiling, who cover themselves by choice and have little or no aversion to women who do not share their conviction, since, as they affirm, faith only concerns the relationship between creature and creator. What is most often postulated as a radical alternative – to be veiled or not – is in reality experienced as a continuum: veiled and nonveiled women rub shoulders, live under the same roofs and are friends irrespective of their vestimentary choices. One can easily cover or uncover oneself without necessarily experiencing the apprehension of conversion or apostasy. *Hijab* separates neither the religious from the secular, nor the subordination of women from their emancipation. It should be understood, rather, as a meeting place – potentially although not necessarily conflictual – between various social facets, between actors themselves and between the past and the present. *Hijab* notably has provided women with access to the public sphere and initiated a practice of negotiations between private and public spaces. In daily life, a woman who practices *hijab* is not confined to the intangible perimeters: not only is she able to remove *hijab* under certain circumstances and in the presence of certain individuals, but she is free to traverse various moments of religious sociability (covered, or covered differently depending on the context), visit administrative offices, markets, family and friends, and travel in neighbouring regions or abroad. This series of social experiences cannot be reduced to the simple alchemy of religion or culture.

In other words, it is necessary to radically readjust our line of inquiry. We must reject our habitual categories in order to start afresh with a sustained reflection on the phenomenon of frontiers. Of course, the idea that the political imposition of the veil functions as a technique of male domination or social control over women is not entirely unfounded. But, considered as such, *hijab* remains a frontier: a place where the exercise of power is practised, where one can either adhere or resist the control of power, or else where one can circumvent or subvert it in various ways. By making the effects of such 'frontiers' the anthropological object par excellence, we might be able to separate ourselves from the current national or nationalistic tendency of the discipline and detach ourselves from the primacy of politics.

Towards an Anthropology of Vestimentary Practices

As far as the anthropology of *hijab* in Iran is concerned, an initial paradox arises from the fact that it has only rarely been understood in its material reality: an article of clothing with its own fabric, style, even its own *imagi-*

naire. Most of the time *hijab* is reified as a meta-code that evokes almost inevitably, photographs of women protesting against imperialism in their black *châdors*. However, in practice *hijab,* as we will see, does not limit itself solely to this one form, which is reserved exclusively for social use in religious places or public services, or for use by certain categories of women, whether elderly or belonging to specific social milieus. Forms of the veil other than the *hijab* include the *maqnaeh*, the *rusari* and the *shâl*, worn in different colours and harmonized with the colouring of the woman's over-coat (*mânto*). And we should not forget the *châdor arabi* with its ornate lace sleeves, which, while difficult to wear in traditionalist circles, is considered more comfortable since it leaves the two hands free. The majority of women alternate between these different forms of *hijab,* modulating their dress according to the circumstances in which they find themselves.

In addition, each form of *hijab* is worn differently by different individuals, in different social categories and in different regions. It provides a repertoire whose interpretation is left open to each individual and changes from one sociopolitical moment to the next. Certain recalcitrant critics, uninterested in serious analysis of Islamic societies, mock the attention that is paid to the length of the locks of hair that hang out from the veils of young women in Tehran – lengths that vary according to changing political climates, weather conditions or even trends in fashion. In the eyes of such critics, these are mere details that distract one's attention from the essential issue: the intolerable oppression of the obligation to wear the veil. They would be right, of course, if the researcher's or analyst's job was to mobilize public opinion, if he or she was charged with the task of 'making people aware' of aspects of Iranian society such as the obligation to wear the veil.

Yet beneath any 'essential' issue – e.g. the wearing of skirts in the West – how many fluctuations, how many debates, how many polemics have been waged! Why deny Iranian women the freedom, the pleasure, the annoyance or the indignation provided by various ways of wearing veils? Why should we expect them to challenge the regime in its entirety or else support it body and soul when it is enough for them to live just like the majority of people in the rest of the world? After all, the moments in history when individuals are called upon to make a clear-cut choice between 'dying for their country' or resisting at the risk of clandestinity are extremely rare. Most of the time, the complexities of the societies in which we live save us from such extremes. Participation in the social realm is not a game of heads-or-tails, and it is sometimes curious to see European women expecting Iranian women to make radical decisions that they themselves would not make on their own with regard to the inequalities that they face in their places of work or in political life. One has the feeling that the denunciation of the Iranian regime, and the condemnation of Islam in general, is a kind of liberation by proxy, irrespective of history, that resembles the raucous cries of encouragement at a boxing match, shouted by spectators who do not themselves risk much in the matter. As the Farsi expression goes, such condemnations are lullabies that will not make the singers fall asleep. Beneath the obligation to wear the veil lies an immense field of negotiations, conflicts and games whose aims are less to exclude others than to win a place to exist. It is for this reason that Iranian society is as dynamic and as mobile as any other.

From this point of view, more attention must be paid to the colours of veils: brown, beige, grey, blue, burgundy and green overcoats coexist with black ones. As for scarves, they are often multicoloured even if they do not all come from Hermès. The material of *hijab* constitutes another element of differentiation. All one needs to do to measure this diversity is to attempt to buy a swath of black fabric for a *chador:* depending on whether it is made in Iran or imported from Switzerland or from Japan, it will have a very different monetary and social value.[11] In other words, beneath the normative meta-discourse, there is a world of social distinction and personal style, as well as games of seduction and fashion.

None of this takes anything away from the fact that the practice of the veil is also the result of a political decision taken on a governmental level.[12] We must not forget that the veil preceded the current political era and will no doubt outlive it, in various forms, as it did following its interdiction in 1935 during the Pahlavi era (Chehabi 1993). It is also necessary to understand that *hijab*, as an indispensable element of the 'respect for Islamic norms' reclaimed by women, has been largely individualized and thus constantly renewed. Following the research that we carried out in the mid 1980s, we might make the following remarks:

- The choice of forms and colours for each woman's *hijab* expresses both spatial differentiations (city/suburb, private/public) and occasional ones (work/leisure, family/friends). The veil is thus a vector of social differentiation, not of uniformity.
- 'The material fabric', writes Sahlins, 'is a total social fact, at once material and conceptual, that weaves together seamlessly the spatial meaning of sex and the sexual meaning of space.' (Sahlins 1980: 245). *Hijab* also guarantees a continuum between private and social life. It is the threshold, the door from one to the other: in affirming an essential biological and sexual difference between men and women, it allows the coherent fusion of the values and ideas of these two spheres.
- It is without a doubt necessary to underscore the naturalist discourse of Islamist women, which confirms traditional sexual differences and fortifies the social ethics that were weakened under the Shah's re-

gime. But at the same time, this discourse carries with it new claims, founded on a dynamic vision of the complementary aspects between the two sexes as I have analysed elsewhere (Adelkhah 1991: chapter 5).

If we ask now about the function of *hijab* in the relationship between the state and female society, we could say, quoting Sahlins, that 'the example of the *hijab* allows one to discover the singular quality of Islamic society, to know that it rests on a symbolic code that functions like an open system that is aware of the events it orchestrates and assimilates in order to produce enlarged versions of itself' (Sahlins 1980: 232)

Hijab crystallizes a claim that is at once ethical, social, religious and political. The political dimension of clothing and jewelry as a symbolic code, of which *hijab* is a perfect illustration, has already been highlighted by others (Goffman 1974, Morris 1978). I have also shown that this code is not simply imposed 'from above', but that it is the product of multiple popular practices, multiple '*arts de faire*' or practices of everyday life, to use Michel de Certeau's expression (1991), that contribute to the invention of Islamic modernity. The practice of *hijab* can be accompanied by women's expanded participation in public life, and here the futility of Western discourse is quite clear, insofar as the latter regards the imposition of *hijab* as a sign of the Islamic regime's repressive character.

Obviously, *hijab* cannot only be analysed as a form of contestation or resistance, but also as a type of participation and conformism. It is therefore necessary to move beyond the traditional dichotomies of dominant/dominated, state/civil society, in order to emphasize the plural invention of a society and, in this case, the plural enunciation of a symbolic code: that of *hijab*. *Hijab* signals perhaps a more fundamental cultural schema than simply Islam or Islamism. Even as we avoid culturalist explanations such as those that speak of the 'specificity of Shi'ism', we are necessarily led to wonder whether *hijab* does not represent a particularly efficient technology of what Michel Foucault calls 'a field of governmentality' (Foucault 1989: 135). If one takes the definition of governmentality as a 'contact between the technologies of domination of others and those of the self', one sees how *hijab* can usefully be interpreted in terms of this debate. That the practice of *hijab* functions as a social and political technique of subjection is undeniable, but one must recognize that this subjection is double-sided: it provides added visibility and constitutes a process of women's affirmation in the public sphere.[13]

At present, however, the practice of wearing the veil has merely given rise to polemics and cookie-cutter arguments rather than inspiring precise anthropological investigations into clearly defined categories of female actors at given historical moments. It was precisely such investigations that allowed me to put forth the argument that the veil functioned, at least for a certain type of woman (those educated and born into a particular social milieu) and within the confines of a particular historical moment (the Revolution, as well as a specific period in Iran's urbanization), as a means of access to the public sphere. At the end of the 1980s this claim was deliberately circumscribed: my intention was to describe one category of women – Islamists – while insisting that not all of these women could be unequivocally classified as such, and situating my analysis at a particular historical juncture rather than attempting to speak of the practice of the veil in general. In reality, I was less interested in the veil as such than in the discourse surrounding the veil or the way in which women appropriated this practice in the aftermath of the Revolution. The wearing of *hijab* has, without a doubt, served as a passport, allowing access to the public sphere and other forms of social life to women who, whether affluent or disadvantaged, felt excluded or marginalized by the 'modernizing' framework of the former regime.

This is not to imply that it is a matter of social or cultural revenge. Rather, participation in the public sphere under the cover of the veil was concomitantly legitimate and exacting. In other words, nobody would have wanted this 'legitimacy' if it meant remaining in seclusion. Nevertheless, as women have grown more self-assured, and as they have consolidated their presence, the security provided by the veil has perhaps become superfluous or, in any case, less imperative. This seems particularly true for the generations that did not experience the prerevolutionary period, when the ideological and cosmetic emancipation of women often went hand in hand with marginalization or self-censure, with the exception of certain urban segments of society.

In the end, the key term for understanding *hijab* during the first decade of the Revolution is without a doubt confidence: both the self-confidence of women themselves and their feeling of confidence in a society that had ceased to function as a trap of alienation and had opened up opportunities for personal, professional or militant fulfillment. But we might also speak of the confidence that the leaders of the Republic and a part of the clergy had to concede to women who contributed to the Revolution, sometimes at the peril of their own lives and liberty. Willfully or not, the new regime ratified a portion of women's social and legal acquisitions inherited from the empire. It renounced assigning women a traditional role.[14] It has tolerated and sometimes encouraged the social participation of women. But it has imposed the wearing of the veil. If this interpretation is justified, *hijab* would be neither a simple apparatus of domination nor a simple instrument of emancipation, but a social contract, by definition concluded between two unequal parties.

It is also necessary to point out that imposing the wearing of the veil, as a device for ideological domination, during the first decade of the Revolution has been a way of controlling men perhaps as much as women: at work or on the public scene, even within the sphere of the family, they had to account for the way their wives, sisters and daughters covered themselves. Subjection is not necessarily always where we think it is. And marriage, for certain top officials of the Islamic Republic of Kurdish descent, has often been a site of great tension: on the one hand, there have been those who defended Kurdish culture, which is resistant to the segregation of men and women, especially during the holidays, and on the other hand some have defended strong power and lauded the state's imposition of Islamic codes, particularly during the conflict in Iraq.

What is the state of affairs today? Twenty-five years after the Revolution, this contract is in crisis, or at least in the process of renegotiation. It finds itself under pressure from one of its contractual parties, which has, following successful legal battles, mobilization and newfound consciousness – as well as an unprecedented debate among religious authorities on the now disputable foundations of a certain number of orders or interdictions, such as barring women from the legal profession – grown rich in symbolic and material resources.

Unfortunately, the current configuration of the female condition has not yet given rise to new empirical research on religious or social practices, nor has it made way for new theoretical debates. Researchers have tended to prefer reiterating the great discovery of the early 1990s that consisted in recognizing the force of society, acknowledging its complexity and its dynamic character by examining each of its modes. Nevertheless, women insist upon the separation between political militantism and their particular demands as women. This is exemplified, for instance, by the 'Campaign for a million signatures'[15] that explicitly targeted legal discriminations, not Islam or the Republic in general. At the same time, women now work, earn money and travel far from their homes, whereas prior to the Revolution women who engaged in commerce or affirmed their right to earn money were stigmatized outright. Of course it is not 'because' of the veil that these transformations have taken place, but women's social affirmation cannot nevertheless be dissociated from the practice of *hijab*: neither outside nor against the veil, the advancement of women is thoroughly encased in the contingencies of Iranian history of the 1980s and 1990s.

Although subject to more ample fieldwork research, the following hypotheses concerning the immediately contemporary period may nonetheless be advanced. The veil has ceased being the object of masculine clerical monopoly. Women now interpret it in their own way. It is no longer an instrument solely for religious expression, but social as well, specifically among artists, fashion designers and actresses. These latter serve as veritable role models for women and have supplanted both tradition and the clerical interpretation of a few sacred verses. The renegotiation of the social contract, materialized in the veil, is carried out through these mediations. It is always easy to appeal to democracy, human rights and the equality of the sexes from abroad in an almost incantatory manner. But to do so is to treat with insufficient respect the history and consciousness of Iranian women and men. In this history, as we have affirmed already, the veil is not Iran's past but its future – both because, in the words of a popular French song, '*la femme est l'avenir de l'homme*' ('woman is the future of man'), and because even the dissidents of the Islamic Republic cannot conceive of themselves outside of the decidedly foundational framework of the Revolution.

Conclusion

As Pierre Tévanian has argued in his excellent work *Le Voile médiatique: Un faux débat: « L'affaire du foulard islamique »* (2005), the question is less the veil or Islam than the effects of a consensus within the university world that reduces the object of research to the domain of power or to that of ancestral religion. Our profession is in danger of being hijacked by the contradictory expectations of the protagonists of political and religious debates from which it has always claimed independence. Because of its critical aspirations, the discipline cannot simply take the middle road, the road of compromise, as has been attempted by Shirin Ebadi – who wears by turns the militant garb of *hijab* and the tailored suit of human rights, and who protested virulently against the ban on the veil in France. Neither can it dissipate itself in the positive themes of reform, promotion of civil society or the defense of Iranianism or religion. As sciences of complexity, the social sciences must not let themselves be enclosed within the simplistic and atemporal narratives of Islamic or national identity, which they know to be historically and socially constructed. Rescuing anthropology from the nation requires us first to accept a reformulation of the latter concept. It compels us to understand how the nation has been formed and conceived of over the last century, rather than accepting it at face value as an obvious idea and a tangible reality.

NOTES

1. Bayart (2005: 181), citing Freud on the subject of the subject of the analysis of dreams.
2. Gilles Kepel wrote: 'The history of Muslim societies, throughout its fourteen centuries, has been marked by an intense tension between two opposed poles,

which have commanded the flux and re-flux of civilization born of Islam: *jihad* and *fitna*' (2005: 335). For a reflection on the media construction of the veil affair in France, see Pierre Tévanian (2005).

3. In this case, we owe to Annie Tual the only article published in French on the veil in the urban milieu before the Revolution: 'Variations et usage du voile dans deux villes d'Iran' (1971).

4. We might cite, for example, Behrang, *Le maillon faible* (1979), which does not devote a single chapter to religion, or the last book published before the Iranian Revolution concerning women in Islamic societies by Lois Beck and Nikki Keddie (eds), *Women in the Muslim World* (1979), where the text concerned with Iran in the chapter on Islam deals with the folklore tradition. This in no way impedes the chapter, or the two books cited, from being excellent reference works.

5. I am borrowing from Nancy L. Green, who advanced the idea for immigration in France in 'Religion et ethnicité: De la comparaison spatiale et temporelle', (2005: 81).

6. Within the context of the Russo-Japanese war and the Russian Revolution of 1905 – and crowning nearly a century of religious effervescence, economic and fiscal crises, and military defeats – the so-called Constitutional Revolution put an end to monarchic absolutism. But historians are quite divided on the respective roles of the clergy, the bazaar, religious dissidents, expatriates, intellectuals and the precise signification of the election of a parliament (*majles*), interpreted either in terms of representative liberalism, or else in Islamic terms as simple consultation (*shoura*). The characterization of events from 1906 to 1909 in terms of revolution, moreover, is subject to caution.

7. In this recent work Homa Katouzian discusses the thesis that he defended more than twenty years earlier in *The Political Economy of Modern Iran: Despotism and Pseudo Modernism 1926–1979* (1981).

8. Cf. likewise Jocelyne Dakhlia (1999).

9. In fact the qualifier 'Islamic' or 'Islamist' does not make sense in Persian, and people substitute for it the classical notion of 'Muslim', opposing it at times to *hezbollahi*, which has a militant and more political connotation. Cf. in particular the conclusion of an article (Adelkhah 1990) published before my thesis.

10. On the practice of the pilgrimage and its sociohistorical dynamics see Adelkhah (2007), cf. likewise the excellent volume published by the Institut Français du Proche-Orient: Chiffoleau and Madoeuf (2005).

11. Even as it imposed the wearing of the veil, the Islamic Republic seems to have been incapable of putting an end to the importation of fabrics used to make the *châdor*. This is a subject of debate insofar as the financial interests at stake were considerable ($300 million between 1996 and 2006). Thus it is easier to obtain, even through force, women's consent to wear veils rather than to prohibit the bazaar from importing such fabrics. Women consume 30 million square meters of fabric per year and naturally prefer imported material. Interestingly, the honour of this Islamic distinction has been saved by Japanese textile manufacturers.

12. This decision, however imperative, has never given rise to a specific law concerning the necessity of wearing the veil. In fact, if there do exist – as is no doubt the case – a considerable number of administrative bills, the Constitution makes no mention of them. Nevertheless, in the penal code a clause in Article 638 indicates a punishment of ten days and two months of prison, or 50,000 to 500,0000 rials (equivalent to $50 to $500 on today's exchange), for women who appear in public without their 'legal *hijab*', even if no indication is made as to the precise form the latter is to take.

13. Nilüfer Göle (1993) has likewise explained this phenomenon in the case of Turkey.

14. In his speech, the Imam Khomeiny honoured at once mothers, Muslim women and female activists.

15. The campaign, which in 2008 is still going on, was launched in June 2006 on the initiative of female activists protesting legal discriminations and was based on the Islamic Republic's signature of different international human rights conventions. http://www.we-change.info/.

REFERENCES

Adelkhah, F. 1991. *La Révolution sous le voile. Femmes islamiques d'Iran*. Paris.

———. 1990. 'Logique étatique et pratiques populaires: la polysémie du *Hejâb* chez les femmes islamiques en Iran', *Cemoti* 10.

———. 2007. 'L'économie morale du pèlerinage', *Politix* 77.

Bayart, J.-F. 2005. *The Illusion of Cultural Identity*. London.

Beck, L. and Keddie, N. (eds). 1979. *Women in the Muslim World*. Cambridge.

Behrang, S. 1979. *Le maillon faible*. Paris.

Chehabi, H. 1993. 'Staging the Emperor's New Clothes: Dress Codes and Nation-Building under Reza Shah', *Iranian Studies* 26(3–4).

Chiffoleau, S. and A. Madoeuf. 2005. *Les pèlerinages au Maghreb et au Moyen-Orient: Espace publics, espaces du public*. Beyrouth.

Dakhlia, J. 1998. *Le divan des rois: Le politique et le religieux dans l'islam*. Paris.

———. 1999. 'Religion et politique en Islam: Pour une approche d'une question entendue', *Prologues: revue maghrébine du livre* 17.

de Certeau, M. 1990. *L'invention du quotidien,1e Arts de faire*. Paris.

Deddie and B. Baron (eds). *Women in Middle Eastern History: Shifting Boundaries in Sex and Gender*. New Haven, CT, and London.

Duara, P. 1995. *Rescuing History from the Nation: Questioning Narratives of Modern China*. Chicago.

Foucault, M. 1988. 'Technologies of the Self', in L.H. Martin, H. Gutman and P.H. Hutton (eds), *Technologies of the Self: A Seminar with Michel Foucault*. Amherst, MA.

———. 1989. *Résumé des cours 1970–1982*. Paris.

Friedl, E. 1991. 'The Dynamics of Women's Spheres of Action in Rural Iran', in N. R.

Göle, N. 1993. *Musulmanes et modernes: voile et civilisation en Turquie.* Paris.

Goffman, E. 1974. *Les rites d'interaction.* Paris.

Green, N.L. 2005. 'Religion et ethnicité: De la comparaison spatiale et temporelle', in R. Kastoryano (ed.), *Les codes de la différence: Race, origine, religion, France, Allemagne, Etats-Unis.* Paris.

Katouzian, H. 2003. *Iranian History and Politics: The Dialectic of State and Society.* London and New York.

Keddie, N. 1972. *Scholars, Saints, and Sufis: Muslim religious institutions in the Middle East since 1500.* Berkeley, CA.

Kepel, G. 2005. *Du Jihad à la Fitna.* Paris.

Khosrokhawar, F. and C. Chafiq. 1995. *Femmes sous le voile. Face à la loi islamique.* Paris.

Lefort, C. 2000. *Les formes de l'histoire: essais d'anthropologie politique.* Paris.

Morris, D. 1978. *La clé des gestes.* Paris.

Sahlins, M. 1980. *Au coeur de sociétés.* Paris.

Shahshahani, S. 1986. 'History of Anthropology in Iran', *Iranian Studies* 19(1): 65–86.

Sohrabi, N. 2005. *Signs taken for Wonder: Nineteenth Century Persian Travel Literature to Europe.* Harvard.

———. 2007. 'The Tyranny of the 1906 Constitutional Revolution of Iran on the Historiography of Qajar Iran', forthcoming, *American Historical Review.*

Tévanian, P. 2005. *Le voile médiatique: Un faux débat: 'L'affaire du foulard islamique'.* Paris.

Tual, A. 1971. 'Variations et usage du voile dans deux villes d'Iran', *Objet et monde* 11(1).

CHAPTER 13

Personal Reflections on Anthropology of and in Iran

Richard Tapper

Introductory Overview

I welcomed this collection as an occasion for stocktaking, in different ways. This is indeed time for an assessment of what our discipline – anthropology of and in Iran – has achieved so far, and where it might or should go in the future. Having recently retired from a career studying and teaching at the School of Oriental and African Studies (SOAS), London, I also personally appreciated this opportunity, right at the start of 'the rest of my life', to reflect on my own trajectory in the discipline, past, present and future.

As I was clearing out my office at SOAS, I discovered a host of forgotten and often intriguing documents. One of them was the typescript of a paper I gave at an informal seminar in 1974, on 'ethical problems in fieldwork'. The participants in this seminar were, as I recall, research students and junior lecturers from different London colleges, and we saw ourselves as part of the movement in anthropology in the late 1960s and 1970s to examine and criticize the ethical and epistemological bases of our discipline. We had all read pieces such as Kathleen Gough's 'Anthropology: Child of Imperialism' (1968), and landmark books like Dell Hymes's *Reinventing Anthropology* (1972) and Talal Asad's *Anthropology and the Colonial Encounter* (1973) had just appeared.

In 1974 I was writing on the basis of research in Iran in the 1960s but was also fairly fresh from the conclusion of a second project, in Afghanistan, which had provided me with a valuable comparative perspective (to which I allude briefly). After that I did further extended fieldwork in a provincial town in Turkey (between 1979 and 1984). Before retirement I had never attempted to publish the essay, but I was delighted to reread it for several reasons, not least because – despite being dated in obvious ways – it raises a number of issues of continuing relevance. I have taken the liberty of presenting it now, in slightly modified form, in the body of the present chapter.

Fieldwork Experiences in Iran and Afghanistan

I lived, for a total of about fifteen months between 1963 and 1966, with Shahsevan pastoral nomads of Eastern Azarbaijan (now in the new Ardabil Province), close to the Iranian frontier with Soviet Azerbaijan. The Shahsevan were tribally organized but had been 'pacified' and brought under Iranian government control in the 1920s. Sedentarization and development programmes, begun after the Second World War (and mainly concentrated in the Dasht-e Moghan) were continuing during my research.

How did I come to choose Iran and the Shahsevan? As I have related this at some length elsewhere,[1] I will summarize relevant points here. In summer 1962, after my first year of studying Archaeology and Anthropology at Cambridge University, I spent two months travelling with a small group of friends in North Africa, especially Egypt – we called ourselves 'The Cambridge Expedition to Abu Simbel'! At the time I was more interested in Egyptology than in studying Arab culture, of which that trip gave us a narrow glimpse. But during my second undergraduate year I thought more seriously about what interested me and found anthropology to offer more exciting intellectual challenges than archaeology – or Egyptology. I started to consider pursuing anthropology beyond my degree. This would involve fieldwork – but where?

In the early 1960s, most British would-be anthropologists did field research in rural/tribal areas of what came to be known (after Worsley 1967) as 'third-world' countries. This was justified with reference to the functionalist dogma of holism: because 'everything' in society and culture was functionally connected, a fieldworker was expected to study 'everything', which was clearly easier where the society was small-scale and 'simple', i.e. 'primitive', though this term was no longer acceptable. A further assumption was that a given society might be studied as though it were isolated from external influences, whether state-level or Westernizing. Indeed, many fieldworkers, in search of 'authenticity', omitted to notice or mention any such influences where they occurred. There was also, of course, the romantic motive of exoticism: going 'out there' to 'discover' a people who were 'unknown', i.e. not known or written about in English.

In 1963, I had no inclination to explore the possibilities of anthropological fieldwork either in the Arab world or in the former 'colonial' territories that were the main subjects of the monographs we were reading, and also of the fieldwork being done by current Ph.D. students. At the start of my career in anthropology, I was most influenced by two fellows of my college: my supervisor, Edmund Leach (an anthropologist who had himself worked in Burma, Ceylon and Sarawak but also, early on, in Kurdistan), and Peter Avery (Lecturer in Persian). When the opportunity came at the end of my second year to attach myself to another 'expedition', this time to Iran, I took it. The attachment was very loose: I raised my own travel funds and travelled independently to Tehran and then to Dasht-e Moghan. There I was joined for a few days by the expedition's anthropologist, Jonathan Parry (now a professor at the London School of Economics), who was busy – despite bouts of serious illness – investigating Shahsevan nomad summer camps on the slopes of Mt. Savalan. In Moghan I conducted my own studies of a number of villages of settled Shahsevan, and in the process I learned a great deal about the pleasures and problems of fieldwork.

The following summer (1964), after graduation, I returned to Iran and the Shahsevan. This time my intention was to make up my mind whether to devote a full-time doctoral research project to the Shahsevan, or to move elsewhere. At the end of the summer I was convinced that the project was worthwhile. Back in the U.K., I decided against continuing at Cambridge, where there was little anthropological expertise or interest in the Middle East. Instead I registered for the Ph.D. programme in social anthropology at SOAS, where, before returning to Iran in summer 1965, I spent nine months preparing for field research. This included language training, guided reading and attendance at graduate seminars, and though 'ethical issues' were not formally part of my programme, I did spend some time pondering them in the light of my two summers' experiences in Iran. In the spring I married Nancy Self (a Junior Year Abroad student at SOAS), who accompanied me to Iran before returning to the U.S. to finish her BA. She rejoined me the following summer for the final months of fieldwork.

I shall also refer more briefly to my second stint of fieldwork, in Afghanistan, where Nancy and I lived for over a year between 1968 and 1972, mostly among nomadic and settled Durrani Pashtuns in the ethnically mixed northern plains and central mountains, where the Durrani were a politically dominant minority. They were under nominal government control, but local politics was run for most purposes by rich and powerful locally based Durrani khans. There were no sedentarization or development programmes, but the nomads spontaneously settled and started agriculture wherever they could.[2]

The following sections of this chapter are taken from my unpublished 1974 paper, with some editorial corrections as well as some current additions and comments in footnotes or square brackets. I have made no attempt to correct anachronisms and naïvetés.

Ethical Issues in Ethnographic Fieldwork

I shall use my own experiences to illustrate and exemplify a number of moral and ethical problems that are likely to affect anyone doing fieldwork. Everyone, in other words, has to make a number of decisions of principle. The first is, clearly, whether to do fieldwork or not; you may decide not, either after considering the complexities of the other moral problems, or as a result of some personal crisis.

I shall refer throughout to John Barnes's article 'Some Ethical Problems in Modern Field Work', first published in the *British Journal of Sociology* in 1963, then revised and republished in Jongmans and Gutkind's landmark collection *Anthropologists in the Field* (1967).[3] I think it is still the best statement of these problems; I first read it in summer 1964, just after graduating and before going to Iran for my second short visit to the Shahsevan.

Barnes begins by comparing the sort of fieldwork done by the Cambridge Torres Straits expeditions and Malinowski – where the fieldworker felt external and looked at his subjects as through a microscope – with more recent conditions:

> Firstly, the ethnographer's field of study is enlarged so that even when focusing on an illiterate tribe he gives some attention to outside agencies. Secondly, the focus of study is no longer always an illiterate tribe but may be a community many of whose members can read, write letters to the newspapers and learned periodicals, and even sue the ethnographer if need be, and who may be his fellow-citizens. Thirdly, the ethnographer hopes not only to publish generalized statements about the customary behaviour but also to describe the actions of individuals whom, for purposes of exposition, he must identify in some way; and these actions may be, in some eyes, reprehensible or illegal. Fourthly, administrators and others realize that ethnographic publications include statements construable as criticism of their activities, and hence are more cautious about giving information. (1967: 196)

The ethnographer is now an integral part of his field of study: 'It begins when he first makes plans to visit his field location and continues at least until the time when his published work is discussed by the people he has studied' (1967: 197). I found this description of fieldwork conditions to be in every way applicable to my own situation in Iran.

Sponsors [and Gatekeepers]

Why do sponsors give money for field research in strange places? To assist in some programme of political or economic exploitation? There were plenty of examples in the 1960s and earlier, not least the American experience in South America and Southeast Asia; but also in the history of the British Colonial Social Science Research Council (SSRC), which sponsored field studies for overt or covert practical purposes. It is clearly as well to be aware of the source of one's funds, which are inevitably going to be 'tainted' somewhere along the line by association with some politically dubious organization; but perhaps one should not worry, so long as one is sure that (a) one's choices of research area and problems were not dictated by the need to make them acceptable to a particular source of funds, and (b) one's results are not going to be directly used by the sponsoring body or made available for economic or political ends with which one may disagree.

For my work on Iran, I felt myself relatively free of such constraints. My Ph.D. studies were financed by a U.K. State Studentship, for which the few details I had to give of my research project were vetted by academics, not bureaucrats; and by grants from the Horniman Fund of the Royal Anthropological Institute, the University of London Central Research Fund and the British Institute of Persian Studies (BIPS) – none of which demanded more than a cursory account of my activities. Although I did consciously phrase my proposals in rather vague terms of 'utility', I did not feel constrained or confined in any way by the terms of my grants, which were in fact very broad. For our Afghan research, Nancy and I had a U.K. SSRC project grant, to which no strings were attached at all: only in the final report were we asked, among other things, to state what use the results might be to the 'community as a whole' (unstated, but presumably in the U.K.) – to which we were able to answer: 'none'.

What about the authorities ['gatekeepers'] in Iran, at all levels? Barnes goes into some details about the ethical problems facing a fieldworker in a situation where the local administration is to some degree influenced by the ethnographer's own government – i.e. a colonial situation:

> now we are not sure over how wide an area we have to suspend moral judgments and to refrain from action. If it is wrong to influence the tribesman, is it wrong to influence the administration? For research purposes, we want to study some at least of the actions of the administration; must we, therefore, treat the administration as though it were another savage tribe? Or is the administration a body to which we can appeal in the name of science? Or again, is it a constitutional body in which we have rights or for which we have responsibilities? Or can we treat with the administration on two levels, seeking intellectual and logistic support at a high administrative level, while at the same time endeavouring not to become identified with the administration at the local level? (1967: 198)

However, he says, the dilemma of relations to government

> is easier to solve in practice when fieldwork is undertaken in territory controlled by an administration that is entirely foreign to the investigator.

Under these circumstances he is likely to have very little influence and is entirely dependent on the co-operation of the foreign administration. The ethnographer will then often try to make his research work appear harmless rather than useful. (1967: 199)

In my situation in Iran, the ethical problems of relating to the administration were not crucial, while the practical problems were. At that time, the early to mid 1960s, Iran was justifiably classified by Gough (1968) as a client or satellite state: the regime was largely held in place by the United States, but American and other political interference did not percolate very deeply into the bureaucracy. At the level of visiting research workers, particularly postgraduate students, the Iranian Ministry of the Interior and the Intelligence and Security Organization (SAVAK) had [so far as one could tell] complete discretion about granting travel and residence permits, and often exercised this with visitors of all nationalities.

The main problem for a foreign researcher in such a situation is to appear both respectable and harmless. In Iran it was slightly different, however. At Tehran University there was a flourishing Institute of Social Studies and Research (ISSR) with a department of tribal studies.[4] Ever since I had first gone there in 1963, it was essential for any foreign anthropologist to work under this institute's auspices. On their part, they cleared you politically through SAVAK, recommended you to various government departments that granted residence and travel permits, and gave letters of introduction to provincial universities and sometimes governors, on a personal basis. Getting all this together, though, was liable to take some time. On your part, you promised to provide a copy of your thesis or relevant published work. You might also get asked to lecture at the institute, or to harbour one or two of their students in your field situation, to give them experience. I was not asked to do either myself, but I gathered from others who had been that the students who accompanied them were unprepared physically and mentally for the ordeal of rural living conditions in their own country, and that when they did accompany a foreign researcher to the field they seldom stayed more than a few days.[5]

If one managed, through good recommendations from one's home university or from the British Institute of Persian Studies (BIPS) in Tehran, to square one's project with the Institute for Social Studies and Research (ISSR), things went smoothly, if slowly, and one eventually arrived in the 'field'. Here, however, one continued, perhaps throughout one's fieldwork, to be a source of political anxiety to the local authorities. First, few local officials really swallowed the 'harmless' label acquired from SAVAK; secondly, they were anxious about possible 'misunderstandings' and often about exposure of their own way of doing things. The first of these is, on the surface at least, the main problem: no matter what one does, one is continually suspected as a 'political agent' [especially if one comes from the U.K. or the U.S.]. It might be useful to go further into this, as it is probably relevant to most fieldwork situations today [i.e. 1974], both with 'unknown' first-time fieldworkers, and with established academics.

Governments in Middle Eastern countries such as Iran and Afghanistan, at least at the time when I worked there, had negative attitudes to anthropologists for several, mostly obvious reasons:

(1) Anthropologists tend to visit the most 'backward' areas of the country, yet the government is anxious to avoid publicity for 'anachronistic' tribal peoples and their primitive customs. This anxiety is often justified; both Iran and Afghanistan have seen the publication abroad of ultra-romantic novels and articles in magazines such as *National Geographic*, which have virtually contradicted the modernizing image that the government puts about, especially among their Western sponsors/supporters.

(2) They don't want publicity for bureaucratic corruption and inefficiency, or for the general conduct of the administration. Almost any ethnographic statement, however detached, is liable to be understood, by such sensitive ears, as criticism.

(3) They don't want exposure of any other undesirable features such as popular anti-government feeling. They are anxious about too close exposure of the people to foreign ideas – and the possibility of direct incitement to opposition. They are particularly concerned by the notion that this is the way British agents have worked in the past.

(4) Fear of military intelligence work, especially by 'big powers', among whom the U.K. still figures largely in popular mythology, used to be well founded, though now it seems a somewhat paranoid attitude.

The situation as seen by Iranians is summed up in the following passage from Parviz Varjavand's *Introduction to the General Study of the Nomad Tribes of Iran,* a publication of the ISSR that appeared at the time of my fieldwork among the Shahsevan:

Nor are foreign studies of the tribes in recent years free of mistakes and deficiencies. Such students usually belong to one of two types. The first includes those who were and are official political agents, and those who conceal their political aims under the disguise of scientific research. The second group comprises a limited number of scholars whose travels into the tribal areas have had only the scientific aims of anthropological research.

Members of the first group enter the field with an eye on the political function of the tribal units. In their investigations they are trying to discover and understand the nature of the tribal organization and political machinery; the basis of the structure of authority positions and the network of links that holds the structure together; the genealogical relations and marriage alliances between them. In general they want to find how the holders of power safeguard their position, whether by their connections with the authorities outside the tribe, or through their relations with other holders of power within the tribe.

Mostly, in the publications of these latter we come across statistics and analysis of tribal economics and politics; that is to say, they do not publish all the results of their studies, but put them at the disposal of their national political organizations. The second type mentioned above comprises scholars mainly from those countries that have no important commercial or political interests in this country. Their aim is to carry out their research with a background knowledge of the development of human societies and the problems of physical and social anthropology. Most of these scholars' studies have a degree of importance and repute; for example the work done by Barth on the Basseri tribe (1961: 15–16).

The importance of this observation is paramount: there is a correlation between the non-involvement of a country in Iran's politics and economics, and the value of the research that scholars from that country carry out. It is striking, of course, that a central theme of Barth's *Nomads of South Persia* (1961) was the very focus of study that Varjavand attributed to the foreign spy: tribal political organization. An anthropologist from the U.S., the U.K., France, or possibly Germany is disadvantaged from the start, especially if interested – as I was – in just these matters. In 1965 I spent some months in Tehran waiting for my residence and research permits. During that time, so I heard, one day the Austrian ambassador to Iran was mistakenly refused permission to land at Mehrabad. When the mistake was discovered, apologies were profuse, and the following week, when two Austrian anthropologists [the Loefflers] arrived from Vienna, within a few days they were granted residence permits and security passes to go to study the Boir Ahmad, politically one of the most sensitive tribal groups of southern Iran!

In Afghanistan, Nancy and I were told almost on arrival (in summer 1968) that 'anthropology' was a dirty word in Afghan administrative circles. Two reasons were clearly given by the minister we talked to [Dr Abdul-Ghafur Rawan Farhadi, himself a specialist in linguistics and recently the Afghan government's permanent representative to the United Nations]: (a) that anthropology was of no use to a government interested in the pressing problems of urban and industrial development rather than the distant rural and tribal sector that was the concern of most anthropologists; and (b) that anthropologists cover 95 per cent the same ground as military intelligence agents (spies).

In fact we managed to work in the area we wanted in 1971–72, for various reasons. We had sponsorship from the SSRC, and I had an academic post at SOAS. We survived a trial period in summer 1968, when we were acutely aware of being 'on probation' [as we conducted a 'survey' of possible research sites and subjects in Afghan Turkistan]. Throughout our time in Afghanistan, we kept our noses clean through subtlety and tact, swallowing pride and prejudice, social and political convictions; otherwise we would have had to abandon our project. [When explaining our activities and attitudes to people] in the field, and to local authorities, a very effective argument was in terms of our responsibilities: we were responsible to our colleagues in the U.K. and to future foreign fieldworkers, and hence could be relied on to observe our responsibilities to the Afghan government and people.[6]

This is all part of the next heading:

Moral Judgments in the Field and Role Definition

This is an area of problems that every fieldworker has to face. With respect to moral judgments, Barnes emphasizes how, under earlier microscope conditions, these were not relevant – a double standard could safely exist. But now, since ethnographers form part of their studies, especially with participant observer techniques, they are going to find themselves torn between at least three different moral codes/value systems: their own, that of their subjects and that of the administration. Objective interest and abstaining from interference are not always possible or desirable. In the eyes of the administration, ethnographers may be concealing illegal acts, or even participating in them; in the eyes of the people they may be required to conceal them, not only in their reports to the administration but also in their publications. Inevitably, there are occasions when one's own personal values come right to the fore – as Barnes says:

> No simple formula will apply to all circumstances. The ethnographer has to define his role, or try to do so, so that he can retain the good will of his informants and of the administration, continue to gain the flow of information essential to his research task, and yet remain true to his own basic values. This ideal may not always been possible, and the ethnographer has to decide which if any of these desiderata he should forgo. If he can-

not reach an acceptable solution, he should not waste everyone's time but
should switch to some other research topic. (1967: 201)

My fieldwork among the Shahsevan was a continual battle to remain
respectable in the eyes of a somewhat corrupt local administration, and yet
to find out as much as possible about what was going on. This was particularly difficult in a situation where I found myself dependent on certain tribal
chiefs who were no longer recognized by government yet continued to wield
considerable local power. Early in my fieldwork, in a running confrontation
between one chief and local gendarmerie officers, I sided, necessarily but
rather openly, with the former. The latter (the officers) spread stories about
my being a foreign spy, harboured by the chief in question and fully equipped
with two-way radio, guns, etc., but such was the gendarmes' corruption, eventually exposed without my help, that they could not push these accusations to
any conclusion, and anyway all the tribesmen knew them to be false.

A result of this particular confrontation, however, was that I was per-
petually, throughout the rest of my fieldwork, suspect from the authorities'
point of view. I was able, and was in fact forced, to identify myself pretty
completely with my Shahsevan hosts. This situation was fine for my fieldwork among the nomads, but it closed local official records to me. I spent
many weeks staying with the above chief, partly to follow the confrontation
in question, but partly because it was long before I could persuade anybody
of the feasibility of my wish to live with non-chiefly nomads in their camps.
I eventually won over one camp headman (from a neighbouring tribe) and
joined his camp. I spent the last eight months of my fieldwork there, but I
was then alienated from the powerful chiefly family of his tribe by a dispute
between them and this headman, in which I now necessarily sided with the
latter.

These were not issues of moral judgment, but of personal and political
intrigue. Probably because I did not then have any very strong moral commitment, I never had any major crises of moral judgment in my fieldwork
in Iran,[7] but as can be understood from my earlier remarks, I had some difficulty with role definition.

My conclusion is a plea that what is needed now, and will be needed
more, is not so much a new anthropology (with new subjects and new theory
– though these might indeed be desirable) as new anthropologists. What is
needed is new awareness on the part of all anthropologists, especially those
entering field situations, of the total extent of their responsibilities: moral,
ethical, academic and political values have to be brought to a balanced
compromise in each case. Anthropologists who do not already realize this
should become aware of the fallacy of academic objectivity (ethical, moral,
intellectual) in the field situation, as well as in theoretical approaches.

Thirty Years On

Happily, anthropology was already moving in the directions for which I was arguing in the last paragraph above; it has indeed, like the world, changed almost unrecognizably in the intervening thirty years. Not least, ethical issues are now a central anthropological concern (see for example AAA 1998 and ASA 1999).

I should add some comments on the degree to which I conformed with Barnes's recommendations. First, in my work in Iran I failed to act on his insistence on widening the time and space limits of fieldwork. My notebooks contain little information on the time I spent in Tehran, and the reconstruction in my 1974 paper is based largely on memory.[8]

Secondly, however, I did make serious efforts to return the results of my research to the Iranian gatekeepers. During my first year back at SOAS (1966–67), I produced the then customary series of four circulated papers for discussion in the post-fieldwork seminar. In 1967 I was appointed assistant lecturer, long before my thesis was finished. Meanwhile, Nancy had completed an M.Phil. thesis (partly based on her field experience among the Shahsevan women), and in summer 1968 we spent two months in Afghanistan exploring the possibilities of fieldwork there (for Nancy's Ph.D.). I completed my own thesis in late 1970; meanwhile we were awarded an SSRC grant for joint research in Afghanistan. On our way there, I took copies of my thesis and lodged them with the three main organizations that had helped or sponsored my 1965–66 fieldwork: the company in Tabriz responsible for development in Dasht-e Moghan, the ISSR in Tehran and BIPS. In the first two cases I have no idea what happened to the copies, or whether anybody ever read them. My first monograph, completed in 1977, came out in early 1979 – at the time of the Revolution. Translations of this book (R. Tapper 1979) into Persian have been attempted, but none has so far been published, though translations of various articles of mine on the Shahsevan and other subjects have appeared. My second Shahsevan monograph (1997) was awarded a 'Best Research of the Year' prize by the Ministry of Culture in 2001, and a translation was published in 2005.

After the Revolution, I did not resume contact with my Shahsevan family and friends until 1992.[9] My closest Shahsevan family was now living in Karaj; I gave them copies of my publications (all in English), together with a VHS copy of the 30-minute black-and-white film I had shot in 1965–66. Around the same time Mehdi Mizban, a nephew of the family, completed his MA in anthropology at Islamic Azad University, Tehran, with a substantial thesis based on his own fieldwork with 'our' family (1992).

Between 1992 and 1995 I spent a total of five months in Iran. I made no attempt to obtain permission to carry out an extended field study such as I had done in the 1960s; rather, one of my main objectives in those short trips was to reestablish contact with the Shahsevan families who had welcomed me so warmly thirty years before – which still necessitated negotiating an official sanction to travel in the border areas of Ardabil Province. Otherwise, I was interested in exploring the possibilities for longer-term field research, if not for myself then at least for students from the U.K. Ziba Mir-Hosseini and I spent some time discussing these possibilities, both with university colleagues in Tehran and Shiraz, and with officials from various ministries in Tehran and elsewhere. The main approach we followed was to open discussion on possible cooperation and exchange, at various levels: this might involve exchanges at both student and faculty level, joint conferences, training programmes, workshops, perhaps a major collaborative research project on change in rural Iran since the Revolution.

What had changed in the research atmosphere between the 1960s and the 1990s – apart from those changes that might be due to my own change in status from a postgraduate research student to a senior academic? How had official attitudes changed towards the conduct of anthropological fieldwork by foreigners, particularly in rural and tribal areas? One major difference I experienced was that, unlike in the 1960s, officials in the 1990s did not hesitate to speak out directly if they suspected foreigners' motives – as they usually did. For example, in late summer 1993, Ziba and I were trying to negotiate a programme of cooperative research with the Ministry of Jihad (the ministry concerned with social and economic development in the countryside, among both villagers and nomads). At a planning meeting chaired by a Deputy Minister, we recorded the following in our notes.

One official begins with quotations from Ayatollah Khomeini to the effect that 'foreigners know about our customs, and this becomes a way of exploiting us, etc. We have this history of being exploited on the basis of this type of research; what sort of guarantees can you give that the research you propose will not be used by foreign universities and spies and governments?'

Another official gave examples, saying, 'we have historical reasons for these fears; for example, the British made Ayatollah Nuri the enemy of the [Constitutional] Revolution, and people had him hanged; and also look at Mossadeq. The British could plan such things because they knew and understood our religious feelings and customs.'

In response, we said: 'We can't give guarantees; knowledge is always a two-edged sword, it can cut both ways; but what matters is who holds the handle, and we want to give you the handle, use the edge in your direction, and take the risk for the other – this is the only way to go forward; the alternative is to remain ignorant and take no risks; you have the choice. If the West has progressed because it has learned which edge to use, there is always the possibility of use by other people; but you can use it better and to better effect. These conspiracy theories are irrelevant and outdated. Academics who come here, like anthropologists, are friends of Iran; they are progressive, and often opposed their own government's policies; they can be the best propagandists for Iran.'

Later we pointed out: 'The same fear you have also exists in the West about jihad; if we make an application for funding in the U.K. for a project involving the Ministry of Jihad, we need to include two pages explaining the term 'jihad', which most people understand to be 'holy war'; this cultural misunderstanding too has historical and political roots ... Times have changed, Iran is a different nation, Iranians can't be manipulated this way, it is an insult to the Iranian people to think so.'

Two years later, in October 1995, a mutual friend asked the security chief in the same ministry in Tehran to give us a simple letter of introduction to his counterpart in Ardabil, the provincial capital where we wanted to go for a couple of weeks in order to visit the Shahsevan. He asked to see us:

> He wanted to find out why there was such a wave (*mowj*) of foreign researchers come to study the tribes at this time; not just us, and Susan Wright among Mamassani, but a young Japanese student who recently went to Boir Ahmad. 'What was behind all this', he asked? The discussion turned towards British politics; he maintained that it was a well-known fact that, although the British don't have much power, they have their agents all over the world, running things. He went on, smiling but apparently serious, that the Zionists control the British media, and somehow manipulate the British government, who isn't aware of it. (From our notes)

My own view of the possibilities of productive cooperative research in Iran changed after an incident at Mehrabad airport (described by Ziba in the preface to her 1999 book) in which Ziba and I had our notes, computer discs and many personal possessions seized by a 'security' person. We have a good idea that the person responsible was not an Iranian government official, but someone whom we had antagonized personally and who had good contacts in the airport. Nonetheless, since that outrage, and despite several official invitations, I have not yet returned to Iran, at first through choice, more recently through lack of opportunity.

One result of my visits to Iran in 1992–95 was a paper on conspiracy theories (CTs) in Iranian political culture.[10] Existing literature on CTs in Iran and the Middle East ranges from racist rubbish by the neoconservative Daniel Pipes (1996) to a brief, insightful essay by anthropologist Jon Anderson (1996). On Iran specifically, there are well-informed and well-documented discussions by historian Ervand Abrahamian (1991, 1993) and sociologist Ahmad Ashraf (1992). Both Abrahamian and Ashraf condemn CTs as paranoid delusions with harmful effects on society and individuals. In my own paper, I ask what kind of theories CTs are, in the wider contexts of political culture and belief systems. I distinguish three levels at which CTs operate: master narratives (the basic CTs), local narratives, and underlying assumptions (about history, agency and power); I also distinguish 'popular' from 'official' CTs. The latter may well be subject to manipulation by oppressive regimes (in reformist Iran the function and credibility of CTs became a political issue), but popular CTs may well be an effective mode of resistance. Drawing analogies between CTs and the witchcraft beliefs described in classic anthropology, I suggest that popular CTs, as theories of human agency, power and knowledge, do not merely provide explanations and compensations for the experience of powerlessness and anxiety, but can be a creative form of political action and participation.

One area in which anthropologists have much to offer the study of Iran, I suggest, is that of political culture and the ethnography of the state, in which we as anthropologists have different and more rounded and insightful perspectives than researchers from other disciplines. For me, the ethnography of the state starts at the 'cutting face': in the office, the classroom, the crime scene, the courtroom and a thousand other situations where the individual confronts the agents, the power and the culture of the state. Of course, various global forces are making themselves felt everywhere, but under the sway of the fashionable late twentieth- and early twenty-first-century obsession with 'globalization' it is too often overlooked that for most people in most countries in the world (and certainly in Iran) the power of the state is far more immediate and pervasive, and will doubtless continue to be for the foreseeable future.

In the 1990s, then, after two decades in which my fieldwork and publication efforts were more concerned with Afghanistan and Turkey, my active research interests returned to Iran, but with a changed focus. My experiences in 1992, 1993 and 1995, together with an interesting sabbatical year (1998–99) during which I accompanied Ziba and her first film (*Divorce Iranian Style*) around the festival circuit in a number of countries, have awakened in me a deeper interest in Iranian political culture, in the notion of the ethnography of the state and, in particular, in Iranian cinema. I have since convened three one-day conferences on Iranian cinema at SOAS, in 1999, 2000 and 2001.[11] The first resulted in an edited book (R. Tapper 2002); another edited book based on the third conference is in preparation. Meanwhile, I taught a one-term MA option course on Iranian cinema in my last three years at SOAS, and had four Ph.D. students working on aspects of the subject.

Although I have a huge backlog of unpublished research materials, one project I hope to pursue in due course concerns aspects of the production and consumption of films about Iran, from *Grass* until the present: consumption particularly in the sense of how different audiences, Iranian and non-Iranian, inside and outside Iran, in different situations, respond to films about Iran. A lively debate among Iranians has probed the main elements of *iraniyat*, national cultural identity, and analysed the dialectic between them: Iran as homeland and Persian as dominant language and culture; modernity, Western or otherwise; and Shi'a Islam. The question is complicated by the large diaspora, which has interacted with many different host cultures and versions of modernity and is now well into a second (and third) generation with hybrid/hyphenated identities, often further compounded by ancestral linguistic and religious differences in Iran. There is now a broad movement in Iran to negotiate a balance between these elements, and to reject the traditional politics of monopolization of power, control, secrecy and violence, in favour of democracy, transparency and political, religious and ethnic pluralism.

Cinema has become a major focus and spur for this debate. Not least of the achievements of Iranian cinema is that it provides both a social critique and a forum for discussion between Iranians inside and outside the country. For many in the diaspora, the international success of Iranian cinema has been both a source of renewed pride in their culture and heritage, and a channel for reconciliation between Iranians of different persuasions inside Iran and in the diaspora. Iranian cinema, or more precisely, the viewing and discussion of films from and about Iran, is becoming an important medium for debating and renegotiating Iranian cultural identity.

NOTES

1. R. Tapper (2005). I have briefly described the conditions of my research in Iran in R. Tapper (1979: Appendix 1); see also Tapper and Tapper (1989).
2. I shall not discuss my field experiences in Turkey, where conditions were rather different, and for which there is no space here; see Tapper and Tapper (1989).
3. Comment, 2006: Barnes wrote over forty years ago, in the new postcolonial atmosphere. Despite the prestructuralist assumptions and prefeminist language, his main categories and statements still have relevance. New and important for the time is the way he insists that research begins the moment you start to plan it, not when you arrive in 'the field', and that it continues until you have finished publication and your subjects have read and responded to your results. See his later developments of the subject (1977, 1979).
4. See Fazeli (2006: 85ff.).
5. For the record, my contemporaries as foreign anthropology students included Brian Spooner (from Oxford University, working among the Baluch, but also

acting as assistant director of BIPS), David Brooks (from Oxford University, working among the Bakhtiari) and William Irons (from University of Michigan, working among the Yamut Turkmen).

6. For an account of our fieldwork in Afghanistan, see N. Tapper (1991: chapter 1); see also Tapper and Tapper (1989).

7. Strikingly, when I revisited members of my former 'host' family in 1993, among the memories they had of my time with them was an occasion I had almost forgotten, when I was upset by what happened when some horses from a neighbouring summer camp strayed onto our pasture: as the men went off to beat the horses with sticks, I ran after them shouting at them not to do this. At the time, and also when they recalled it, they found my behaviour weird but amusing.

8. In Afghanistan, however, Nancy and I did keep a fairly detailed record of all our dealings with officials in Kabul.

9. My last visit to Iran had been in 1977, to the Isfahan Festival of Popular Traditions; on that occasion I had been unable to visit the Shahsevan.

10. Presented in various versions, starting with the joint meeting of the British Society for Middle Eastern Studies and the Association française pour l'étude du monde arabe et musulman at Aix-en-Provence in 1996, as a lecture to BIPS in London in the same year, and elsewhere; as yet unpublished.

11. The first ('New Iranian Cinema: Politics, Representation and Identity') and the third ('Behind the Lens, Beyond the Veil: Women in Iranian Cinema') were on behalf of the Iran Heritage Foundation and coincided with major London festivals of Iranian cinema at the National Film Theatre and the Barbican respectively. The second, on 'Young Iranian Cinema', was on behalf of Forum Iran.

REFERENCES

AAA (American Anthropological Association). 1998. *Code of Ethics*. Downloadable from http://www.aaanet.org/committees/ethics/ethcode.htm (accessed 14 August 2007).

Abrahamian, E. 1991. 'Fekr-e "towte'eh-chini" dar farhang-e siyasi-ye Iran', *Kankash* 7(winter 1369 AHS): 96–104.

———. 1993. *Khomeinism: Essays on the Islamic Republic*. Berkeley, CA.

Anderson, J.W. 1996. 'Conspiracy Theories, Premature Entextualization, and Popular Political Analysis', *Arab Studies Journal* 4(1): 96–102.

ASA (Association of Social Anthropologists). 1999. *Ethical Guidelines for Good Research Practice*. Found at http://www.theasa.org/ethics.htm (accessed 14 August 2007).

Asad, T. (ed.). 1973. *Anthropology and the Colonial Encounter*. London.

Ashraf, A. 1992. 'Conspiracy Theories', *Encyclopedia Iranica* 6: 138–147. [Translated as 'Tavahom-e toute'eh', *Goftogu* 8 (summer 1374 AHS/1995): 7–45.]

Barnes, J.A. 1967. 'Some Ethical Problems in Modern Fieldwork', in D.G. Jongmans and P.C.W. Gutkind (eds), *Anthropologists in the Field*. Assen. [Revised version of 'Some Ethical Problems in Modern Fieldwork', *British Journal of Sociology* 14 (1963): 118–134.]

————. 1977. *The Ethics of Inquiry in Social Science.* Delhi.

————. 1979. *Who Should Know What? Social Science, Privacy and Ethics.* Harmondsworth.

Barth, F. 1961. *Nomads of South Persia: The Basseri Tribe of the Khamseh Confederacy.* Oslo.

Fazeli, N. 2006. *Politics of Culture in Iran: Anthropology and Politics in the Twentieth Century.* London and New York.

Gough, K. 1968. 'Anthropology: Child of Imperialism', *Monthly Review* 19(11): 12–27. Also published as 'New Proposals for Anthropologists', *Current Anthropology* 9(5): 403–407.

Hymes, D. (ed.). 1972. *Reinventing Anthropology.* New York.

Jongmans, D.G. and P.C.W. Gutkind (eds). 1967. *Anthropologists in the Field.* Assen.

Mir-Hosseini, Z. 1999. *Islam and Gender: The Religious Debate in Contemporary Iran.* Princeton, NJ.

Mizban, M. 1992. *Il-e Shahsevan: Mowred-e Motale'e-ye Tayfe-ye Geiklu, Tire-ye Hajji-Imanlu*, MA dissertation. Tehran: Islamic Azad University (1371 AHS).

Pipes, D. 1996. *The Hidden Hand: Middle East Fears of Conspiracy.* New York and London.

Tapper, N. 1991. *Bartered Brides: Politics, Gender and Marriage in an Afghan Tribal Society.* Cambridge.

Tapper, N. and R. Tapper. 1989. 'A Marriage with Fieldwork', in I. Ariëns and R. Strijp (eds), *Anthropological Couples*, special issue of *Focaal, Tijdschrift voor Antropologie* (Nijmegen) 10: 54–60.

Tapper, R. 1979. *Pasture and Politics: Economics, Conflict and Ritual among Shahsevan Nomads of Northwestern Iran.* London.

————. 1997. *Frontier Nomads of Iran: A Political and Social History of the Shahsevan.* Cambridge. [Translated by H. Asadi as *Tarikh-e Siasi-ejtema'i-ye Shahsevan-ha-ye Moghan.* Tehran, 1384 AHS].

————. (ed.). 2002. *The New Iranian Cinema: Politics, Representation and Identity.* London.

————. 2005. Interview in *Farhang wa Ensan* 1(1):194–202. Tehran: Nazar.

Varjavand, P. 1344/1965. *Ravesh-e Bar-rasi va Shenakht-e Kolli-ye Ilat-e 'Ashayer.* Tehran.

Worsley, P. 1967. *The Third World.* 2.ed. London.

ℵ Select Bibliography for Anthropology of Iran

This bibliography, collated by Mary Elaine Hegland, offers a comprehensive compilation of English-language publications on anthropological studies in and of Iran. We are most grateful for Professor Mary Hegland's agreement to publish this bibliography and thus make it accessible to all those who are interested in further literature on the anthropology of Iran.

Adelkhah, F. 1999. *Being Modern in Iran*. London.

Akcapar, S.K. 2006. 'Iranian Transit Migrants in Turkey', Ph.D. dissertation. Leuven: Catholic University of Leuven (Belgium).

Alberts, R.C. 1963. 'Social Structure and Culture Change in an Iranian Village', Ph.D. dissertation. Madison, Wisconsin: University of Wisconsin.

Amanolahi, S. 1975a. 'The Baharvand: Former Pastoralists of Iran', Ph.D. dissertation. Houston: Rice University.

———. 1975b. 'Luti, an Outcaste Group of Iran', in *Rice University Studies* 61(2): 1–12.

———. 1985. 'Lurs of Iran', *Cultural Survival Quarterly* 9(1): 65–9.

———. 1986a. 'Ecological Adaptation of the Lutfi Herder-Horticulturists of South Iran', *Human Ecology* 14(3): 355–60.

———. 1986b. *Tales from Luristan (Matalyâ Lurissu): Tales, Fables, and Folk Poetry from the Lur of Bâlâ-Garîva* (with W. M. Thackston). Cambridge, MA.

———. 1989. 'Tribes of Iran', *Human Relations Area Files* 1.

———. 2002. 'Reza Shah and the Lurs: The Impact of the Modern State on Luristan', *Iran and the Caucasus* 6881–29: 193–218.

———. 2003. 'Socio-Political Changes among the Basseri of South Iran', *Iran and the Caucasus* 7(1–2): 261–78.

———. 2004a. 'Fieldwork among Pastoral Nomads and in Sedentary Communities of Iran', *Iranian Studies: Special Issue: Ethnographic Fieldwork in Iran* 37(4): 613–21.

———. 2004b. 'The Status of Women among the Qashqai of South Iran', *Iran and the Caucasus* 8(1): 131–40.

Amir-Moez, Y. 2002. 'The Qashqa'i', in R. Tapper and J. Thompson (eds), *The Nomadic Peoples of Iran*. London: 190–251.

Antoun, R. 1976. 'The Gentry of a Traditional Peasant Community Undergoing Rapid Technological Change: An Iranian Case Study', *Iranian Studies* 9(1): 2–21.

———. 1981a. 'Key Variables Affecting Muslim Local-Level Religious Leadership in Iran and Jordan', in F. Khuri (ed.), *Leadership and Development in Arab Society*. Beirut: 92–101.

————. 1981b. 'The Complexity of the Lower Stratum: Sharecroppers and Wage Laborers in an Iranian Village', *Iranian Studies* 14(3–4): 215–46.

Antoun, R. and M. Hegland (eds). 1987. *The Islamic Resurgence in Comparative Perspective*. Syracuse, N.Y.

Ardehali, P.E. (Drew). 1987. 'Arranging Marriages in Iran', Ph.D. dissertation. New Brunswick: State University of New Jersey.

Atkinson, J. 1832. *Customs and Manners of the Women of Persia and Their Domestic Superstitions*. London.

Balasescu, A. 2003. '"Tehran Chic": Islamic Headscarfs, Fashion Designers, and New Geographies of Modernity', *Fashion Theory* 7(1): 39–56.

————. 2004. 'Fashioning Subjects, Unveiling Modernity: The Co-motion of Aesthetics between Paris and Tehran (France, Iran)', Ph.D. dissertation. Irvine: University of California.

Barth, F. 1953. 'Principles of Social Organisation in South Kurdistan', *Universitetets Etnografiske Museum Bulletin* 7. Oslo.

————. 1969. 'Introduction', in F. Barth (ed.), *Ethnic Groups and Boundaries: The Social Organization of Culture Difference*. Long Grove, Illinois: Waveland Press, Inc: 9–38.

Bateson, M.C. et al. 1977. 'Safa-yi Batin: A Study of the Interrelation of a Set of Iranian Ideal Character Types', in L. C. Brown and N. Itzkowitz (eds), *Psychological Dimensions of Near Eastern Studies*. Princeton, NJ.

————. 1979. '"This Figure of Tinsel": A Study of Themes of Hypocrisy and Pessimism in Iranian Culture', *Daedalus* 108(3): 125–34.

Bauer, J. 1983a. 'Women, the Veil, and the Islamic Revolution in Iran', *Sacramento Anthropological Society, California State University, Sacramento* 16: 120–27.

————. 1983b. 'Poor Women and Social Consciousness in Revolutionary Iran', in G. Nashaht (ed.), *Women and Revolution in Iran*. Boulder, CO.

————. 1983c. 'Women's Images of Women: The Case of Iran', *Sacramento Anthropological Society, California State University, Sacramento* 16: 2–14.

————. 1984. 'New Models and Traditional Networks: Migrant Women in Tehran', in J. T. Fawcett, S.-E. Khoo and P. C. Smith (eds.), *Women in the Cities of Asia*. Boulder, CO: 269–93.

————. 1985. 'Demographical Change, Women and Family in Migrant Neighbourhood of Tehran', in A. Fathi (ed.), *Women and Family in Iran*. Leiden.

————. 1986. 'Sexuality and the Moral "Construction" of Women in an Islamic Society', *Anthropological Quarterly* 58(3): 120–29.

————. 1991. 'A Long Way Home: Islam in the Adaptation of Iranian Women Refugees in Turkey and West Germany', in A. Fathi (ed.), *Iranian Refugees and Exiles since Khomeini*. Costa Mesa, CA: 102–19.

Beck, L. 1978. 'Women among Qashqa'i Nomadic Pastoralists in Iran', in L. Beck and N. Keddie (eds), *Women in the Muslim World*. Cambridge: 351–73.

————. 1980a. 'Herd Owners and Hired Shepherds: The Qashqa'i of Iran', *Ethnology* 19(3): 327–51.

————. 1980b. 'Tribe and State in Revolutionary Iran: The Return of the Qashqa'i Khans', *Iranian Studies* 13(1–4): 215–55.

————. 1980c. 'The Religious Lives of Muslim Women' in J. Smith (ed.), *Women in Contemporary Muslim Societies*. Lewisburg, PA.

————. 1980d. 'Revolutionary Iran and Its Tribal Peoples', *Middle East Report* (MERIP), 87 (10): 14–20.

————. 1983. 'Iran and the Qashqai Tribal Confederacy', in R. Tapper (ed.), *The Conflict of Tribe and State in Iran and Afghanistan*. London: 284–313.

————. 1984. 'Qashqa'i of Iran', *Cultural Survival Quarterly* 8(1): 19–22.

————. 1986. *The Qashqa'i of Iran*. New Haven, CT.

————. 1990. 'Tribes and the State in Nineteenth and Twentieth-Century Iran', in P. Khoury and J. Kostiner (eds), *Tribes and State Formation in the Middle East*. Berkeley, CA.

————. 1991. *Nomad: A Year in the Life of a Qashqa'i Tribesman in Iran*. Berkeley, CA.

————. 1992. 'Qashqa'i Nomads and the Islamic Republic', *Middle East Report* (MERIP) 22(4): 36–41.

————. 1993a. 'With My Daughter', *Natural History* 102(3): 6–13.

————. 1993b. 'Rostam: Qashqa'i Rebel', in E. Burke (ed.), *Struggle and Survival in the Modern Middle East*. Berkeley, CA.

————. 1998. 'Use of Land by Nomadic Pastoralists in Iran, 1970–1998', *Bulletin of the Yale School of Forestry and Environmental Studies* 103: 58–80.

————. 2000. 'Local Histories: A Longitudinal Study of a Qashqa'i Subtribe in Iran', in R. Matthee and B. Baron (eds), *Iran and Beyond: Essays in Middle Eastern History in Honor of Nikki R. Keddie*. Costa Mesa, CA: 262–88.

Beck, L. and N. Keddie (eds). 1978. *Women in the Muslim World*. Cambridge, MA.

Beck, L. and G. Nashat (eds). 2003. *Women in Iran from the Rise of Islam to 1800*. Champaign/Urbana, IL.

———— (eds). 2004. *Women in Iran from 1800 to the Islamic Republic*. Champaign/Urbana, IL.

Beeman, W.O. 1976a. 'You Can Take Music Out of the Country, But ... : The Dynamics of Change in Iranian Musical Tradition', *Asian Music* 7(2): 6–19.

————. 1976b. 'What is Iranian National Character? A Sociolinguistic Approach', *Iranian Studies* 9(1): 22–48.

————. 1977. 'Hows and Whys of Persian Style: A Pragmatic Approach', in *Colloquium on New Ways of Analyzing Variation, 3d. Georgetown University, 1974, Studies in Language Variation*. Washington, D.C.: 269–82.

————. 1978. 'Toward an Assessment of the Social Role of Rural Midwives and Its Implication for the Family Planning Program: An Iranian Case Study', *Human Organization* 37(3): 295–300.

————. 1979. 'Cultural Dimensions of Performance Conventions in Iranian Ta'ziyeh', in P. Chelkowski (ed.), *Ta-ziyeh: Ritual and Drama in Iran*. New York: 24–32.

————. 1981a. 'A Full Arena: The Development and Meaning of Popular Performances in Iran', in E. Bonine and N. R. Keddie (eds), *Modern Iran: Dialectics of Continuity and Change*. Albany.

————. 1981b. 'Why do they Laugh? An Interactional Approach to Humor in Traditional Iranian Improvisatory Theater', *Folk Drama: Journal of American Folklore* 94: 374.

———. 1983. 'Images of the Great Satan: Representations of the United States in the Iranian Revolution', in N. R. Keddie (ed.), *Religion and Politics in Iran*. New Haven, CT: 191–217.

———. 1984. 'The Cultural Role of the Media in Iran', in A. Arno and W. Dissanayake (eds), *The News Media in National and International Conflict*. Boulder, CO.

———. 1986. *Language, Status and Power in Iran*. Bloomington.

———. 1992. 'Mimesis and Travesty in Iranian Traditional Theatre', in L. Senelick (ed.), *Gender in Performance: The Presentation of Difference in the Performing Arts*. Hanover, NH: 14–25.

———. 2001. 'Emotion and Sincerity in Persian Discourse: Accomplishing the Representation of Inner States', *International Journal of the Sociology of Language* 148: 31–57.

———. 2003. 'Iran and the United States: Postmodern Culture Conflict in Action', *Anthropological Quarterly* 76(4): 671–91.

———. 2005. *The 'Great Satan' vs. the 'Mad Mullahs': How the United States and Iran Demonize Each Other*. Westport, CT.

Betteridge, A. 1983a. 'Muslim Women and Shrines in Shiraz', in S.J. Palmer (ed.), *Mormons and Muslims*. Provo, UT: 127–38.

———. 1983b. 'To Veil or Not to Veil: A Matter of Protest or Policy', in G. Nashat (ed.), *Women and Revolution in Iran*. Boulder, CO: 109–28.

———. 1985a. 'Gift Exchange in Iran: The Locus of Self-Identity in Social Interaction', *Anthropological Quarterly* 58(4): 190–202.

———. 1985b. 'Ziarat: Pilgrimage to the Shrines of Shiraz', Ph.D. dissertation. University of Chicago.

———. 1989. 'The Controversial Vows of Urban Muslim Women in Iran', in N.A. Falk and R.M. Gross (eds), *Unspoken Worlds: Women's Religious Lives in Non-Western Culture*. San Francisco, CA: 102–11.

———. 1992. 'Specialists in Miraculous Action: Some Shrines in Shiraz', in A. Morinis (ed.), *Sacred Journeys: The Anthropology of Pilgrimage*. Westport, CT: 189–209.

———. 1993. 'Women and Shrines in Shiraz', in D. Bowen and E. Early (eds), *Everyday Life in the Muslim Middle East*. Bloomington: 239–47.

Borghei, M. 1981. 'Social Stratification and Political Organization in Bent and Fannudge (Baluchistan)', Ph.D. dissertation. Manchester: University of Manchester.

———. 1993. 'Iran's Religious Establishment: The Dialectics of Politicization', in S. Farsoun and M. Mashayekhi (eds), *Iran: Political Culture in The Islamic Republic*. London: 57–81.

Bradburd, D. 1983. 'National Conditions and Local-Level Political Structures: Patronage in Prerevolutionary Iran', *American Ethnologist* 10(1): 23–40.

———. 1984. 'Ritual and Southwest Asian Pastoralists: Implications of the Komachi Case', *Journal of Anthropological Research* 40(3): 380–93.

———. 1989. 'Producing their Fates: Why Poor Basseri Settled But Poor Komachi and Yomut Did Not', *American Ethnologist* 16(3): 502–17.

———. 1994. 'Historical Bases of the Political Economy of Kermani Pastoralists: Tribe and World Markets in the Nineteenth and Early Twentieth Centuries', in C. Chang and H. A. Foster (eds), *Pastoralists at the Periphery: Herders in a Capitalist World*. Tucson, AZ: 42–61.

———. 1996. 'Toward an Understanding of the Economics of Pastoralism: The Balance of Exchange between Pastoralists and Nonpastoralists in Western Iran, 1815–1975', *Human Ecology* 24(1): 1–38.

———. 1997. 'Nomads and Their Trade Partners: Historical Context and Trade Relations in Southwest Iran, 1840–1975', *American Ethnologist* 24(4): 895–909.

———. 1998. *Being There: The Necessity of Fieldwork*. Washington, D.C.

Bromberger, C. 1989. 'Habitat, Architecture and Rural Society in the Gilan Plain (Northern Iran)', *Bonner Geographische Abhandlungen* 80.

———. 1994. 'Eating Habits and Cultural Boundaries in Northern Iran', in S. Zubaida and R. Tapper (eds), *Culinary Cultures of the Middle East*. London: 185–201.

Brooks, D. 1983. 'The Enemy Within: Limitations of Leadership in the Bakhtiari', in R. Tapper (ed.), *The Conflict of Tribe and State in Iran and Afghanistan*. London: 337–63.

Digard, J.-P. 1978. 'The Segmental System: Native Model or Anthropological Construction?: Discussion of an Iranian Example', in *Nomadic Alternative, Papers of the Ninth International Congress of Anthropological and Ethnological Sciences*. The Hague: 315–17.

———. 1983. 'On the Bakhtiari: Comments on "Tribes, Confederation and the State"', in R. Tapper (ed.), *The Conflict of Tribe and State in Iran and Afghanistan*. London: 331–36.

———. 1990. 'Evolution of Nomadic Pastoralism in Iran 1960–1978: Problems and Interpretations', in *Nomads in a Changing World: First Conference, Revised Papers*. Naples: 165–75.

Dillon, R. 1976. *Carpet Capitalism and Craft Involution in Kirman, Iran: A Study in Economic Anthropology*. (Ph.D. dissertation. Department of Anthropology, Columbia University, New York.

Drew, P.E. 1997. 'Sexuality', in R. T. Francoeur (ed.), *The International Encyclopaedia of Sexuality* 2. New York: 620–49.

Doostdar, A. 2004. '"The Vulgar Spirit of Blogging": on Language, Culture, and Power in Persian Weblogestan'. *American Anthropologist* 106(4), 651–662.

Fazeli, N. 2006. *Politics of Culture in Iran: Anthropology, Politics and Society in the Twentieth Century*. London.

Fazel, R. 1977. 'Social and Political Status of Women among Pastoral Nomads: The Bohr Ahmad of Southwest Iran', *Anthropological Quarterly* 50 (2): 77–89.

———. 1979. 'Economic Bases of Political Leadership among Pastoral Nomads: The Boyr Ahmad Tribe of Southwest Iran', in M.B. Leons and F. Rothstein (eds), *New Directions in Political Economy*. Westport, CT: 33–48.

Field, H. 1939. *Contributions to the Anthropology of Iran*, Anthropological Series, Field Museum of Natural History 29(1). Chicago.

———. 1953. *The Track of Man: Adventures of an Anthropologist*. Garden City, NY.

Fischer, M. 1973. 'Zoroastrian Iran Between Myth and Praxis', Ph.D. dissertation. Chicago: University of Chicago.

———. 1978a. 'On Changing the Concept and Position of Persian Women', in L. Beck and N. Keddie (eds), *Women of the Muslim World*. Cambridge, MA.

———. 1978b. 'In Defense of Ayesha: Women in Iran', *New Society* 44: 537–38.

———. 1980a. *Iran: From Religious Dispute to Revolution*. Cambridge.

———. 1980b. 'Becoming Mollah: Reflections on Iranian Clerics in a Revolutionary Age', *Iranian Studies* 13(1–4): 83–117.

———. 1982. 'Islam and the Revolt of the Petit Bourgeoisie', *Daedalus* 3(1): 101–25.

———. 1983. 'Imam Khomeini: Four Levels of Understanding' in J. L. Esposito (ed.), *Voices of Resurgent Islam*. New York: 150–174.

———. 1990. 'Legal Postulates in Flux: Justice, Wit, and Hierarchy in Iran', in D. H. Dwyer (ed.), *Law and Islam in the Middle East*. New York: 115–42.

———. 1990. *Debating Muslims: Cultural Dialogues in Postmodernity and Tradition*. Madison, WI.

Friedl, E. 1970. 'On the Physical Anthropology of the Boir Ahmedi in Southwest Iran', *Homo* 21(4): 227–50.

———. 1978. 'Women in Contemporary Persian Folktales' in L. Beck and N. R. Keddie (eds), *Women in the Muslim World*. Cambridge, MA: 629–50.

———. 1979. 'Colors and Culture Change in Southwest Iran', *Language in Society* 8(1): 51–68.

———. 1981. 'Women and the Division of Labor in an Iranian Village', *Middle East Report* (MERIP) 95: 12–18.

———. 1983. 'State Ideology and Village Women', in G. Nashat (ed.), *Women and Revolution in Iran*. Boulder, CO: 217–30.

———. 1989. 'Islam and Tribal Women in a Village in Iran', in N. A. Falk and R. M. Gross (eds), *Unspoken Worlds: Women's Religious Lives*. Belmont, CA: 125–33.

———. 1991a. *Women of Deh Koh: Lives in an Iranian Village*. New York.

———. 1991b. 'The Dynamics of Women's Spheres of Action in Rural Iran', in N. R. Keddie and B. Baron (eds), *Women in Middle Eastern History: Shifting Boundaries in Sex and Gender*. New Haven, CT: 195–214.

———. 1992. 'Moonrose Watched through a Sunny Day', *Natural History* 8: 34–45.

———. 1993. 'Legendary Heroines: Ideal Womanhood and Ideology in Iran', in M. Womack and J. Marti (eds), *The Other Fifty Percent: Multicultural Perspectives on Gender Relations*. Prospect Heights, IL: 261–66.

———. 1994a. 'Sources of Female Power in Iran', in M. Afkhami and E. Friedl (eds), *In the Eye of the Storm: Women in Post-Revolutionary Iran*. Syracuse: 151–67.

———. 1994b. 'Notes from the Village: On the Ethnographic Construction of Women in Iran', in F. M. Gocek and S. Balaghi (eds), *Reconstructing Gender in the Middle East: Tradition, Identity, and Power*. New York.

———. 1997a. 'Ideal Womanhood in Postrevolutionary Iran', in J. Brink and J. Mencher (eds), *Mixed Blessings: Gender and Religious Fundamentalism Cross Culturally*. New York: 143–57.

———. 1997b. *Children of Deh Koh: Young Life in an Iranian Village*. Syracuse, New York.

––––––. 2004a. 'The Ethnography of Children', *Iranian Studies* 37(4): 655–63.

––––––. 2004b. 'Stories as Ethnographic Dilemma in Longitudinal Research', *Anthropology and Humanism* 29(1): 5–21.

Friedl, E. and M.E. Hegland. 2004a. 'Guest Editors' Introduction', *Journal of Iranian Studies: Special Issue on Ethnography in Iran* 37(4): 569–73.

–––––– (eds). 2004b. *Journal of Iranian Studies: Special Issue on Ethnography in Iran* 37(4).

Friedl, E. and A. Loeffler. 1994. 'The Ups and Downs of Dwellings in a Village in West Iran: The History of Two Compounds', *Archiv fur Völkerkunde* 48: 1–44.

Gazagnadou, D. 2006. 'Diffusion of Cultural Models, Body Transformations and Technology in Iran: Iranian Women and Cosmetic Nose Surgery', *Anthropology of the Middle East* 1(1): 106–11.

Ghorashi, H. 2003. *Ways to Survive, Battles to Win: Iranian Women Exiles in the Netherlands and the US*. New York.

Good, B. 1977a. 'The Heart of What's the Matter: The Structure of Medical Discourse in a Provincial Iranian Town', Ph.D. dissertation. Chicago: University of Chicago.

––––––. 1977b. 'The Heart of What's the Matter. The Semantics of Illness in Iran', *Culture, Medicine and Psychiatry* 1(1): 25–58.

Good, B. and M.-J. DelVecchio Good. 1982. 'Toward a Meaning-Centered Analysis of Popular Illness Categories: "Fright Illness" and "Heart Distress" in Iran', in A. J. Marsella and G. M. White (eds), *Cultural Conceptions of Mental Health and Therapy*. Dordrecht: 141–66.

Good, M.-J. DelVecchio and J. Byron. 1988. 'Ritual, the State, and the Transformation of Emotional Discourse in Iranian Society', *Culture, Medicine and Psychiatry* 12(1): 43–63.

Good, B., M.-J. DelVecchio Good and R. Moradi. 1985. 'The Interpretation of Iranian Depressive Illness and Dysphoric Affect', in A. Kleinman and B. Good (eds), *Culture and Depression: Studies in the Anthropology and Cross-Cultural Psychiatry of Affect and Disorder*. Berkeley, CA: 369–428.

Goodell, G. 1985. 'Paternalism, Patronage, and Potlatch: The Dynamics of Giving and Being Given To', *Current Anthropology* 26(2): 247–66.

––––––. 1986. *The Elementary Structures of Political Life: Rural Development in Pahlavi Iran*. New York.

Gulick, J. 1974. 'Private Life and Public Face: Cultural Continuities in the Domestic Architecture of Isfahan', *Iranian Studies* 7(3–4): 629–51.

Gulick, M. and J. Gulick. 1974. 'Varieties of Domestic Social Oranization in the Iranian City of Isfahan', in A. L. LaRuffa et al. (eds), *City and Peasant: A Study in "Sociocultural Dynamics"*. New York.

––––––. 1975. 'Kinship, Contraception and Family Planning in the Iranian City of Isfahan', in M. Nag (ed.), *Population and Social Organization*. The Hague.

––––––. 1976. 'Migrant and Native Married Women in the Iranian City of Isfahan', *Anthropological Quarterly* 49(1): 53–61.

––––––. 1978. 'The Domestic Social Environment of Women and Girls in Isfahan, Iran' in L. Beck and N. R. Keddie (eds), *Women in the Muslim World*. Cambridge, MA: 501–21.

Haeri, S. 1980. 'Women, Law and Social change in Iran', in J. Smith (ed.), *Women in Contemporary Muslim Societies*. Lewisburg: 209–34.

———. 1983. 'The Institution of *Mut'a* Marriage in Iran: A Formal and Historical Perspective', in G. Nashat (ed.), *Women and Revolution in Iran*. Boulder, CO: 231–52.

———. 1986. 'Power of Ambiguity: Cultural Improvisations on the Theme of Temporary Marriage', *Iranian Studies* 19(2): 123–54.

———. 1989. *Law of Desire: Temporary Marriage in Shi'i Iran*. Syracuse, NY.

———. 1993. 'Obedience Versus Autonomy: Women and Fundamentalism in Iran and Pakistan', in M.E. Marty and R.S. Appleby (eds), *Fundamentalisms and Society: Reclaiming the Sciences, the Family, and Education*, The Fundamentalism Project vol. 2. Chicago: 181–213.

———. 1994. 'Temporary Marriage: An Islamic Discourse on Female Sexuality in Iran', in M. Afkhami and E. Friedl (eds), *In the Eye of the Storm: Women in Post-revolutionary Iran*. Syracuse, NY: 98–114.

———. 1995a. 'Of Feminism and Fundamentalism in Iran and Pakistan', *Contention: Debates in Society, Culture, and Science* 4(3): 129–49.

Hakimzadeh, S. 2006. 'Iran: A Vast Diaspora Abroad and Millions of Refugees at Home', *Migration Information Source*. Retrieved September 2006 from http://www.migrationinformation.org/Profiles/display.cfm?ID=424.

Hakimzadeh, S. and D. Dixon. 2006. 'Spotlight on the Iranian Foreign Born', *Migration Information Source*. Retrieved June 2006 from http://www.migrationinformation.org/USfocus/print.cfm?ID=404.

Hamdhaidari, S. and S. Wright. 2001. 'Participation and Participatory Development among the Kalhor Nomads of Iran', *Community Development Journal* 36(1): 53–62.

Harbottle, L. 1996. '"Bastard" Chicken or Ghormeh-Sabzi? Iranian Women Guarding the Health of the Migrant Family', in S. Edgell, K. Hetherington and A. Warde (eds), *Consumption Matters*. Oxford: 224–226.

———. 1997. *Fast Food/Spoiled Identity: Iranian Migrants in the British Catering Trade*. London.

———. 2000. *Food for Health, Food for Wealth: The Performance of Ethnic and Gender Identities by Iranian Settlers in Britain*. Oxford.

Hegland, M.E. 1980. 'One Village in the Revolution', *Middle East Report* (MERIP) 10(4): 7–12.

———. 1982a. 'Religious Ritual and Political Struggle in an Iranian Village', *Middle East Report* (MERIP) 12(1): 10–17, 23.

———. 1982b. '"Traditional" Iranian Women: How They Cope', *The Middle East Journal* 36(4): 483–501.

———. 1983a. 'Two Images of Husain: Accommodation and Revolution in an Iranian Village', in N. R. Keddie (ed.), *Religion and Politics in Iran: Shi'ism from Quietism to Revolution*. New Haven, CT: 218–36.

———. 1983b. 'Ritual and Revolution in Iran', in M.J. Aronoff (ed.), *Political Anthropology: Culture and Political Change*, vol. 2. New Brunswick, NJ: 75–100.

———. 1983c. 'Aliabad Women: Revolution as Religious Activity', in G. Nashat (ed.), *Women and Revolution in Iran*. Boulder, CO: 171–94.

————. 1986a. 'Political Roles of Iranian Village Women', *Middle East Report* (MERIP) 16(10): 14–9.

————. 1986b. 'Imam Khomaini's Village: Recruitment to Revolution', Ph.D. dissertation. Binghamton: State University of New York.

————. 1987a. 'Introduction', in R. Antoun and M. Hegland (eds), *The Islamic Resurgence in Comparative Perspective*. Syracuse, NY: 1–12.

————. 1987b. 'Conclusion: Religious Resurgence in Today's World - Refuge from Dislocation and Anomie or Enablement for Change?' in R. Antoun and M. Hegland (eds), *The Islamic Resurgence in Comparative Perspective*. Syracuse, NY: 233–56.

————. 1987c. 'Islamic Revival or Political and Cultural Revolution? An Islamic Case Study', in R. Antoun and M. Hegland (eds), *The Islamic Resurgence in Comparative Perspective*. Syracuse, NY: 194–219.

————. 1991. 'Political Roles of Aliabad Women: The Public/Private Dichotomy Transcended', in N.R. Keddie and B. Baron (eds), *Shifting Boundaries: Gender Roles in the Middle East, Past and Present*. New Haven, CT: 215–30.

————. 1998. 'Women and the Iranian Revolution: A Village Case Study', in M. J. Diamond (ed.), *Women and Revolution: Global Expressions*. Dordrecht: 211–25.

————. 1999a. 'Gender and Religion in the Middle East and South Asia: Women's Voices Rising', in J. Tucker and M. Meriwether (eds), *Social History of Women and Gender in the Modern Middle East*. Boulder, CO: 177–212.

————. 1999b. 'Wife Abuse and the Political System: A Middle Eastern Case Study', in D. Counts, J. Brown and J. Campbell (eds), *To Have and to Hit: Cultural Perspective on Wife Beating*. Urbana, IL: 234–51.

————. 2003. 'Talking Politics: A Village Widow in Iran', in L.S. Walbridge and A.K. Sievert (eds), *Personal Encounters: A Reader in Cultural Anthropology*. Boston, MA: 53–59.

————. 2004. 'Zip In and Zip Out Fieldwork', *Iranian Studies* 37(4): 275–583.

————. 2006a. 'Women of Karbala: Moving to America', in K.S. Aghai (ed.), *Women of Karbala: Ritual Performance and Symbolic Discourses in Modern Shi'i Islam*. Austin: 199–227.

————. 2006b. 'Iranian-American Elderly in California's Santa Clara Valley: Crafting Selves and Composing Lives', in H. Moghissi (ed.), *Muslim Diaspora: Gender, Culture and Identity*. London: 205–19.

————. forthcoming a. 'Aliabad of Shiraz: From Village to Suburb', *Iran Nameh*.

————.2008. 'Esmat Khanum and a Life of Travail: "God, Help Me; Son of Musa Ibn-e Jaafar, You Yourself Help Me"', in F. Trix and J. Walbridge (eds), *Muslims Around the World*. New York: 57–69.

————. forthcoming c. *Imam Khomeini's Village: Recruitment to Revolution*.

Higgins, P. 1976. 'The Conflict of Acculturation and Enculturation in Suburban Elementary Schools of Tehran', *Journal of Research and Development in Education* 9(4): 102–12.

————. 1984a. 'Minority-State Relations in Contemporary Iran', *Iranian Studies* 17(1): 37–71.

————. 1984b. 'Anthropologists and Issues of Public Concern: the Iran Crisis', *Human Organization* 43: 132–45.

———. 1985. 'Women in the Islamic Republic of Iran: Legal, Social and Ideological Changes', *SIGNS* 10(3): 477–95.

———. 1997a. 'Intergenerational Stress: Parents and Adolescents in Iranian Immigrant Families', in D. Baxter and R. Krulfeld (eds), *Beyond Boundaries: Selected Papers on Refugees and Immigrants*, vol. 5. Arlington, VA: 189–213.

———. 1997b. 'Adolescent Ethnic Identities: Iranians in the U.S.', *DANESH Bulletin* 1(2): 10–4.

———. 2004. 'Interviewing Iranian Immigrant Parents and Adolescents', *Iranian Studies* 37(4): 706.

Higgins, P.J. and P. Shoar-Ghaffari. 1994. 'Women's Education in the Islamic Republic of Iran', in M. Afkhami and E. Friedl (eds), *In the Eye of the Storm: Women in Post-revolutionary Iran*. Syracuse, NY: 19–43.

Hoffman, D.M. 1989. 'Language and Culture Acquisition among Iranians in the United States', *Anthropology and Education Quarterly* 20: 118–132.

———. 1989b. 'Self and Culture Revisited: Culture Acquisition among Iranians in the United States', *Ethos* 17(1): 32–49.

Hoodfar, H. 1994a. 'Devices and Desires: Population Policy and Gender Roles in the Islamic Republic', *Middle East Report* (MERIP) 190: 11–17.

———. 1994b. 'Situating the Anthropologist: Personal Account of Ethnographic Fieldwork in Three Urban Settings: Tehran, Cairo, and Montreal', in V. Amit-Talai and H. Lustiger-Thaler (eds), *Urban Lives: Fragmentation and Resistance*. Toronto: 206–26.

———. 1995a. 'State Policy and Gender Equity in Post-Revolutionary Iran', in C. M. Oberymeyer (ed.), *Family, Gender and Population Policy in the Middle East*. Cairo.

———. 1995b. 'The Veil in Their Mind and on Our Heads', *Resources for Feminist Research* 22(3–4): 5–18.

———. 1996. 'Bargaining with Fundamentalism: Women and the Politics of Population Control in Iran', *Reproductive Health Matters* 8(November): 30–40.

———. 1997. 'The Veil in their Minds and on Our Heads: The Persistence of Colonial Images of Muslim Women', in D. Lloyd and L. Lowe (eds), *The Politics of Culture in the Shadow of the Capital*. Durham, NC: 248–79.

———. 1999. *The Women's Movement in Iran: Women at the Crossroads of Secularization and Islamization*. Montpellier.

———. 2000. 'Iranian Women at the Intersection of Citizenship and the Family Code: The Perils of "Islamic Criteria"', in S. Joseph (ed.), *Gender and Citizenship in the Middle East*. Syracuse, NY: 287–313.

Inhorn, M.C. 2006. 'Islam, IVF and Everyday Life in the Middle East: The Making of Sunni versus Shi'ite Test-Tube Babies', *Anthropology in the Middle East* 1(1): 42–50.

Irons, W. 1969. 'The Yomut Turkmen: A Study of Social Organization among a Central Asian Turkic Speaking Population', Ph.D. dissertation. Ann Arbor: University of Michigan,

———. 1974. 'Nomadism as a Political Adaptation: the Case of the Yomut Turkmen', *American Ethnologist* 1(4): 635–58.

———. 1975. 'The Yomut Turkmen: A Study of Social Organization Among a Central Asian Turkic Speaking Population', *Anthropological Paper* 58, Museum of Anthropology, University of Michigan.

———. 1979. 'Political Stratification Among Pastoral Nomads', in L'Equipe Ecologie et Anthropologie des Sociétes Pastorales (ed.), *Pastoral Production and Society.* New York: 361–374.

———. 1994. 'Why Are the Yomut Not More Stratified?', in C. Chang and H.A. Koster (eds), *Pastoralists at the Periphery: Herders in a Capitalist World.* Tucson, AZ: 175–96.

Ishaya, A. 1977. 'The Role of Minorities in the State: History of the Assyrian Experience', *Anthropology Papers* 19. Winnipeg.

Kalinock, S. 2003a. 'Between Party and Devotion: *Mowludi* of Tehran Women', *Critique. Critical Studies of the Middle East* 12(2): 173–88.

———. 2003b. 'Supernatural Intercession to Earthly Problems: *Sofreh* Rituals among Shiite Muslim and Zoroastrian Women in Iran', in M. Strausberg (ed.), *Zoroastrian Rituals in Context.* Leiden: 531–46.

———. 2004. 'Touching a Sensitive Topic: Research on Shiite Rituals of Women in Tehran', *Iranian Studies* 37(4): 665–74.

Kamalkhani, Z. 1988. *Iranian Immigrants and Refugees in Norway.* Bergen.

———. 1993a. 'Women's Everyday Religious Discourse in Iran', in H. Afshar (ed.), *Women in the Middle East: Perceptions, Realities and Struggles for Liberation.* London: 102–13.

———. 1993b. 'Family and Household Economic Management in the Context of Change: A Case Study in Shiraz', *International Journal of Comparative Family and Marriage* 1(1): 125–33.

———. 1996. 'Religious Education in the Islamic Republic and Women as Fundamentalists', *Journal of Iranian Studies* 1: 27–31.

———. 1997. *Women's Islam: Religious Practice Among Women in Today's Iran.* London.

———. 1998. 'Reconstruction of Islamic Knowledge and Knowing: A Case of Islamic Practices among Women in Iran', in K. Ask and M. Tjomsland (eds), *Women and Islamization: Contemporary Dimensions of Discourse on Gender Relations.* Oxford: 177–93.

Keshavjee, R. 1989. 'Power of Games and the Games of Power in Rural Iran', *Iranian Studies* 22(2–3): 87–97.

———. 1998. Mysticism and the Plurality of Meaning: The Case of the Ismailis of Rural Iran. Tauris.

Kestenberg Amighi, J. 1990. *The Zoroastrians of Iran: Conversion, Assimilation, or Persistence.* New York.

Khosravi, S. 1996. 'Can a Khan Be an Anthropologist?' *Antropologiska studier* 54(5): 71–79.

———. 1999. 'Displacement and Entrepreneurship: Iranian Small Businesses in Stockholm', *Journal of Ethnic and Migration Studies* 25(3): 493–508.

———. 2000. 'An Ethnographic Approach to an Online Diaspora', *ISIM Newsletter* 6: 13.

Khosronejad, P. forthcoming. 'A Zoomorphic Tombstone in Shiite Context', Ph.D. dissertation.

Lindisfarne-Tapper, N. 1997. 'The Dress of the Shahsevan Tribespeople of Iranian Azerbaijan', in N. Lindisfarne-Tapper and B. Ingham (eds), *Languages of Dress in the Middle East*. Richmond: 67–79.

Loeb, L. 1970. *The Jews of Southwest Iran*. Ph.D. dissertation, Columbia University, New York.

———. 1977. *Outcaste: Jewish Life in Southern Iran*. New York.

———. 1982. 'Prestige and Piety in the Iranian Synagogue', in S. Deshen and W.P. Zenner (eds), *Jewish Societies in the Middle East*. Washington, D.C: 285–97.

Loeffler, A. 1998. 'Memories of Difference: From Lur to Anthropologist', *Anthropology and Humanism* 23(2): 146–56.

———. 2004. 'The Double-edged Foreign Connection', *Iranian Studies* 37(4): 633–42.

———. 2007a. *Allopathy Goes Native: Mind, Models and Motives in Iran*. London.

———. 2007b. 'Individual Constitutions vs. Universal Physiology: Iranian Responses to Allopathic Medicine', Body & Society 13(3): 103–123.

Loeffler, R. 1971. 'The Representative Mediator and the New Peasant', *American Anthropologist* 73(2): 1077–91.

———. 1973. 'The National Integration of Boir Ahmad', *Iranian Studies* 6(2–3): 127–35.

———. 1976. 'Recent Economic Changes in Boir Ahmad: Regional Growth without Development', *Iranian Studies* 9(4): 266–87.

———.1978. 'Tribal Order and the State: The Political Organization of Boir Ahmad', in A. Banani (ed.) *Iranian Studies*, Special Volume, *State and Society in Iran* 11: 145–71.

———. 1986. 'Economic Changes in a Rural Area Since 1979', in N.R. Keddie and E. Hooglund (eds), *The Iranian Revolution and the Islamic Republic*. Syracuse, NY: 93–109.

———. 1988. *Islam in Practice: Religious Beliefs in a Persian Village*. Albany.

———. 2004. 'The Making of a Historical Document', *Iranian Studies* 37(4): 585–93.

———. forthcoming. 'Change and Continuity in Sisakht, Iran', *Iran-Nameh*.

Magnarella, P. 1969. 'A Note on Aspects of Social Life among the Jewish Kurds of Sanandaj, Iran', *Jewish Journal of Sociology* 11(1): 51–58.

———. 1981. 'Iranian Diplomacy in the Khomeini Era', *Studies in Third World Societies* 12: 1–15.

Mahdavi, P. 2007. 'Passionate Uprisings: Young People, Sexuality and Politics in Post-Revolutionary Iran' *Culture, Health and Sexuality*, Sep–Oct; 9(5): 445–457.

Manoukian, S. 1996. 'Fatwa as Asymmetrical Dialogues', in K. Masud, B. Messick and D.S. Powers (eds), *Islamic Legal Interpretation: Mufti and their Fatwas*. Cambridge, MA.

Manoukian, S. 2005. 'Power, Religion, and the Effects of Publicness in 20th-Century Shiraz', in Armando Salvatore and Mark LeVine (eds), *Religion, Social Practice, and Contested Hegemonies*. New York: Palgrave Macmillan: 57–83.

Martin, M. 1980a. 'Making a Living in Turan: Animals, Land and Wages', *Expedition* 22(4): 29–35.

———. 1980b. 'Pastoral Production. Milk and Firewood in the Ecology of Turn', *Expedition* 22(4): 24–7.

———. 1987. 'Production Strategies, Herd composition, and Offtake Rates: Reassessment of Archaeological Models', *MASCA Journal* 4(4): 154–65.

———. 1989. 'National and Regional Context of Local Level Agricultural Strategies: The Case of Small Holders in Northeastern Iran', in S. Smith and E. Reeves (eds), *Human Systems Ecology: Studies in the Integration of Political Economy, Adaptation, and Socionatural Regions*. Boulder, CO: 148–69.

Mir-Hosseini, Z. 1986. 'Divorce in Islamic Law and Practice: The Case of Iran', *Cambridge Anthropology* 11(1): 41–69.

———. 1987. 'Impact of Wage Labour on Household Fission in Rural Iran', *Journal of Comparative Family Studies* 18(3): 445–61.

———. 1989. 'Some Aspects of Changing Marriage in Rural Iran: The Case of Kalardasht, A District in the Northern Provinces', *Journal of Comparative Family Studies* 20(2): 215–31.

———. 1992–93. 'Paternity, Patriarchy and Matrifocality in the Sharia and in Social Practice: The Cases of Morocco and Iran', *Cambridge Anthropology* 16(2): 22–40.

———. 1993a. 'Women, Marriage and the Law in Post-Revolutionary Iran', in H. Afshar (ed.), *Women in the Middle East: Perceptions, Realities and Struggles for Liberation*. London: 59–84.

———. 1993b. *Marriage on Trial: A Study of Islamic Family Law, Iran and Morocco Compared*. London.

———. 1996a. 'Women and Politics in Post-Khomeini Iran: Divorce, Veiling and Emerging Feminist Voices', in H. Afshar (ed.), *Women and Politics in the Third World*. New York, London: 149–69.

———. 1996b. 'Stretching the Limits: A Feminist Reading of the Shari'a in Post-Khomeini Iran', in M. Yamani (ed.), *Feminism and Islam: Islamic Law and Feminism*. Ithaca, NY: 285–319.

———. 1998. 'Hojjat ol-Islam Sa'idzadeh-Iran', *Women Living under Muslim Laws*, dossier 21. London.

———. 1999. *Islam and Gender: The Religious Debate in Contemporary Iran*. Princeton, NJ.

———. 2000. *Marriage on Trial: A Study of Islamic Family Law in Iran and Morocco*. London.

———. 2001. 'Iran: Emerging Feminist Voices', in L. Walter (ed.), *Women's Rights: A Global View*. Westport, CT: 113–25.

———. 2002a. 'Religious Modernists and the "Woman Question"', in E. Hooglund (ed.), *Twenty Years of Islamic Revolution: Political and Social Transition in Iran since 1979*. Syracuse, NY: 74–95.

———. 2002b. 'Negotiating the Politics of Gender in Iran: An Ethnography of a Documentary', in R. Tapper (ed.), *The New Iranian Cinema: Politics, Representation and Identity*. London: 167–99.

———. 2002c. 'Tamkin: Stories from a Family Court in Iran', in D. Bowen and E. Early (eds), *Everyday Life in the Muslim Middle East*. Bloomington: 136–50.

Mir-Hosseini, Z. and K. Longinotto. 1998. *Divorce Iranian Style*. Documentary film.

————. 2001a. *Runaways*. Documentary film.

Mir-Hosseini, Z. and R. Tapper. 2006. *Eshkevari and the Quest for Reform: Islam and Democracy in Iran*. London.

Mobasher, M. 2004. 'Ethnic Resources and Ethnic Economy: The Case of Iranian Immigrants in Dallas', in M. Mobasher and M. Sadri (eds), *Migration Globalization, and Ethnic Relations: An Interdisciplinary Approach*. Upper Saddle River, NJ: 297–306.

————. 2006. 'Cultural Trauma and Ethnic Identity Formation among Iranian Immigrants in the United States', *American Behavioral Scientist* 50(1): 100–17.

————. forthcoming a. 'Iranian Immigrant Entrepreneurs in the United States', in L. Dana (ed.), *The Handbook of Research on Ethnic Minority Entrepreneurship*. Cheltenham.

————. forthcoming b. *Iranians in Diaspora*. Video film. With Hakakk and Mahmoud Sadri.

Naderi, N.A. 1982. 'Some Considerations Regarding Anthropological Dilemmas', in H. Fahim (ed.), *Indigenous Anthropology in Non-Western Countries*. Durham, NC: 242–49.

Nadjmabadi, S. 1993. 'Reconstruction without Foreign Assistance: The Iranian Reconstruction Organization Jehad e Sazandeqi', *Sociologus* 43(2): 168–82.

————. 2004. 'From "Alien" to "One of Us" and Back: Field Experiences in Iran', *Iranian Studies* 37(4): 603–12.

Nassehi-Behnam, V. 1985. 'Change and the Iranian Family', *Current Anthropology* 26(5): 557–62.

————. 2005. 'Transnational Identities: A Generational Study of Iranian Immigrants in France', The Japan Center for Area Studies (JCAS) *Symposium Series*, 17: 251–268.

Naseri, M. 2003. 'Medical Pluralism among Iran's Nomadic Pastoralist Ethnic Minorities', MA thesis. Milwaukee: University of Wisconsin.

Osanloo, A. 2002. 'At the Juncture of Islam and Republic: Socio-legal Constructions of Women's Rights in Iran', Ph.D. dissertation. Stanford: Stanford University.

————. 2004. 'Doing the "Rights" Thing: Methods and Challenges of Fieldwork in Iran', *Iranian Studies* 37(4): 675–84.

————. 2006a. 'Islamico-civil "Rights Talk": Women, Subjectivity, and Law in Iranian Family Court', *American Ethnologist* 33(2): 191–209.

————. 2006b. 'The Measure of Mercy: Islamic Justice, Sovereign Power, and Human Rights in Iran', *Cultural Anthropology* 21(4): 570–602.

Pardini, E. 1975. 'Anthropological Research in Sistan, Preliminary Report', *East and West* 25(3–4): 267–86.

Pliskin, K. 1980. 'Camouflage, Conspiracy, and Collaborators: Rumors of the Revolution', *Iranian Studies* 13(1–4): 55–81.

————. 1987. *Silent Boundaries: Cultural Constraints on Sickness and Diagnosis of Iranians in Israel*. New Haven, CT.

Pourzal, R. 1981. 'Other Nomads of South Persia: The Baraftowi Koohaki of Jahrom', *Nomadic Peoples* 8: 24–26.

Putzey, D. deBaun. 1961. 'The Mountain Tribes of Iran', *Harvard University. Department of Anthropology: Anthropology 213. Seminar. Peoples and Cultures of the Middle East*. 1–19.

————. 2004. 'Multiple Sites of Fieldwork: A Personal Reflection', *Iranian Studies* 37(4): 685–93.

Razavi, S. 1993. 'Fieldwork in a Familiar Setting: The Role of Politics at the National, Community and Household Levels', in S. Devereux and J. Hoddinott (eds.), Fieldwork in Developing Countries. Boulder, CO: 152–163.

Rice, C. 1923. *Persian Women and Their Ways*. London.

Safa, K. 1988. 'Reading Saedi's Ahl-e Hava: Pattern and Significance in Spirit Possession Beliefs on the Southern Coasts of Iran', *Culture, Medicine and Psychiatry* 12(1): 85–111.

Safa-Isfahani, K. 1980. 'Female Centered World Views in Iranian Culture: Symbolic Representations of Sexuality in Dramatic Games', *SIGNS: Journal of Women in Society* 6(1): 33–53.

Safizadeh, F. 1984. *The Shahsavan Nomads of Iran*. Ethnographic film.

————. 1985. 'Agrarian Change, Migration and Impact of the Islamic Revolution in a Village Community in Azerbaijan, Iran', Ph.D. dissertation. Cambridge: Harvard University and Center for Middle Eastern Studies.

————. 1986. *The Winnowers of Azerbaijan*. Anthropological documentary film. Harvard Film Study Center.

————. 1991. 'Peasant Protest and Resistance in Rural Iranian Azerbaijan', in F. Kazemi and J. Waterbury (eds), *Peasants and Politics in the Modern Middle East*. Miami, FL: 312–326.

————. 1996. 'Children of the Revolution: Transnational Identity among Young Iranians in Northern California' in M. Bozorgmehr and A. Feldman (eds), *Middle Eastern Diaspora Communities in America, The Proceedings of the 17th Summer Institute of the Joint Center for Near Eastern Studies of New York University and Princeton University*. New York: 124–44.

————. 1999. 'Children of the Revolution', in P.M. Karim and M.M. Khorrami (eds), *A World in Between: Poems, Stories and Essays by Iranian Americans*. New York: 255–276.

Sahraee-Smith, A. 2001. 'The Political Economy of Mourning: A Study of Practised Islam and Gender in Urban Iran', Ph.D. dissertation. London: University of London.

Salzman, P. 1971. 'National Integration of the Tribes in Modern Iran', *Middle East Journal* 25(3): 325–36.

————. 1978. 'Does Complementary Opposition Exist?' *American Anthropologist* 80: 43–70.

————. 1979. 'Inequality and Oppression in Nomadic Society', in L'Equipe Ecologie et Anthropologie des Sociétes Pastorales (ed.), *Pastoral Production and Society*. Cambridge.

————.1988.'Labor Formations in a Nomadic Tribe', in D. W. Attwood and B. S. Baviskar, (eds) *In Who Shares? Co-operatives and Rural Development*. Delhi, India: Oxford University Press: 233–258.

————. 1986. 'Dates to Meet, Dates to Eat: Oasis Life in Tribal Baluchistan', *Newsletter of Baluchistan Studies* 3: 48–62.

————. 1994. 'Baluchi Nomads in the Market', in C. Chang and H.A. Koster (eds), *Pastoralists at the Periphery: Herders in a Capitalist World*. Tucson, AZ: 165–74.

————. 1995. 'Studying Nomads: An Autobiographical Reflection', *Nomadic Peoples* 36(7): 157–65.

————. 2000. 'Hierarchical Image and Reality: The Construction of a Tribal Chiefship', *Comparative Studies in Society and History* 42(1): 49–66.

————. 2000. *Black Tents of Baluchistan*. Washington, D.C.

————. 2002. 'Pastoral Nomads: Some General Observations Based on Research in Iran', *Journal of Anthropological Research* 58(2): 245–64.

Sanadjian, M. 1990. 'From Participant to Partisan Observation: An Open End', *Critique of Anthropology* 10(1): 113–35.

————. 1996. 'Public Flogging in South-Western Iran: Juridical Rule, Abolition of Legality and Local Resistance', in O. Harris (ed.), *Inside and Outside the Law: Anthropological Studies of Authority and Ambiguity*. London: 157–83.

————. 1996. 'An Anthology of "the People", Place, Space and "Home": (Re)Constructing the Lur in South-Western Iran', *Social Identities* 2(1): 5–36.

————. 2001. 'Witnessing an Islamic Rite of Passage and a Local/Non-Local Articulation', *Social Identities* 7(2): 203–19.

Schumacher, P. 1950. 'Report on the Second Iran Expedition: Ethnography', *Philadelphia Anthropological Society Bulletin* 4(2): 3–4.

Schwartz, R.M. 1985. 'The Structure of Christian-Muslim Relations in Contemporary Iran', Ph.D. dissertation. Halifax, N:S: Saint Mary's University.

Shahbazi, M. 1998 'Formal Education, Schoolteachers, and Ethnic Identity among the Qashqa'i of Iran', Ph.D. dissertation. St. Louis: Washington University.

————. M. 2001. 'Qashqa'i Nomads of Iran (Part I): Formal Education', *Nomadic Peoples* 5(1): 37–64.

————. 2002. 'The Qashqa'i Nomads of Iran (Part II): State-Supported Literacy and Ethnic Identity', *Nomadic Peoples* 6(1): 95–123.

————. 2003. 'Anthropological Fieldwork Endeavour and Indigenous Researchers', *Nomadic Peoples* 7(2): 98–107.

————. 2004. 'Insider/Outsider: An Indigenous Anthropologist Bridges a Gap', *Iranian Studies* 37(4): 593–602.

Shahrokhi, S. forthcoming. 'Female Runaways: Gender Crossing, Teen Prostitution, and Other Subversive Sexual Praxis', Ph.D. dissertation. Berkeley: University of California.

Shahshahani, S. 1981. 'The Four Seasons of the Sun: An Ethnography of the Sedentarized Village of the Mamasani Pastoral Nomads of Iran', Ph.D. dissertation. New York: Graduate Faculty of the New School for Social Research.

————.1984. 'Religion, Politics and Society: A Historical Perspective on the Women's Movement in Iran', *Samya Shakti* 1–2: 100–20.

————. 1986. 'History of Anthropology in Iran', *Iranian Studies* 19(1): 65–86.

————. 1995. 'Tribal Schools in Iran: Sedentarization through Education', *Nomadic Peoples* 36/37: 145–55.

————. 2000. 'Ambiguity in Law and the Marginalisation of Sedentarised Nomads of the Southern Zagros Mountains of Iran', *Nomadic Peoples* 4(1): 23–36.

————. 2003a. 'Nomads and Nomadism in Post-Revolutionary Iran', *Nomadic Peoples* 7(2).

————. 2003b. 'The Mamassani of Iran: At the Juncture of Two Modes of Subsistence', *Nomadic Peoples* 7(2): 87–97.

————. 2006. 'Editorial: Everyday Life in the Middle East', *Anthropology in the Middle East* 1(1): v–vi.

Simpson-Herbert, M. 1987. 'Women, Food and Hospitality in Iranian Society', *Canberra Anthropology* 10(1): 24–34.

Singer, A. 1972. 'The Jamshidi of Khurasan: A Historical Note', *Iran: Journal of the British Institute of Persian Studies* 10: 151–55.

Spooner, B. 1963. 'The Function of Religion in Persian Society', *Iran: Journal of the British Institute of Persian Studies* 1: 83–95.

————. 1965a. 'Kinship and Marriage in Eastern Persia', *Sociologus* 15(1): 22–31.

————. 1965b. 'Arghiyan, the Area of Jajarm in Western Khurasan', *Iran: Journal of the British Institute of Persian Studies* 3: 97–107.

————. 1966. 'Iranian Kinship and Marriage', *Iran: Journal of the British Institute of Persian Studies* 4: 51–59.

————. 1969. 'Politics, Kinship, and Ecology in Southeast Persia', *Ethnology* 8(2): 139–52.

————. 1970. 'The Evil Eye in the Middle East', in M. Douglas (ed.), *Witchcraft Confessions and Accusations*. London: 311–20.

————. 1971. 'Cultural Anthropology in Iran: Beginnings and Prospects', *Expedition* 13(3–4): 66–71.

————. 1972. 'The Iranian Deserts', in B. Spooner (ed.), *Population Growth: Anthropological Implications*. Cambridge, MA: 245–68.

————. 1973. 'The Cultural Ecology of Pastoral Nomads', *Addison-Wesley Module in Anthropology* 45.

————. 1974. 'City and River in Iran: Urbanization and Irrigation of the Iranian Plateau', *Iranian Studies* 7(3–4): 681–713.

————. 1980. 'Introduction', in B. Spooner and L. Horne (eds), *Cultural and Ecological Perspectives from the Turan Program, Iran*. Expedition, 22: 4–10.

————. 1987. 'Anthropology, Social and Cultural, in Iran', *Encyclopaedia Iranica*, vol. 2: 107–116.

————. 1997 'Ethnography', *Encyclopaedia Iranica* 8: 9–45.

Street, B. 1995. *Social Literacies: Critical Approaches to Literacy in Development, Ethnography, and Education*. London.

————. 1992. 'Reply to "Method in Our Critique of Anthropology" by F. Barth', *Man* 27(1): 1977–79.

Suzuki, Y. 2004. 'Negotiations, Concessions, and Adaptations during Fieldwork in a Tribal Society', *Iranian Studies* 37(4): 623–32.

Sykes, Sir P. 1902. 'Anthropological Notes on Southern Persia', *Journal of the Anthropological Institute* 32: 339–49.

————. 1921. 'The Gypsies of Persia', *Journal of the Anthropological Institute* 36: 302–11.

Tapper(-Lindisfarne), N. 1978. 'The Women's Subsociety Among the Shahsevan Nomads of Iran', in L. Beck and N.R. Keddie (eds), *Women in the Muslim World*. Cambridge, MA: 374–98.

————. 1980. 'Matrons and Mistresses: Women and Boundaries in Two Middle Eastern Tribal Societies', *European Journal of Sociology* 21: 374–98.

Tapper, R. 1966. 'Black Sheep, White Sheep and Red-Heads: A Historical Sketch of the Shahsavan of Azarbaijan', *Iran: Journal of the British Institute of Persian Studies* 4: 61–84.

———. 1979a. *Pasture and Politics: Economics, Conflict and Ritual among Shahsevan Nomads of Northwestern Iran.* London.

———. 1979b. 'Access to Grazing Rights and Social Organization among the Shahsevan Nomads of Azerbaijan', in L'Equipe Ecologie et Anthropologie des Sociétes Pastorales (ed.), *Pastoral Production and Society.* New York: 95–114.

———. 1980. 'Tribe and State in Iran and Afghanistan', *Social Science Research Council Newsletter* 42: 13–15.

———. 1983a. 'Introduction', in R. Tapper (ed.), *The Conflict of Tribe and State in Iran and Afghanistan.* London: 1–82.

———. 1983b. 'Nomads and Commissars in the Mughan Steppe: The Shahsevan Tribes in the Great Game', in R. Tapper (ed.), *The Conflict of Tribe and State in Iran and Afghanistan.* London: 401–35.

———. 1988. 'History and Identity among the Shahsevan', *Iranian Studies* 21(3–4): 84–108.

———. 1989. 'Ethnic Identities and Social Categories in Iran and Afghanistan', in E. Tonkin et al. (eds), *History and Ethnicity.* London: 232–46.

———. 1990. 'Anthropologists, Historians, and Tribespeople on Tribe and State Formation in the Middle East', in P. Khoury and J. Kostiner (eds), *Tribes and State Formation in the Middle East.* Berkeley, CA: 48–73.

———. 1994. 'Blood, Wine and Water: Social and Symbolic Aspects of Drinks and Drinking in the Islamic Middle East', in S. Zubaida and R. Tapper (eds), *Culinary Cultures of the Middle East.* London: 215–31.

———. 1997. *Frontier Nomads of Iran: A Political and Social History of the Shahsevan.* Cambridge.

——— (ed.). 2002. *The New Iranian Cinema: Politics, Representation and Identity.* London.

Tavakolian, B. 2003. 'Multiplicities of Nomadism and Varieties of Anthropological Theory', *Reviews in Anthropology* 32(4): 297–314.

Thaiss, G.E. 1971. 'The Bazaar as a Case Study of Religion and Social Change', in E. Yar-Shater (ed.), *Iran Faces the Seventies.* New York: 45–76.

———. 1972a. 'Unity and Discord: The Symbol of Husayn in Iran', in C.J. Adams (ed.), *Iranian Civilization and Culture.* Montreal: 111–19.

———. 1972b. 'Religious Symbolism and Social Change: The Drama of Husain', in N.R. Keddie (ed.), *Scholars, Saints and Sufis: Muslim Religious Institutions since 1500.* Berkeley, CA: 349–66.

———. 1973. 'Religious Symbolism and Social Change: The Drama of Husain', Ph.D. dissertation. St. Louis: Washington University.

———. 1978a. 'The Conceptualization of Social Change through Metaphor', *Journal of Asian and African Studies* 13(1–2): 1–13.

Thompson, C.T. 1979. 'A Persian Miniature: The Value of Tradition in a Mazandaran Village', Ph.D. dissertation. Austin: University of Texas.

———. 1983. 'Shir Mohammad Kerbali: A Trader in the Village Markets of Mazandaran', *Lambda Alpha Journal of Man* 15: 59–80.

Tober, D. 2004. 'Children in the Field and Methodological Challenges of Research in Iran', *Iranian Studies* 37(4): 643–54.

———. forthcoming. *A Path to Isfahan: Iran with my Two Sons.*

Tober, D., M.-H. Taghdisi and M. Jalali. 2006. '"Fewer Children, Better Life" or "As Many as God Wants?" Family Planning among Low-Income Iranian and Afghan Refugee Families in Isfahan', Iran. *Medical Anthropology Quarterly* 20(1): 50–71.

Torab, A. 1996. 'Piety as Gendered Agency: A Study of *Jalasa* Ritual Discourse in an Urban Neighbourhood in Iran', *Journal of the Royal Anthropological Institute* 2(2): 235–51.

———. 1998. 'Neighbourhoods of Piety: Gender and Ritual in South Tehran', Ph.D. dissertation. London: University of London, London.

———. 2002. 'The Politicization of Women's Religious Circles in Post-Revolutionary Iran', in S. Ansari and V. Martin (eds), *Women, Religion, and Culture in Iran.* London: 143–67.

———. 2005. 'Vows, Mediumship and Gender: Women's Votive Meals in Iran', in I. M. Okkenhaug and I. Flaskerud (eds), *Gender, Religion and Change in the Middle East: Two Hundred Years of History.* New York: 207–22.

———. 2006. *Performing Islam: Gender and Ritual in Iran.* Leiden.

Tremayne, S. 2004. 'And Never Shall the Twain Meet: The Reproductive Health Policies of the Islamic Republic of Iran', M. Unnithan (ed.), *Reproductive Change, Agency and the State: Cultural Transformations in Childbearing.* Oxford: 181–202.

———. 2006a. 'Modernity and Early Marriage in Iran: A View from Within', *Journal of Middle East Women's Studies* 2(1): 65–94.

———. 2006b. 'Change and "Face" in Modern Iran', *Anthropology of the Middle East* 1(1): 25–41.

Varzi, R. 2006. *Warring Souls: Youth, Media, and Martyrdom in Post-Revolution Iran.* Durham, NC: Duke University Press.

Wright, S. 1978. 'Prattle and Politics. The Position of Women in Dushman-Ziari', *Anthropological Society of Oxford Journal* 9: 98–112.

———. 1981. 'Place and Face: Of Women in Doshman Ziari, Iran', in S. Ardener (ed.), *Women and Space.* New York: 136–57.

———. 1985. 'Identities and Influence: Political Organisation in Doshman Ziari, Iran', Ph.D. dissertation. Oxford: University of Oxford.

———. 1992. 'Concepts and Experience of Development in Doshman Ziari, Mamasani', *Zakhayer-e Enghelab Special Issue: International Conference on Nomadism and Development* 19: 72–4.

———. 1995. 'Understanding Tribal Identity in Iran and Beyond: Reply to Salzman', *Journal of the Royal Anthropological Institute* (incorporating *Man*) 1: 404–6.

———. 1996. 'Patterns and Representations', in E. Hallam and N. Levell (eds), *Communicating Otherness: Cultural Encounters.* Sussex: 45–62.

Wright, S. and S.H. Haidari. 2001. 'Participation and Participatory Development among the Kalhor Nomads of Iran', *Community Development Journal* 36(1): 53–62.

ℵ Contributors

Fariba Adelkhah, a senior researcher at the CERI (Centre d'Etudes et de Recherches Internationales), obtained her PhD in anthropology from Ecole des Hautes Etudes en Scieces Sociales, Paris. Specializing in gender and modernity in postrevolutionary Iran, she has published various articles and two well-known books on these subjects: *La révolution sous le voile. Femme islamique d'Iran* (1991), translated into Arabic in 1995, and *Being Modern in Iran* (1999). Together with J. F. Bayart she published *Voyages du développement. Emigration, commerce, exil* (2007).

Lois Beck is a professor of anthropology at Washington University in Saint Louis. As a specialist on the cultural anthropology of Iran, especially tribally organized nomadic pastoralists, she has conducted research there since 1969, including twelve visits since the Revolution in 1979. She has also worked with Iranians in the diaspora, particularly those who are part of ethnic, tribal and religious minorities. Her books include *Women in the Muslim World* (1978, with Nikki Keddie), *The Qashqa'i of Iran* (1986), *Nomad: A Year in the Life of a Qashqa'i Tribesman in Iran* (1991), *Women in Iran from the Rise of Islam to 1800* (2003, with Guity Nashat) and *Women in Iran from 1800 to the Islamic Republic* (2004, with Guity Nashat). She is working on: *Nomads Move On: Qashqa'i Tribespeople in Post-Revolutionary Iran.*

Christian Bromberger is a professor of anthropology at the University of Provence in Aix-en-Provence (France) and a senior member of the Institut Universitaire de France (general anthropology). He was in charge of the Institut Français de Recherche en Iran from 2006 to 2008. His interest lies in the study of collective identities through different themes. He has carried out field research in Gilân, a northern province of Iran, in Provence (France) and in Piemonte and Campania (Italy).

Ali A. Bulookbashi is a member of the High Scientific Council and director of the Department of Anthropology in the Center for the Great Islamic Encyclopedia, director of the Department of Anthropology at the Cultural Research Bureau, chief editor and scientific director of the Encyclopedia of Iran in the Center For Cultural and International Studies, and a member of the board of scientific editors of the *Iranian Journal of Anthropology.*

He specializes in Iranian popular culture and literature, with a particular focus on Iranian religious behaviours and beliefs. His major publications, all in Persian, include *Popular Culture of Iran*, 2 vols. (1977), *Iran Coffeehouses* (1996), *Tribal Society in Iran* (2003) and *The Ancient Games in Iran* (2007).

Jean-Pierre Digard, an anthropologist, is directeur de recherche émérite au Centre National de la Recherche Scientifique (unité 'Monde Iranien et Indien', Paris). He specializes in Iran, with particular emphasis on nomadic tribes and animal domestication. His major publications include *Techniques des nomades Baxtyâri d'Iran* (1981), and he edited *Le fait ethnique en Iran et en Afghanistan* (1988), *L'homme et les animaux domestiques. Anthropologie d'une passion* (1990), *L'Iran au XXe siècle. Entre nationalisme, islam et mondialisation* (with Bernard Hourcade and Yann Richard, 2007 [1996]), *Chevaux et cavaliers arabes dans les arts d'Orient et d'Occident* (2002) and *Une histoire du cheval. Art, techniques, société* (2007 [2004]).

Nasser Fakouhi, an associate professor of anthropology at the University of Tehran, specializes in the applied, development and ethnic problems of Iranian urban areas with particular emphasis on western Iran. His major publications include *Political Violence* (1997), *Political Mythology of Iran* (1998), *Urban Anthropology* (2000), *In the Labyrinths of Globalization* (2004) and *Anthropological Pieces* (2006). A founding member and president of the Iranian Anthropological Society, he is also vice president of the Iranian Sociological Association.

Nematollah Fazeli is an associate professor of social anthropology and cultural studies at the University of Allameh Tabatabai in Tehran and a research associate of SOAS (University of London). He specializes in the contemporary culture of Iran, with particular emphasis on anthropology and ethnography. His major publications include *Politics of Culture in Iran: Anthropology, Politics and Society in the Twentieth Century* (2006) and in Persian *Culture and University: Anthropological and Cultural Studies Approaches* (2008).

Mary Elaine Hegland teaches for the Anthropology Department and Women and Gender Studies Program at Santa Clara University in California. She has conducted research in Iran, Tajikistan, Turkey, Pakistan, Afghanistan and the U.S. among Iranian immigrants about aging, religion, ritual, politics, revolution and gender. After twenty-five years away from Iran, Hegland returned four times since 2003 to conduct field research in a village near Shiraz. Recent publications include: 'Methods Applied: Political Transformation and Recent Ethnographic Fieldwork' in *Anthropology of the Middle East, Special Issue on Methodology* (with Erika Friedl, 2007), 'Modernization and Social Change: Impact on Iranian Elderly Social Networks and Care Systems' in *Anthropology of the Middle East* (with Zahra Sarraf and Mohammad Shahbazi, 2007) and 'Esmat Khanum and a Life of Travail: "God, Help Me; Son of Musa Ibn-e Jaafar, You Yourself Help Me" in *Muslim Voices and Lives in the Contemporary World* (2008).

Ulrich Marzolph is a professor of Islamic studies at Georg-August-University in Göttingen, Germany, and a senior member of the editorial committee of the *Enzyklopädie des Märchens*. He specializes in the narrative culture of the Near East, with particular emphasis on Arab and Persian folk narrative and popular literature. His recent publications include *The Arabian Nights Encyclopedia* (together with Richard van Leeuwen, 2004), *The Arabian Nights Reader* (2006) and *The Arabian Nights in Transnational Perspective* (2007).

Ziba Mir-Hosseini is an independent consultant, researcher and writer on Middle Eastern issues, based at the London Middle East Institute and the Centre for Middle Eastern and Islamic Law, both at SOAS, University of London. She specializes in gender, family relations, Islamic law and development. She has a BA in Sociology from Tehran University (1974) and PhD in Social Anthropology from University of Cambridge (1980), and has held numerous research fellowships and visiting professorships; she has been Hauser Global Law Visiting Professor at New York University since 2002. She is a Council member of Women Living Under Muslim Laws, and a founding member of Musawah Global Movement for Equality and Justice in the Muslim Family. Her publications include *Marriage on Trial: A Study of Islamic Family Law in Iran and Morocco* (I. B. Tauris, 1993, 2002), *Islam and Gender: The Religious Debate in Contemporary Iran* (Princeton University Press, 1999) and (with Richard Tapper) *Islam and Democracy in Iran: Eshkevari and the Quest for Reform* (I. B. Tauris, 2006). She has also directed (with Kim Longinotto) two award-winning feature-length documentary films on contemporary issues in Iran: *Divorce Iranian Style* (1998) and *Runaway* (2001).

Shahnaz R. Nadjmabadi is a senior research fellow and teaches at the Department of Ethnologie at the Goethe-Universität/Frankfurt am Main (Germany). She obtained her PhD in anthropology at the University of Heidelberg and worked at UNESCO in Paris from 1977 to 1984, where she supervised programme activities at the Department of Human Settlement and Socio-Cultural Environment. She was also a member of the working group

Le Monde Iranien Contemporain of the Centre National de la Recherche Scientifique in Paris. Her research is focused on the interrelationships of the populations living in Iranian coastal areas and their neighbours in the Arab countries of the Persian Gulf. She has published articles on questions of identity, locality and the history of settlement in the province of Hormozgan (Persian Gulf), including '"The Sea Belongs to God, the Land Belongs to Us:" Resource Managment in a Multi-resource Community in the Persian Gulf' (1992), '„Arabisiert" oder „iranisiert?" Siedlungsgeschichte am Persischen Golf' (2005), and 'The Arab Presence on the Iranian Coast of the Persian Gulf' (2008).

Mohammad Shahbazi is a professor of public health, and chair of the Department of Behavioral and Environmental Health, School of Health Sciences, at Jackson State University, Jackson, MS, United States. His research interests include cultural impacts of state-supported formal education and health services on ethnic minorities in the Middle East; health status of ethnic minorities (nationally and internationally) with a focus on women and schoolchildren; community outreach, health-related information-sharing and stroke awareness and social determinants of rural health in Mississippi. Some of his publications are: 'Challenging Health Disparities at Home and Abroad' (2007), 'The Qashqa'i, Formal Education, and the Indigenous Educator' (2006), and 'Global Health Disparities and a Qashqa'i Nomadic Pastoralist Tribesman's Tale as a Health Worker' (2007).

Soheila Shahshahani is an associate professor at Shahid Beheshti University in Tehran, Iran. She is editor of *Anthropology of the Middle East* (in English and French) and *Culture and the Human Being* (in Persian). She received her doctorate from the New School for Social Research in New York in 1981. She is senior vice-president of the International Union of Anthropological and Ethnological Sciences and chair of the Commission on the Middle East of the same union. She is author of *The Four Seasons of the Sun* (1987), an ethnography of women of Oyun, a village of settled Mamassani pastoral nomads of Iran; in Persian *A Pictorial History of Iranian Headdresses* (1995) and *Meymand, We Were One People One Territory* (2005), an ethnographic study of a grotto-village. She is guest editor of *Nomadic Peoples: Nomads and Nomadism in Post-revolutionary Iran* (7(2), 2003) and editor of *Body as Medium of Meaning* (2004).

R. L. Tapper, MA (Cambridge) and PhD (London), is emeritus professor of anthropology with reference to the Middle East at the University of London. His main research interests are Iran, Afghanistan and Turkey, pastoral nomadism, ethnicity, tribe/state relations, anthropology of Islam, documentary film and Iranian cinema. His most recent books are *Frontier Nomads of Iran* (CUP, 1997), *Islam and Democracy in Iran: Eshkevari and the Quest for Reform* (co-authored with Ziba Mir-Hosseini, Tauris, 2006), and the edited volumes *The New Iranian Cinema* (Tauris, 2002), *The Nomadic Peoples of Iran* (co-edited with Jon Thompson, Azimuth, 2002) and *Technology, Tradition and Survival: Aspects of Material Culture in the Middle East and Central Asia* (co-edited with Keith McLachlan, Frank Cass, 2003). He is working on a book provisionally entitled *Afghan Village Voices*.

ℵ Index

Indexed terms have been rendered according to the spelling used in the respective contribution. However, efforts have been made to cross-reference to alternative orthographies.